PERFORMANCE STUDIES

"Richard Schechner's work is crucial to exploring the tricky and sometimes dangerous territories of performance. Not only is he responsible for continually expanding the boundaries of the field but also for demystifying esoteric issues. His work reaches wide constituencies."

Guillermo Gómez-Peña, performance artist
and writer, *San Francisco*.

"Desperately needed. I like the textbook features, especially the quotations from primary sources."

Philip Auslander, *Georgia Institute of Technology*

"Well written, thoughtful, provocative, an essential purchase. The material is presented in a clear and accessible way and is structured logically and helpfully. The diagrams are the mark of a great visual thinker."

Sally Harrison-Pepper, *Miami University*

"This textbook is excellent and sure to excite classroom discussion. Whether teaching World Theatre or Performance Theory it provides a provocative guide to questions that arise when performance is approached in a global perspective. I will certainly adopt it in my classroom."

Rebecca Schneider, *Cornell University*

"The text is very cleverly put together with a clear idea of how its features contribute to the reading of the material. I frankly cannot imagine it being done better."

Simon Shepherd, *Central School of Speech and Drama, London*

"It will make the teaching of performance studies a lot easier."

Colin Counsell, *University of North London*

"Exactly what I have longed for. It provides linkages between concepts, gives historical perspective, and explains theoretical ideas in a language accessible to undergraduate students. It will be required reading."

Takahashi Yuichiro, Professor of Performance Studies, *Dokkyo University, Tokyo*

This important new introductory textbook by a prime mover in the emergent field of Performance Studies is a defining moment for the discipline. It provides a lively and accessible overview of the full range of performance for undergraduates at all levels and beginning graduate students in performance studies, theatre, performing arts, and cultural studies. It includes discussion of the performing arts and popular entertainments, rituals, play, and games as well as the performances of everyday life. Supporting examples and ideas are drawn from the performing arts, anthropology, post-structuralism, ritual theory, ethology, philosophy, and aesthetics. The text has been fully developed with input from leading teachers and trialled with students.

User-friendly, with a special text design, it also includes the following features:

- Extracts from primary sources giving alternative voices and viewpoints
- Short biographies of key thinkers
- "Things to think about" and "things to do" to stimulate fieldwork, classroom exercises, and discussion
- Key reading lists for each chapter and an extensive final bibliography
- 20 line drawings and 173 photos drawn from private and public collections around the world

Richard Schechner is one of the pioneers of the field of Performance Studies. A scholar and director, he is University Professor of Performance Studies at the Tisch School of the Arts at New York University and Editor of *TDR: The Journal of Performance Studies*. He is the author of *Public Domain, Environmental Theater, The End of Humanism, Performance Theory, Between Theater and Anthropology* and *The Future of Ritual*. His books have been translated into Spanish, Korean, Chinese, Japanese, Serbo-Croatian, German, Italian, Hungarian, and Bulgarian. He is the general editor of the Worlds of Performance series published by Routledge.

PERFORMANCE

Usually, people say that a truly artistic show will always be unique,
impossible to be repeated: never will the same actors,
in the same play, produce the same show.
Theatre is Life.

People also say that, in life, we never really do anything
for the first time, always repeating
past experiences, habits, rituals, conventions.
Life is Theatre.

Richard Schechner, with his sensibility and intelligence,
leads us to explore the limits between Life and Theater,
which he calls Performance. With his knowledge,
he allows us to discover other thinkers,
stimulating us to have our own thoughts.

Augusto Boal

PERFORMANCE STUDIES

An introduction

Richard Schechner

Routledge
Taylor & Francis Group

LONDON AND NEW YORK

First published 2002 by Routledge
11 New Fetter Lane, London EC4P 4EE

Reprinted 2003

Simultaneously published in the USA and Canada
by Routledge
29 West 35th Street, New York, NY 10001

Routledge is an imprint of the Taylor & Francis Group

Designed and typeset in Perpetua and Benguiat Gothic by
Keystroke, Jacaranda Lodge, Wolverhampton
Printed and bound in Great Britain by
St Edmundsbury Press, Bury St Edmunds, Suffolk

British Library Cataloguing in Publication Data
A catalogue record for this book is available from the British Library

Library of Congress Cataloging in Publication Data
Schechner, Richard, 1934–
    Performance studies : an introduction / Richard Schechner.
    p. cm.
    Includes bibliographical references and index.
    1. Theater—Anthropological aspects.   2. Rites and ceremonies.
    3. Performing arts.   I. Title.
    PN2041 .A57 S34 2002
    792—dc21   2001048687

ISBN 0–415–14620–8 hbk
ISBN 0–415–14621–6 pbk

To

Barbara Kirshenblatt-Gimblett

Peggy Phelan

Diana Taylor

CONTENTS

PREFACE

Whoever cannot seek
the unforeseen sees nothing,
for the known way
is an impasse.

Heraclitus, Fragment 7
(Brooks Haxton, translator)

No one knows better than an editor that writing a book is a collective effort. There are a lot of people I want to thank. Foremost is Professor Carol Martin, my wife, whose supportive critical and organizational skills helped me keep this work coherent and focused. Carol knows me very well. No one can speak to me in as direct and forceful a manner (and live to tell what happened next). No one has been more helpful in making this book into a reality.

Next is Professor Henry Bial, who wrote the short bio-notes and subject definitions that enliven almost every page of this book. He wrote the first drafts of the "Things to Think About" and "Things to Do" and helped select the suggested readings that end each chapter. Henry also read every word more than once, making constructive comments, keeping my spirits up during the weeks when I thought Sisyphus had it easy. Henry is also editing a companion performance studies reader that, along with this book, gives to students and their teachers the basis for a compact course in performance studies.

Then, my children, Sam MacIntosh Schechner and Sophia Martin Schechner. I know that usually "the family" are thanked last, but that's not the way it is with me. I have not only jabbered the ideas of this book with them, but have witnessed performance-in-action through their growth and development. Sam is now a professional editor and writer in his own right and Sophia a poet, painter, and equestrian of formidable talent.

I want to thank my editors at Routledge, first Talia Rodgers, who commissioned this book (and waited years for me to earn my advance). Talia has always been enthusiastic and supportive, not only of this project but of so much else that is fine at Routledge. Along with her far-reaching vision Talia has a very clear editor's eye for what's what. And then Moira Taylor, Senior Textbook Development Editor and the Project Manager for this book. Moira has educated me in

constructing a textbook, for which I cannot thank her enough. Talia, Moira, and their colleagues at Routledge have worked from instigation to completion, advising, cajoling, and insisting. I feel supported also by a team of readers, designers, and sales personnel – including cover designer Sutchinda Rangsi-Thompson and production editor Ruth Bourne. Altogether, I felt part of a team effort. Writing can be a woeful, solitary occupation, but producing a book is something else again.

My colleagues at the Department of Performance Studies, Tisch School of the Arts, sustained me in several ways. Professors Barbara Kirshenblatt-Gimblett and Diana Taylor read portions of the book and offered detailed, clear suggestions, many of which I took. I turn porcupine when criticized, but after a little while, I am grateful to friends who tell me in plain English what I need to do to make my work better. My other colleagues – Professors Peggy Phelan, Barbara Browning, José Muñoz, Fred Moten, and Ngugi wa Thiong'o, and more recently, Anna Deavere Smith and Andre Lepecki – have also helped by creating a department where ideas come first, internecine war has been abolished, and intellectual, artistic, and personal diversity are cherished and practiced. Believe it or not, most of our faculty meetings are fun, some downright stimulating.

Nor could this book have been completed without the efforts of the home office, the contributing editors, and those whose work appears in *TDR: The Journal of Performance Studies*. I especially want to thank Associate Editor Mariellen Sandford, my long-time partner at *TDR*, who worked extra hard, so that I had both the time and peace of mind necessary for writing. Also the student editors during the final year of work on this book: Jennifer Chan, Cathlyn Harris, Alice Reagan, and Sara Brady. The entire *TDR* community deserves thanks. I am in regular contact with the Contributing Editors, as active and broad-ranging a group of persons one could ever hope to work with – Philip Auslander, Eugenio Barba, John Bell, Augusto Boal, Guillermo Goméz-Peña, Barbara Kirshenblatt-Gimblett, Rebecca Schneider, William H. Sun, Diana Taylor, Ngugi wa Thiong'o, Tadashi Uchino, and Susanne Winnacker. No wonder that some of their work is featured in this book. Also, reading submissions and editing accepted manuscripts helps keep me abreast of the field.

Writing a textbook demands feedback from people who are expert in the field. In performance studies, this encompasses many different kinds of persons, approaches, and specialties. In writing this book I have benefited greatly during its development from the comments of reviewers in North America and the UK including Baz Kershaw, Head of Drama, University of Bristol; Colin Counsell, Programme Director, Theatre Studies, University of North London; Simon Shepherd, Director of Programmes, Central School of Speech and Drama, London; Rebecca Schneider, Department of Theater, Film, and Dance, Cornell University; and Sally Harrison-Pepper, School of Interdisciplinary Studies, Miami University, Ohio.

In writing this kind of prefatory memorandum, I fear I've omitted persons who are absolutely crucial. So in that spirit let me thank most wholeheartedly the Forgotten Colleagues, whoever you may be.

Finally, what kind of book is this? To whom is it addressed? How might it be useful? All the effort of my writing and the team at Routledge is to make an accessible and useful textbook suitable for any course in Performance Studies wherever it may be taught in the world. What this means in practical terms is that *Performance Studies: An Introduction* will be used primarily as a textbook in departments of, or programs in, performance studies, theatre,

communications, speech, cultural studies, and the like. Already there is a significant worldwide interest in performance studies. I want this book to help those already involved in performance studies and stimulate others to become involved. As I emphasize in the text that follows, performance studies is unsettled, open, diverse, and multiple in its methods, themes, subjects, arts, and persons.

The reference list at the end of the text includes every writing I have consulted or cited, as well as key writings of persons who are mentioned in the text. Some of these writings are ancient, some very contemporary – the range is from classics to newspaper articles and internet sites. There are some discrepancies between dates of first publication or composition given in the main body of the book and the dates given in the reference list. For the most part, in compiling the reference list I selected editions and translations that I feel are readable and available. My goal is to provide an extensive, if not comprehensive, set of writings that in some way characterizes the field of performance studies as I am in the process of envisioning it.

My hope is that this book will stimulate the growth of many new courses in performance studies. Not only courses concerning one or another aspect of performance studies, but broad-ranging courses that serve as an "introduction." An introduction to what? Well, life. My goal is nothing less than making performance studies a method of analysis, a way to understand the world as it is becoming, and a necessary tool for living.

Richard Schechner
Hanover, New Hampshire
July 2001

1 WHAT IS PERFORMANCE STUDIES?

Introducing This Book, This Field, and Myself

The book you hold in your hand is "an" introduction to performance studies. There will be others, and that suits me just fine. The one overriding and underlying assumption of performance studies is that the field is wide open. There is no finality to performance studies, either theoretically or operationally. There are many voices, opinions, methods, and subjects. As I will show in chapter 2, anything at all can be studied "as" performance. But this does not mean performance studies as an academic discipline does not have certain specific subjects that it focuses on. Theoretically, performance studies is wide open; practically, it has developed in a certain way which I will discuss in this chapter.

Nor does this kind of openness mean there are no values. People want, need, and have standards by which to live, write, think, and act. As individuals and as parts of communities and nations people participate and interact with other people, other species, the planet, and whatever else is out there. But the values that guide people are not "natural," transcendent, God-given, or inalienable (despite the claim of the US Declaration of Independence). Values belong to ideology, science, the arts, religion, and other areas of human endeavor. Values are hard-won and contingent, changing over time according to social and historical circumstances. Values are a function of cultures, groups, and individuals. Values can be used to protect and liberate or to control and oppress. In fact, the difference between what is "liberty" and what is "oppression" depends a lot on where you are coming from.

This book embodies the values, theories, and practices of a certain field of scholarship as understood by one particular person in the seventh decade of his life. This person is a Jewish Hindu Buddhist atheist living in New York City, married, and the father of two children. He is a Professor of Performance Studies at New York University and the Editor of *TDR: The Journal of Performance Studies*. He directs plays, writes, lectures, and leads workshops. He has traveled and worked in many parts of the world. Who I am is not irrelevant. I will be leading you on a journey. You ought to know a little about your guide.

Because performance studies is so broad-ranging and open to new possibilities, no one can actually grasp its totality or press all its vastness and variety into a single book. My points of departure are my own teaching, research, artistic practice, and life experiences. But I am not limited by these. I will offer ideas far from my center, some even contrary to my values.

The Boxes

Before going on, I want to point out a feature of this book. My text includes almost no quotations, citations, or notes. Ideas are drawn from many sources, but the voice is my own. I hope this gives the reader a smoother ride than many scholarly texts. At the same time, I want my readers to hear many voices. The boxes offer alternative opinions and interruptions. The boxes open the conversation in ways I may not be able to reach. They are hyperlinks. They help enact some of the diversity of performance studies. I want the effect to be of a seminar with many hands raised or of a computer desktop with many open windows.

What Makes Performance Studies Special

Performances are actions. As a discipline, performance studies takes actions very seriously in four ways. First, behavior is the "object of study" of performance studies. Although performance studies scholars use the "archive" extensively — what's in books, photographs, the archaeological record, historical remains, etc. — their dedicated focus is on the "repertory" — namely, what people do in the activity of their doing it. Second, artistic practice is a big part of the performance studies project. A number of performance studies scholars are also practising artists working in the avantgarde, in community-based performance, and elsewhere; others have mastered a variety of non-Western and Western traditional forms. The relationship between studying performance and doing performance is integral.

Third, fieldwork as "participant observation" is a much-prized method adapted from anthropology and put to new uses. In anthropological fieldwork, participant observation is a way of learning about cultures other than that of the fieldworker. In anthropology, for the most part, the "home culture" is Western, the "other" non-Western. But in performance studies, the "other" may be a part of one's own culture (non-Western or Western), or even an aspect of one's own behavior. That positions the performance studies fieldworker at a Brechtian distance allowing for criticism, irony, and personal commentary as well as sympathetic participation. In an active way, one performs fieldwork. Taking this critical distance from the objects of study and self invites revision, the recognition that social circumstances – including knowledge itself – are not fixed, but subject to the "rehearsal process" of testing and revising. Fourth, it follows that performance studies is actively involved in social practices and advocacies. Many who practice performance studies do not aspire to ideological neutrality. In fact, a basic theoretical claim is that no approach or position is "neutral." There is no such thing as neutral or unbiased. The challenge is to become as aware as possible of one's own stances in relation to the positions of others – and then take steps to maintain or change positions.

Performances – as I will show in some detail in chapter 2 – occur in many different instances and kinds. Performance must be construed as a "broad spectrum" or "continuum" of human actions ranging from ritual, play, sports, popular entertainments, the performing arts (theatre, dance, music), and everyday life performances to the enactment of social, professional, gender, race, and class roles, and on to healing (from shamanism to surgery), the media, and the internet. Before performance studies, Western thinkers believed they knew exactly what was and what was not "performance." But in fact, there is no historically or culturally fixable limit to what is or is not "performance." Along the continuum new genres are added, others are dropped. The underlying notion is that any action that is framed, presented, highlighted, or displayed is a performance. Many performances belong to more than one category along the continuum. For example, a football player spiking the ball and pointing a finger in the air after scoring a touchdown is performing a dance and enacting a ritual as part of his professional role as athlete and popular entertainer.

As a method of studying performances, this new discipline is still in its formative stage. Performance studies draws on and synthesizes approaches from a wide variety of disciplines in the the social sciences, feminist studies, gender studies, history, psychoanalysis, queer theory, semiotics, ethology, cybernetics, area studies, media and popular culture theory, and cultural studies. But as **Barbara Kirshenblatt-Gimblett** (birthdate withheld), the founding chair of NYU's Department of Performance Studies, notes, "performance studies is more than the sum of its inclusions" (**see Kirshenblatt-Gimblett box 1**). Performance studies does not study texts, architecture, visual arts, or any other item or artifact of art or culture as such. When texts, architecture, visual arts, or anything else are looked at, they are studied "as" performances (a concept I will develop in chapter 2). That is, they are regarded as practices, events, and behaviors, not as "objects" or "things." The question of "liveness," as Kirshenblatt-Gimblett points out, is at the heart of performance studies. Thus, performance studies does not "read" an action or ask what "text" is being enacted. Rather the emphasis is on inquiring about the "behavior" of, for example, a painting: the ways it interacts with those who view it, thus evoking different reactions and meanings; and how it changes meaning over time and in different contexts. The performance studies scholar examines the circumstances in which the painting was created and exhibited; and looks at how the gallery or building displaying it shapes its presentations. These kinds of performance studies questions can be asked of any event or material object. Of course, when performance studies deals with behavior – artistic, everyday, ritual, playful, and so on – the questions asked are closer to how performance theorists have traditionally approached theatre and the other performing arts. I discuss and apply this kind of analysis more fully in every chapter of this book.

Barbara Kirshenblatt-Gimblett (prefers not to have her birthdate disclosed): American performance theorist specializing in the aesthetics of everyday life, Jewish performance, and folklore. She was the founding chair of NYU's Department of Performance Studies from 1981 to 1993. Author of *Destination Culture* (1998).

In performance studies, questions of embodiment, action, behavior, and agency are dealt with interculturally. This approach recognizes two things. First, in today's world, cultures are always interacting – there is no totally isolated group. Second, the differences among cultures are so profound that no theory of performance is universal: one size does not fit all. Nor are the playing fields where cultures interact level. The current means of cultural interaction – globalization – enacts extreme imbalances of power, money, access to media, and control over resources. Although this is reminiscent of colonialism, globalization is also different from

globalization as a means of cultural interaction

Barbara Kirshenblatt-Gimblett

Performance Studies is more than a sum of its Inclusions

Performance studies starts from the premise that its objects of study are not to be divided up and parceled out, medium by medium, to various other disciplines – music, dance, dramatic literature, art history. The prevailing division of the arts by medium is arbitrary, as is the creation of fields and departments devoted to each.

To study performance, as an artform that lacks a distinctive medium (and hence uses any and all media), requires attending to all the modalities in play. This distinguishes performance studies from those that focus on a single modality – dance, music, art, theatre, literature, cinema. For this and other reasons, performance studies is better equipped to deal with most of the world's artistic expression, which has always synthesized or otherwise integrated movement, sound, speech, narrative, and objects.

A provisional coalescence on the move, performance studies is more than the sum of its inclusions. While it might be argued that "as an artform, performance lacks a distinctive medium" (Carroll 1986: 78), embodied practice and event is a recurring point of reference within performance studies. What this means, among other things, is that presence, liveness, agency, embodiment, and event are not so much the defining features of our objects of study as issues at the heart of our disciplinary subject. While some may address these issues in relation to plays performed on a stage, others may address them in relation to artifacts in a museum vitrine.

We take our lead form the historical avant-garde and contemporary art, which have long questioned the boundaries between modalities and gone about blurring them, whether those boundaries mark off media, genres, or cultural traditions. What they found interesting – Chinese opera, Balinese barong, circus – we find interesting.

Such confounding of categories has not only widened the range of what can count as an artmaking practice, but also gives rise to performance art that is expressly not theatre and art performance that dematerializes the art object and approaches the condition of performance.

1999, adapted by Kirshenblatt-Gimblett from "Performance Studies," a report written for the Rockefeller Foundation, http://www.nyu.edu/classes/bkg/ps.htm

colonialism in key ways. Proponents of globalization promise that "free trade," the internet, and advances in science and technology are leading to a better life for the world's peoples. Globalization also induces a sameness at the level of popular culture – "world beat" and the proliferation of American-style fast foods and films are examples. The two ideas are related. Cultural sameness and seamless communications make it easier for transnational entities to get their messages across. This is crucial because governments and business alike increasingly find it more efficient to rule and manage with the collaboration rather than the opposition of workers. In order to gain their collaboration, information must not only move with ease globally but also be skillfully managed. The apparent victory of "democracy" and capitalism goes hand in hand with the flow of controlled media. Whether or not the internet will be, finally, an arena of resistance or compliance remains an open question. There are areas of resistance to the new world order, but these are often stigmatized as "rogue states" or "fundamentalists." I further discuss these questions in chapter 8.

Performance studies explores a wide array of subjects and uses many methodologies to deal with this contradictory and turbulent world. But unlike more traditional academic disciplines, performance studies does not organize its subjects and methods into a unitary system. These days many intellectuals know that knowledge cannot be easily, if at all, reduced to coherence. In fact, performance studies scholars consciously and eagerly express the tensions and partialities driving today's world. No one in performance studies is able to profess the whole field. This is because performance studies has a huge appetite for encountering, even inventing, new kinds of performing while insisting that cultural knowledge can never be complete (**see Geertz box**). If performance studies were an art, it would be avant-garde.

As a field, performance studies is sympathetic to the avant-garde, the marginal, the offbeat, the minoritarian, the subversive, the twisted, the queer, people of color, and the formerly colonized. Projects within performance studies often act on or act against strictly ordered or settled hier-archies of ideas, organizations, or people. Therefore, it is hard

Bring my ideas about ritual as art into TDR article ' but backup assertion that ritual pertends to be divine

Clifford Geertz

The Pitfalls of Cultural Analysis

Cultural analysis is intrinsically incomplete. And, worse than that, the more deeply it goes the less complete it is. It is a strange science whose most telling assertions are its most tremulously based, in which to get somewhere with the matter at hand is to intensify the suspicion, both your own and that of others, that you are not quite getting it right. But that, along with plaguing subtle people with obtuse questions, is what being an ethnographer is like.

1973, *The Interpretation of Cultures*, 29.

> **James Joyce (1882–1941):** Irish ground-breaking writer. Author of *Ulysses* (1922) and *Finnegan's Wake* (1939).

> **Andy Warhol (1928?–87):** American artist and filmmaker. Leader of the Pop Art movement in the 1960s and 1970s. Warhol appropriated images from American popular culture — Campbell's soup cans, Marilyn Monroe — and repositioned them as high art.

to imagine performance studies getting its act together, or even wanting to. Those working in the field resist creating a new, singular body of knowledge or methodology of the kind cosmologists dream of in their quest for the "theory of everything."

Literacies, Performatives, and Texters

Some people complain that literacy is declining not only in terms of basic reading skills, but also in what people read and how they write. The universality of television plus the growing global availability of the internet gives speech and visual communication a strong lift over conventional literacy. This affects all strata of culture from the ways ordinary people communicate to the art of writing. Few novelists in the early twenty-first century care to write panoptic, "big" novels such as **Leo Tolstoy**'s (1828–1910) *War and Peace* or even hyper-literate works such as **James Joyce**'s (1882–1941) *Ulysses* or *Finnegan's Wake*. **Andy Warhol** (1928?–87) was more than a little right when he predicted that everyone would have fifteen minutes of fame. Life is lived too fast; events and "stars" come and go before we can really take them in. The form and pressure of such an age is expressed more in the compact disc, music video, or hyperlinked email than it is in the considered piece of literature.

> **Leo Tolstoy (1828–1910):** Russian author. Novels include *War and Peace* (1863–69, Eng. 1886) and *Anna Karenina* (1875–77, Eng. 1886).

Another way of understanding what's happening is to regard our time as witnessing an explosion of multiple literacies. People are increasingly "body literate," "aurally literate," "visually literate," and so on. Films come at all levels of sophistication, as do recorded musics. Email is a burgeoning of letter writing. Not the elegant hand-written correspondence of eighteenth and nineteenth century Europe and Europeanized America, but a rapid part-words-part-pictures hypertext type of communication. People not only gab on their cell phones to converse via instant messaging, but they also read each other's body languages across cultures. They travel actually or virtually to far-away places interacting across ethnic, national, linguistic, religious, and gender boundaries. Operating at these levels and in so many directions takes multiple literacies. These multiple literacies are "performatives." Writing, speaking, and just about everything else is being transformed into performances. Exactly what that means and how it is being accomplished is a principal subject of this book. A world of multiple performatives is the purview of performance studies. Or to put it another way, the academic discipline of performance studies is emerging as a response to an increasingly performative world.

Traditional literacy is being forced to the extremes — a low-level pulp-and-tabloid literacy and a high-level specialized literacy. What is being squeezed is mid-level, or ordinary, literacy. The ability to read, write, and calculate above a basic level is probably declining in so-called "advanced" societies. Whether literacy will ever be achieved globally is open to question. Computers are taking over basic tasks. For example, a clerk in a store simply swipes a bar-coded item past the scanner, enters the amount of money proffered, and waits for the computerized cash register to read out how much to give in change. Efficient voice-recognition programs transcribe speaking into writing. A short time from now, a person will speak in one language and her words will be typed out (or spoken) in another. Many web pages already automatically translate into several languages. At least at the level of basic comprehension and

[handwritten: hypertext]

communication, the curse of the Tower of Babel is about to be history.

What is gaining in importance is hypertext, in the broadest meaning of that word. Hypertext combines words, images, and various shorthands. People who own cell phones use the keypads to punch out messages that combine letters, punctuation marks, and other graphics. This widespread practice is called "texting." Texting is not writing as taught in schools, nor is it voice telephony, or even email. Texting leaves lots of room for interpretation. What's not said or depicted explicitly is read in – a very wide range of implied feelings, requests, and desires. As in chat rooms, the persons of texters can be partly or fully fabricated. Texters perform their assumed identities, which may or may not be who they "really are." This kind of writing is unliterary but highly performative. It demands that senders and receivers use their imagination in transmitting and interpreting the dynamic cloud of possibilities that surrounds each message. As with indeterminacy in physics, only when someone "pins down" a message does it take a definite shape. And as in a jazz improvisation, what happens is a once only interaction.

High-level literacy is fast becoming the specialty of researchers and academics who investigate, expand, and preserve many different, often esoteric and technical, knowledges. Some of these knowledges – in cybernetics,

biotechnology, medicine, and economics – are having a huge impact on the world's peoples. Whole industries are devoted to "translating" research into marketable applications. At the same time, many academics do not feel the need to address a broad public or to explain exactly what the bases for the new knowledges are. Unfortunately, this is true of performance studies too. For example, performance studies scholars are able to "read" pop culture, but have yet to write about what they have discovered in ways that ordinary people – those who practice pop culture – find necessary to read.

Many Players, Few Departments, One Emergent Field

At colleges and universities around the world there are thousands of performing arts departments, an even greater number of English, anthropology, dramatic literature, and comparative literature departments, and many cultural studies programs. But as of 2001, there were only a handful of full-fledged performance studies departments or programs, including three in the USA, one at the University of Wales, Aberystwyth, and one at the University of Sydney, Australia (**see Maxwell box**). Two of the three in the USA

Ian Maxwell

Performance Studies at the University of Sydney, Australia

[. . .] at the Department of Performance Studies we set out from the premise that performance is not limited to those forms traditionally marked as being "artistic," and that any theory of performance must, accordingly, be generalisable to a wide range of performative practices, across and between cultures, history, and conventional social categories. [. . .] This means that scholars and students in Performance Studies need to develop new tools with which to develop a sense of the object of their analysis: not a text, but the living, breathing (and often ephemeral) performance itself. [. . .]

[handwritten margin note: not just write books to present scholarship but video interactive CD-Roms etc]

Performance Studies has developed over the last twenty years from an interdisciplinary exchange between traditional theatre studies and anthropology, in particular at New York University. At the University of Sydney, the Department has grown out of a collaboration between, initially, scholars from French Studies, Italian Studies, English, Asian Studies, Architecture, and a range of professional practitioners. Over the years, that initial core group expanded to include scholars from Anthropology, Music, Electrical Engineering, Semiotics and, more recently, contributions from History, Archaeology, Germanic Studies, Modern Greek, Classics, Medieval Studies and the Faculty of Law. At the same time, the discipline itself has evolved through a range of approaches, from semiotics to phenomenology, from functional linguistics to sociology, all of which have left their trace on current practice. Additionally, the department's staffing profile now includes permanent and casual teachers with backgrounds in a range of performance practices, in addition to their scholarly work. All of this adds up to a rich, varied, challenging and colourful learning experience in a discipline which is still very much in the early phase of its development.

2001, "Learning at the Department of Performance Studies,"
http://www.arts.usyd.edu.au/Arts/departs/perform/Learning%20at%20Perf%20Studies.html

[handwritten bottom notes: get funding for acquiring / commissioning Yakurr Picasso etc.; Dreamweaver website project; project of figuring out Final Cut to performance itself my book should include a CD-Rom; all pertains to idea that the Yakurr rituals can be interpreted from a global perspective – that they can perform in more than one cultural system.]

– at New York University and Northwestern University – offer PhDs in performance studies. At the University of California, Berkeley, performance studies is part of an amalgam called the Department of Theater, Dance, and Performance Studies. There is a tendency to change departmental names or append "performance studies" to existing names without concurrently revising the curriculum or disciplinary approach. On the other hand, performance studies is sometimes practiced under a different name, as at the University of California Los Angeles's Department of World Arts and Cultures. The fact is that most people professing performance studies work in non-performance studies environments. But this minority is a strong cohort reshaping a broad range of fields and professions.

Barbara Kirshenblatt-Gimblett

NYU's Department of Performance Studies

When I was recruited in 1980 the then Graduate Drama Department at NYU's School of the Arts was adrift. At first, I thought I was an unlikely candidate for chair. I had a PhD in folklore, not theatre. I studied performance in everyday life, not on the stage. Soon I realized there was no mistake. A mark of NYU's seriousness in making the transformation to performance studies was hiring a chair who did not come from drama or theatre. I brought a performance perspective to the study of culture that was remarkably aligned with what was emerging as performance theory and in a broad range of experimental and popular performance. By having someone who was not a theatre scholar chair, the faculty was ensuring a more radical break between the former Graduate Department of Drama and emerging Department of Performance Studies.

At the time that I was being recruited, the department consisted of four men – Richard Schechner, Brooks McNamara, Michael Kirby, and Theodore Hoffman. The department had never had a woman on the faculty. There were more than 400 MA and PhD students on the books, some of them deceased.

The idea for performance studies that I encountered had been developing in the context of contemporary experimental performance, with links to the historical avant-garde. Richard Schechner, Michael Kirby, and Brooks McNamara were themselves active in the off off Broadway movement. Performance studies would let them align their artistic practice with their pedagogy. This meant abandoning a traditional curriculum in European and American drama and theatre. EuroAmerican theatre would thenceforth find its place within an intercultural, intergeneric, and interdisciplinary intellectual project as one of many objects of study. Taking their lead from the historical avant-garde and contemporary experimental performance, they determined that Western theatre and the dramatic text would not be at the center of the new Performance Studies curriculum, though it continues to play an important role.

I built on the foundation of Schechner's landmark Performance Theory courses, McNamara's curriculum in popular entertainments, and Kirby's offerings on the historical avant-garde and stage design and technology. I set out to make what I saw as an extraordinarily exciting vision of Performance Studies an academic reality. Over more than a decade, we got our departmental house in order. We increased our office staff from one graduate student to a professional staff of three. We increased our faculty from four to eight. If this seems still a small faculty, remember we were a graduate-only department. We offered MA and PhD degrees.

Over the 12 years of my chairing (1980–92), we developed a rich Performance Studies curriculum that came to include dance research, thanks to Marcia Siegel, and feminist theory, thanks to Peggy Phelan. We placed greater emphasis on theory across the curriculum than had previously been the case. We raised academic and admission standards, reduced and transformed our student body so that everyone was full-time, increased financial aid, restructured requirements, and increased the pace and likelihood of completing the degree. We created a Performance Studies Archive. And, on our tenth anniversary, we organized the first Performance Studies International conference.

2001, personal correspondence

How is performance studies distinct from theatre studies, cultural studies, or other closely allied fields? One can construct several intellectual histories explaining the specific outlook of performance studies in its various manifestations as practiced by different schools of thought. In this book, I am developing my own version of the "NYU School of Performance Studies." My colleagues at NYU have different versions (**see Kirshenblatt-Gimblett box 2, Taylor box, and Phelan box**). At this point, I offer one narrative outlining how performance studies developed at NYU. This narrative concerns interactions among Western and Indian philosophy, anthropology, feminism, the aesthetics of everyday life, race theory, area studies, popular entertainments, queer theory, and postcolonial studies. These interactions have been heavily inflected by an ongoing contact with the avant-garde – both the Euro-American "historical avant-garde" (from symbolism and surrealism through to dada and happenings) and the more current avant-gardes being practiced in many parts of the world. Many students, and some professors, of performance studies at NYU are also practicing artists – in performance art, dance, theatre, and music. Preponderantly, their approach has been experimental – to stretch the limits of their arts in ways analogous to how performance studies stretches the limits of academic discourse.

The philosophical antecedents to performance studies include questions addressed in ancient times, in the

Diana Taylor

Performance Studies: A Hemispheric Focus

My particular investment in performance studies derives less from what it *is* than what it allows us to *do*. What I want performance studies to *do* is provide a theoretical lens for the sustained historical analysis of performance practices – the Americas being my special area of interest. The many definitions of the word "performance," as everyone has noted more or less generously, result in a complex, and at times contradictory, mix. For some it is a process, for others the "result" of a process. For some it is that which disappears, while others see it as that which remains as embodied memory. As the different uses of the term rarely engage each other, "performance" has a history of untranslatability. Ironically, the word is stuck in the disciplinary boxes it defies, denied the universality and transparency that some claim it promises its objects of analysis. These many points of "untranslatability," of course, are what make the term and the practices so culturally revealing. While performances may not give us access and insight into another culture, they certainly tell us a great deal about our desire for access and the politics of our interpretations.

"Performance" has no equivalent in Latin America. Translated simply but nonetheless ambiguously as masculine ("el performance") or feminine ("la performance"), it usually refers to performance art. Nonetheless, scholars and artists have started to use the term to refer more broadly to social dramas and embodied practices. What this "performance studies" approach allows us to *do* is crucial: rethink cultural production and expression from a place other than the written word which has dominated Latin American thought since the conquest. While writing was used before the conquest – either in pictogram form, hieroglyphs or knotting systems – it never replaced the performed utterance. Writing was a prompt to performance, a mnemonic aid, not a separate form of knowing. With the conquest, the legitimation of writing over other epistemic and mnemonic systems assured that colonial power could be developed and enforced without the input of the great majority of the population – the indigenous and marginal populations without access to systematic writing. While some scholars engage in "indigenismo" by focusing on oral traditions, the schism does not lie between the written and spoken word but rather between discursive and performative systems.

Western culture, wedded to the word, whether written or spoken, enables language to usurp epistemic and explanatory power. Performance studies allows us to take seriously other forms of cultural expression as both praxis and episteme. Performance traditions also serve to store and transmit knowledge. Performance studies, additionally, functions as a wedge in the institutional understanding and organization of knowledge. In the United States, departments of Spanish and Portuguese limit themselves to "language and literature" to the exclusion of much else. In Latin American institutions, "departamentos de letras" assure a similar schism between literary and embodied cultural practice. The resulting exclusions of many forms of embodied knowledge from analysis effect their own performance of erasure.

So perceive the Yakurr ritual not only as performing identity, but also of as a ~~means~~ form of knowledge.

not paying attention to ritual as an embodied knowledge involves a form of erasure.

Text as the preferred mode of form of knowing in West b/c in is exclusive to those who can read & write.

Preponderantly,

> Performance is as much about forgetting as about remembering, about disappearing as about re-appearing. A "hemispheric" focus indicates just how much "America," as the U.S. likes to think of itself, has forgotten about America, whose name, territory, and resources it has fought so hard to dominate. Domination by culture, by "definition," by claims to "originality" and "authenticity," functions in tandem with military and economic supremacy. Though a-historical in much of its practice, performance studies can allow us to engage in a sustained historical analysis of performance practices. That's what I'm asking it to do.
>
> 2001, personal communication

Renaissance, and in the 1950s to 1970s, the period immediately before performance studies came into its own. Early philosophers both in the West and in India pondered the relationship between daily life, theatre, and the "really real." Plato (c.427–c.347 BCE) felt that the really real, the ideal, existed only as pure forms. In the *Republic*, he argued that ordinary reality is but the shadows puppets cast on the wall of the dark cave of ignorance. (One wonders if shadow puppetry, so popular in Asia from ancient times, was known to Plato.) Theatre imitates these shadows and is therefore even further removed from the really real. As if this weren't enough, Plato also distrusted theatre because it appealed to the emotions rather than to reason. Therefore, the Greek philosopher banned theatre from his ideal republic. It was left to his student Aristotle (384–322 BCE) to redeem the theatre. Aristotle argued that the really real was "indwelling" in each being as a plan or potential, somewhat like a genetic code. In the *Poetics* Aristotle reasoned that by imitating actions, and the logical line of consequences flowing from actions, one might learn about these indwelling forms. Far from wanting to avoid the emotions, Aristotle wanted to understand, arouse, and purge them.

> **Plato (c. 427– c. 347 BCE):** Greek philosopher, advocate of reason, restraint, and logic. Developed the dialogical or dialectical style of discourse – reasoning by means of dialogue and the confrontation of opposites. His works include many "dialogues" as well as *The Republic* (c. 370 BCE) – a work in which Plato urged that poets and actors be excluded from his ideal republic.

> **Aristotle (384–322 BCE):** Greek philosopher, student of Plato. Aristotle published numerous philosophical treatises, including the *Poetics* (c. 335 BCE), which lays out principles of Greek tragic drama.

Indian philosophers had a different idea altogether. Writing at roughly the same time as the Greeks, they felt that the whole universe, from ordinary reality to the realm of the gods, was *maya* and *lila* – illusion, play, and theatre on a grand scale. These were far from being terms of debasement. The theory of maya–lila asserts that the really real is playful, ever-changing, and illusive. What is "behind" maya–lila? On this, Indian philosophers differed. Some said that nothing was beyond maya–lila. Others proposed realities too awesome for humans to experience. When Arjuna, the hero-warrior of the *Mahabharata*, asks Krishna to show his true form, the experience is terrifying in the extreme. Still other philosophers proposed the existence of Brahman, an absolute unity-of-all which a person can enter through meditation, yoga, or living a perfected life. At the achievement of *moksha*, or release from the cycle of birth–death–rebirth, a person's individual *atman* becomes one with Brahman. But for most people most of the time, reality is maya–lila. The gods also enter the world of maya–lila. The gods take human form, as Krishna does in the performance of Raslila (Krishna's dance with adoring female cow-herders and with his favorite lover, Radha) or as Rama does in the performance of Ramlila (when Vishnu incarnates himself to rid the world of the demon Ravana). Raslila and Ramlila are performed today. Hundreds of millions of Indian Hindus believe in these enacted incarnations – where young boys become the gods. Notions of maya–lila are discussed more fully in chapter 4.

In Renaissance Europe a widely accepted opinion was that the world was a great theatre, a *theatrum mundi*. In **William Shakespeare**'s (1564–1616) *As You Like It*, Jaques puts it this way: "All the world's a stage | And all the men and women merely players; | They have their exits and their entrances; | And one man in his time plays many parts" (2, 7: 139–42). Hamlet, in his instructions to the players, had a somewhat different opinion, more in keeping with Aristotle's theory of mimesis: "[. . .] the purpose of playing, whose end, both at the first and now, was and is, to hold, as 't were, the mirror up to nature; to show virtue her own feature, scorn her own image, and the very age and body of the time his form and pressure" (3, 2: 21–25). Everyday life was theatrical; conversely, theatre offered a working model of how life was lived. To use terms familiar to those living in seventeenth-century England: theatre and nature resembled each other.

[handwritten: like embodiment performance is a mode of investigation?]

Peggy Phelan

Another History, Another Future of Performance Studies

One potent version of the history of performance studies is that the field was born out of the fecund collaborations between Richard Schechner and Victor Turner. In bringing theatre and anthropology together, both men saw the extraordinarily deep questions these perspectives on cultural expression raised. If the diversity of human culture continually showed a persistent theatricality, could performance be a universal expression of human signification, akin to language? [. . .] Was "theatre" an adequate term for the wide range of "theatrical acts" that intercultural observation was everywhere revealing? Perhaps "performance" better captured and conveyed the activity that was provoking these questions. Since only a tiny portion of the world's cultures equated theatre with written scripts, performance studies would begin with an intercultural understanding of its fundamental term, rather than enlisting intercultural case studies as additives, rhetorically or ideologically based postures of inclusion and relevance.

This is the story that surrounded me when I first began teaching in the Department of Performance Studies [. . .] in 1985. I was immediately fascinated by the idea that two men gave birth. [. . .]

When I first began reading Turner's and Schechner's work I was struck by its generosity and porousness, its undisguised desire to be "taken up." [. . .] But I was also a little suspicious of their ease, their sense that all could be understood if we could only see widely and deeply enough. [. . .] As the institutionalization of performance studies spread throughout the eighties (sometimes under other names) in the United States and internationally, the openness of the central paradigm sometimes made it seem that performance studies was (endlessly?) capable of absorbing ideas and methods from a wide variety of disciplines. [. . .]

But institutionalization is hardly ever benign, and one could easily tell the story of the consolidation of the discipline of performance studies in a much less flattering manner. Many people (including some of my own inner voices), did tell me such stories, but I'll use the conditional here to muffle echoes and because I love the guilty. To wit: one could accuse the discipline of practicing some of the very colonialist and empire-extending arts it had critiqued so aggressively. One could argue that performance studies was a narrow, even small-minded, version of cultural studies. One could say that performance studies had so broad a focus precisely because it had nothing original to say. One could suggest that the famous "parasitism" of J. L. Austin's linguistic performative was actually a terrific description of performance studies itself. One could even argue that the whole discipline was created as a reactionary response to the simulations and virtualities of postmodernism; a discipline devoted to live artistic human exchange could easily be taken up by the universities in the eighties precisely because its power as a vital form of culture exchange had been dissipated. A new discipline just in time to commemorate a dead art would be in keeping with the necrophilia of much academic practice.

But each of these (conditional) claims misses what I believe are the most compelling possibilities realized by performance studies. While theatre and anthropology certainly played a central role in the generative disciplines of performance studies, other "points of contact" have also had exceptional force in the field. [. . . W]e must begin to imagine a post-theatrical, post-anthropological age. [. . .]

Thinking of performance in the expanded field of the electronic paradigm requires that we reconsider the terms that have been at the contested center of performance studies for the past decade [since 1988]: simulation, representation, virtuality, presence, and above all, the slippery indicative "as if." The electronic paradigm places the "as if" at the foundation of a much-hyped "global communication," even while it asks us to act "as if" such a network would render phantasmatic race, class, gender, literacy, and other access differentials. [. . .]

The electronic paradigm as an epistemic event represents something more than a new way to transmit information; it redefines knowledge itself into that which can be sent and that which can be stored. Performance studies [. . .] is alert to the Net's potential to flatten and screen that which we might want most to remember, to love, to learn. We have created and studied a discipline based on that which disappears, art that cannot be preserved or posted. And we know performance knows things worth knowing. As the electronic paradigm moves into the center of universities, corporations, and other systems of power-knowledge, the "knowing" that cannot be preserved or posted may well generate a mourning that transcends the current lite Luddite resistance to technology.

1998, Introduction to *The Ends of Performance*, 3–5,8

[handwritten: performance studies is about art that cannot be preserved or posted (on the Net).]

William Shakespeare (1564–1616): English playwright, poet, and actor. Among his many plays are *Hamlet*, *King Lear*, *Othello*, *The Merchant of Venice*, *Macbeth*, *Measure for Measure*, *As You Like It*, and *The Tempest*.

Erving Goffman (1922–82): Canadian-born anthropologist. Was among the first to make comprehensive studies of performance in everyday life. His books include *The Presentation of Self in Everyday Life* (1959), *Interaction Ritual* (1967), and *Frame Analysis* (1974).

The most recent version of the *theatrum mundi* idea in Western thought took shape with the convergence of a variety of approaches beginning shortly after the end of the Second World War and continuing to the present. In 1949, **Jacques Lacan** (1901–81) published "The Mirror Stage," his influential psychoanalytic study proposing that when very young children begin to recognize themselves in the mirror, they actually see themselves as "another." In 1955, **Gregory Bateson** (1904–80) wrote "A Theory of Play and Fantasy." Bateson emphasized the importance of what he termed "metacommunication," the message that tells the receiver that a message of a certain kind is being sent – social communications exist within a complex of frames. Bateson's ideas were elaborated on by **Erving Goffman** (1922–82) in a series of works about performing in everyday life, the most influential of which is his 1959, *The Presentation of Self in Everyday Life*. At roughly the same time, philosopher **J. L. Austin** (1911–60) developed his notion of "performativity." Austin's lectures on the performative were published posthumously in 1962 as *How To Do Things With Words*. According to Austin, performatives are utterances such as bets, promises, namings, and so on that actually do something, that perform. A little later, in France, **Jean-François Lyotard** (1924–98), **Gilles Deleuze** (1925–95), **Michel Foucault** (1926–84), **Jean Baudrillard** (1929–), **Jacques Derrida** (1930–), **Guy Debord** (1931–94), and **Félix Guattari** (1930–92) argued for radical new ways to understand history, social life, and language. I discuss performativity, postmodernism, simulations, and poststructuralism in chapter 5.

[handwritten: meta-communi-cation.]

[handwritten: performativity]

J. L. Austin (1911–60): English philosopher and linguist. His Harvard lectures on the concept of the "performative" were posthumously published as *How To Do Things With Words* (1962).

Jean-François Lyotard (1924–98): French philosopher. Major works include *The Postmodern Condition* (1979, Eng. 1984), *The Differend* (1982, Eng. 1988) and *Peregrinations: Law, Form, Event* (1988).

Gilles Deleuze (1925–95): French philosopher and proponent of poststructuralism. With collaborator **Félix Guattari (1930–92)**, wrote *Anti-Oedipus* (1972, Eng. 1977) and *A Thousand Plateaus* (1980, Eng. 1987).

Gregory Bateson (1904–80): British-born anthropologist, cyberneticist, and communications theorist. Major works include *Steps to an Ecology of Mind* (1972) and *Mind and Nature* (1979).

Jean Baudrillard (1929–): French intellectual and cultural critic, known for his work on the concept of the *simulacra*. Major works include *Simulations* (1981, Eng. 1983) and *The Illusion of the End* (1992, Eng. 1994).

Jacques Derrida (1930–): Algerian-born French philosopher. Author of *Of Grammatology* (1967, Eng. 1976) *Writing and Difference* (1967, Eng. 1976), and many other works concerning the philosophical movement he pioneered, "deconstruction."

Jacques Lacan (1901–81): French psychoanalyst and interpreter of Freud's theories in terms of structural linguistics. Lacan suggested that the formation of the self (or "I") was largely a function of the subject's alienation from one's own self. A selection of his writings is availabe as *Ecrits* (1966, Eng. 1977).

Guy Debord (1931–94): French writer and filmmaker, leader of the Situationists (1957–72), a revolutionary group of artists and writers who came to prominence during the Paris riots of May 1968. Author of *The Society of the Spectacle* (1967, Eng. 1994).

Michel Foucault (1926–84): French philosopher and historian whose work explored the power relationships entwined in the organization of knowledge and social interactions. Among numerous major works are *Madness and Civilization* (1961, Eng. 1965), *The Order of Things* (1966, Eng. 1970), *Discipline and Punish* (1975, Eng. 1977), and *The History of Sexuality* (1976, Eng. 1978).

My own role in the formation of performance studies goes back to the mid-1960s. My 1966 essay "Approaches to Theory/Criticism" was a formulation of an area of study I called "the performance activities of man" (*sic*): play, games, sports, theatre, and ritual. "Actuals," published in 1970, related rituals in non-Western cultures to avant-garde performances.

[handwritten: Schechner]

[handwritten: my rendering Yakut ritual as art akin to avant-garde perf.]

In 1973, as guest editor of a special *TDR* issue on "Performance and the Social Sciences," I outlined seven "areas where performance theory and the social sciences coincide":

1 Performance in everyday life, including gatherings of every kind.
2 The structure of sports, ritual, play, and public political behaviors.
3 Analysis of various modes of communication (other than the written word); semiotics.
4 Connections between human and animal behavior patterns with an emphasis on play and ritualized behavior.
5 Aspects of psychotherapy that emphasize person-to-person interaction, acting out, and body awareness.
6 Ethnography and prehistory – both of exotic and familiar cultures [from the Western perspective].
7 Constitution of unified theories of performance, which are, in fact, theories of behavior.

I saw these nodes connected to each other either as a "fan" or a "web" (**see figure 1.1**). In 1977, the first edition of *Performance Theory* appeared, revised and expanded in 1988. I published *Between Theater and Anthropology* in 1985 and *The Future of Ritual* in 1993. I also co-edited several books as well as serving twice as editor of *TDR* (1962–69,

1987–present). I related my theories to my artistic work and research activities in various parts of the world, and to my growing sense of the broad spectrum of performance (**see figures 1.2 and 1.3**).

The Victor Turner Connection

This network of ideas and practice was nourished by my relationship with anthropologist **Victor Turner** (1917–83). Though we knew each other's work earlier, Turner and I met in 1977 when he invited me to participate in a conference he was organizing on "Ritual, Drama, and Spectacle." The conference was so successful, and the chemistry between Turner and me so positive, that we joined to plan a "World Conference on Ritual and Performance" which developed into three related conferences held during 1981–82. The first focused on the performances of the Yaquis of northern Mexico and the US Southwest; the second on the work of **Suzuki Tadashi** (1939–). The culminating meeting took place in New York from 23 August to 1 September 1982. Attending were artists and scholars from the Americas, Asia, Europe, and Africa. All in all, 74 participated, 49 at the New

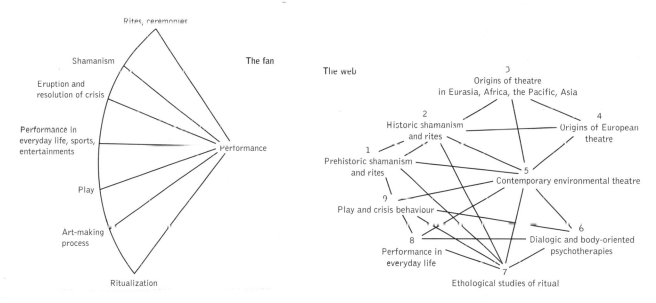

fig 1.1. Performance can be graphically configured as either a fan or a web. This open fan depicts an orderly panorama ranging from "ritualization" on one end through the "performances of everyday life" in the center to "rites and ceremonies" at the other end. Ritualization is an ethological term; rites and ceremonies are uniquely human.

The web depicts the same system more dynamically – and therefore more experientially. Each node interacts with all the others. It's no accident that I place my "contemporary environmental theatre" in the center. This arbitrary and subjective positioning expresses my life practice. Others might place something else at the center. In actual fact, there is no center – one ought to imagine the system as in continuous motion and realignment. Furthermore I place historical events alongside speculations and artistic performances. This method is similar to that of Australian First Peoples who credit dreams with a reality maybe even stronger than awake-time events. My method is also similar to the classic theatre exercise wherein "as if" = "is".

Drawing: "Fan" and "Web" from p. ii of *Performance Theory*, 1977 and all subsequent editions.

fig. 1.2. A selection of performances directed by Richard Schechner.

Dionysus in 69, based on Euripides' *The Bacchae*. The Ecstasy Dance led by Dionysus played by William Finley. The Performance Group, New York, 1968. Photograph by Frederick Eberstadt. Photograph courtesy of Richard Schechner.

Cherry Ka Bagicha (The Cherry Orchard), Anton Chekhov. Act 2, Dunyasha flirting with Yepikhodov. With the Repertory Company of the National School of Drama, New Delhi, 1982. Photograph by Richard Schechner.

Ma Rainey's Black Bottom, August Wilson. Act 2, Ma Rainey (seated, played by Sophie Mcina), her girl Dussie Mae, played by Baby Cele, and her nephew, Sylvester. Grahamstown Festival, Republic of South Africa, 1992. Photograph by Richard Schechner.

Three Sisters, Anton Chekhov. Act 2, Vershinin, played by Frank Wood, orating about the future. With East Coast Artists, New York 1997. Photograph by Richard Schechner.

The Oresteia, Aeschylus (in Chinese). Agamemnon, played by Wu Hsing-kuo, steps on the purple carpet. With the Contemporary Legend Theatre, Taipei, 1995. Photograph by Richard Schechner.

York conference – only Victor and **Edith Turner** (1921–), **Phillip Zarrilli**, and I were at all three meetings. Turner exulted in the meetings as utopian gatherings (**see Turner box**). *By Means of Performance (1990)* was edited from the proceedings of the three episodes of the World Conference.

Suzuki Tadashi (1939–): Japanese founding artistic director of the Suzuki Company of Toga, with whom he has directed a number of influential works including *The Trojan Women* and *Dionysus*. He advocates an intensely physical approach to actor-training which he outlines in *The Way of Acting* (1986).

Phillip Zarrilli (1947–): American director, writer, and actor trainer employing a psychophysical process developed from Asian martial and meditation arts. His books include *Acting (Re)Considered* (editor, 1995), *When the Body Becomes All Eyes* (1998), and *Kathakali Dance Drama* (2000).

Victor Turner (1917–83): Scottish-born anthropologist. Major works include *Forest of Symbols* (1967), *The Ritual Process* (1969), *Dramas, Fields, and Metaphors* (1974), and *From Ritual to Theatre* (1982). His wife, anthropologist **Edith Turner (1921–)**, collaborated with him on many of his works. Among Edith Turner's writings are *Experiencing Ritual* (1992) and *The Hands Feel It* (1996).

Victor Turner

By Their Performances Shall Ye Know Them

Cultures are most fully expressed In and made conscious of themselves in their ritual and theatrical performances. [. . .] A performance is a dialectic of "flow," that is, spontaneous movement in which action and awareness are one, and "reflexivity," in which the central meanings, values and goals of a culture are seen "in action," as they shape and explain behavior. A performance is declarative of our shared humanity, yet it utters the uniqueness of particular cultures. We will know one another better by entering one another's performances and learning their grammars and vocabularies.

1980, From a Planning Meeting for the World Conference on Ritual and Performance quoted in introduction to Richard Schechner and Willa Appel (eds), *By Means of Performance*, 1.

[margin handwritten notes:] we all have bodys. perf. primary modality through which one can grasp another culture

---

What made Turner's conferences so special was that they were extended get-togethers of relatively few people, lasting from five days to two weeks. Participants had plenty of time to trade ideas, view performances together, tell stories, and socialize. These conferences helped shape my ideas about what performance studies could become. In my courses at NYU, I invited many of those who were at one or another of the conferences to lecture or guest teach. Friends reached out to friends. Tilting performance studies toward anthropology – which was particularly strong in the 1970s and 1980s – is linked to working with Turner and the people he introduced me to; other possibilities for performance studies have since come into play strongly.

After Turner's death in 1983, I planned another conference in his style – a 1990 meeting on "intercultural performance" attended by about 20 artists and scholars at the

Northwestern University's Department of Performance Studies

Mission Statement

The department of performance studies educates students, produces research, and supports public art Initiatives that extending deep in the understanding of performance are central to the human condition. Performance has become a keyword in recent intellectual history, functioning as a lens to focus thinking about human experience and philosophy, literature on the amount is, sociology, cultural anthropology, lInguistics, education, outlaw, and other disciplines. The department contributes to the strong academic interest in "performance" as a concept or metaphor that foregrounds the creative, constructed, collaborative, and contingent nature of human communication and interaction. At the same time, the department has strengthened its historical commitment to performance as a method as well as a subject to research. In the midst of the proliferation of performance theory for all corners of the economy, the department remains anchored in its long-standing tradition of human performance as an experiential practice and pedagogy, an embodied way of knowing, and not just an abstract concept.

2000, from "The Department of Performance Studies," a pamphlet distributed by Northwestern University

[handwritten bottom note:] performance is collaborative construction contingent on communication.

fig 1.3. A photographic array of some examples of the "broad spectrum of performance."

Ritual:
Masked performer during carnival in Guinea-Bissau, 1980s. Photograph by Eve L. Crowley. Photograph courtesy of Richard Schechner.

Ritual:
Bishop Fulton J. Sheen celebrating mass. Photograph by Karsh of Ottawa. Copyright Camera Press, London.

Play:
Sam and Kate Taylor and their cousin Bridget Caird playing "dress up" in New Zealand, 1979. Photograph by Moira Taylor.

Sports:
The New York Mets baseball team playing at Shea Stadium, New York, 2001. Photograph by Henry Bial.

Popular Entertainment:
Woodstock Festival of music, 1968. Photograph by Ken Regan.

Performing Arts:
Peter Brook's 1970 production of Shakespeare's *A Midsummer Night's Dream*, Royal Shakespeare Theatre. On the swings, Alan Howard as Oberon and John Kane as Puck. Below, Sara Kestelman as Titania and David Waller as Bottom. Copyright Shakespeare Birthplace Trust.

Performing Arts:
Azuma Katsuko performing kabuki dance, Japan, 1980s. Photograph by Torben Huss. Photograph courtesy of Eugenio Barba.

Performance in Everyday Life:
Ascot, the Royal Enclosure. Copyright Popperfoto.

Performing Arts:
Isadora Duncan at around the turn of the 20th century. Photograph courtesy of New York Public Library.

Political Performance:
Students in a sitdown demonstration confronting the National Guard at the University of California, Berkeley, 1969. Copyright Hulton-Deutsch Collection/ Corbis.

Rockefeller Foundation's villa in Bellagio, Italy. Many of the participants were closely associated with what was by then being called the "emerging field of performance studies." The three conferences – stretching over 15 years – were important as field-defining events, as means of dissemination, and as prototypes for the yet-to-be convened "Points of Contact" conferences of the Centre for Performance Research in Wales and the annual conferences of Performance Studies International.

The Centre for Performance Research and PSi

Journals + Conferences

From the early 1980s onward, performance studies developed rapidly. In 1980, the NYU Graduate Drama Department became the Department of Performance Studies, the first such in the world. TDR added the subtitle, *The Journal of Performance Studies*. In Wales, under the guidance of **Richard Gough** (1956–), the Centre for Performance Research (CPR) convened a series of conferences entitled "Points of Contact" (named after the introduction to my *Between Theater and Anthropology*) and in 1996 launched its own journal, *Performance Research*. In 1993 performance studies scholars formed a "focus group" within ATHE (American Theatre in Higher Education). By 2001, there were about 450 participants in the focus group. In 1997, many of the same group, joined by people from the Speech Communications Association and artists, formed Performance Studies International (PSi) – the first worldwide association devoted solely to performance studies. But before there was an official organization there were several performance studies conferences. The first – entitled "Performance Studies International" – was convened at NYU in 1991 to celebrate the tenth anniversary of the founding of the Department. Several hundred persons attended. From 1995 onward, there have been annual conferences drawing upward of 500 people. The first was at NYU, the second at Northwestern University. Other annual meetings took place at the Georgia Institute of Technology in Atlanta, at the Centre for Performance Research in Aberystwyth, at

Arizona State University in Phoenix, and at the Johannes Gutenberg University in Mainz, Germany. The 2002 conference will take place at NYU. *The Ends of Performance* (1998), edited by **Peggy Phelan** (birthdate withheld) and **Jill Lane** (1967–), is a collection of papers based on the 1995 PSi conference.

Carol **Simpson Stern** and Bruce **Henderson**

A Whole Field of Human Activity

The term *performance* incorporates a whole field of human activity. It embraces a verbal act in everyday life or a staged play, a rite of invective played in urban streets, a performance in the Western traditions of high art, or a work of performance art. It includes cultural performances, such as the personal narrative or folk and fairy tales, or more communal forms of ceremony – the National Democratic Convention, an evensong vigil march for people with AIDS, Mardi Gras, or a bullfight. It also includes literary performance, the celebration of individual genius, and conformity to Western definitions of art. In all cases a *performance act, interactional* in nature and involving *symbolic forms* and *live bodies*, provides a way to constitute meaning and to affirm individual and cultural values.

1993, *Performance Texts and Contexts*, 3

Richard Gough: (1956–): Founder and director of the Centre for Performance Research (CPR) of Aberystwyth, Wales. Gough organized a series of conferences, "Points of Contact," in the 1990s which helped define performance studies. He is a founding editor of the journal *Performance Research*.

Peggy Phelan (prefers not to have her birthdate disclosed): American feminist scholar, chair of NYU's Department of Performance Studies from 1993 to 1996. Author of *Unmarked* (1993) and *Mourning Sex* (1997).

Jill Lane (1967–): American performance theorist. One of the organizers of the First Annual Performance Studies Conference (1995) and editor (with Peggy Phelan) of *The Ends of Performance* (1998).

Northwestern's Brand of Performance Studies

It was no accident that the 1996 PSi conference took place at Northwestern University in Evanston, Illinois. Along with NYU, NU is the only other fully vested department of performance studies in the USA. Northwestern's brand of performance studies, which took its present shape during the 1980s, emerged from speech communications, oral interpretation (the performance of literature other than dramas), rhetoric (debate and public speaking), and urban anthropology (**see Northwestern box**). Adherents of the NU approach take a very broad view of what constitutes "text" (**see Stern and Henderson box**). In the 1980s, two historians of performance studies felt it was "too early" to assert that the new name at Northwestern signaled a shift in paradigm from oral interpretation and theatre to performance studies (**see Pelias and VanOosting box**). By the start of the new millennium the paradigm shift was clear.

Ronald J. Pelias and James VanOosting

A Magical Renaming that Opens Doors

The term "performance studies" as a disciplinary title enjoys increasing currency, often used in place of the more familiar label, "oral interpretation." [. . .] Between the two terms exist many possible tensions. Is the relationship between performance studies and oral interpretation an instance of magical renaming, a natural stage of evolutionary development, a revisionist reading, or a revolutionary denial? To examine this question, we shall assume the broadest possible distinction between oral interpretation and performance studies by granting paradigmatic status to the newer term. [. . .]

Performance studies calls into question the privilege of academic authority by including all members of a speech community as potential artists, all utterances as potentially aesthetic, all events as potentially theatrical, and all audiences as potentially active participants who can authorize artistic experience. By rejecting canonical security and exclusionary conventions, performance studies practitioners eschew artistic imperialism in favor of aesthetic communalism. These claims, then, yield an ideology that is racially democratic and counterelitist. [. . .]

[T]he move to performance studies institutionalizes what oral interpretation sanctioned as experimentation. [. . .] While positioned squarely within the field of speech communication, [the name] "performance studies" suggests clear links to theatre, ethnography and folklore, popular culture, and contemporary literary criticism. However, the new nomenclature is hardly arbitrary or mercenary; it is justified by the long evolutionary development of oral interpretation. That performance studies is a natural phase in disciplinary development is manifest by the contemporary research thrusts pushing out the conventional limits of oral interpretation. To recommend performance studies as an evolutionary stage demands a certain revisionist reading of the history of oral interpretation. [. . .] Performance studies, thus, is an act of magical renaming, a stage of evolutionary development, and a revisionist reading. But does the name change point to a paradigm shift? It is too early to say.

1987, "A Paradigm for Performance Studies," 219, 221, 228–29

Impetus for the shift came strongly from **Dwight Conquergood** (1949–), a principal theorist and practitioner of the NU model. Conquergood argues for a performance-based rather than text-based approach that combines scholarly and artistic training and practice (**see Conquergood box 1**). In the mid-1990s Conquergood called for performance studies adherents to "rethink" five areas of study (**see Conquergood box 2**):

Dwight Conquergood (1949–): American ethnographer and performance theorist. Former chair of Northwestern University's Department of Performance Studies. Co-director (with Taggart Siegel) of the video documentary *The Heart Broken in Half* (1990).

1 Performance and cultural process.
2 Performance and ethnographic praxis.
3 Performance and hermeneutics.
4 Performance and scholarly representation.
5 The politics of performance.

As general principles, these "rethinkings" are not far from what goes on at NYU. But the two approaches differ considerably when the theories are put into practice. They both enact their disciplinary genealogies.

Dwight Conquergood

Performance Studies at Northwestern

What is really radical about theatre, performance, and media studies at N U is that we embrace BOTH written scholarship AND creative work, texts and performance. [. . .] Printed texts are too important and powerful for us to cede that form of scholarship. But it is not enough. We also engage in creative work that stands alongside and in metonymic tension with conventional scholarship. We think of performance and practical work as a supplement to – not substitute for – written scholarship. [. . .]

Speaking from my home department, we sometimes refer to the three A's of performance studies: artistry, analysis, activism. Or to change the alliteration, a commitment to the three C's of performance studies: creativity, critique, and community. By community, I mean citizenship and civic struggles for social justice. Theatre, performance, and media studies at N U all struggle to forge a unique and unifying mission around the triangulation of these three perspectives on performance and creative work:

1. Accomplishment (the making of art and culture; creativity; embodiment; the work of imagination; artistic process and form; knowledge that comes from doing, participatory understanding, practical consciousness, performing as a way of knowing).

2. Analysis (the interpretation of art and culture; critique; thinking about and with performance; performance as an optic, a metaphor or theoretical model for understanding culture; knowledge that comes from contemplation and comparison – concentrated attention and contextualization as a way of knowing).

3. Application (activism, the connection to community; social contexts and articulations; action research; artistic and research projects that reach outside the academy and are rooted in an ethic of reciprocity and exchange; knowledge that is tested by practice within a community – social commitment, collaboration, and contribution/intervention as a way of knowing: praxis).

The ongoing challenge of our collaborative agenda is to refuse and supersede the deeply entrenched division of labor, apartheid of knowledges, that plays out inside the academy as the difference between thinking and doing, interpreting and making, conceptualization and creativity. The division of labor between theory and practice, abstraction and embodiment, is an arbitrary and rigged choice, and like all binarisms it is booby-trapped. It's a Faustian bargain. If we go the one-way street of abstraction, then we cut ourselves off from the nourishing ground of participatory experience. If we go the one-way street of practice, then we drive ourselves into an isolated cul de sac, a practitioner's workshop or artist's colony. Our radical move is to turn, and return, insistently, to the crossroads.

1999, From a talk at the "Cultural Intersections" conference, Northwestern University.

Dwight **Conquergood**

The Five Areas of Performance Studies

1. *Performance and Cultural Process.* What are the conceptual consequences of thinking about culture as a *verb* instead of a *noun*, a process instead of product? Culture as an unfolding performative invention instead of reified system, structure, or variable? What happens to our thinking about performance when we move it outside of aesthetics and situate it at the center of lived experience?

2. *Performance and Ethnographic Praxis.* What are the methodological implications of thinking about fieldwork as the collaborative performance of an enabling fiction between observer and observed, knower and known? How does thinking about fieldwork as performance differ from thinking about fieldwork as the collection of data? [. . .]

3. *Performance and Hermeneutics.* What kinds of knowledge are privileged or displaced when performed experience becomes a way of knowing, a method of critical inquiry, a mode of understanding? [. . .]

4. *Performance and Scholarly Representation.* What are the rhetorical problematics of performance as a complementary or alternative form of "publishing" research? What are the differences between reading an analysis of fieldwork data, and hearing the voices from the field interpretively filtered through the voice of the researcher? [. . .] What about enabling people themselves to perform their own experience? [. . .]

5. *The Politics of Performance.* What is the relationship between performance and power? How does performance reproduce, enable, sustain, challenge, subvert, critique, and naturalize ideology? How do performances simultaneously reproduce and resist hegemony? How does performance accommodate and contest domination?

1991, "Rethinking Ethnography," 190

The "Inter" of Performance Studies

Performance studies resists fixed definition. Performance studies does not value "purity." It is at its best when operating amidst a dense web of connections. Academic disciplines are most active at their ever-changing interfaces. In terms of performance studies, this means the interactions between theatre and anthropology, folklore and sociology, history and performance theory, gender studies and psychoanalysis, performativity and actual performance events — and more. New interfaces will appear as time goes on, and older ones will disappear. Accepting "inter" means opposing the establishment of any single system of knowledge, values, or subject matter. Performance studies is open, multivocal, and self-contradictory. Therefore, any call for a "unified field" is, in my view, a misunderstanding of the very fluidity and playfulness fundamental to performance studies.

At a more theoretical level, what is the relation of performance studies to performance proper? Are there any limits to performativity? Is there anything outside the purview of performance studies? These questions will be discussed more fully in chapters 2 and 5. For now, let me say that the performative occurs in places and situations not traditionally marked as "performing arts," from dress-up and drag to certain kinds of writing and speaking. Accepting the performative as a category of theory makes it increasingly difficult to sustain a distinction between appearances and reality, facts and make-believe, surfaces and depths. Appearances are actualities — neither more nor less so than what lies behind or beneath appearances. Social reality is constructed through and through. In modernity, what was "deep" and "hidden" was thought to be "more real" than what was on the surface (Platonism dies hard). But in postmodernity, the relationship between depths and surfaces is fluid; the relationship is dynamically convective.

Ethical Questions

Many who practice performance studies resist or oppose the global forces of capital. Fewer will concede that these forces know very well — perhaps even better than we — how to perform, in all meanings of that word. The interplay of

that is what is really behind globilization = capital moves perhaps continued desire to own the other

efficiency, productivity, activity, and entertainment – in a word, performance – informs and drives countless operations. In many key areas of human activity "performance" is crucial to success. The word crops up in apparently very different circumstances. These divergent uses indicate a basic overall similarity at the theoretical level. Performance has become a major site of knowledge and power (**see McKenzie box**). In relation to this relatively new situation, many ethical questions remain nakedly open. The most important concern "intervention" – biologically, militarily, culturally. When, if ever, ought force be used to "save" or "protect" people – and why say yes to Kosovo and no to Rwanda? Who has the right and/or the responsibility to say yes or no? What about genetic intervention? Who can be against preventing or curing diseases and increasing crop yields? But what about cloning? Or modifying human traits? What constitutes a "disease" and what traits are "bad"? The nineteenth and twentieth centuries saw some very nasty things done under the aegis of a eugenic "improvement" of the human species. What about genetically engineering "super athletes" (**see Longman box**)? In terms of art and scholarship, what, if any, ought to be the limits to creativity and cultural borrowings? I will take up some of these questions in chapter 8.

Jon McKenzie

Performance is a New Subject of Knowledge

[. . . P]erformance will be to the 20th and 21st centuries what discipline was to the 18th and 19th, that is, an onto-historical formation of power and knowledge [italics in original].[. . .]

Like discipline, performance produces a new subject of knowledge, though one quite different from that produced under the regime of panoptic surveillance. Hyphenated identities, transgendered bodies, digital avatars, the Human Genome Project – these suggest that the performative subject is constructed as fragmented rather than unified, decentered rather than centered, virtual as well as actual. Similarly, performative objects are unstable rather than fixed, simulated rather than real. They do not occupy a single, "proper" place in knowledge; there is no such thing as the thing-in-itself. Instead, objects are produced and maintained through a variety of sociotechnical systems, overcoded by many discourses, and situated in numerous sites of practice. While disciplinary institutions and mechanisms forged Western Europe's industrial revolution and its system of colonial empires, those of performance are programming the circuits of our postindustrial, postcolonial world. More profoundly than the alphabet, printed book, and factory, such technologies as electronic media and the Internet allow discourses and practices from different geographical and historical situations to be networked and patched together, their traditions to be electronically archived and played back, their forms and processes to become raw materials for other productions. Similarly, research and teaching machines once ruled strictly and linearly by the book are being retooled by a multimedia, hypertextual metatechnology, that of the computer.

2001, *Perform Or Else*, 18

Jere Longman

Genetically Altered Athletes

Genes serve as a script that directs the body to make proteins. It seems fantastic today to think that injecting a gene could result in more fast-twitch muscle fibers, enabling a sprinter to run 100 meters in six seconds instead of just under 10. Or injecting a gene that could increase oxygen-carrying capacity so that a marathoner could run 26.2 miles in one and a half hours instead of just over two. Some scientists and Olympic committee members think genetic engineering in sports is a decade away. Some believe it may appear in two years. Still others believe crude forms might already be in use, at great health risk to athletes. [. . .] Instead of repeatedly ingesting pills or taking injections, an athlete may be able, with a single insertion of genetic material, to sustain bulked-up muscle mass or heightened oxygen-carrying capacity for months or even years. Such genetic manipulation would be extremely difficult, if not virtually impossible to detect [. . .].

2001, "Someday Soon, Athletic Edge May Be From Altered Genes," *The New York Times*, 11 May, A1, D5.

panoptic surveillance

Conclusion

Performance studies came into existence because of a radically changed intellectual and artistic landscape emerging during the last third of the twentieth century. Combined with a dissatisfaction with the status quo was an explosion of knowledge and a new means of distributing this knowledge via the internet. The world no longer appeared as a book to be read but as a performance to participate in. The academic discipline of performance studies – a fully vested department only in a few places but a presence in many – arose to deal with these swiftly changing circumstances. But even as performance studies scholars began to research, organize, and interrogate the performatives they experienced everywhere, they were faced with ethical and political questions. Ought there to be any limit to the ways information is gathered, processed, and distributed? Should one intervene in the interest of "human rights" or respect local cultural autonomy at whatever cost? Artists and scholars are playing decisive roles in raising these ethical questions. One job of this textbook is to help you think about and act on these questions.

THINGS TO THINK ABOUT

1. From what academic disciplines or fields does performance studies draw its issues and methods? To what fields or disciplines can performance studies be applied?
2. Why do you think "performance studies" can/cannot be helpful in dealing with some of the world's great problems, such as the environment, oppression and exploitation of people, over-population, and war?

THINGS TO DO

1. Form a circle. Let each person give her/his name. Let others ask questions of the speaker. Different kinds of questions. "Why are you taking this course?" "Where do you live?" "Do you have friends in the class?" Go around the circle, but not in any particular order. Continue until everyone in the class knows everyone else's name.
2. Have someone walk across the room. Someone else describes that simple action. Then let the person walk across the room again, this time "showing" what previously they were just "doing." The second person again describes the action. The class discusses the differences between "just walking" and "showing just walking."

SUGGESTED READINGS

Conquergood, Dwight. "Performance Studies: Interventions and Radical Research." *TDR: The Drama Review* 46.3 (2002).

Dolan, Jill. "Geographies of Learning." *Theatre Journal* 45 (1993): 427–32.

Kirshenblatt-Gimblett, Barbara. "Performance Studies." Unpublished paper. New York, Rockefeller Foundation, 1999. Available at: http://www.nyu.edu/classes/bkg/ps.htm.

Pelias, Ronald J., and James VanOosting. "A Paradigm for Performance Studies." *Quarterly Journal of Speech* 73 (1987): 219–31.

Schechner, Richard. "Performance Studies: The Broad Spectrum Approach." *The Drama Review* 32.3 (T119) (1988): 4–6.

Worthen, W. B. "Disciplines of the Text/Sites of Performance." *The Drama Review* 39.1 (T145) (1995): 13–28.

2 WHAT IS PERFORMANCE?

What Is "To Perform"?

In business, sports, and sex, "to perform" is to do something up to a standard – to succeed, to excel. In the arts, "to perform" is to put on a show, a play, a dance, a concert. In everyday life, "to perform" is to show off, to go to extremes, to underline an action for those who are watching. In the twenty-first century, people as never before live by means of performance.

"To perform" can also be understood in relation to:

- Being
- Doing
- Showing doing
- Explaining showing doing

"Being" is existence itself. "Doing" is the activity of all that exists, from quarks to sentient beings to super galactic strings. "Showing doing" is performing: pointing to, underlining, and displaying doing. "Explaining 'showing doing'" is the work of performance studies.

It is very important to distinguish these from each other. "Being" may be active or static, linear or circular, expanding or contracting, material or spiritual. Being is a philosophical category pointing to whatever people theorize is the "ultimate reality." "Doing" and "showing doing" are actions. Doing and showing are always in flux, always changing – the world of the pre-Socratic Greek philosopher **Heraclitus** (*c.* 535–475 BCE), who said, "No one can step twice into the same river, nor touch mortal substance twice in the same condition." (fragment 41). The fourth term, "explaining showing doing," is a reflexive effort to comprehend the world of performance and the world as performance. This comprehension is usually the work of critics and scholars. But sometimes, in Brechtian theatre where the actor steps outside the role to comment on what the character is doing and in critically developed performance art such as **Guillermo Gómez-Peña**'s (1955–) and **Coco Fusco**'s (1960–) *Couple in the Cage* (1992), a performance is reflexive. I discuss this sort of critically conscious performance in chapters 5, 6, and 8.

Heraclitus of Ephesus (*c.* 535–475 BCE): Greek philosopher credited with the creation of the doctrine of "flux," the theory that change is always happening. This is illustrated by his statement that "You cannot step into the same river twice," because the flow of the river insures that new water continually replaces the old.

Reflexive: Referring back to oneself.

Guillermo Gómez-Peña (1955–): Mexican-born bi-national performance artist and writer. His works include both writings – *Warrior for Gringostroika* (1993), *The New World Border* (1996), *Codex Espangliensis* (2000), and *Dangerous Border Crossers* (2000) – and performances: *Border Brujo* (1990), *El Naftazeca* (1994), *Border Stasis* (1998), and *Brownout: Border Pulp Stories* (2001).

Coco Fusco (1960–): Cuban-born interdisciplinary artist based in New York City. Collaborated with Guillermo Goméz-Peña on the performance *The Couple in the Cage* (1992). Author of *English is Broken Here* (1995) and *The Bodies that were Not Ours* (2001).

Performances

Performances mark identities, bend time, reshape and adorn the body, and tell stories. Performances – of art, rituals, or ordinary life – are made of "twice-behaved behaviors," "restored behaviors," performed actions that people train to do, that they practice and rehearse (**see Goffman box**). That training and conscious effort go into making art is clear. But everyday life also involves years of training, of learning appropriate bits of behavior, of finding out how to adjust and

Restored behavior: Physical or verbal actions that are not-for-the-first time, prepared, or rehearsed. A person may not be aware that she is performing a strip of restored behavior. Also referred to as **twice-behaved behavior**.

perform one's life in relation to social and personal circumstances. The long infancy and childhood specific to the human species is an extended training and rehearsal period for the successful performance of adult life. "Graduation" into adulthood is marked in many cultures and religions by initiation rites. But even before adulthood, some persons more comfortably adapt to the life they are assigned than do others who resist or rebel. Most people live in a tension between acceptance and rebellion. Social action – politics, protests, revolutions, and the like – are large-scale collective efforts either to maintain the status quo or to change the world. The whole span of individual human development can be studied "as" performance (a concept I will discuss later in this chapter). This includes large-scale events such as social actions, revolutions, and politics. Every action, no matter how small or encompassing, consists of twice-behaved behaviors.

Erving Goffman

Defining Performance

A "performance" may be defined as all the activity of a given participant on a given occasion which serves to influence in any way any of the other participants. Taking a particular participant and his performance as a basic point of reference, we may refer to those who contribute to the other performances as the audience, observers, or co-participants. The pre-established pattern of action which is unfolded during a performance and which may be presented or played through on other occasions may be called a "part" or a "routine." These situational terms can easily be related to conventional structural ones. When an individual or performer plays the same part to the same audience on different occasions, a social relationship is likely to arise. Defining social role as the enactment of rights and duties attached to a given status, we can say that a social role will involve one or more parts and that each of these different parts may be presented by the performer on a series of occasions to the same kinds of audiences or to an audience of the same persons.

1959, *The Presentation of Self in Everyday Life*,
15–16

What about actions that are apparently "once-behaved" – the Happenings of **Allan Kaprow** (1927–), for example, or an everyday life occurrence (cooking, dressing, taking a walk, talking to a friend)? Even these are constructed from behaviors previously behaved. In fact, the everydayness of everyday life is precisely its familiarity, its being built from known bits of behavior rearranged and shaped in order to suit specific circumstances. "Lifelike" art – as Kaprow calls much of his work – is close to everyday life. Kaprow's art slightly underlines or highlights ordinary behavior – paying close attention to how a meal is prepared, looking back at one's footsteps after walking in the desert. Paying attention to simple activities performed in the present moment is developing a Zen consciousness in relation to the daily, an honoring of the ordinary. Honoring the ordinary is noticing how ritual-like daily life is, how much daily life consists of repetitions. There is no such thing as "once-behaved behavior."

Allan Kaprow (1927–): American artist who coined the term "Happening" to describe his 1959 installation/performance *18 Happenings in 6 Parts*. Author of *Assemblage, Environments and Happenings* (1966) and *Essays on the Blurring of Art and Life* (1993, with Jeff Kelley).

There is a paradox here. Can both Heraclitus and the theory of restored behavior be right? Performances are made from bits of restored behavior, but every performance is different from every other. First, fixed bits of behavior can be recombined in endless variations. Second, no event can exactly copy another event. Not only the behavior itself — nuances of mood, tone of voice, body language, and so on, but also the specific occasion and context make each instance unique. What about mechanically, digitally, or biologically reproduced replicants or clones? It may be that a film or a digitized performance art piece will be the same at each showing. But the context of every reception makes each instance different. Even though every "thing" is exactly the same, each event in which the "thing" participates is different. In other words, the uniqueness of an event is not in its materiality but in its interactivity. If this is so with regard to film and digitized events, how much more so in live performance, where both production and reception vary from instance to instance. Or in daily life, where context is impossible to perfectly control. Thus, ironically, performances resist that which produces them.

Which leads to the question, Where do performances take place? A painting "takes place" in the physical object; a novel takes place in the words. But a performance (even of a painting or a novel, when treated "as" performance, a concept I will explain shortly) takes place only in action, interaction, and relation. Performance isn't "in" anything, but "between." Let me explain. A performer in ordinary life, in a ritual, at play, or in the performing arts does/shows something – performs an action. For example, a mother lifts a spoon to her own mouth and then to a baby's mouth to show the baby how to eat cereal. The performance is the action of lifting the spoon, bringing it to mother's mouth, and then to baby's mouth. The baby is at first the spectator of its mother's performance. At some point, the baby becomes a co-performer as she takes the spoon and tries the same action – often at first missing her mouth and messing up her lips and chin with food. Father videotapes the whole show. Later, maybe many years later, the baby is a grown woman showing to her own baby a home video of the day when she began to learn how to use a spoon. Viewing this video is another performance existing in the complex relation between the original event, the memory of parents now old or maybe dead, and the present moment of delight as mother points to the screen and tells her baby, "That was mommy when I was your age!" The first performance "takes place" in between the action of showing baby how to use the spoon and baby's reaction to this action. The second performance takes place between the videotape of the first performance and the reception of that first performance by both the baby-now-mother and her own baby (or anyone else watching the videotape). What is true of this "home movie" performance is true of all performances. To treat any object, work, or product "as" performance – a painting, a novel, a shoe, or anything at all – means to investigate what the object does, how it interacts with other objects or beings, and how it relates to other objects or beings. Performances exist only as actions, interactions, and relationships.

Bill Parcells Wants You to Perform

A 1999 full-page advertisement in *The New York Times* selling the Cadillac Seville car features American legendary football coach **Bill Parcells** (1941–) staring out at the reader (**see figure 2.1**). One of Parcells' eyes is in shadow, the darkness blending into the background for the stark large white-on-black text:

> **Bill Parcells (1941–):** American football coach. Winner of two Superbowls (1987, 1991) with the New York Giants.

IF YOU WANT TO IMPRESS

BILL PARCELLS

YOU HAVE TO

PERFORM

Underneath a photograph of a Seville, the text continues in smaller type, "Great performers have always made a big impression on Bill Parcells. That explains his strong appreciation for Seville [. . .]."

The ad conflates performing in sports, business, sex, the arts, and technology. Parcells excels as a football coach. By making demands upon his players he motivates them and they

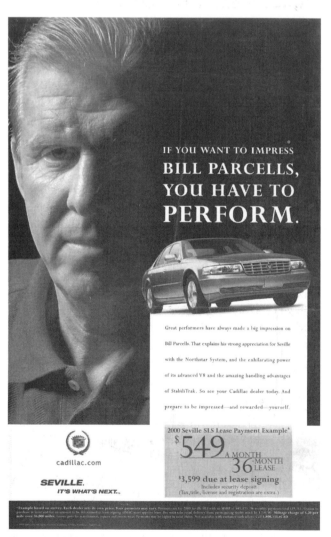

fig 2.1. Football coach Bill Parcells in an advertisement for Cadillac automobiles that appeared in *The New York Times* in 1999. Photograph courtesy of General Motors Corporation.

respond on the field with winning performances. Parcells' excellence derives from his drive, his ability to organize, and his insistence on careful attention to each detail of the game. His stare has "sex appeal" – his penetrating gaze is that of a potent man able to control the giants who play football. He combines mastery, efficiency, and beauty. At the same time, Parcells displays an understated flash; he knows he is playing to the camera and to the crowds. All of this informs the ad, which tries to convince viewers that the Cadillac, like Parcells, is at the top of its game, is sexy and powerful, well made down to the last detail, dependable, the leader in its field, and something that will stand out in a crowd.

Eight Kinds of Performance

Performances occur in eight sometimes separate, sometimes overlapping situations:

1 in everyday life – cooking, socializing, "just living"
2 in the arts
3 in sports and other popular entertainments
4 in business
5 in technology
6 in sex
7 in ritual – sacred and secular
8 in play.

This list does not exhaust the possibilities (**see Carlson box**). If examined rigorously as theoretical categories, the eight situations are not commensurate. "Everyday life" can encompass most of the other situations. The arts take as their subjects materials from every what and every where. Ritual and play are not only "genres" of performance but present in all of the situations as qualities, inflections, or moods. I list these eight to indicate the large territory covered by performance. Some items – those occurring in business, technology, and sex – are not usually analyzed with the others, which have been the loci of arts-based performance theories. And the operation of making categories such as these eight is the result of a particular kind of thinking that is far from universal.

Even notions of history and culture are culture-specific, not universal. It is impossible to come at a subject except from one's own cultural biases. But once a project such as this book is undertaken, the best I can do is to be aware of, and share with the reader, this limitation. That having been noted, designating music, dance, and theatre as the "performing

Marvin **Carlson**

What Is Performance?

The term "performance" has become extremely popular in recent years in a wide range of activities in the arts, in literature, and in the social sciences. As its popularity and usage has grown, so has a complex body of writing about performance, attempting to analyze and understand just what sort of human activity it is. [. . .] The recognition that our lives are structured according to repeated and socially sanctioned modes of behavior raises the possibility that all human activity could potentially be considered as "performance," or at least all activity carried out with a consciousness of itself. [. . .] If we consider performance as an essentially contested concept, this will help us to understand the futility of seeking some overarching semantic field to cover such seemingly disparate usages as the performance of an actor, of a schoolchild, of an automobile.

1996, *Performance: A Critical Introduction*, 4–5

arts" may seem relatively simple. But as categories even these are ambiguous. What is designated "art," if anything at all, varies historically and culturally. Objects and performances called "art" in some parts of the world are like what is made or done in many other places without being so designated. Many cultures do not have a word for, or category called, "art" even though they create performances and objects demonstrating a highly developed aesthetic sense.

Not only making but evaluating "art" occurs everywhere. People in different cultures all around the world know how to distinguish "good" from "bad" dancing, singing, orating, story-telling, sculpting, fabric design, pottery, painting, and so on. But what makes something "good" or "bad" varies greatly from place to place and even occasion to occasion. The ritual objects of one culture or one historical period become the art works of other cultures or periods. Museums of art are full of paintings and objects that once were regarded as sacred (and still may be by pillaged peoples eager to regain their ritual objects and sacred remains). Furthermore, even if a performance has a strong aesthetic dimension, it is not necessarily "art." The moves of basketball

fig 2.2. Ice skater Denise Biellmenn does a triple toe-loop as seen in a time-lapse photograph, no date. Photograph by Alberto Venzago. Copyright Camera Press, London

players are as beautiful as those of ballet dancers, but one is termed sport, the other art. Figure skating and gymnastics exist in both realms (**see figure 2.2**). Deciding what is art depends on context, historical circumstance, use, and local conventions.

Separating "art" from "ritual" is particularly difficult. I have noted that ritual objects from many cultures are featured in art museums. But consider also religious services with music, singing, dancing, preaching, speaking in tongues, and healing. At a Christian evangelical church service, for example, people go into trance, dance in the aisles, give testimony, receive anointment and baptism. In African-American churches, the gospel music is closely related to blues, jazz, and rock-and-roll. Are such services art or ritual? Church authorities in medieval Europe such as **Amalarius** (780–850), the Bishop of Metz, asserted that the Mass was the theatre equivalent to ancient Greek tragedy (**see Hardison box**). Indeed, more than a few people attend religious services as much for aesthetic pleasure and social interaction as for reasons of belief. Composers, visual artists, and performers have long made works of fine art for use in rituals. In many cultures, participatory performing is the core of ritual practices. In ancient Athens, the great theatre festivals were ritual, art, sports-like competition, and popular entertainment simultaneously. Today, sports are both live and media entertainment combining competition, ritual, and big business.

Amalarius of Metz (780–850): Roman Catholic bishop and theologian, author of several major treatises on the performance of liturgical rites, including *Eclogae de ordine Romano (Pastoral Dialogues on the Roman Rite)* (814) and *Liber officialis (Book of the Service)* (821).

As noted, some sports are close to fine arts. Gymnastics, figure skating, and high diving are recognized by the Olympics. But there are no quantitative ways to determine winners, as there is in racing, javelin throwing, or weight lifting. Instead, these "aesthetic athletes" are judged qualitatively on the basis of "form" and "difficulty." Their performances are more like dancing than competitions of speed or strength. But with the widespread use of slow-motion photography and replay even "brute sports" like football, wrestling, and boxing attain an aesthetic dimension that is more apparent in the re-viewing than in the swift, tumultuous action itself. An artful add-on is the taunting and victory displays of athletes who dance and prance their superiority.

For all that, everyone knows the difference between going to church, watching a football game, or attending one of the performing arts. The difference is based on function, the circumstance of the event within society, the venue, and the behavior expected of the players and spectators. There is even a big difference between various genres of the performing arts. Being tossed around a mosh pit at a

o. b. Hardison

The Medieval Mass was Drama

That there is a close relationship between allegorical interpretation of the liturgy and the history of drama becomes apparent the moment we turn to the Amalarian interpretations. Without exception, they present the Mass as an elaborate drama with definite roles assigned to the participants and a plot whose ultimate significance is nothing less than the "renewal of the whole plan of redemption" through the re-creation of the "life, death, and resurrection" of Christ. [. . .] The church is regarded as a theatre. The drama enacted has a coherent plot based on conflict between a champion and an antagonist. The plot has a rising action, culminating in the passion and entombment. At its climax there is a dramatic reversal, the Resurrection, correlated with the emotional transition from the Canon of the Mass to the Communion. Something like dramatic catharsis is expressed in the *gaudium* [joy at the news of the Resurrection] of the Postcommunion. [. . .]

Should church vestments then, with their elaborate symbolic meanings, be considered costumes? Should the paten, chalice, sindon, sudarium, candles, and thurible be considered stage properties? Should the nave, chancel, presbyterium, and altar of the church be considered a stage, and its windows, statues, images, and ornaments a "setting"? As long as there is clear recognition that these elements are hallowed, that they are the sacred phase of parallel elements turned to secular use on the profane stage, it is possible to answer yes. Just as the Mass is a sacred drama encompassing all history and embodying in its structure the central pattern of Christian life on which all Christian drama must draw, the celebration of the Mass contains all elements necessary to secular performances. The Mass as the general case — for Christian culture, the archetype. Individual dramas are shaped in its mold.

1965, *Christian Rite and Christian Drama in the Middle Ages*, 39–40, 79

rock concert is very different from attending the American Ballet Theatre's *Giselle* at New York's Metropolitan Opera House. Theatre emphasizes narration and impersonation, sports emphasize competition, and ritual emphasizes participation and communication with transcendent forces or beings.

In business, to perform means doing a job efficiently with maximum productivity. In the corporate world, people, machines, systems, departments, and organizations are required to perform. At least since the advent of the factory in the nineteenth century, there has been a merging of the human, the technical, and the organizational. This has led to an increase in material wealth — and also the sense that individuals are just "part of the machine" (**see figure 2.3**). But also this melding of person and machine has an erotic quality. There is something sexual about high performance in business, just as there is a lot that's businesslike in sexual performance. Sexual performance also invokes meanings drawn from the arts and sports. Consider the range of meanings attached to the phrases "performing sex," "How did s/he perform in bed?" and being a "sexual performer."

The first refers to the act in itself and the second to how well one "does it," while the third implies an element of either going to extremes or of pretending, of putting on a show and therefore maybe not really doing it at all.

fig 2.3. Charlie Chaplin turning, and being turned by, the wheels of industry in *Modern Times*, 1936.

Restoration of Behavior

Let us examine the notion of restored behavior more closely. We all perform more than we realize. As noted, daily life, ceremonial life, and artistic life consist largely of routines, habits, and rituals; and the recombination of already behaved behaviors. What's "new," "original," "shocking," or "avant-garde" is mostly either a different combination of known behaviors or the displacement of a behavior from where it is acceptable or expected to a venue or occasion where it is not expected. Thus, for example, nakedness caused a stir in the performing arts when it first was used in a widespread way in the 1960s. But why the shock, why was nudity new? Simply because the nakedness took place in "high-art" live-performance venues. Previously people saw naked bodies only at home or in gymnasium shower rooms. Naked performers were seen only in striptease shows. But this prohibition applied only to live naked bodies. Art museums were full of representations of naked bodies. The "cover" for this nakedness was that the art displays were presumed to be non-erotic. Of course, in many cultures nakedness is the norm. In others, such as Japan, it has long been acceptable in certain public circumstances and forbidden in others. By the year 2000 no one in any Western metropolitan venue could get a rise out of spectators or critics by performing naked. But don't try it in Kabul.

The habits, rituals, and routines of life are restored behaviors. Restored behavior is living behavior treated as a film director treats a strip of film. These strips of behavior can be rearranged or reconstructed; they are independent of the causal systems (personal, social, political, technological, etc.) that brought them into existence. They have a life of their own. The original "truth" or "source" of the behavior may not be known, or may be lost, ignored, or contradicted – even while that truth or source is being honored. How the strips of behavior were made, found, or developed may be unknown or concealed; elaborated; distorted by myth and tradition. Restored behavior can be of long duration as in ritual performances or of short duration as in fleeting gestures such as waving goodbye.

Restored behavior is the key process of every kind of performing, in everyday life, in healing, in ritual, in play, and in the arts. Restored behavior is "out there," separate from "me." To put it in personal terms, restored behavior is "me behaving as if I were someone else," or "as I am told to do," or "as I have learned." Even if I feel myself wholly to be myself, acting independently, only a little investigating reveals that the units of behavior that comprise "me" were not invented by "me." Or, quite the opposite, I may experience being "beside myself," "not myself," or "taken over" as in trance. The fact that there are multiple "me's" in every person is not a sign of derangement but the way things are. The ways one performs one's selves are connected to the ways people perform others in dramas, dances, and rituals. In fact, if people did not ordinarily come into contact with their multiple selves, the art of acting and the experience of trance possession would not be possible. Most performances, in daily life and otherwise, do not have a single author. Rituals, games, and the performances of everyday life are authored by the collective "Anonymous" or the "Tradition." Individuals given credit for inventing rituals or games usually turn out to be synthesizers, recombiners, compilers, or editors of already practiced actions.

Restored behavior includes a vast range of actions. In fact, all behavior is restored behavior – all behavior consists of recombining bits of previously behaved behaviors. Of course, most of the time people aren't aware that they are doing any such thing. People just "live life." Performances are marked, framed, or heightened behavior separated out from just "living life" – restored restored behavior, if you will. However, for my purpose here, it is not necessary to pursue this doubling. It is enough to define restored behavior as marked, framed, or heightened. Restored behavior can be "me" at another time or psychological state – for example, telling the story of or acting out a celebratory or traumatic event. Restored behavior can bring into play non-ordinary reality as in the Balinese trance-dance enacting the struggle between the demoness Rangda and the Lion-god Barong (**see figure 2.4**). Restored behavior can be actions marked off by aesthetic convention as in theatre, dance, and music. It can be actions reified into the "rules of the game," "etiquette," or diplomatic "protocol" – or any other of the myriad, known-beforehand actions of life. These vary enormously from culture to culture. Restored behavior can be a boy not shedding tears when jagged leaves slice the inside of his nostrils during a Papua New Guinea initiation; or the formality of a bride and groom during their wedding ceremony. Because it is marked, framed, and separate, restored behavior can be worked on, stored and recalled, played with, made into something else, transmitted, and transformed.

Restored behavior is symbolic and reflexive (**see Geertz box**). Its meanings need to be decoded by those in the know. This is not a question of "high" versus "low" culture. A sports fan knows the rules and strategies of the game, the statistics of key players, the standings, and many other historical and technical details. Ditto for the fans of rock bands. Sometimes the knowledge about restored behavior is esoteric, privy to only the initiated. Among Australian Native Peoples,

fig 2.4. The lion god Barong, right, does battle against the demon Rangda in Balinese ritual dance theatre, 1980s. Photograph by Richard Schechner.

Clifford Geertz

Human Behavior as Symbolic Action

Once human behavior is seen as [. . .] symbolic action — action which, like phonation in speech, pigment in painting, line in writing, or sonance in music, signifies — the question as to whether culture is patterned conduct or a frame of mind, or even the two somehow mixed together, loses sense. [. . .] Behavior must be attended to, and with some exactness, because it is through the flow of behavior — or more precisely, social action — that cultural forms find articulation. They find it as well, of course, in various sorts of artifacts, and various states of consciousness; but these draw their meaning from the role they play [. . .] in an ongoing pattern of life [. . .].

1973, *The Interpretation of Cultures*, 10, 17

the outback itself is full of significant rocks, trails, water holes, and other markings that form a record of the actions of mythical beings. Only the initiated know the relationship between the ordinary geography and the sacred geography. To become conscious of restored behavior is to recognize the process by which social processes in all their multiple forms are transformed into theatre. Theatre not in the limited sense of enactments of dramas on stages (which, after all, is a practice that until it became very widespread as part of colonialism belonged to relatively few cultures), but in the broader sense outlined in chapter 1. Performance in the restored behavior sense means never for the first time, always for the second to *n*th time: twice-behaved behavior.

Caution! Beware of Generalizations

I need to emphasize a point. Performances can be generalized at the theoretical level of restoration of behavior. However, as embodied practices each and every performance is specific and different from every other. The differences enact the conventions and traditions of a genre, the personal choices made by the performers, various cultural patterns, historical circumstances, and the particularities of reception. Take wrestling, for example. In Japan, the moves of a sumo wrestler are well determined by long tradition. These moves include the athlete's swaggering circulation around the ring,

his adjusting his groin belt, the throwing of handfuls of salt, the eyeing of his opponent and the final, often very brief, grapple of the two enormous competitors (**see figure 2.5**). Knowing spectators see in these carefully ritualized displays a centuries-old tradition linked to Shinto, the native Japanese religion. By contrast, American professional wrestling is a noisy sport for "outlaws" where each wrestler flaunts his own raucous identity (**see figure 2.6**). During the matches referees are clobbered, wrestlers are thrown from the ring, and cheating is endemic. All this is spurred on

fig 2.5. Japanese sumo wrestlers grappling in the ring. The referee in ritual dress is in the left foreground. Photograph by Michael MacIntyre. Copyright Hutchison Picture Library.

fig 2.6

"The Road Warriors" professional American wrestlers posing with their manager. Copyright Superstar Wrestling.

"Macho Man" displaying himself for his admiring fans. Copyright Sharon Mazer.

by fans who hurl epithets and objects. However, everyone knows that the outcome of American wrestling is determined in advance, that the lawlessness is play-acting – it's pretty much "all a show." Fans of sumo and fans of World Wrestling Federation matches know their heroes and villains, can tell you the history of their sport, and react according to accepted conventions and traditions. Both sumo and what occurs under the banner of the World Wrestling Federation are "wrestling"; each enacts the values of its particular culture.

What's true of wrestling is also true of the performing arts, political demonstrations, the roles of everyday life (doctor, mother, cop, etc.), and all other performances. Each genre is divided into many sub-genres. What is American theatre? Broadway, off Broadway, off off Broadway, regional theatre, community theatre, community-based theatre, college theatre, and more. Each sub-genre has its own particularities – similar in some ways to related forms but also different. And the whole system could be looked at from other perspectives – in terms, for example, of comedy, tragedy, melodrama, musicals; or divided according to professional–amateur, issue-oriented or apolitical, and so on. Nor are categories fixed or static. New genres emerge, and others fade away. Yesterday's avant-garde is today's mainstream is tomorrow's forgotten practice. Particular genres migrate from one category to another.

Take jazz, for example. During its formative years at the start of the twentieth century, jazz was not regarded as an art. It was akin to "folk performance" or "popular entertainment." But as performers moved out of red-light districts into respectable clubs and finally into concert halls, scholars increasingly paid attention to jazz. A substantial repertory of

music was archived. Particular musicians' works achieved canonical status. By the 1950s jazz was regarded as "art." Today's popular music includes rock, rap, and reggae, but not "pure jazz." But that is not to say that rock and other forms of pop music will not someday be listened to and regarded in the same way that jazz or classical music is now. The categories of "folk," "pop," and "classical" have more to do with ideology, politics, and economic power than with the formal qualities of the music.

"Is" Performance

What is the difference between "is" performance and "as" performance? Certain events are performances and other events less so. There are limits to what "is" performance. But just about anything can be studied "as" performance. Something "is" a performance when historical and social context, convention, usage, and tradition say it is. Rituals, play and games, and the roles of everyday life are performances because convention, context, usage, and tradition say so. One cannot determine what "is" a performance without referring to specific cultural circumstances. There is nothing inherent in an action in itself that makes it a performance or disqualifies it from being a performance. From the vantage of the kind of performance theory I am propounding, every action is a performance. But from the vantage of cultural practice, some actions will be deemed performances and others not; and this will vary from culture to culture, historical period to historical period.

Let me use the European tradition as an example to explain in more detail how definitions operate within contexts. What "is" or "is not" performance does not depend on an event in itself but on how that event is received and placed. Today the enactment of dramas by actors "is" a theatrical performance. But it was not always so. What we today call "theatre" people in other times did not. The ancient Greeks used words similar to ours to describe the theatre (our words derive from theirs), but what the Greeks meant in practice was very different from what we mean. During the epoch of the tragedians **Aeschylus** (*c.* 525–*c.* 456 BCE), **Sophocles** (*c.* 496–*c.* 406 BCE), and **Euripides** (*c.* 485–*c.* 405 BCE) the enactment of tragic dramas was more a ritual infused with competitions for prizes for the best actor and the best play than it was theatre in our sense. The occasions for the playing of the tragedies were religious festivals. Highly sought-after prizes were awarded. These prizes were based on aesthetic excellence, but the events in which that excellence was demonstrated were not artistic but ritual. It was Aristotle, writing a century after the high point of Greek tragedy as embodied performance, who codified the aesthetic understanding of theatre in its entirety – in all of its "six parts," as the philosopher parsed it. After Aristotle, in Hellenic and Roman times, the entertainment-aesthetic aspect of theatre became more dominant as the ritual-efficacious elements receded.

Aeschylus (*c.* 525–*c.* 456 BCE): Greek playwright and actor, regarded as the first great tragedian. Surviving works include *The Persians* (*c.* 472 BCE) and *The Oresteia* (458 BCE).

Sophocles (*c.* 496–*c.* 406 BCE): Greek playwright, credited with introducing the third actor onto the stage of tragedy. Surviving plays include *Oedipus Tyrannus* (*c.* 429 BCE), *Electra* (date uncertain), and *Antigone* (*c.* 441 BCE).

Euripides (*c.* 485–*c.* 405 BCE): Greek playwright whose surviving works include *Medea* (431 BCE), *Hyppolytus* (428 BCE), *The Trojan Women* (415 BCE), and *The Bacchae* (*c.* 405 BCE).

Let us skip ahead a millennium or more. During much of the medieval period in Europe, acting written dramas on public stages was "forgotten" or at least not practiced. But this did not mean there was a scarcity of performances. On the streets, in town squares, in castles and mansions a wide range of popular entertainments held people's attention. There were a multitude of mimes, magicians, animal acts, acrobats, puppet shows, and what would later become the commedia dell'arte. Also from early medieval times, the Church offered a rich panoply of feasts, services, and rituals. By the fourteenth century these had joined to form the basis for the great cycle plays celebrating and enacting the history of the world from Creation through the Crucifixion and Resurrection to the Last Judgment. These we would now call "theatre," but they were not called that at the time. The anti-theatrical prejudice of the Church disallowed any such designation. But then, in the fifteenth and sixteenth centuries the revolution in thought and practice called the Renaissance began. Renaissance means "rebirth," and what the humanists of the Renaissance thought they were bringing back to life was the classical culture of Greece and Rome. When works were staged in Vicenza's Teatro Olympico (Theatre of Olympus), the makers felt they were reinventing Greek . . . theatre (not ritual). Whether an event is theatre or not, performance or not, depends on the dominant thinking of the day.

Make another leap in time to the last third of the nineteenth century. The notion of theatre as an art was by then well established. In fact, so well founded that counter-movements called "avant-garde" erupted frequently as efforts among radical artists to disrupt the status quo. Each new wave attempted to dislodge what went before. Some of yesterday's avant-garde became today's establishment. The list of avant-garde movements is long, including realism, naturalism, symbolism, futurism, surrealism, constructivism, dada, expressionism, cubism, theatre of the absurd, Happenings, Fluxus, environmental theatre, performance art . . . and more. Sometimes works in these styles were considered theatre, sometimes dance, sometimes music, sometimes visual art, sometimes multimedia, etc. Often enough, events were attacked or dismissed as not being art at all – as were Happenings, an antecedent to performance art. Allan Kaprow, creator of the first Happening, jumped at this chance to make a place for what he called "lifelike art" (**see Kaprow box**). The term "performance art" was coined in the 1970s as an umbrella for works that otherwise resisted categorization.

The outcome is that today many events that formerly would not be thought of as art or performance are now so designated. These kinds of actions are performed everywhere, not just in the West. The feedback loop is very complicated. The work of a Japanese butoh dancer may effect a German choreographer whose dances in turn are elaborated on by a Mexican performance artist . . . and so on without definite national or cultural limits. Beyond composed art works is a blurry world of "accidental" or "incidental" performance. Webcams broadcast what people

Allan Kaprow

Artlike Art and Lifelike Art

Western art actually has two avantgarde histories: one of artlike art, and the other of lifelike art. [. . .] Simplistically put, artlike art holds that art is separate from life and everything else, while lifelike art holds that art is connected to life and everything else. In other words, there's art at the service of art, and art at the service of life. The maker of artlike art tends to be a specialist; the maker of lifelike art, a generalist. [. . .]

Avantgarde artlike art occupies the majority of attention from artists and public. It is usually seen as serious and a part of the mainstream Western art-historical tradition, in which mind is separate from body, individual is separate from people, civilization is separate from nature, and each art is separate from the other. [. . .] Avantgarde artlike art basically believes in (or does not eliminate) the continuity of the traditionally separate genres of visual art, music, dance, literature, theatre, etc. [. . .]

Avantgarde lifelike art, in contrast, concerns an intermittent minority (Futurists, Dadas, guatai, Happeners, fluxartists, Earthworkers, body artists, provos, postal artists, noise musicians, performance poets, shamanistic artists, conceptualists). Avantgarde lifelike art is not nearly as serious as avantgarde artlike art. Often it is quite humorous. It isn't very interested in the great Western tradition either, since it tends to mix things up: body with mind, individual with people in general, civilization with nature, and so on. Thus it mixes up the traditional art genres, or avoids them entirely – for example, a mechanical fiddle playing around the clock to a cow in the barnyard. Or going to the laundromat. Despite formalist and idealist interpretations of art, lifelike art makers' principal dialogue is not with art but with everything else, one event suggesting another. If you don't know much about life, you'll miss much of the meaning of the lifelike art that's born of it. Indeed, it's never certain if an artist who creates avantgarde lifelike art is an artist.

1983, "The Real Experiment," 36, 38

do at home over the internet. Television frames the news as entertainment. Performance theorists argue that everyday life is performance – courses are offered in the aesthetics of everyday life. At present, there is hardly any human activity that is not a performance for someone somewhere. Generally, the tendency over the past century has been to dissolve the boundaries separating performing from not-performing, art from not-art. At one end of the spectrum it's clear what a performance is, what an art work is; at the other end of the spectrum no such clarity exists.

"As" Performance

In her studies of cooking as performance, Barbara Kirshenblatt-Gimblett proposes a theory very close to my own. She says that to perform is to do, to behave, and to show (**see Kirshenblatt-Gimblett box**). I want to go further. Any behavior, event, action, or thing can be studied "as" performance, can be analyzed in terms of doing, behaving, and showing. Take maps, for example.

Everyone knows the world is round, but flat maps are extremely useful. You can't see the whole world or even a significant part of it at the same time on a globe. Globes can't be folded and easily carried. Maps flatten the world the better to lay out territories on a table, tack them to a wall, or tuck them in a briefcase. Maps depict anything from nations to topography to demography. On common world maps, nations are separated from each other by colors and lines, and cities appear as circles, rivers as lines, and oceans as large, usually blue, areas. Everything is named – achieving status is being "on the map." But the "real earth" does not look like its mapped representations – or even like a globe. People were astonished when they first saw photographs taken from space of the white-flecked blue ball earth (**see figure 2.7**). There was no sign of a human presence at all.

Nation-states seem so natural that when most people picture the world as a map they see it divided into nation-states. But maps are not neutral. They perform a particular interpretation of how the world ought to be. A map is a "projection," a particular way of representing a sphere on a flat surface. On maps, nations do not overlap or share territories.

Barbara Kirshenblatt-Gimblett

Food as Performance

Food and performance converge conceptually at three junctures. First, *to perform is to do*, to execute, to carry out to completion, to discharge a duty – in other words, all that governs the production, presentation, and disposal of food. To perform in this sense is to make food, to serve food. It is about materials, tools, techniques, procedures, actions. It is about getting something done. It is in this sense, first and foremost, that we can speak of the performing kitchen.

Second, *to perform is to behave*. This is what Erving Goffman calls the performance in everyday life. Whether a matter of habit, custom, or law, the divine etiquette of ritual, codifications of social grace, the laws governing cabarets and liquor licenses, or the health and sanitation codes, performance encompasses the social practices that are part and parcel of what Pierre Bourdieu [(1930–)] calls *habitus*. To perform in this sense is to behave appropriately in relation to food at any point in its production, consumption, or disposal, each of which may be subject to precise protocols or taboos. Jewish and Hindu laws of ritual purity and formal etiquette stipulate the requirements in exquisite detail. They involve the performance of precepts as well as precepts of performance.

Third, *to perform is to show*. When doing and behaving are displayed, when they are shown, when participants are invited to exercise discernment, evaluation, and appreciation, food events move towards the theatrical and, more specifically, towards the spectacular. It is here that taste as a sensory experience and taste as an aesthetic faculty converge. The conflation of the two meanings of taste can be found in Enlightenment aesthetics and in the Hindu concept of *rasa* alike.

1999, "Playing to the Senses:
Food as a Performance Medium," 1–2

fig 2.7. The western hemisphere of planet earth as photographed by a geostationary satellite in 1995. Copyright Popperfoto.

Gerardus Mercator (1512–94): Flemish geographer-cartographer whose basic approach to map-making is still practiced today. His actual name was Gerhard Kremer, but like many European scholars of his day, he used a latinized version of his name.

Boundaries are definite. For more than one nation to enforce its claim to the same space means war, as between Pakistan and India over Kashmir or Palestine and Israel over Jerusalem. The most common projection in use today is derived from the Mercator projection, developed in the sixteenth century by the Flemish geographer-cartographer **Gerardus Mercator** (1512–94) (**see figure 2.8**).

The Mercator projection distorts the globe wildly in favor of the northern hemisphere. The further north, the relatively bigger the territory appears. Spain is as large as Zimbabwe, North America dwarfs South America, and Europe is one-fourth the size of Africa. In other words, Mercator's map enacts the world as the colonial powers wished to view it. Although times have changed since the sixteenth century, the preponderance of world economic and military power remains in the hands of Europe and its North American inheritor, the USA. Perhaps it won't be this way in another century or two. If so, a different projection will be in common use. Indeed, with satellite photography a detailed remapping of the globe is taking place. There are also maps showing the world "upside down," that is, with south on top; or drawn according to population, showing China and India four times the size of the USA. The Peters Projection developed in 1974 by **Arno Peters** (1916–) is an "area accurate" map showing the world's areas sized correctly in relation to each other (**see figure 2.9**). No longer is Greenland the same size as Africa when in fact Africa is fourteen times larger than Greenland. But the Peters map has its own inaccuracies. It is

fig 2.8. A contemporary version of the Mercator Projection map of the world. Copyright Worldview Publications.

fig 2.9. The Peters Projection "area accurate" world map. Copyright Oxford Cartographers.

not correct in terms of shape – the southern hemisphere is elongated, the northern squashed. Making a flat map of a round earth means that one must sacrifice either accurate shape or size. If the Peters map looks "unnatural," then you know how much the Mercator projection – or any other map – is a performance.

> **Arno Peters (1916–):** German historian. Developed in 1974 an area-accurate world map, known as the Peters Projection.

One of the meanings of "to perform" is to get things done according to a particular plan or scenario. Mercator's maps proved very helpful for navigating the seas because straight lines on the projection kept to compass bearings. Mercator drew his maps to suit the scenarios of the mariners, merchants, and military of an expansionist, colonizing Western Europe. Similarly, the authors of the new maps have scenarios of their own which their maps enact. Interpreting maps this way is to examine map-making "as" performance. Every map not only represents the earth in a specific way, but also enacts power relationships.

It's not just maps. Everything and anything can be studied "as" any discipline of study – physics, economics, law, etc. What the "as" says is that the object of study will be regarded "from the perspective of," "in terms of," "interrogated by" a particular discipline of study. For example, I am composing this book on a Dell Dimension 4001 desktop computer. If I regard it "as physics," I would examine its size, weight, and other physical qualities, perhaps even its atomic and subatomic qualities. If I regard it "as mathematics," I would delve into the binary codes of its programs. Regarding it "as law" would mean interpreting networks of patents, copyrights, and contracts. If I were to treat the computer "as performance" I would evaluate the speed of its processor, the clarity of its display, the usefulness of the pre-packaged software, its size and portability, and so on. I can envision Bill Parcells staring out at me telling me how well my computer performs.

Make Believe Versus Make Belief

What about the many performances in everyday life? Playing professional roles, gender and race roles, and shaping one's identity are not make-believe actions (as playing a role on stage or in a film most probably is). The performances of everyday life (which I will discuss in more detail in chapters 5 and 6) "make belief" – create the very social realities they enact. In "make-believe" performances, the distinction between what's real and what's pretended is kept clear. Children playing "doctor" or "dress-up" know that they are pretending. On stage, various conventions – the stage itself as a distinct domain, the opening and closing a curtain or dimming the lights, the curtain call, etc. – mark the distinction between pretending and being. When people go to the movies or the theatre they know that the social and personal worlds enacted are not those of the actors but those of the characters. Of course, it is this distinction that first the avant-garde and later the media and the internet have successfully sabotaged.

> **Make-believe** performances maintain a clearly marked boundary between the world of the performance and everyday reality. **Make-belief** performances intentionally blur that boundary.

Public figures are often making belief – enacting the effects they want the receivers of their performances to accept "for real." When an American President signs an important piece of legislation, or makes a grave announcement of national importance, his handlers stage the event in the Oval Office of the White House where the President can perform his authority. Behind him is an array of VIPs, including the Vice-President. A large Presidential Seal provides an appropriately patriotic foreground (**see figure 2.10**). At other times, the national leader may wish to appear as a friend or a good neighbor talking informally with "fellow citizens" (**see figure 2.11**).

By now, everyone knows these kinds of activities are staged in every detail. Today's American Presidency – at least its public face – is a totally scripted performance. The President's words are written by professional speech-writers, the backdrops and settings carefully designed for maximum effect, the Chief Executive himself well rehearsed. Teleprompters insure that the President will appear to be speaking off the cuff while he is actually reading every word. Each detail is choreographed, from how the President makes eye contact (with the camera, with the selected audience at a town meeting), to how he uses his hands, dresses, and is made-up. The goal of all this is to "make belief" – first, to build the public's confidence in the President, and second, to sustain the President's belief in himself. His performances convince himself even as he strives to convince others.

Arguably, the President is an important personage by virtue of his position of authority. But with the exponential growth of media, hordes of citizens have jumped into the make-belief business. Some are hucksters selling everything from cooking utensils and firm buttocks to everlasting salvation in the blood of Jesus. Others are venerable network "anchors," familiar voices and faces holding the public in place amidst the swift currents of the news. Still others are "experts" – economists, lawyers, retired generals, etc. – whose authority is sometimes created simply by their frequent appearances. Then come the "spin masters," employed by politicians and corporations to turn bad news into good. As for the producers behind the scenes, their job is to make certain that whatever is going on is dramatized enough to attract viewers. The greater the number watching, the higher the revenues from sponsors. Some news is inherently exciting – disasters, wars, crimes, and trials. But media masters have learned how to dramatize the stock market and the weather. How to build the "human interest" angle into every story. The producers know that the same information is available from many different venues, so their job is to develop attractive sideshows. Paradoxically, the result is a public less easy to fool. With so many kinds of performances on view, people are sophisticated and suspicious deconstructors of the theatrical techniques deployed to lure them.

fig 2.10. In a formally arranged "photo op," President Bill Clinton, flanked by Vice President Al Gore and other VIPs, makes a pitch for a piece of legislation – using the Oval Office as his stage set, 1997. Photograph by Win McNamee. Copyright Popperfoto.

fig 2.11. British Prime Minister Tony Blair acts the part of a "man of the people" in an "informal meeting" with some "ordinary citizens." Of course, such meetings are carefully planned, staged, and photographed. Copyright *The Independent* Picture Syndication.

Blurry Boundaries

Let's return to Mercator's map. The world represented there is one of neatly demarcated sovereign nation-states. That world no longer exists, if it ever did (in Mercator's day the European nations were constantly at war with each other over who controlled what). Today national boundaries are extremely porous, not only to people but even more so to information and ideas. The newest maps can't be drawn because what needs to be represented is not territories but networks of relationships. Mapping these takes fractals or streams of numbers continually changing their shapes and values. The notion of fixity has been under attack at least since 1927, when **Werner Heisenberg** (1901–76) proposed his "uncertainty principle." Few people outside of a select group of quantum physicists could really understand Heisenberg's theory. But "uncertainty" or "indeterminacy" rang a bell. It was a very appropriate and powerful metaphor for the epoch. It affected thought in many disciplines. It was a call to the making of a certain kind of art. **John Cage** (1912–92) used indeterminacy as the basis for his music, influencing a whole generation of artists and theorists in many fields.

> **Werner Heisenberg (1901–76):** German physicist, winner of the Nobel Prize for Physics in 1932, is best known for his uncertainty principle.

> **John Cage (1912–92):** American composer and music theorist whose interests spanned using indeterminacy to make art, Zen Buddhism, and mushrooms. Author of *Silence: Selected Lectures and Writings* (1961) and *A Year from Monday* (1967). His many musical compositions include *Fontana Mix* (1960) and *Roaratorio* (1982).

Boundaries are blurry in different ways. On the internet people participate effortlessly in a system that transgresses national boundaries. Even languages present less of a barrier than before. Already you can login, write in your own language, and know that your message will be translated into the language of whomever you are addressing. At present, this facility is available in only a limited number of languages. But the repertory of translatables will increase. It will be routine for Chinese speakers to address Kikuyu speakers or for someone in a remote village to address a message to any number of people globally. Furthermore, for better or worse, English has become a global rather than national language. At the United Nations, 120 countries representing more than 97 percent of the world's populations choose English as their medium for international communication.

> **Heisenberg uncertainty principle:** A principle of quantum mechanics which states that accurate measurement of one of two related observable quantities (for example, position) produces uncertainty in the measurement of the other (for example, velocity), so that while each quantity may be measured accurately on its own, both together cannot be measured beyond a certain degree of accuracy. First formulated by German physicist **Werner Heisenberg** (1901–76).

The dissolution of national boundaries is occurring in relation to manufactured objects as well as with regard to politics and information. If, for example, you drive an American or Japanese or Swedish or German or Korean car, you may believe it came from the country whose label it displays. But where were the parts manufactured? Where was the car assembled, where designed? The brand name refers to itself, not to a place of origin. Japanese cars are made in Tennessee and Fords roll off assembly lines in Canada, Europe, and elsewhere. Mexico is a major assembly point for many cars. And what about your clothes? Look at the labels of the clothes you are wearing right now. Do your dress, pants, shoes, and blouse come from the same country? Do you even know where they were stitched or by whom and at what wage or under what kind of working conditions?

But more than cars and clothes are transnational. Cultures are also blurring. "Globalization" is accelerating. Airports are the same wherever you travel; standardized fast food is available in just about every major city in the world. American television and movies are broadcast everywhere. But the USA itself is increasingly intercultural in both its populations and its living styles. The profusion of international arts festivals and the hosts of artists touring all parts of the world are a major means of circulating styles of performing. "World beat" music combines elements of African, Asian, Latin American, and Euro-American sounds. New hybrids are emerging all the time. People are arguing whether or not all this mixing is good or bad. Is globalization the equivalent of Americanization? Questions of globalization and intercultural performance will be taken up in chapter 8.

The Functions of Performance

I have touched on what performance is and what can be studied as performance. But what do performances accomplish? It is difficult to stipulate the functions of performance. Over time, and in different cultures, there have been a number of proposals. One of the most inclusive is that of the Indian sage **Bharata Muni** (*c.* second century BCE–*c.* second century CE), who felt that performance was a comprehensive repository of knowledge and a very powerful vehicle for the expression of emotions (**see Bharata box**). The Roman poet-scholar **Horace** (65–8 BCE) in his *Ars Poetica* argued that theatre ought to entertain and educate, an idea taken up by many Renaissance thinkers and later by the German playwright and director **Bertolt Brecht** (1898–1956).

Bharata Muni

The Functions of Natya
(Dance-Music-Theatre)

I [The god Brahma] have created the Natyaveda to show good and bad actions and feelings of both the gods and yourselves. It is a representation of the entire three worlds and not only of the gods or of yourselves. Now dharma [duty], now artha [strategies], now kama [love], now humor, now fights, now greed, now killing. Natya teaches right to people going wrong; it gives enjoyment for those who are pleasure seekers; it chastises those who are ill-behaved and promotes tolerance in the well-behaved. It gives courage to cowards, energy to the brave. It enlightens people of little intellect and gives wisdom to the wise. Natya provides entertainment to kings, fortitude to those grief stricken, money to those who want to make a living, and stability to disturbed minds. Natya is a representation of the ways of the world involving various emotions and differing circumstances. It relates the actions of good, bad, and middling people, giving peace, entertainment, and happiness, as well as beneficial advice, to all. It brings rest and peace to persons afflicted by sorrow, fatigue, grief, or helplessness. There is no art, no knowledge, no learning, no action that is not found in natya.

1996 [second century BCE–second century CE],
The Natyasastra, chapter 1

Bharata Muni (*c.* second century BCE–second century CE): Indian sage credited with authorship of *The Natyasastra*, the primary theoretical treatise of classical Indian theatre and dance.

Horace (65–8 BCE): Roman poet whose *Ars Poetica* (*The Art of Poetry*) offers advice on the construction of drama. His basic instruction that art should both "entertain and educate" is very close to Brecht's ideas on the function of theatre.

Bertolt Brecht (1898–1956): German playwright, director, and performance theorist. In 1949 he and actress Helene Weigel (1900–71), his wife, founded the Berliner Ensemble. Major works include *The Threepenny Opera* (1928), *The Rise and Fall of the City of Mahagonny* (1930), *Mother Courage and her Children* (1941), *Galileo* (1943), *The Good Woman of Szechwuan* (1943), and *The Caucasian Chalk Circle* (1948 Eng; 1954 Ger.) The dates refer to stage premieres. Many of his theoretical writings are anthologized in English, in *Brecht on Theatre* (1964).

Putting together ideas drawn from various sources, I find seven functions of performance:

- To entertain
- To make something that is beautiful
- To mark or change identity
- To make or foster community
- To heal
- To teach, persuade, or convince
- To deal with the sacred and/or the demonic.

These are not listed in order of importance. For some people one or a few of these will be more important than others. But the hierarchy changes according to who you are and what you want to get done. No performance accomplishes all of these functions, but many performances emphasize more than one.

Very rarely does a performance focus on one or even two functions. A street demonstration or propaganda play may be mostly about teaching, persuading, and convincing – but such a show also has to entertain and may foster community. Shamans heal, but they entertain also, foster community, and deal with the sacred and/or demonic. A doctor's "bedside manner" is a performance of encouragement, teaching, and healing. A charismatic Christian church service heals, entertains, maintains community solidarity, invokes both the sacred and the demonic, and, if the sermon is tolerable, teaches. If someone at the service declares for Jesus and is reborn, that person's identity is marked and changed. The President addressing the nation wants to convince and foster community – but he had better entertain also if he wants people to listen. Rituals tend to have the greatest number of functions, commercial productions the fewest. A Broadway musical will entertain, but little else. The seven functions are best represented as overlapping and interacting spheres, as a network (**see figure 2.12**).

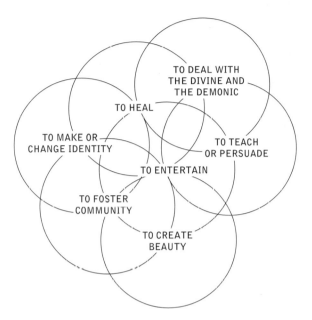

fig 2.12. The seven interlocking spheres of performance. Drawing by Richard Schechner.

Whole works, even genres, can be shaped to very specific functions. Examples of political or propaganda performances are found all over the world. El Teatro Campesino of California, formed in the 1960s in order to support Mexican migrant farm workers in the midst of a bitter strike, built solidarity among the strikers, educated them to the issues involved, attacked the bosses, and entertained. Groups such as Greenpeace and ACTUP use performance militantly in support of a healthy ecology and to gain money for AIDS research and treatment. "Theatre for development" as practiced widely since the 1960s in Africa, Latin America, and Asia educates people in a wide range of subjects and activities, from birth control and cholera prevention to irrigation and the protection of endangered species. **Augusto Boal**'s (1931–) Theatre of the Oppressed empowers "spectactors" to enact, analyze, and change their situations.

Augusto Boal (1931–): Brazilian director and theorist, founder of Theatre of the Oppressed. His books include *Theatre of the Oppressed* (1985), *Games for Actors and Non-Actors* (1980, Eng. 1992), *Legislative Theatre* (1998), and his autobiography, *Hamlet and the Baker's Son* (2001).

Boal's Theatre of the Oppressed is based to some degree on Brecht's work, especially his *Lehrstücke* or "learning plays" of the 1930s such as *The Measures Taken* or *The Exception and the Rule* (**see figure 2.13**). During China's Cultural Revolution (1966–75), which she helped orchestrate, **Jiang Qing** (1914–91) produced a series of "model operas" carefully shaped to teach, entertain, and put forward a new kind of community based on the values of Chinese Communism as Jiang interpreted them. These theatre and ballet pieces employed both traditional Chinese performance styles modified to suit the ideological purposes of the Cultural Revolution and elements of Western music and staging (**see figure 2.14**). The utopian vision of the model operas contradicted the terrible fact of the millions who were killed, tortured, and displaced by the Cultural Revolution. But by the turn of the twenty-first century, the model operas were again being performed, studied, and enjoyed for their entertainment value, technical excellence, and artistic innovations (see **Melvin and Cai box**).

Jiang Qing (1914–91): Chinese Communist leader, wife of Chairman Mao Zedong (1893–1976). As Deputy Director of China's Cultural Revolution (1966–76), Jiang Qing sought to redefine all forms of artistic expression in strict adherence to revolutionary ideals. She oversaw the development of "model operas" and "model ballets," versions of Chinese traditional performance genres that made heroes of peasants and workers instead of aristocrats. After the Cultural Revolution, she was tried as one of the Gang of Four. She died in prison.

Entertainment means something produced in order to please a public. But what may please one audience may not please another. So one cannot specify exactly what constitutes entertainment – except to say that almost all performances strive, to some degree or other, to entertain. I include in this regard both fine and popular arts, as well as rituals and the performances of everyday life. What about performances of avant-garde artists and political activists designed to offend? Guerrilla theatre events disrupt and may even destroy. These are not entertaining. However, "offensive" art usually is aimed at two publics simultaneously: those who do not find the work pleasant, and those who are entertained by the discomfort the work evokes in others.

Beauty is hard to define. Beauty is not equivalent to being "pretty." The ghastly, terrifying events of kabuki, Greek tragedy, Elizabethan theatre, and some performance art are not pretty. Nor are the demons invoked by shamans. But the skilled enactment of horrors can be beautiful and yield aesthetic pleasure. Is this true of such absolute horrors as

fig 2.13. *The Measures Taken*, by Bertolt Brecht and Hans Eisler, a *Lehrstück* or "teaching play" – a play with a clear message. At the Berlin Philharmonnie, 1930. Copyright Bertolt Brecht Archive, Berlin.

fig 2.14. *The Red Lantern*, one of five "model operas" performed in China during the Cultural Revolution (1966–76). Copyright David King Collection.

Sheila **Melvin** and Jindong **Cai**

The Model Operas

"The Communist Party of China is like the bright sun," sang Granny Sha, her face glowing through wrinkles of sorrow as she told of abuse at the hands of a "poisonous snake, bloodsucker" landlord in Kuomintang-ruled China. Her words, soaring and elongated in the lyrical gymnastics of Beijing Opera, were punctuated by a roar of applause from the audience in the Yifu theatre here. [. . .] While the scene on stage closely resembled Cultural Revolution-era performance, the audience members – mostly middle-aged and stylishly dressed, casually taking cell phone calls, slurping Cokes and licking ice cream bars as the opera proceeded – were decidedly Shanghai 2000. [. . .] As the number of performances increases, so do attempts to analyze the artistic value of this genre created expressly to serve politics. "Naturally, this is sensitive," said Wang Renyuan, a Nanjing-based professor who wrote a book on the music in model operas. "We oppose the Cultural Revolution now, so of course products from then are also criticized. But model operas were very special, and we can't just ignore them. If we say that the Cultural Revolution was politics raping art, then we shouldn't still be doing this today. Criticize the Cultural Revolution, criticize Jiang Qing, but why can't we analyze model operas artistically?" [...] Most intellectuals, even those who detest the genre, are willing to concede that if people want to watch model operas, they should have that right. "I don't want to watch them," said Mr. Luo Zhengrong, the composer. "I don't want to hear them. But they were created well, and if they didn't have a political purpose, they wouldn't exist. The fact is, there's a market for them. If there wasn't a market, they wouldn't be performed."

2000, "Why This Nostalgia for Fruits of Chaos?" 1, 31

slavery, the Shoah, or the extermination of Native Americans? **Francisco de Goya y Luciente**'s (1746–1828) *The Disasters of War* show that nothing is beyond the purview of artistic treatment (**see figure 2.15**). Philosopher **Susanne K. Langer** (1895–1985) argued that in life people may endure terrible experiences, but in art these experiences are transformed into "expressive form" (**see Langer box**). One of the differences between "art" and "life" is that in art, we do not experience the event itself but its representation. Langer's classical notions of aesthetics are challenged in this epoch of simulation, digitization, performance artists, and webcam

fig 2.15. From Goya's *Disasters of War*, 1810–14. From www.napoleonguide.com/goya18.html.

performers who "do" the thing itself in front of our very eyes. A considerable amount of postmodern art does not offer viewers objects or actions for contemplation.

> **Francisco de Goya y Luciente (1746–1828):** Spanish artist. Often referred to simply as "Goya." His series of etchings titled *The Disasters of War* chronicled the Peninsular Wars (1808–14) among Spain, Portugal, and France.

> **Susanne K. Langer (1895–1985):** American philosopher and aesthetician. Her major works include *Philosophy in a New Key* (1942), *Feeling and Form* (1953), and *Problems of Art* (1957).

Susanne K. Langer

Every Good Art Work is Beautiful

A work of art is intrinsically expressive; it is designed to abstract and preset forms for perception — forms of life and feeling, activity, suffering, selfhood — whereby we conceive these realities, which otherwise we can but blindly undergo. Every good work of art is beautiful; as soon as we find it so, we have grasped its expressiveness, and until we do we have not seen it as good art, though we may have ample intellectual reason to believe that it is so. Beautiful works may contain elements that, taken in isolation, are hideous. [...] The emergent form, the whole, is alive and therefore beautiful, as awful things may be — as gargoyles, and fearful African masks, and the Greek tragedies of incest and murder are beautiful. Beauty is not identical with the normal, and certainly not with charm and sense appeal, though all such properties may go to the making of it. Beauty is expressive form.

1953, *Feeling and Form*, 395–96

Conclusion

There are many ways to understand performance. Any event, action, or behavior may be examined "as" performance. Using the category "as" performance has advantages. One can consider things provisionally, in process, and as they change over time. In every human activity there are usually many players with different and even opposing points of view, goals, and feelings. Using "as" performance as a tool, one can look into things otherwise closed off to inquiry. One asks performance questions of events: How is an event deployed in space and disclosed in time? What special clothes or objects are put to use? What roles are played and how are these different, if at all, from who the performers usually are? How are the events controlled, distributed, received, and evaluated?

"Is" performance refers to more definite, bounded events marked by context, convention, usage, and tradition. However, at the start of the twenty-first century, clear distinctions between "as" performance and "is" performance are vanishing. This is part of a general trend toward the dissolution of boundaries of all kinds. The internet, globalization, and the ever-increasing presence of media is affecting human behavior at all levels. More and more people experience their lives as a connected series of performances: dressing up for a party, interviewing for a job, experimenting with sexual orientations and gender roles, playing a life role such as mother or son, or a professional role such as doctor or teacher. The sense that "performance is everywhere" is heightened by the increasingly mediatized environment we live in where people communicate by fax, phone, and the internet; where an unlimited quantity of information and entertainment comes through the air.

One way of ordering this complex situation is to arrange the performance genres, performative behaviors, and performance activities into a continuum (**see figure 2.16**). These genres, behaviors, and activities do not each stand alone. As in the spectrum of visible light, they blend into one another; their boundaries are indistinct. They interact with each other. The continuum is drawn as a straight line to accommodate the printed page. If I could work in three dimensions, I would shape the relationships as more of an overlapping and interlacing spheroid network. For example, though they stand at opposite ends of the straight-line continuum, playing and ritualizing are closely related to each other. In some ways, they underlie all the rest as a foundation.

With regard to figure 2.16: games, sports, pop entertainments, and performing arts include many genres each with its own conventions, rules, history, and traditions. An enormous range of activities comes under these banners. Even the same activity – cricket, for example – varies widely. Cricket at a test match is not the same as that played on a neighborhood oval. And cricket in the Trobriand Islands, where it was changed into a ritual encounter between towns, with the home team always winning, and where it features dancing as much as hitting and fielding, is something else again. On the other hand, certain generalizations can be made. Even though genres are distinct, and no one would confuse the Superbowl with *Les Sylphides*, both ballet and football are about movement, contact, lifting, carrying, falling, and rushing to and fro. In many cultures, theatre, dance, and music are so wholly integrated that it is not possible to place a given event into one or the other category. Kathakali in India, a Makishi performance in Zambia, and the Deer Dance of the Yaquis are but three examples among many that integrate music, dance, and theatre (**see figure 2.17**).

The middle terms on the right side – performances in everyday life and identity constructions – are relatively fluid when compared to the strict governance on the left side. But that is not to say that there are no rules. Even the most apparently casual social interaction is rule-guided and culture-specific. Politeness, manners, body language, and the like all operate according to known scenarios. The specifics of the rules differ from society to society, circumstance to circumstance. But there is no human social interaction that is not "lawful," that is not rule-bound.

The remaining chapters of this book explore these matters in more detail. Chapter 3 deals with ritual and chapter 4 with play. Chapter 5 concerns performativity, the extension of the idea of performance into all areas of human life. Chapter 6 is about the different kinds of performing

a   **PLAY–GAMES–SPORTS–POP ENTERTAINMENTS–PERFORMING ARTS–DAILY LIFE–RITUAL**

b   **GAMES–SPORTS–POP ENTERTAINMENTS–PERFORMING ARTS–DAILY LIFE**
PLAY AND RITUAL

fig 2.16. The performance continuum showing the range, unity, and comprehensivity of performance. In 2.16a the continuum is depicted as a continuous range. In 2.16b "play" and "ritual" are shown as underlying, supporting, and permeating the range.

fig 2.17. All of these performance genres integrate dance, theatre, and music.

A kathakali performer in Kerala, India, a heroic role displaying vigor and energy. Copyright Performing Arts Library.

Makishi mask performer, Zambia. Photograph courtesy of Richard Schechner.

Yaqui Deer Dancer, New Pascua, Arizona, 1980s. Photograph by Richard Schechner.

– from everyday life to theatre to trance. Chapter 7 is about performance processes – generating, presenting, and evaluating performances; and about how performers train, rehearse, warm-up, perform, and cool-down. Chapter 8 is an examination of globalization and its relationship to intercultural performances. It is neither possible nor advisable to fence these topics off from each other – so although each chapter develops a basic theme, there is also a good deal of overlap and interplay among the chapters.

THINGS TO THINK ABOUT

1. Pick an action that would not usually be thought of as a performance. For example, a waiting on line at a supermarket checkout counter, a traffic light at a busy intersection, a person visiting a sick friend. Analyze these "as" performances.
2. Select an event from each of the following performance

genres – a sports match, a religious ritual, an everyday life occurrence, and a performing art. Discuss their similarities and differences with regard to venue, function, audience involvement, event-structure, and historical-cultural context.

THINGS TO DO

1. Observe an everyday encounter of people you do not know. Intervene in the encounter yourself with a definite goal in mind. Afterwards, discuss how your intervention changed the performances of the others. Did they welcome or resent your invention? Why?

2. In small groups, take turns reproducing for your group a bit of behavior which you ordinarily do only in private. How did the behavior change when you were self-consciously performing for others?

SUGGESTED READINGS

Carlson, Marvin. "Introduction: What is Performance?" *Performance: A Critical Introduction*. London and New York: Routledge, 1996. 1–9.

Geertz, Clifford. "Blurred Genres: The Refiguration of Social Thought." *Local Knowledge*. New York: Basic Books, 1983. 26–30.

Goffman, Erving. "The Presentation of Self in Everyday Life." *The Presentation of Self in Everyday Life*. New York: Doubleday, 1959. 17–36.

Kaprow, Allan. "Art Which Can't Be Art (1986)." *Essays on the Blurring of Art and Life*. Berkeley: University of California Press, 1993. 219–22.

Schechner, Richard. "Restoration of Behavior." *Between Theater and Anthropology*. Philadelphia: University of Pennsylvania Press, 1985. 35–116.

3 RITUAL

Ritual, Play, and Performance

Performances – whether in the performing arts, sports, or everyday life – consist of ritualized gestures and sounds. Even when we think we're being spontaneous and original, most of what we do and utter has been done and said before – by us even. Performing arts frame and mark their presentations, underlining the fact that artistic behavior is "not for the first time" but enacted by trained persons who take time to prepare and rehearse. The performance may feature highly stylized behavior such as in kabuki, kathakali, ballet, or the dance dramas of Australian native peoples. Or it may be congruent to everyday behavior as in naturalism. In addition to the performing arts are sports and popular entertainments ranging from circus to rock music. And of course the roles of everyday life.

In chapter 2 I pointed out that performances consist of twice-behaved, coded, transmittable behaviors. This twice-behaved behavior is generated by interactions between ritual and play. In fact, one definition of performance may be: Ritualized behavior conditioned/permeated by play. Rituals are a way people remember. Rituals are memories in action, encoded into actions. Rituals also help people (and animals) deal with difficult transitions, ambivalent relationships, hierarchies, and desires that trouble, exceed, or violate the norms of daily life. Play gives people a chance to temporarily experience the tabu, the excessive, and the risky. You may never be Oedipus or Electra, but you can perform them "in play." Ritual and play both lead people into a "second reality," separate from ordinary life. This reality is one where people can become selves other than their daily selves. When they temporarily become or enact another, people perform actions different from what they do ordinarily. Thus, ritual and play transform people, either permanently or temporarily. Rituals that transform people permanently. These are called "rites of passage," some examples of which are initiations, weddings, and funerals. In play, the transformations are temporary, bounded by the rules of the game. The performing arts, sports, and games are playful, but they often use the processes of ritual. In this chapter, I consider ritual, and in the following chapter, play.

Varieties of Ritual

We cannot go through a day without performing dozens of rituals. There are religious rituals, the rituals of everyday life, the rituals of life roles, the rituals of each profession, the rituals of politics, business, and the judicial system. Even animals perform rituals.

Many people identify ritual with practicing a religion. In religion, rituals give form to the sacred, communicate doctrine, and mold individuals into communities. If people enact most of the secular rituals of everyday life hardly noticing they are doing so (in daily living, it is difficult to distinguish among "ritual," "habit," and "routine"), religious rituals are clearly marked. We know when we are performing them.

Billions of human beings encounter ritual directly through religion. Evidence of religious rituals dates back to the earliest periods of human history, and even to pre-history. Numerous cave sites and burial sites dating back 20,000–30,000 years before the present are full of objects and "art" that experts agree are of ritual significance. Present-day life throughout the world is saturated with religion and religious rituals. There are Passover seders, the five daily prostrations toward Mecca of Muslims, the Roman Catholic Eucharist, the waving of a camphor flame at the climax of a Hindu *puja*, the dances, songs, and utterances of a person possessed by an *orixa* of Umbanda or Candomble – and too many more to list even a small fraction of (**see figure 3.1**). Religious rituals are as various as religion itself.

Nor is religion limited to the normative practices of the "world religions" – Islam, Buddhism, Christianity, Hinduism, and Judaism. There are many local, regional, and sectarian variations of the world religions. There are Shaman, Animist, Pantheist, and New Age religions. Most people, even if they don't openly admit it, actually follow more than one religion. A devout Christian may carry in her pocket a "good luck charm" or regularly consult her horoscope. Diasporic, formerly colonized and missionized peoples combine the religions of their homelands with what was imposed on them. When under stress, people who ordinarily would not do so seek out healers and seers.

fig 3.1. Religious rituals of various faiths.

Muslims praying outside the Registan complex of mosques in Samarkand, 1996. Photograph by Shamil Zhumatov. Copyright Popperfoto.

An Animist Ndembu woman in trance, possessed by a spirit during a girl's initiation rite, Zambia 1985. Copyright Edith Turner, Victor and Edith Turner Collection, Center for the Study of World Religions at Harvard Divinity School Image Bank.

Roman Catholic priest Adolphe Hardy reads his sermon at Saint-Francois-Xavier Church in Paris. Photograph by Jean-Philippe Charbonnier. Copyright Camera Press.

Worship of the Hindu goddess Durga during Durga Puja, Calcutta, 1980s. Photograph by Richard Schechner.

A Jewish Passover seder in New Jersey, USA, 1980s. Photograph by Richard Schechner.

Sacred and Secular

Rituals are frequently divided into two main types, the sacred and the secular. Sacred rituals are those associated with, expressing, or enacting religious beliefs. It is assumed that religious belief systems involve communicating with, praying, or otherwise appealing to supernatural forces.

religious rituals include activities that are decidedly worldly or non-transcendent, such as the masking, playing, drinking, and sexuality of Carnival (**see figure 3.3**). Additionally, many, perhaps most, rituals are both secular and sacred. A wedding, for example, is the performance of a state-

fig 3.2. Uluru – a geological formation sacred to Australian Native Peoples. This same formation is called "Ayer's Rock" by non-Native Australians. Photograph courtesy of Ernest Bial.

These forces may reside in, or be symbolized by, gods or other superhuman beings. Or they may inhere in the natural world itself – rocks, rivers, trees, mountains – as in Native American and Native Australian religions (**see figure 3.2**). Secular rituals are those associated with state ceremonies, everyday life, sports, and any other activity not specifically religious in character.

But this neat division is spurious. Many state ceremonies take on the quality of a religious ritual, with the state playing the role of the transcendent or godly other. Hitler and his Nazi party were particularly adept at this kind of quasi-religious presentation of the state. The great party rallies at Nuremberg in the 1930s were secular-sacred ritual performances of party-state power. The Memorial Day observance at the US Arlington National Cemetery is a secular-sacred state ritual. On the other side of the coin, many

sanctioned contract, a religious ceremony, and a gathering of family and friends. The rituals of American weddings are both secular and sacred. Secular wedding rituals include "cutting the cake," "throwing the bridal bouquet," "the first dance with the bride," and so on (**see figure 3.4**). Many weddings also enact sacred rituals featuring clergy and prayers. Some weddings are presided over by a judge or a ship's captain – in these cases, state rituals are performed. Sometimes the sacred portion of a wedding is separated from the secular by having the wedding ceremony in church and the party elsewhere. What is true of weddings is also so of many other

Carnival: Period of feasting and revelry which precedes the start of Lent on Ash Wednesday. The term "Carnival" includes, but is not limited to, Mardi Gras celebrations.

fig 3.3. Trinidad Carnival combines the secular and the sacred, the ecstatic and solemn, the celebratory and the erotic.

A line of young people "wining" – rotating the hips and rubbing up close to one another – during carnival in Port of Spain, Trinidad, 1990s. Photograph by Pablo Delano.

Maskers "bloody" and ecstatic celebrate carnival in Trinidad, 1990s. Photograph by Jeffrey Chock.

fig 3.4. Bob and Joy Hall "cutting the cake," one of the secular rituals of a traditional British or American wedding. Wanganui, New Zealand, 1970. Photograph by Moira Taylor.

observances, celebrations, and life-passage events such as birthday parties, job-related celebrations honoring years of service or retirement, Thanksgiving Day dinner in the US, and so on.

In a number of cultures, there is no rigid separation between sacred and secular. Sometimes there is no separation whatsoever. To those Native Australians who continue to live traditionally, everything and every place has a "sacred" quality to it (**see Gould box**). This idea of the sacredness of the ordinary is a major theme of New Age religions and of some performance art. Dancer-choreographer **Anna Halprin** (1920–) works with many different kinds of groups to locate and consciously perform the rituals of everyday life – eating, sleeping, greeting, touching, moving – and to invent new rituals that "honor" the body and the earth. For example, Halprin's 1987 *Planetary Dance*, a two-day "dance ritual," consisted of groups of dancers in 25 countries performing in moving synchrony to make a "wave" of dance circling the earth. The dance was repeated in 1994.

Richard A. Gould

Ritual is an Inseparable Part of the Whole

The daily lives of the Aborigines is rewarding but routine. There is a kind of low-key pace to the everyday round of living. In their ritual lives, however, the

Aborigines attain a heightened sense of drama. Sharp images appear and colors deepen. The Aborigines are masters of stagecraft and achieve remarkable visual and musical effects with the limited materials at hand. [. . .] Gradually I experienced the central truth of Aboriginal religion: that it is not a thing by itself but an inseparable part of a whole that encompasses every aspect of daily life, every individual and every time – past, present, and future. It is nothing less than the theme of existence, and as such constitutes one of the most sophisticated and unique religious and philosophical systems known to man.

1969, *Yiwara*, 103–104

Anna Halprin (1920–): American dancer and choreographer. A pioneer in the use of expressive arts for healing. Her work in the 1960s had a profound influence on postmodern dance. Her most recent book is *Dance as a Healing Art* (2000).

Structures, Functions, Processes, and Experiences

Rituals and ritualizing can be understood from at least four perspectives:

- structures – what rituals look and sound like, how they use space, who performs them, and how they are performed.
- functions – what rituals accomplish for groups, cultures, and individuals.
- processes – the underlying dynamic driving rituals; how rituals enact and bring about change.
- experiences – what it's like to be "in" a ritual

These four aspects of ritual have been explored from many angles.

Ethologists study the continuities between animal and human rituals – particularly how rituals control and redirect aggression, establish and maintain hierarchy, and mark and defend territory. Neuro-psychologists believe that certain repetitive rhythms stimulate the brain, leading to an "oceanic experience" of ultimate well-being. Paleo-historians studying the cave "art" of Europe surmise that hunting and fertility rituals were probably performed in association with the paintings and sculptings. The "art" may have been a repository

of group memory before writing (**see Pfeiffer box**). (I use quotation marks because no one knows what the makers of these works thought of them.) Anthropologists observe and theorize about the myriad ritual practices of today's human societies. Performance theorists investigate the ritual processes underlying workshops, rehearsals, and performances.

Ethology is the science of biologically driven behavior, whether in humans or other animals. **Ethnology** is the science of human societies. Adherents of the two sciences, who one might suppose would benefit from each other's research and theories, have in fact often been in conflict.

John **Pfeiffer**

Paleolithic Cave Performances

Meat meant survival, and people did everything in their power, and more, to assure success in the hunt. Above all, they killed animals ritually by drawing them on cave walls and piercing them with spears and arrows, essentially a variation on the sympathetic-magic theme [. . .]. Another variety of ritual, designed to avoid overkill and guarantee a continuing abundance of game, involved fertility cults and the drawing of pregnant animals and sex organs. [. . .] An information explosion occurred together with the explosion of ceremony and the explosion of art. [. . .] The collective knowledge of the band-society was on the rise, demanding far more powerful systems of record-keeping – and there was no writing.[. . .] The here-and-now emergency gave rise to measures of a different sort, measures created to transmit the expanding contents of "the tribal encyclopedia" intact and indelibly from generation to generation. [. . .] This was not art for art sake, no play, nothing casual. It was bare survival-necessity. The development of prehistoric, preliterate mnemonics must have been the result of considerable trial and error. [. . .] It implies a system of classification, bodies of information separated by increasing difficulty of access, degrees of concealment, a hierarchy of knowledge.

1982, *The Creative Explosion*, 119, 123, 127

Only some of the vast literature on ritual is relevant to performance studies. I have identified seven key themes to explore further:

1   ritual as actions, as performances.
2   similarities/differences of human and animal rituals.
3   rituals as liminal performances taking place "betwixt and between" life-stages and social identities.
4   the ritual process.
5   social dramas.
6   the relation between ritual and theatre in terms of the efficacy–entertainment dyad.
7   the "origins" of performance in ritual, or not?

Rituals as Actions, as Performances

The idea that rituals are performances was proposed nearly a century ago. **Emile Durkheim** (1858–1917) theorized that performing rituals created and sustained "social solidarity." He insisted that although rituals may communicate or express religious ideas, rituals were not ideas or abstractions, but performances enacting known patterns of behavior and texts. The relationship between "ritual action" and "thought" is complex (**see Bell box**). Rituals don't so much express ideas as embody them. Rituals are thought-in/as-action. This is one of the qualities that makes ritual so theatre-like, a similarity Durkheim recognized (**see Durkheim box**).

Emile Durkheim (1858–1917): French social scientist. One of the founding theorists of anthropology, sociology, and psychology. Author of *The Elementary Forms of the Religious Life* (1911, Eng. 1915).

Catherine Bell

Ritual Structure

[. . .] ritual is to the symbols it dramatizes as action is to thought; on a second level, ritual integrates thought and action; and on a third level, a focus on ritual performances integrates *our* thought and *their* actions.

1992, *Ritual Theory, Ritual Practice*, 32

Emile Durkheim

Ritual and Theatre

We have already had occasion to show that they [rites performed by Native Australians] are closely akin to dramatic representations. [. . .] Not only do they employ the same processes as real drama, but they also pursue an end of the same sort: being foreign to all utilitarian ends, they make men forget the real world and transport them into another where their imagination is more at ease; they distract. They sometimes even go so far as to have the outward appearance of a recreation: the assistants may be seen laughing and amusing themselves openly. [. . .] Art is not merely an external ornament with which the cult has adorned itself in order to dissimulate certain of its features which may be too austere and too rude; but rather, in itself, the cult is something aesthetic.

1965 [1915], *The Elementary Forms of the Religious Life*, 424, 426–27

Arnold van Gennep (1873–1957) also recognized the theatrical dynamics of ritual. In his study of the "rites of passage," van Gennep proposed a three-phase structure of ritual action: the preliminal, liminal, and postliminal. He pointed out that life was a succession of passages from one phase to another and that each step along the way was marked by ritual (**see van Gennep box**). In the 1960s, Victor Turner developed van Gennep's insight into a theory of ritual that has great importance for performance studies. Later in this chapter, I will discuss van Gennep's and Turner's work. But first I need to explain ritual from an evolutionary perspective.

Arnold van Gennep (1873–1957): French ethnographer and folklorist. Author of *The Rites of Passage* (1908, Eng. 1960).

Arnold van Gennep

The Rites of Passage

The life of an individual in any society is a series of passages from one age to another and from one occupation to another. [. . .] Life comes to be made up of a succession of stages with similar ends and beginnings: birth, social puberty, marriage, fatherhood, advancement to a higher class, occupational specialization, and death. For every one of these events there are ceremonies whose essential purpose is to enable the individual to pass from one defined position to another which is equally well defined.

1960 [1908], *The Rites of Passage*, 3

Human and Animal Rituals

All animals, including homo sapiens, exist within the same ecological web subject to the same evolutionary processes. But animals are not all alike. Homologies and analogies must be put forward cautiously. It is not correct to call the abdominal waggle and footwork of honeybees communicating to other bees the whereabouts of nectar "dances" in the human sense. The bees cannot improvise, change the basic patterns of movement, or express their feelings (which they don't have in any human understanding of that word). Where everything is genetically determined, where there is no learning, where no improvisation is possible, where error and/or lying cannot occur, art is not. So what are the bees doing? They are communicating by means of a symbolic system of movements. This kind of communication suggests a connection, one of very many, linking human and animal rituals.

Charles Darwin (1809–82): English naturalist who developed the theory of evolution by natural selection. In addition to his landmark *The Origin of Species* (1859), Darwin also authored the increasingly influential *The Expression of the Emotions in Man and Animals* (1872).

Julian Huxley (1887–1975): English biologist, author of *Evolution: The Modern Synthesis* (1942) and *Essays of a Humanist* (1964) among many other works.

Konrad Lorenz (1903–89): Austrian ethologist, winner (with Karl von Frisch and Nikolaas Tinbergen) of the 1973 Nobel Prize in medicine. His books include *On Aggression* (1963, Eng. 1966) and *The Foundations of Ethology* (1978, Eng. 1981).

E. O. (Edward Osborne) Wilson (1929–): American entymologist and pioneer of sociobiology. His works include *Sociobiology* (1975), *On Human Nature* (1978), and *Consilience* (1998).

Charles Darwin (1809–82), in his 1872 book *The Expression of the Emotions in Man and Animals*, noted many similarities in behavior between humans and animals. He felt these indicated a common evolutionary development of feelings and the expression of emotions as well as of anatomy and brain structure. Darwin's work led **Julian Huxley** (1887–1975) to assert that human and animal rituals were related through evolution; this idea has been developed by many ethologists and sociobiologists including **Konrad Lorenz** (1903–89) and **Edward O. Wilson** (1929–) (**see Lorenz and d'Aquili boxes**).

Konrad Lorenz

Ritualization in Animals and Humans

[Julian] Huxley discovered the remarkable fact that certain movement patterns lose, in the course of phylogeny, their original specific function and become purely "symbolic" ceremonies. He called this process ritualization and used this term without quotation marks; in other words, he equated the cultural processes leading to the development of human rites with the phylogenetic processes giving rise to such remarkable "ceremonies" in animals. From a purely functional point of view this equation is justified, even bearing in mind the difference between the cultural and phylogenetic processes. [. . .]

The triple function of suppressing fighting within the group, of holding the group together, and of setting it off, as an independent entity, against other, similar units, is performed by culturally developed ritual in so strictly analogous a manner as to merit deep consideration. [. . .]

The formation of traditional rites must have begun with the first dawning of human culture, just as at a much lower level phylogenetic rite formation was a prerequisite for the origin of social organization in higher animals. [. . .] In both cases, a behavior pattern by means of which a species in the one case, a cultured society in the other, deals with certain environmental conditions, acquires an entirely new function, that of communication. The primary function may still be performed, but it often recedes more and more into the background and may disappear completely so that a typical change of function is achieved. Out of communication two new equally important functions may arise, both of which still contain some measure of communicative effects. The first of these is the channeling of aggression into innocuous outlets, the second is the formation of a bond between two or more individuals. [. . .] The display of animals during threat and courtship furnishes an abundance of examples, and so does the culturally developed ceremonial of man. [. . .] Rhythmical repetition of the same movement is so characteristic of very many rituals, both instinctive and cultural, that it is hardly necessary to describe examples. [. . .]

This "mimic exaggeration" results in a ceremony which is, indeed, closely akin to a symbol and produces that theatrical effect that first struck Sir Julian Huxley as he watched his Great Crested Grebes. [. . .] There is hardly a doubt that all human art primarily developed in the service of rituals and that the autonomy of "art for art's sake" was achieved only by another, secondary step of cultural progress.

1966, *On Aggression*, 54–55, 72–74

Eugene G. **d'Aquili,**
Charles D. **Laughlin** Jr., and
John **McManus**

The Biological Foundations of Ritual

We may say then that the primary biological function of ritual behavior is cybernetic: ritual operates to facilitate both intraorganismic and interorganismic coordination. Such coordination is necessary to form coherent, corporate responses, with common motive and drive, for the completion of some effect or task that could not be completed by conspecifics acting alone. Human ceremonial ritual is not a simple institution unique to man but rather a nexus of variables shared by other species. [. . .] One may trace the evolutionary progression of ritual behavior from the emergence of formalization through the coordination of formalized communicative behavior and sequences of ritual behavior to the conceptualization of such sequences and the assignment of symbols to them by man.

1979, *The Spectrum of Ritual*, 33, 36–37

The evolutionary scheme of ritual can be depicted as a "ritual tree" (**see figure 3.5**). Animals with simple nervous systems, such as insects and fish, enact genetically fixed rituals. Further up the evolutionary ladder, mammal and bird species – dogs and parrots, for example – elaborate on what is genetically given and are able to learn, mimic, and improvise. Much closer to humans are the non-human

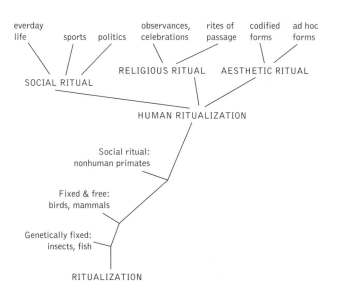

fig 3.5. The evolution of ritual from an ethological perspective can be depicted as a "tree." The further up the tree, the more complex the rituals. Nonhuman primates enact social rituals, but only humans enact religious and aesthetic rituals. Drawing by Richard Schechner.

primates. Among these, some species of chimpanzee and gorilla perform in ways quite like humans but with nowhere near the complexity, diversity, or cognitive qualities of human rituals. Humans have developed ritual into complex and sophisticated systems divisible into three main categories: social ritual, religious ritual, and aesthetic ritual. As noted earlier, these are not locked out from each other, but often overlap or converge.

To glimpse just how close some of the higher primates are to humans, one must turn to field studies as well as some of the laboratory experiments concerning language acquisition and use. **Jane Goodall** (1934–) described a performance by a juvenile male chimpanzee in the Gombe Stream Reserve in Tanzania in which a young animal challenged the alpha male not by means of combat, but through ritual display (**see Goodall box 1**). Not long after his

show, "Mike" replaced "Goliath" as the troupe's alpha male. Note that the animals Goodall observed were not trained or tamed. Goodall gave them names for identification purposes only. Where does ritual come in? Like so many other encounters among animals concerning dominance, mating, territory, and food, Mike's challenge was played out as a ritual, as symbolic display, not as the "real thing," deadly combat. Goodall observed other performances by chimpanzees that she thought were very like human theatre (**see Goodall box 2**).

Jane Goodall (1934–): British ethologist, known for her research among the chimpanzees in Tanzania's Gombe Stream National Park. Her books include *In the Shadow of Man* (1971) and *The Chimpanzees of Gombe: Patterns of Behavior* (1986).

Jane Goodall

Chimpanzee Ritual Challenge

All at once Mike [a young male chimp] calmly walked over to our tent and took hold of an empty kerosene can by the handle. Then he picked up a second can and, walking upright, returned to the place where he had been sitting. Armed with his two cans Mike continued to stare toward the other males. After a few minutes he began to rock from side to side. At first the movement was almost imperceptible, but Hugo and I were watching him closely. Gradually he rocked more vigorously, his hair slowly began to stand erect, and then softly at first, he started a series of pant-hoots. As he called, Mike got to his feet and suddenly he was off, charging toward the group of males, hitting the two cans ahead of him. The cans, together with Mike's crescendo of hooting, made the most appalling racket: no wonder the erstwhile peaceful males rushed out of the way. Mike and his cans vanished down a track, and after a few moments there was silence. [. . .]

After a short interval that low-pitched hooting began again, followed almost immediately by the appearance of the two rackety cans with Mike closely behind them. Straight for the other males he charged, and once more they fled. This time, even before the group could reassemble, Mike set off again; but he made straight for Goliath [the alpha male] – and even he hastened out of Mike's way like all the others. Then Mike stopped and sat, all his hair on end, breathing hard.

1971, *In the Shadow of Man*, 122–23

Jane Goodall

Chimpanzee Theatre

At about noon the first heavy drops of rain began to fall. The chimpanzees climbed out of the tree and one after the other plodded up the steep grassy slope toward the open ridge at the top. There were seven adult males in the group [. . .], several females, and a few youngsters. At that moment the storm broke. The rain was torrential, and the sudden clap of thunder, right overhead, made me jump. As if this were a signal, one of the big males stood upright and as he swayed and swaggered rhythmically from foot to foot I could just hear the rising crescendo of his pant-hoots above the beating of the rain. Then he charged flat-out down the slope toward the trees he had just left. He ran some thirty yards, and then, swinging round the trunk of a small tree to break his headlong rush, leaped into the low branches and sat motionless.

Almost at once two other males charged after him. One broke off a low branch from a tree as he ran and brandished it in the air before hurling it ahead of him. The other, as he reached the end of his run, stood upright and rhythmically swayed the branches of a tree back and forth before seizing a huge branch and dragging it farther down the slope. A fourth male, as he too charged leaped into a tree and, almost without breaking his speed, tore off a large branch, leaped with it to the ground, and continued down the slope. As the last two males called and charged down, so the one who had started the whole performance climbed from his tree and began plodding up the slope again. The others, who had also climbed into trees near the bottom of the slope, followed suit. When they reached the ridge, they started charging down all over again, one after the other, with equal vigor.

The females and youngsters had climbed into the trees near the top of the rise as soon as the displays had begun, and there they remained watching throughout the whole performance. As the males charged down and plodded back up, so the rain fell harder, jagged forks or brilliant flares of lightning lit the leaden sky, and the crashing of the thunder seemed to shake the very mountains.

My enthusiasm was not merely scientific as I watched, enthralled, from my grandstand seat on the opposite side of the narrow ravine, sheltering under a plastic sheet. [. . .] I could only watch, and marvel at the magnificence of those splendid creatures. With a display of strength and vigor such as this, primitive man himself might have challenged the elements.

1971, *In the Shadow of Man*, 52–53

George Schaller (1933–), who studied the mountain gorilla in Uganda, also underscores similarities between human and non-human primates. Schaller shows how cheering, stomping, waving, and throwing things by involved fans at sports events is very much like what gorillas do (**see Schaller box**) (**see figure 3.6**). Recent studies confirm that sports fans are involved to such a degree that they undergo both physiological and psychological changes (**see McKinley box**). Enthusiastic, even violent displays are not infrequent at football games and wrestling matches. In sports such as golf and tennis, impulses to full-fledged emotional displays are dampened by the traditions of the game. But the situation is not static. In recent years, tennis fans (and players) have become more demonstrative, if not rowdy.

George B. Schaller (1933–): American ethologist, author of *The Mountain Gorilla* (1963) and *The Serengeti Lion* (1972).

And not only sports events. Large-scale rhythmic formations of many kinds – marching, movement choirs, hymn singing, disco-dancing, and parades, to name some of many – are examples of the same genetically based behavior. Only a few of these allow for individual expression. Mass demonstrations and rallies, religious revivals, the

George **Schaller**

Gorillas and Sports Fans

Various aspects of the chest-beating display sequence are present in the gibbon, orangutan, chimpanzee, and man, although the specificity is sometimes lacking. [. . .] Man behaves remarkably like a chimpanzee or a gorilla in conflicting situations. Sporting events are ideal locations for watching the behavior of man when he is generally excited and emotionally off-guard. A spectator at a sporting event perceives actions which excite him. Yet he cannot participate in them directly, nor does he want to cease observing them. The tension thus produced finds release in chanting, clapping of hands, stamping of feet, jumping up and down, throwing of objects. This behavior is sometimes guided into a pattern by the efforts of cheerleaders who, by repeating similar sounds over and over again, channel the displays into a violent, synchronized climax. The intermittent nature of such behavior, the transfer of excitement from one individual to the next, and other similarities with the displays of gorillas are readily apparent.

1963, *The Mountain Gorilla*, 235

fig 3.6. The expressive displays of humans and the great apes can be very similar.

A mountain gorilla displaying, Congo (Zaire). Photograph by D. Parer and E. Parer Cook. Copyright Ardea, London Ltd.

Liverpool football fans displaying, Wembley Stadium, London. Copyright Popperfoto.

streets of Tehran crowded with people chanting their support for or opposition to the mullahs, party conventions in the UK and USA, the gathering of a million people in Beijing's Tiananmen Square – all trade in the same emotional currency (**see figure 3.7**). When mood displays are ritualized into mass actions, individual expression is discouraged or prohibited and replaced by exaggerated, rhythmically coordinated, repetitive actions and chanting. Aggression is evoked and channeled for the benefit of the sponsor, team, corporation, politician, party, religion, or state.

> **Mood display:** An ethological term indicating how an animal communicates through movements, postures, sounds, and faces that it is happy, angry, sad, etc.

But what exactly happens to ordinary behavior when it is ritualized? Are there any patterns? Is there a non-ideological system to ritual? Ethologists say that rituals are the result of a process that over millions of years evolved behaviors that have an "adaptive advantage." In other words, rituals help animals survive, procreate, and pass on their genes. The qualities of ritualization, according to ethologists, are that:

- some ordinary behaviors (movements, calls) are freed from their original functions.
- the behavior is exaggerated and simplified; movements are often frozen into postures; movements and calls become rhythmic and repetitive.
- conspicuous body parts for display develop, such as the peacock's tail and the moose's horns. In humans, these are artificially provided – uniforms, sound-makers, masks, etc.
- the behavior is "released" (performed) on cue according to specific "releasing mechanisms" (stimuli resulting in conditioned responses).

One can see similarities to "restoration of behavior." As in restored behavior, rituals are "strips of behavior" that develop on their own regardless of their "origins" or original functions. The movements, utterances, and postures of human rituals are often ordinary actions that have been exaggerated, simplified, and made repetitive. Humans have not developed conspicuous body parts, but are extremely skilled at masks, costumes, makeup, jewelry, scarification, cosmetic surgery, and other ways to modify either temporarily or permanently how the body looks and moves. The

James C. McKinley Jr.

Root, Root, Root for the Home Team!

It has long been assumed that ardent sports fans derive excitement and a sense of community from rooting for a big-time team. But a growing body of scientific evidence suggests that for some fans, the ties go much deeper.

Some researchers have found that fervent fans become so tied to their teams that they experience hormonal surges and other physiological changes while watching games, much as the athletes do.

The self-esteem of some male and female fans also rises and falls with a game's outcome, with losses affecting their optimism about everything from getting a date to winning at darts, one study showed. [. . .]

One theory traces the roots of fan psychology to a primitive time when human beings lived in small tribes, and warriors fighting to protect tribes were true genetic representatives of their people, psychologists say.

In modern society, professional and college athletes play a similar role for a city in the stylized war on a playing field, the theory goes. Even though professional athletes are mercenaries in every sense, their exploits may re-create the intense emotions in some fans that tribal warfare might have in their ancestors. It may also be these emotions that have in large part fueled the explosion in the popularity of sports over the last two decades.

"Our sports heroes are our warriors," Robert Cialdini, a professor of psychology at Arizona State, said about sports fans. "This is not some light diversion to be enjoyed for its inherent grace and harmony. The self is centrally involved in the outcome of the event. Whoever you root for represents you." [. . .]

Some recent studies suggest that some fans experience physiological changes during a game or when shown photos of their team. A study in Georgia has shown, for instance, that testosterone levels in male fans rise markedly after a victory and drop just as sharply after a defeat. The same pattern has been documented in male animals who fight over a mate: biologists theorize that mammals may have evolved this way to ensure quick resolutions to conflicts.

James Dabbs, a psychologist at Georgia State University, tested saliva samples from different groups of sports fans before and after important games. In one test, Dr. Dabbs took saliva samples from 21 Italian and Brazilian men in Atlanta before and after Brazil's victory over Italy in soccer's 1994 World Cup. The Brazilians' testosterone rose an average of 28%, while the Italians' levels dropped 27%. [. . .]

Charles Hillman, a psychologist now at the University of Illinois, found that ardent football fans at the University of Florida experience extreme physiological arousal when they viewed pictures of Gator football stars making game-winning plays, but responded indifferently to pictures of other athletes and teams. [. . .]

Among zealous male and female fans, Dr. Hillman's study found, the levels of arousal – measured by heartrate, brain waves, and perspiration – was comparable to what the fans registered when shown erotic photos or pictures of animal attacks, he said. [. . .]

Edward Hirt of Indiana University has demonstrated that an ardent fan's self-esteem tends to track a team's performance. [. . . M]en and women who were die-hard fans were much more optimistic about their sex appeal after a victory. They were also more sanguine about their ability to perform well at mental and physical tests, like darts and word games, Dr. Hirt found. When the team lost, that optimism evaporated. [. . .]

In most cases, this deep attachment to a team can be healthy, studies have shown. Daniel Wann, a psychologist at Murray State University in Kentucky, has done several studies showing that an intense interest in a team can buffer people from depression and foster feelings of self-worth and belonging.

2000, "It Isn't Just a Game: Clues to Rooting," 1–2, 4, 6–7

fig 3.7. The People's Liberation Army on parade in Tiananmen Square, Beijing, 1951. Copyright AP/Wide World Photographs.

munications can lead to violent or even fatal encounters. Rituals appear designed to enhance clear communications. Rituals are over determined, redundant, exaggerated, and repetitious. Ritual's metamessage is, "You get the message, don't you?!" This message is both imploring and problematic. Is God listening? Is the trance real? Was that a miracle or a hoax?

> **Metamessage:** A message that refers back to itself. For example, a message that says, "This is a message." A metamessage of prayer would be praying in such a way that everyone knows, "Now I am praying." The idea is based on Gregory Bateson's notion of "metacommunication," which will be discussed in chapter 4.

Human rituals go beyond animal ritualization in two key regards. Human rituals mark a society's calendar. Human rituals transport persons from one life phase to another. Animals are not conscious of puberty, Easter, marriage, or death as "life passages." Animals do not wonder about life after death or reincarnation. Animals don't take oaths of fealty, or exchange gifts on a birthday. Human rituals are bridges across life's troubled waters.

"important parts" of the human body have been replicated in untold representations, often highly exaggerated. Exactly what is "important" varies culturally, though there are some favorites – phallus, breasts, buttocks, and face.

These qualities of ritual enhance its functions. From an ethological perspective, the functions are to reduce deadly fighting within a group, to determine and maintain hierarchy, to enhance group cohesion, to mark out and protect territory, to share food, and to regulate mating. Ethologists argue that these functions carry over into human cultures, with the significant addition of belief, ideology, and cognition. In other words, human rituals accomplish the same tasks as animal rituals – but in addition, human rituals are meaningful. Exactly what those meanings are depends upon the specific ritual practice and upon the specific culture, religion, society, or kin group.

Are ethologists begging the question? Do they call some animal behavior "ritual" because it looks like what people do? Are those female and juvenile chimps sitting in the trees watching the big males perform really spectators as at the theatre? Or was Goodall projecting? Is there really a link connecting human behavior with the behavior of other animals analogous to the evolutionary development of body structure? This is not an easy question to settle, though recent work in genetics and neurology suggests a single bio-evolutionary web that would include behavior.

In both animals and humans, rituals arise or are devised around, and to regulate, disruptive, turbulent, dangerous, and ambivalent interactions. In these areas faulty com-

Rituals as Liminal Performances

Everywhere people mark the passing from one life stage to another – birth, social puberty (which may occur before or after the biological changes associated with the onset of adolescence), marriage, parenthood, social advancement, job specialization, retirement, and death. As I pointed out earlier, Van Gennep noted that these rites of passage consist of three phases – the preliminal, liminal, and postliminal. The key phase is the liminal – a period of time when a person is "betwixt and between" social categories or personal identities (**see Turner box 1**). During the liminal phase, the actual work of rites of passage takes place. At this time, in specially marked spaces, transitions and transformations occur. The liminal phase fascinated Turner because he recognized in it a possibility for ritual to be creative, to make the way for new situations, identities, and social realities by means of what Turner called "anti-structure."

The work of the liminal phase is twofold: first, to reduce those undergoing the ritual to a state of vulnerability so that they are open to change. Persons are stripped of their former identities and assigned places in the social world; they enter a time-place where they are not-this-not-that, neither here nor there, in the midst of a journey from one social self to

Victor Turner

Liminality

Liminal entities are neither here nor there; they are betwixt and between the positions assigned and arrayed by law, custom, convention, and ceremonial. As such, their ambiguous and indeterminate attributes are expressed by a rich variety of symbols in the many societies that ritualize social and cultural transitions. Thus, liminality is frequently likened to death, to being in the womb, to invisibility, to darkness, to bisexuality, to the wilderness, and to an eclipse of the sun or moon. Liminal entities, such as neophytes in initiation or puberty rites, may be represented as possessing nothing. [. . .] Their behavior is normally passive or humble; they must obey their instructors implicitly, and accept arbitrary punishment without complaint. It is as though they are being reduced or ground down to a uniform condition to be fashioned anew and endowed with additional powers to enable them to cope with their new stations in life. Among themselves, neophytes tend to develop an intense comradeship and egalitarianism.

1969, *The Ritual Process*, 95

another. For the time being, they are literally powerless and often identityless. Second, during the liminal phase, persons are inscribed with their new identities and initiated into their new powers. There are many ways to accomplish the transformation. Persons may take oaths, learn lore, dress in new clothes, perform special actions, be scarred or circumcised. The possibilities are countless, varying from culture to culture, group to group, ceremony to ceremony. As I will explain later in this chapter, the workshop-rehearsal phase of performance composition is analogous to the liminal phase of the ritual process.

At the conclusion of the liminal phase of a ritual, actions and objects take on, and radiate, significances in excess of their practical use or value. These actions and objects are symbolic of the changes taking place. The "I do" and exchange of rings at a wedding, the snipping of an 8-day-old Jewish boy's foreskin in a circumcision, the handful of earth thrown on the coffin at a funeral, the giving of a diploma at a graduation, the placing of a red cap on a new-made Cardinal's head signify a change in status, identity, or what-have-you. A transformation is taking place.

But liminality need not require pomp or the use of valuables in order to signify. In Hindu India, the corpse is wrapped in plain cloth, carried on a wooden palett to the burning grounds, and set ablaze. The body must be consumed, the skull cracked open to release the *atman*, or soul, the ashes scattered. Only then, when all the rituals have been performed, can the self fly free from the body – to final release or on its journey to another reincarnation. The Zoroastrian Parsis of Mumbai expose the dead body atop the Doongarwadi, the Tower of Silence, where vultures swiftly consume the flesh and smaller bones. Bones too large for the birds are buried or crushed to dust.

Limens, Lintels, and Stages

A limen is a threshold or sill, a thin strip neither inside nor outside a building or room linking one space to another, a passageway between places rather than a place in itself. In ritual and aesthetic performances, the thin space of the limen is expanded into a wide space both actually and conceptually. What usually is just a "go between" becomes the site of the action. And yet this action remains, to use Turner's phrase, "betwixt and between." It is enlarged in time and space yet retains its peculiar quality of passageway or temporariness. Architecturally, the empty space of a limen is bridged at the top by a lintel, usually made of lumber or stone. This provides reinforcement. Conceptually, what happens within a liminal time-space is "reinforced," emphasized.

Limen: Literally a threshold or sill, an architectural feature linking one space to another – a passageway between places rather than a place in itself. A limen is often framed by a **lintel**, which outlines the emptiness it reinforces. In performance theory, "liminal" refers to "in-between" actions or behaviors, such as initiation rituals.

This conceptual-architectural detail remains visible in the design of many proscenium theatres. The front frame of a proscenium stage, from the forestage to a few feet behind the curtain, is a limen connecting the imaginary worlds performed onstage to the daily lives of spectators in the house. The house is permanently decorated, while the stage is often fully dressed in settings indicating specific times and places. But most of the world's stages are empty spaces, to use **Peter Brook**'s (1925–) phrase (**see figure 3.8**). An empty theatre space is liminal, open to all kinds of possibilities – that space by means of performing could become anywhere. The orchestra circle of the ancient Greek amphitheatre was

fig 3.8. The empty space of performance in different cultures.

The Greek theatre at Epidaurus, 4th–2nd centuries BCE. This theatre, still in use, holds up to 17,000 spectators. Copyright Ancient Art and Architecture Collection.

The interior of the Swan Theatre as drawn in Elizabethan times by Johannis de Witt. Notice how close the audience is to the performers. Copyright British Museum.

A Bira village dancing ground in Congo (Zaire), 1950s. Here ordinary space is transformed into a performance arena by the action taking place. The women are performing a maipe ritual dance. Photograph by Colin Turnbull. Photograph courtesy of Richard Schechner.

Paul Claudel's *La Femme et son Ombre* (A Woman and Her Shadow) as performed by Izumi Yoshio, left, and Izumi Yasutake in Nagoya, 1972. Performing in an empty space emphasizes the performers, not the scenery. Photograph by Tanaka Masao. Photograph courtesy of Karen Brazell.

Scene 8 of Bertolt Brecht's *Mother Courage and Her Children*, with The Performance Group, directed by Richard Schechner, in the New School Gymnasium, New Delhi, 1976. Stephen Borst as The Chaplain threatens Jim Griffiths as The Cook. The surrounding audience focuses the otherwise empty space. Photograph by Pablo Bartholomew. Photograph Courtesy of Richard Schechner.

unadorned except for the altar of Dionysus at its center. The noh stage is made of smoothed *hinoki*, Japanese cypress. The only decorations are a painting of bamboo to the side and a backdrop painting of a large pine tree – the Yogo Pine at the Kasuga Shrine in Nara – where each year for centuries the noh season begins. Under the noh stage are large hollow earthen jugs so that when the actors stamp on the wooden stage a deep reverberation swells. The Elizabethan stage was likewise simple and empty, hardly more than "two boards and a passion." The dancing ground of an African village and the temporary erection of a screen for Javanese *wayang kulit* (shadow puppets) are both liminal spaces ready to be populated by imagined realities. Illusionistic stage sets, so familiar in the West since the nineteenth century, are actually the exception to the rule. The spaces of film, television, and computer monitors are more traditional. Apparently full of real things and people, they are actually empty screens, populated by shadows or pixels.

Peter Brook (1925–): British director working in Paris from 1970 when he founded the International Centre for Theatre Research. His many theatre credits include Peter Weiss' *Marat / Sade* (1964), *A Midsummer's Night Dream* (1970), *The Mahabharata* (1985), and *Hamlet* (2000). His books include *The Empty Space* (1968), *The Shifting Point* (1987), and *The Threads of Time* (1998).

Turner realized that there was a difference between what happens in traditional cultures and in modern cultures. With industrialization and the division of labor, many of the functions of ritual were taken over by the arts, entertainment, and recreation. Turner used the term "liminoid" to describe types of symbolic action that occurred in leisure activities which were like ritual. If the liminal includes "communication of sacra" and "ludic recombinations and inversions," the liminoid includes all the different kinds of art and popular entertainments (**see figure 3.9**). Generally, liminoid activities are voluntary, while liminal rites are obligatory.

Victor Turner used the term "liminoid" to describe types of symbolic action or leisure activity occurring in contemporary societies that serve a function similar to rituals in pre-modern or traditional societies. Generally speaking, **liminoid** activities are voluntary, while **liminal** activities are required. Recreational activities and the arts are often liminal.

Turner felt that the counter-culture of the 1960s was in part an attempt to recuperate the force and unity of traditional liminality. Shortly before his death in 1983, Turner recognized that the counter-culture had moderated into the New Age with its alternative religions and medicines, concerns for ecology, and increasing tolerance of different

fig 3.9. Victor Turner's diagram of the ritual process in relationship to the liminal, liminoid, and theatre. Figure from *On the Edge of the Bush: Anthropology as Experience*, by Victor Turner. Copyright The Arizona Board of Regents. Reprinted by permission of the University of Arizona Press.

sorts of non-traditional lifestyles. Turner was an optimist, if not an outright utopian. He predicted that "the liberated and disciplined body itself, with its many untapped resources for pleasure, pain, and expression," would lead the way to a better world.

The decades since Turner's death indicate that his utopianism is probably unjustified. At the turn of the twenty-first century, sacred and secular rituals, staged in central, symbolically loaded places – major avenues, civic centers, cathedrals, stadiums, and Capitols – reinforce officialdom and mainstream values. Liminoid artistic and social activities take place at the margins and in the creases of established cultural systems, off the beaten track in "bad" neighborhoods, and in remote rural areas. The internet pulls these distant and disparate venues and tendencies together, allowing for unity and dispersal at the same time. The question remains whether or not official culture – by means of regulation and commercialization – will reign in the vibrancy and diversity of the internet. Struggles over "intellectual property" are evidence that the internet will not be as free – in all senses of that word – as it has been. Some of these issues will be explored further in chapter 8.

Anti-Structure and Communitas

Rituals are more than structures and functions; they can also be among the most powerful experiences life has to offer. While in a liminal state, people are freed from the demands of daily life. They feel at one with their comrades, all personal and social difference erased. People are uplifted, swept away, taken over. Turner called the liberation from the constraints of ordinary life "anti-structure" and the experience of ritual camaraderie "communitas" (**see Turner box 2**).

Communitas A feeling of group solidarity, usually short-lived, generated during ritual. According to Victor Turner, communitas comes in several varieties. Normative communitas is the sometimes dry and unfeeling display of group solidarity. Spontaneous communitas is a sincere outflowing of warmth for others in the group.

Communitas is a complex term. As Turner defined it, communitas comes in several varieties, including the "normative" and the "spontaneous." Normative communitas is what happens during communion in an Episcopal or Roman Catholic service. The congregation is united "in Christ" by the Eucharist. However, not every congregant may feel "in Christ" at that moment. The communitas is "official,"

Victor Turner

Anti-Structure and Communitas

I have used the term "anti-structure" mainly with reference to tribal and agrarian societies, to describe both liminality and what I have called "communitas." I meant by it not a structural reversal, a mirror-imaging of the "profane": workaday socioeconomic structure, or a fantasy-rejection of structural "necessities," but the liberation of human capacities of cognition, affect, volition, creativity, etc., from the normative constraints incumbent upon occupying a sequence of social statuses, enacting a multiplicity of social roles, and being acutely conscious of membership in some corporate group [. . .]

In the workshop, village, office, lecture-room, theatre, almost anywhere people can be subverted from their duties and rights into an atmosphere of communitas. What then *is* communitas? [. . .]

For me, communitas preserves individual distinctiveness [. . .]. Martin Buber's notions of the *I-and-Thou* relationship and the *Essential We* formed by people moving towards a freely chosen common goal are intuitive perceptions of a non-transactional order or quality of human relationship, in the sense that people do not necessarily initiate action towards one another in the expectation of a reaction that satisfies their interests. [. . .]

Is there any of us who has not known this moment when compatible people – friends, congeners – obtain a flash of lucid mutual understanding on the existential level, when they feel that all problems, not just their problems, could be resolved, whether emotional or cognitive, if only the group which is felt (in the first person) as "essentially us" could sustain its intersubjective illumination? [. . .]

In industrial societies, it is within leisure, and sometimes aided by the projections of art, that this way of experiencing one's fellows can be portrayed, grasped, and sometimes realized.

1982 *From Ritual to Theatre*, 44–48

"ordained," "imposed." Spontaneous communitas – Turner's favorite – is different, almost the opposite. Spontaneous communitas happens when a congregation or group catches fire in the Spirit. It can also be secular, as when a sports team is playing so well that each player feels inside the others' heads.

Spontaneous communitas abolishes status. People encounter each other directly, "nakedly," in the face-to-face intimate encounter theologian **Martin Buber** (1878–1965) called the intimate "I–you" (*ich–du*) dialogue. Once, during a theatre workshop I was leading, when we reached a state of high spontaneous communitas, a man looked deeply and at length at each of the ten or so of us standing in a circle. "There's a little bit of you in each of me," he said. I never knew whether he intended this locution or its opposite – but certainly he expressed the feeling in the circle at that moment.

Martin Buber (1878–1965): Jewish philosopher, born in Austria and emigrated to Israel. First president of the Israeli Academy of Science and Humanities. Author of *I and Thou* (1922, German, Eng. 1937), and *The Origin and Meaning of Hasidism* (1960).

Spontaneous communitas rarely "just happens." It is generated by certain procedures. Across a ritual limen, inside of a "sacred space/time," normative communitas usually reigns, with occasional moments of spontaneous communitas. Those in the ritual are all treated equally, reinforcing a sense of "we are all in this together." People wear the same or similar clothing; they set aside indicators of wealth or poverty, low rank or privilege. Formal titles are done away with; sometimes even first names are not used. Instead, people call each other "sister," "brother," "comrade," or some other generic term. In workshops (liminoid experiences), I encourage people to give themselves new names. More than once, a new name sticks: a transformation takes place.

Ritual experiences are not always pleasant or fun. They can also be terrifying. One may encounter enormous forces and memories, demonic or divine. When Arjuna in the *Bhagavad Gita* glimpses Krishna in his true form, the warrior turns to jelly. It is not "good" or "evil" that frightens Arjuna, but coming face-to-face with the Absolute. Initiation rites are often frightening for the young neophytes, who are taken to strange and forbidding locations and forced through ordeals, some of which may be painful or bloody. Even ultimately pleasant ritual occasions such as a wedding can be very scary to the bride and groom, and a time of high anxiety mixing sadness and joy for the parents.

Ritual Time/Space

Because rituals take place in special, often sequestered places, the very act of entering the "sacred space" has an impact on participants. In such spaces, special behavior is required. One must remove one's shoes before entering a mosque or a Hindu temple. In the synagogue men are asked to wear *yamulkas* (skull caps) and *talisem* (prayer shawls). It is customary for women in Roman Catholic churches to keep their heads covered. When the sacred space is a natural place – a sacred tree, cave, or mountain, for example – one approaches and enters the space with care. But ordinary secular spaces can be made temporarily special by means of ritual action. Dance and yoga classes often require a careful preparation of the space and the participants. When I lead a performance workshop I insist that participants wear no street clothes, shoes, watches, or jewelry for the duration of the workshop. No one has a watch, so time is defined by our mutual experience. Each session begins with a careful sweeping and mopping of the floor. Once everyone is in the space, there is no more socializing. Daily life is left behind as participants clean the space making it ready for work. Such simple actions as sweeping and mopping in silence transport the workshoppers to a different place mentally and emotionally. These ritualized procedures help create a feeling of communitas even before the exercises begin.

Transportations and Transformations

Liminal rituals permanently change who people are. These are transformations. Liminoid rituals effect a temporary change – sometimes nothing more than a brief experience of spontaneous communitas or a several-hours-long performance of a role. These are transportations. From a spectator's point of view, one enters into the experience, is "moved" or "touched" (apt metaphors) and is then dropped off about where she or he entered. For performers, the situation is more complex and long-lived. **Figure 3.10** is a model of a transportation performance from the point of view of a performer in a dance, play, or sports contest; or even a deeply religious person at a church service or a practitioner of Candomble in trance.

A person can fall into a trance, speak in tongues, handle snakes, "get happy" with the Spirit – experiencing overwhelmingly powerful emotions. But no matter how strong the experience, sooner or later, most people return to their ordinary selves. At the Institutional Church of God in Christ in Brooklyn, New York, I have seen women go into trance and dance, speak in tongues, and tremble with the Spirit at 11 o'clock in the morning, while by 1 in the afternoon they are chatting and joking in the church kitchen as they prepare

fig 3.10. A "transportation performance" from the point of view of a performer. A performer leaves her daily world and by means of preparations and warm ups enters into performing. When the performance is over, the performer cools down and re-enters ordinary life. For the most part, the performer is "dropped off" where she entered. She has been "transported" – taken somewhere – not "transformed" or permanently changed.
Drawing by Richard Schechner.

the "fellowship lunch." In a suburb of Rio de Janeiro I witnessed a young Brazilian man being seized by an *orixa* (god) of Candomble, sing, speak in an African language, dance, and yank others into trance with him. After four hours of intense performing, the *orixa* left his body, he came back to himself, and he served supper to the many neighbors assembled in his mother's home, which was also her *terrero* (sacred place).

These examples are more complex than they may at first appear. The entranced Brooklyn women and the Candomble *filho de santo* (initiated medium), at the moment of their decisive life-changing experience – not at the time I saw them – were transformed. The women had "declared for Christ" and were "twice born." The man was a Candomble filho de santo. But once they were transformed, they were enabled to participate in any number of transportation performances. The two kinds of performing are not mutually exclusive, but they do occur with different frequencies. A person is transformed once or only a few times in life, if ever. However, a person may experience transportations on an almost daily basis.

Transportations occur not only in ritual situations but also in aesthetic performances. In fact, this is where all kinds of performances converge. Actors, athletes, dancers, shamans, entertainers, classical musicians – all train, practice, and/or rehearse in order to temporarily "leave themselves" and be fully "in" whatever they are performing. In theatre, actors onstage do more than pretend. The actors exist in the field of a double negative. They are not themselves, nor are they the characters they impersonate. A theatrical perform-ance takes place between "not me . . . not not me." The actress is not Ophelia, but she is not not Ophelia; the actress is not **Paula Murray Cole** (1964–), but she is not not Paula Murray Cole. She is in that highly charged in-between liminal

space. Spectators help by not reminding Cole who she "really is" in her ordinary life. But during the curtain call, they applaud Cole, not Ophelia. Or rather they applaud Cole's ability to perform Ophelia.

> **Paula Murray Cole (1964–):** American actor, member of East Coast Artists. She has worked with Schechner on several productions, including Chekhov's *Three Sisters* (1997) and *Hamlet* (1999).

Of course, it's not so simple. Many actors try to believe in the actuality of whom they are representing. And from the mid-1950s, Happeners and performance artists have explored many different ways of performing themselves. But even someone so insistent on performing his own life as **Spalding Gray** (1941–) plays a character called "Spalding", a persona who is a framed and edited version of the "real" Spalding. Gray develops his life-narratives by tape-recording early in-process appearances, listening to the recordings, and editing his text. By the time Gray appears onstage at Lincoln Center, his apparently casual self-presentation is honed in every detail, including slips and "mistakes." The audience enjoys "Spalding" as presented by Gray.

> **Spalding Gray (1941–):** American actor, performance artist, and author. His well-known autobiographical performance pieces include *Three Places in Rhodes Island* (1979) (with The Wooster Group), *Swimming to Cambodia* (1985), *Slippery Slope* (1996), and *Morning, Noon and Night* (2000). His books include *Gray's Anatomy* (1994) and *Morning, Noon, and Night* (1999).

There are performers — actors as well as musicians — who improvise, for whom each instance is "original." But even in these cases, the restoration of behavior applies. A careful comparison of a number of instances would reveal strips of behavior repeated regularly as well as recurring patterns of presentation (timing, tone of voice, gestures). It is these repetitions that give each performer her or his own style.

Transformation performances bring together two kinds of performers — those who are being transformed and those who oversee the transformation. Rites of passage such as initiations are transformation performances. Every initiation rite depends both on performers who are being transformed, the initiates, and those who are being transported, the initiators. This will become clearer if we look at a specific example of an initiation rite.

Asemo's Initiation

In the 1950s, Asemo was a boy of the Gahuku people living in Susaroka, a settlement in the mountainous highlands of Papua New Guinea. Asemo's initiation is described in detail by **Kenneth E. Read** (1917–) in *The High Valley*. Read tells how Asemo, then about 10 years old, was abruptly snatched from his mother's house and secluded along with his age-mates in the bush for two weeks, where they underwent extreme ordeals such as forced vomiting and nose-bleeding. During this phase of the initiation, the boys were literally being emptied, prepared to receive the knowledge of their tribe.

Kenneth Read (1917–): Australian anthropologist specializing in Papuan New Guinea cultures. His books include *The High Valley* (1965) and *Return to the High Valley* (1986).

fig 3.11. Men and newly initiated boys – one can be seen in the center – dancing on the final day of Asemo's initiation. Photograph by Kenneth E. Read.

After two weeks, the tired, bedraggled boys were brought back to the village. Riding on the shoulders of the men, they ran a gauntlet of women wielding stones, wood, an axe or two, and even bows and arrows. The attacks were "ritualized," but severe nonetheless, terrifying the boys. Reed writes, "There was no mistaking the venom in the assault of the women," which "teetered on the edge of virtual disaster." On the edge, but not over: the attack was contained within its performative boundaries, much the way a bloody hockey game barely but reliably remains a game.

Next, the boys were returned to the bush for six more weeks of indoctrination and training. They were in a liminal time-space during the process of being transformed into Gahuku men. Read was not allowed to witness the details of this education. But the outcome made it clear that what happened during the six weeks was enough to make a real change in Asemo. The day Asemo and his age-mates returned to Susaroka was a time of feasting and dancing (**see figure 3.11**). This time the women did not attack the men, but greeted them with a "rising chorus of welcoming calls." The newly conferred men, the initiates, danced without the assistance or protection of the older men (**see Read box**).

Read wrote in 1965 that he felt he had seen the last Gahuku initiation rite. If that was so, then this signals a big shift in the basis of Gahuku society. That is because the initiation rites didn't merely "mark" a change – as, say, graduation ceremonies in Western style schools do. Asemo's initiation, taken as an eight-week whole, was the machine that transformed Asemo from a boy into a Gahuku man. This status – whatever its personal meanings and effects, whatever

Kenneth H. **Read**

Asemo Transformed

They moved unsteadily under the ungainly decorations, and I failed to see the splendid stirring change that had been apparent to their elders' eyes. But dignity touched them when they began to dance, a slow measure based on the assertive stepping of the men but held to a restrained, promenading pace by the weight [of their headdresses [. . .] For a moment I was one with the crowd of admirers. [. . .] Asemo was in the front rank of the dancers, his legs moving in unison with his age mates, his face, like theirs, expressionless, his eyes fixed on some distant point only he could see.

1965, *The High Valley*, 177

private styles it accommodates – is at its heart social, public, and objective. It did not determine what kind of Gahuku man Asemo became, or even how he felt about it, any more than a wedding ceremony determines what kind of husband the groom will be. But definite acts were performed that forever made Asemo into a Gahuku man. These acts were not symbolic of a change accomplished elsewhere. The ritual acts were themselves the system of transformation.

All the same, the men training Asemo and his cohort were not transformed. They had been transformed earlier in life, at the time of their own initiations. At Asemo's initiation their job was to see that Asemo and his age-mates were properly instructed and made it through. They were the boys' teachers, guides, models, protectors, tormentors, and elders. They were the transporters of those who were transformed. The relationship between transporters and transformers is depicted in **figure 3.12**. The transporters were experienced performers. They shared in the bleeding, vomiting, gauntlet running, and dancing. But when the performance was over, the previously initiated Gahuku men re-entered ordinary life approximately where they left it. If any change occurred among them, it was subtle: some achieved more respect, or lost it, through performing what was required of them.

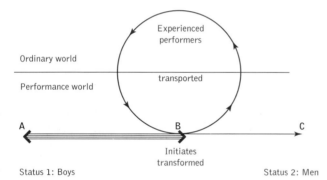

fig 3.12. The transportation-transformation system works like a printing press. At point B – where the "press" meets the "paper" – permanent impressions are imprinted by the transporters on the transformed. In Asemo's case, the already initiated men, all experienced performers, temporarily leave their ordinary lives and enter a performance world where they lead the boys through their initiation. During the initiation period, Asemo and his cohorts move from point A to point B again and again. Each ordeal or instruction makes a permanent impression on them. Finally, at the conclusion of the initiation period they enter the village dancing – for the first time as men, C. Drawing by Richard Schechner.

Social Drama

One of Turner's most fruitful yet problematic ideas was his theory of social drama (**see Turner box 3**). Every social drama develops in four phases, one following the other:

1 breach
2 crisis
3 redressive action
4 reintegration or schism.

Victor **Turner**

Social Dramas

Social dramas are units of aharmonic process, arising in conflict situations. Typically, they have four main phases of public action. [. . .] These are: 1. *Breach* of regular, norm-governed social relations. [. . .] 2. *Crisis* during which [. . .] there is a tendency for the breach to widen. [. . .] Each public crisis has [. . .] liminal characteristics, since it is a threshold between more or less stable phases of the social process, but it is not a sacred limen, hedged around by taboos and thrust away from the centers of public life. On the contrary, it takes up its menacing stance in the forum itself and, as it were, dares the representatives of order to grapple with it. [. . .] 3. *Redressive action* [ranging] from personal advice and informal mediation or arbitration to formal judicial and legal machinery, and, to resolve certain kinds of crisis or legitimate other modes of resolution, to the performance of public ritual. [. . .] Redress, too, has its liminal features, its being "betwixt and between," and, as such, furnishes a distanced replication and critique of the events leading up to and composing the "crisis." This replication may be in the rational idiom of a judicial process, or in the metaphorical and symbolic idiom of a ritual process. [. . .] 4. The final phase [. . .] consists either of the *reintegration* of the disturbed social group or of the social recognition and legitimization of an inseparable *schism* between contesting parties.

1974, *Dramas, Fields, and Metaphors* 37–41

A breach is a situation that threatens the stability of a social unit – family, corporation, community, nation, etc. A crisis is a widening of the breach into an open or public display. There may be several successive crises, each more public and threatening than the last. Redressive action is what is done to deal with the crisis, to resolve or heal the breach. Often enough, at this phase of a social drama, each crisis is answered by a redressive action which fails, evoking new, even more explosive crises. Reintegration is the resolution of the original breach in such a way that the social fabric is knit back together. Or a schism occurs.

Take, for example, the great social drama of sixteenth-century Europe called the Protestant Reformation. The conflict in this social drama was between the established Church of Rome and rebels such as **Martin Luther** (1483–1546) and **John Calvin** (1509–64). Each attempt by Rome to suppress or appease the Protestants failed. Year by year, the Protestants grew stronger. Crisis by crisis, the breach widened, generating a schism yet to be healed. Other examples of social dramas are the ongoing conflicts in Northern Ireland or between the Palestinians and the Israelis. Social dramas can be extremely long-lived, bitter, and all but intractable. On the other hand, some social dramas are resolved relatively swiftly, at least on the surface. The conflict in the USA over slavery led to the secession of 11 southern states. The Civil War (1861–65) resolved the crisis in favor of the Union with a reintegration enforced by arms. The breach was the inability of slave states and free states to agree on the future of the Union. The crisis began with the Confederate attack on Fort Sumter, South Carolina, in April 1861. The Civil War that followed was a main portion of the redressive action. The Confederate surrender at Appomattox, Virginia in 1865 was the start of reintegration. However, the end of the war did not settle the matter. Questions of equality, civil liberties, racism and economic justice brought to the fore in the Civil War era are still in the process of being resolved.

These brief "applications" of Turner's theory expose its weaknesses. The theory reduces and flattens out events. Precise details, the ups and downs, nuances and differences, that make cultural analysis interesting and enlightening are pressed into sameness. Any conflict can be analyzed "as" social drama – but what new insights does such an analysis yield? The one advantage to the theory is that it is helpful in distilling very complicated circumstances into manageable units. As a teaching device, the social-drama theory has its good points. One can select a starting point and a finishing point, framing a set of social or historical events so that a cluster of occurrences that may at first appear inchoate become manageable "as" drama. It makes closure appear inevitable. Such framing is always arbitrary.

What Turner's theory does is twist worlds of difference into the shape of a Western aesthetic genre, the drama. The progression from breach and crisis through redressive action to reintegration/schism is the underlying scheme of the Greek tragedies, the Elizabethan theatre, and modern realist drama. It is what Aristotle meant when he wrote "plot is the soul of tragedy" and "every tragedy has a beginning, middle, and end." This is the theatre Turner was most familiar with. However, this sharply edged structure is not so apparent in the theatre of the absurd or other counter-dramatic pieces, such as **Samuel Beckett**'s (1906–89) *Waiting for Godot* or even Brecht's *Mother Courage and her Children* with its episodic plot, each scene comprising a small drama in itself. It doesn't apply at all to many Happenings or performance art. Nor is it present in the extended, episodic works of many non-Western cultures. Peter Brook was roundly criticized in the 1980s for turning *The Mahabharata* into a Western-style drama. Similarly, Turner can be taken to task for turning all the world's conflicts into Western-style dramas. Perhaps today's world of terrorism, guerrilla warfare, prolonged civil wars, and economic espionage are better modeled by performance art or the seemingly endless episodes of *The Mahabharata*. It may be that life mirrors art as much as the other way round – and that social theorists need to choose very carefully among the aesthetic genres.

Turner integrated his social drama theory into his theory of ritual process (**see figure 3.13**). During the redressive action phase of a social drama, people turn to political process (from legislation to war), to the legal process (from arbitration to formal trials), and to the ritual process. The ritual process employs a wide range of devices – divination, sacrifice, and, in Turner's words, the "ludic deconstruction and recombination of familiar cultural configurations." In other words, art. But exactly how art helps resolve social conflict Turner does not make clear.

What is clearer and more useful is noting the very fluid relationship between aesthetic processes and social processes, including aesthetic and social dramas. This relationship can be depicted as a horizontal numeral 8 or infinity symbol (**see figure 3.14**). This model proposes that in an ongoing and never-ending process social dramas affect aesthetic dramas and vice versa. That is to say, the visible actions of any given social drama are informed, shaped, and guided by aesthetic principles and performance/rhetorical devices. Reciprocally, fig 3.13. Victor Turner's diagram of the relationship between social drama and the ritual process. Figure from *On the Edge of the Bush: Anthropology as Experience*, by Victor Turner. Copyright The Arizona Board of Regents. Reprinted by permission of the University of Arizona Press.

Ludic: Playful, or relating to playful behavior.

a culture's visible aesthetic practices are informed, shaped, and guided by the processes of social interaction (**see Turner box 4**). The politician, activist, lawyer, or terrorist all use techniques of performance — staging, ways of addressing various audiences, setting, etc. — to present, demonstrate, protest, or support specific social actions — actions designed to maintain, modify, or overturn the existing social order. Reciprocally, artists draw on actions performed in social life, "real events," not only as materials to be enacted but as themes, rhythms, and models of behavior and representation. As figure 3.14 indicates with its arrows, there is a positive feedback flow between social and aesthetic drama. This model demands that each social drama, each aesthetic drama

fig 3.14. The mutual positive feedback relationship of social dramas and aesthetic performances. Drawing by Richard Schechner.

(or other kind of performance), be understood in its specific cultural and historical circumstances. The word "drama" is used not to assert Western hegemony, but as a cipher representing any kind of specific cultural enactment. Another way of putting this relationship is to say that every performance — aesthetic or social — is both efficacious and entertaining. That is, each event proposes something to get done and each event gives pleasure to those who participate in it or observe it. Let me give a concrete example of what I mean.

Victor Turner

Social Drama/Aesthetic Drama

Notice that the *manifest* social drama feeds into the latent realm of stage drama; its characteristic form in a given culture, at a given time and place, unconsciously, or perhaps preconsciously, influences not only the form but also the content of the stage drama of which it is the active or "magic" mirror. The stage drama, when it is meant to do more than entertain — though entertainment is always one of its vital aims — is a metacommentary, explicit or implicit, witting or unwitting, on the major social dramas of its social context (wars, revolutions, scandals, institutional changes). Not only that, but its message and its rhetoric feed back into the *latent* processual structure of the social drama and partly accounts for its ready ritualization. Life itself now becomes a mirror held up to art, and the living now *perform* their lives, for the protagonists of a social drama, a "drama of living," have been equipped by aesthetic drama with some of their most salient opinions, imageries, tropes, and ideological perspectives. Neither mutual mirroring, life by art, art by life, is exact, for each is not a planar mirror but a matricial mirror; at each exchange something new is added and something old is lost or discarded. Human beings learn through experience, though all too often they repress painful experience, and perhaps the deepest experience is through drama; not through social drama, or stage drama (or its equivalent) alone but in the circulatory or oscillatory process of their mutual and incessant modification.

1985, *On the Edge of the Bush*, 300–301

The Pig-Kill Dancing at Kurumugl

In March 1972 at "council grounds" in the vicinity of Kurumugl, a village in the Papua New Guinea highlands, I observed a two day pig kill celebration. The performance I saw was in danger of tipping over into actual combat. The dances and songs were adapted from combat movements and war chants. The armed dancers dressed partly for battle and partly for dancing (**see figure 3.15**). The first day consisted of setting up house in long rectangular huts and digging cooking pits. The second day began with the slaughter of about 200 pigs. As each owner killed his animal he melodically orated a speech saying how hard it was to raise the pig, who it was promised to, what a fine animal it was, etc. These recitatives were applauded with laughs and roars, as they often were full of jokes and obscene invective. Then the pigs were gutted, butchered in halves, and lowered into the pits to roast over hot rocks. The guts were hung in nets over the ovens and steamed. Bladders were blown into balloons for children to play with. A festive scene.

As the cooking started, the men retired to the huts. I watched a man set up a mirror and apply blue, red, and black pigment to his arms, face, and torso. He painted half his nose red, the other half blue. I asked him what the patterns meant. He said he chose them because he liked the way they looked. When he was done he emerged, his casual air evaporating as he literally thrust his chest forward and up, gave a long whooping call, put on his four-foot long peacock and cassowary feather headdress, and displayed himself.

He was costumed not for a fictional role in a play, but for a life role – displaying his strength, his power, his wealth, and his position in the group. He joined his comrades, whose costumes were like his, amalgams of traditional—local and new—imported: bones and sunglasses, cigarette holders and

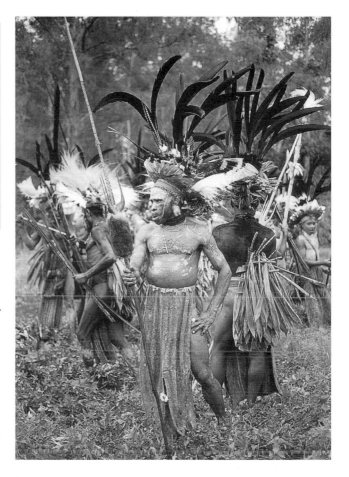

fig 3.15. Men dressed for dancing at Kurumugl, Papua-New Guinea Highlands, 1972. Photograph by Richard Schechner.

homemade pipes, khaki shorts under grass skirts. But despite what a purist might call intrusions, a traditional ritual of "payback" was being enacted. The pig kill at Kurumugl was very like the *kaiko* that anthropologist **Roy A. Rappaport** (1926–97) witnessed in 1963 – a traditional performance enacted regularly at least since the beginning of the twentieth century. As at the *kaiko*, the dances at Kurumugl were adapted from military moves (**see Rappaport box**).

Roy Rappaport (1926–97): American anthropologist who analyzed the ritual performances of the Tsembaga of Papua New Guinea. He also published essays on a general theory of ritual. His books include *Pigs for the Ancestors* (1968) and *Ecology, Meaning, and Religion* (1979).

The visitors approaching Kurumugl came not as friends to a party but as invaders seizing what they were owed. As the invaders – armed with fighting spears – danced their assault

Roy A. Rappaport

From Fighting to Dancing

The visitors approach the [village] gate silently, led by men carrying fight packages [full of materials to give a warrior courage and improve his chances of killing an enemy], swinging their axes as they run back and forth in front of their procession in the peculiar crouched fighting prance. Just before they reach the gate they are met by one or two of those locals who have invited them and who now escort them over the gate. Visiting women and children follow behind the dancers and join the other spectators on the sidelines. There is much embracing as the local women and children greet visiting kinfolk. The dancing procession charges to the center of the dance ground shouting the long, low battle cry and stamping their feet, magically treated before their arrival [. . .] to enable them to dance strongly. After they charge back and forth across the dance ground several times, repeating the stamping in several locations while the crowd cheers in admiration of their numbers, their style, and the richness of their finery, they begin to sing.

1968, *Pigs for the Ancestors*, 187

on the council grounds, they were repelled by armed campers – men plus about twenty fully armed women dancing their defense of the meat. The invaders launched vigorous assaults dozens of times. A valuable peanut field was trampled to muck. Each assault was met by a determined counter-attack. But foot-by-foot, the invaders penetrated to the heart of the council grounds, to the pile of meat and the altar of jawbones and flowers at its center. Once the invaders reached the meat they merged with their "enemies" forming one whooping, chanting, dancing doughnut of warriors. They danced around the meat for nearly an hour.

I was pinned against a tree, between warriors and meat. Then suddenly the dancing stopped. Orators plunged into the meat, pulling out a leg or a flank, shouting-singing things like (in pidgin English), "This pig I give you in payment for the pig you gave my father three years ago! Your pig was scrawny, no fat on it at all! But my pig is enormous, with tons of fat, and lots of good meat – see! see! – much better than what you gave my father! My brothers and I will remember that we are giving you today better than what you gave us. If we call you to help us in a fight, you must come! You owe us bigtime!"

Sometimes the speechifying rose to song. Insults were hurled back and forth. The fun in orating, and the joking, teetered on the edge. Participants did not forget that not so long ago they were blood enemies. After more than an hour of orating, the meat was distributed. Hoisted onto sleds, the booty was carried shoulder-high as whole families, with much singing, departed with their share. This meat found its way by means of the network of ritual obligations to places far from Kurumugl and to many who were not present that day in the council grounds.

Instead of a secret raiding party there were dancers; instead of taking human victims, they took meat. Instead of entering enemy territory on the sly as would occur in war, the whole performance took place on the council grounds, a no man's land. And instead of doubt about the outcome, everyone knew what was going to happen. A ritualized social drama – as war in the highlands had been – had been transformed into something approaching an aesthetic drama.

What are the differences between social and aesthetic dramas? Aesthetic dramas create symbolic times, spaces, and characters; the outcome of the story is pre-determined by the drama. Aesthetic dramas are fictions. Social dramas have more variables, their outcomes are in doubt, and they are like games. Social dramas are "real," they happen "here and now". But aspects of social dramas, as with aesthetic dramas, are pre-arranged, foreknown, and rehearsed. The celebration at Kurumugl was somewhere between a social and an aesthetic drama.

Figure 3.16 depicts what happens at a successful pig-kill celebration. The transformations "above the line" convert dangerous encounters into mostly benign aesthetic and economic performances. Those "below the line" show how the situation existing between groups is changed by the ritual. The pig kill and dancing at the council grounds managed a complicated and potentially dangerous exchange of goods and obligations with a minimum of danger and a maximum of pleasure. This success was due to performing.

war parties	. . .	transformed into	. . .	dancing groups
human victims				pig meat
battledress				costumes
combat				dancing
two groups	. . .	become	. . .	one group
debtors				creditors
creditors				debtors

fig 3.16. At a successful pig kill celebration a set of transformations is effected. Those transformations "above the line" change potentially lethal encounters into aesthetic and economic performances. Those "below the line" depict the changes wrought by the ritual performance.

Performing was the way the participants achieved "real results." The dancing, orating, and giving out meat did not mark or "represent" the results, but created the results they celebrated. Those at the council grounds performed in two senses: they put on a show, and they got something done.

As "above-line right-side" activities in figure 3.16 grow in importance, the entertainment value of the event increases relative to its efficacy value. Maybe the first times groups gathered at the council grounds, they danced so that they might exchange pigs to fulfill social obligations. But over time, they came to the grounds and exchanged pigs so that they could dance. Or at least the motives for the gathering blurred. It was not only that creditors and debtors changed positions, but also that people wanted to show off, dance, and have a good time. It was not only to "perform results" that the dances were staged, but because people enjoyed the sing-sing (festive celebration) for its own sake.

The Efficacy–Entertainment Dyad

Efficacy and entertainment are not binary opposites. Rather, they form the poles of a continuum (**see figure 3.17**). The basic polarity is between efficacy and entertainment, not ritual and theatre. Whether one calls a specific performance "ritual" or "theatre" depends mostly on context and function. A performance is called one or the other because of where it is performed, by whom, in what circumstances, and for what purpose. The purpose is the most important factor determining whether a performance is ritual or not. If the performance's purpose is to effect change, then the other qualities under the heading "efficacy" in figure 3.17 will also be present, and the performance is a ritual. But if the performance's purpose is mostly to give pleasure, to show off, to be beautiful, or to pass the time, then the performance

is an entertainment. The fact is that no performance is pure efficacy or pure entertainment.

Origins of Performance: If Not Ritual, Then What?

Performance doesn't originate in ritual any more than it originates in one of the aesthetic genres. Performance originates in the creative tensions of the binary efficacy–entertainment. Think of this figure not as a flat binary, but as a braid or helix, tightening and loosening over time and in specific cultural contexts. Efficacy and entertainment are not opposites, but "dancing partners" each depending on and in continuous active relationship to the other.

No "first performance" will ever be identified either specifically or in terms of genre. That has not stopped Western scholars since the end of the nineteenth century trying to prove that the performing arts originated in ritual. The first scholars to propose such an origin were influenced by several factors. Early European and American anthropologists derived their theories from the observations of colonists, missionaries, and adventurers who wrote reports about so-called "primitive peoples" in Africa, Native America, Australia, and elsewhere performing rituals using dance, music, and theatre. In one of the distortions of social Darwinism, "primitive peoples" were thought to be still "living in the stone age," their practices evidence of how all peoples once lived. If these "primitives" performed rituals but had not yet "reached the level" of the performing arts in the West, then this indicated that the arts originated in/as ritual. Second, a particular group of scholars centered at Cambridge University – **Gilbert Murray** (1866–1957) **Francis Cornford** (1874–1943), and **Jane Ellen Harrison** (1850–1928) – believed they found in ancient Greek tragedy evidence of a "primal ritual" or "*sacer ludus*" (sacred game) re-enacting the sacrifice–rebirth of a god (**see**

EFFICACY/RITUAL ← → ENTERTAINMENT/PERFORMING ARTS	
Results	For fun
Link to transcendent Other(s)	Focus on the here and now
Timeless time – the eternal present	Historical time and/or now
Performer possessed, in trance	Performer self-aware, in control
Virtuosity downplayed	Virtuosity highly valued
Traditional scripts/behaviors	New and traditional scripts/behaviors
Transformation of self possible	Transformation of self unlikely
Audience participates	Audience observers
Audience believes	Audience appreciates, evaluates
Criticism discouraged	Criticism flourishes
Collective creativity	Individual creativity

fig 3.17. The efficacy/ritual-entertainment/aesthetic performance dyad. Although typeset as a binary, the figure ought to be read as a continuum. There are many degrees leading back forth from "results" to "fun," from "collective creativity" to "individual creativity," and so on.

Murray box). Third, medievalists traced the origins of Renaissance theatre to church ritual.

> **Jane Ellen Harrison (1850–1928), Gilbert Murray (1866–1957),** and **Francis Cornford (1874–1943)** were classicists based at Cambridge and Oxford Universities in the early part of the twentieth century. They proposed several influential theories on the relationship of ritual to theatre. Their works included Harrison's *Themis: A Study of the Social Origins of Greek Religion* (1912), Cornford's *The Origins of Attic Comedy* (1914), and Murray's *Five Stages of Greek Religion* (1925).

Gilbert Murray

The Ritual Origins of Greek Tragedy

The following note presupposes certain general views about the origin and essential nature of Greek Tragedy. It assumes that tragedy is in origin a Ritual Dance, a *Sacer Ludus* [. . .] Further, it assumes in accord with the overwhelming weight of ancient tradition, that the dance in question is originally or centrally that of Dionysus, performed at his feast, in his theatre. [. . .] It regards Dionysus in this connection as an "Eniautos-Daimon," or vegetation God, like Adonis, Osiris, etc., who represents the cyclic death and rebirth of the earth and the world, i.e., for practical purposes, of the tribe's own lands of the tribe itself. It seems clear, further, the Comedy and Tragedy represent different stages in the life of this Year Spirit.

1912, "Excursus on the Ritual Forms Preserved in Greek Tragedy," 341

But each of these arguments is spurious. There is no such thing as "primitive" peoples. Social Darwinism mistakenly assumes a hierarchy of cultures. Difference does not prove superiority. The "primal ritual" of the Cambridge Anthropologists (as Murray and his associates were called) is provable only if one uses circular reasoning. The primal ritual exists because of remnants of it in Greek tragedy; Greek tragedy contains remnants of a primal ritual; therefore there must be such a ritual. As for the origins of modern European theatre in the Mass or other church celebrations such as the cycle plays of the fourteenth to sixteenth centuries, there is no doubt that these great civic and religious events abutted the emergent popular theatre.

But it is also true that the medieval period enjoyed many popular entertainments as well as a variety of "private" or indoor theatricals, dances, and musical performances. The epoch was not "empty" of performing arts.

The fact is that at any given point in time, in every part of the world and in every culture, people were and are making dances, music, and theatre. They are using performances for a variety of purposes, including entertainment, ritual, community building, and socializing. These functions can be summarized as the dynamic tension between efficacy and entertainment. The desire to imagine a "first performance" tells us more about what scholars of a certain culture desire than about what may have actually happened. Theoretically, the "first performance" is a situation, not an event or a genre. Performance originates in the need to make things happen and to entertain; to get results and to fool around; to show the way things are and to pass the time; to be transformed into another and to enjoy being oneself; to disappear and to show off; to embody a transcendent other and to be "just me" here-and-now; to be in trance and to be in control; to focus on one's own group and to broadcast to the largest possible audience; to play in order to satisfy a deep personal, social, or religious need; and to play only under contract for cash. The shift from ritual to aesthetic performance occurs when a participating community fragments into occasional, paying customers. The move from aesthetic performance to ritual happens when an audience of individuals is transformed into a community. The tendencies to move in both these directions are present in all performances.

Changing Rituals or Inventing New Ones

Rituals provide stability. They also help people accomplish change in their lives, transforming them from one status or identity to another. But what about rituals themselves? They give the impression of permanence, of "always having been." That is their publicly performed face. But only a little investigation shows that as social circumstances change, rituals also change (**see Drewal box**). Sometimes the change is accomplished informally as ritual practitioners – shamans, Hindu priests, tribal elders – adjust their performances to suit new circumstances. Introducing newer technology sometimes subtly and sometimes more obviously changes the ritual. Electric lighting, microphones, and more recently the use of the internet have all resulted in changes in the performance of rituals. In other circumstances, official changes are introduced to bring rituals into line with new social realities. Thus Vatican II, meeting in Rome from 1962 to 1965 with the stated purpose of bringing the church more into harmony with the modern world, actually deeply changed Roman Catholic rituals. The liturgy was reformed in order to bring ordinary people closer to the service. Latin was abandoned as the language of the Mass in favor of vernacular languages. Non-priests were given more of a chance to participate in services.

Margaret Thompson **Drewal**

Revising Rituals

Practitioners of Yoruba religion are aware that when ritual becomes static, when it ceases to adjust and adapt, it becomes obsolete, empty of meaning, and eventually dies out. They often express the need to modify rituals to address current social conditions. Sometimes change is the result of long deliberations, oftentimes it is more spontaneous. Many revisions are not particularly obvious, unless the observer is thoroughly familiar with the ritual process by having followed a number of its performances, much in the same way a critic follows the productions of a dance or theatre piece.

1992, *Yoruba Ritual*, 8

But rituals may also be invented — both by official culture and by individuals. In fact, one job of official culture is to make relatively new rituals and the traditions they embody appear old and stable. Such an appearance helps support a sense of social stability. It is no accident that dictatorships thrive on state ceremony, much of it concocted to suit the needs of a particular regime. To a large degree, the emergence of the idea of a "nation" from the eighteenth century onward was buttressed by new rituals enacting national consciousness. Designating and singing a "national anthem," "saluting the flag," and even the pomp surrounding the British monarchy are not anywhere near as old or set as they appear to be (**see Hobsbawm box**). Schools are hotbeds of invented rituals pertaining to sororities and fraternities, "school spirit," and the awarding of degrees at graduation. A set order of behavior and annual repetition rather quickly ritualizes behavior such as hazings and initiations, academic processions, and cheers at sports matches (**see figure 3.18**). The fact that there is a quick turnover in the student population helps establish new rituals swiftly. In real life a generation takes 20 or 30 years to turn over; at college it is four years.

Eric **Hobsbawm**

Inventing Traditions

Nothing appears more ancient, and linked into an immemorial past, than the pageantry which surrounds British monarchy in its public ceremonial manifestations. Yet [. . .] in its modern form it is the product of the late 19th and 20th centuries. [. . .] "Invented tradition" is taken to mean a set of practices, normally governed by overtly or tacitly accepted rules and of a ritual or symbolic nature, which seek to inculcate certain values and norms of behavior by repetition, which automatically implies continuity with the past. In fact, where possible, they normally attempt to establish continuity with a suitable historic past. A striking example is the deliberate choice of the Gothic style for the 19th-century rebuilding of the British Parliament and the equally deliberate decision after World War II to rebuild the parliamentary chamber on exactly the same basic plan as before. [. . .]

To establish the clustering of "invented traditions" in western countries between 1870 and 1914 is relatively easy. [These include] Bastille Day and the Daughters of the American Revolution, May Day, [. . .] the Olympic Games, the Cup Final, and the Tour de France as popular rites, and the institution of flag worship in the U.S.A. [. . .] Moreover, the construction of formal ritual spaces, already consciously allowed for in German nationalism, appears to have been systematically undertaken even in countries which had hitherto paid little attention to it. [. . .] New constructions for spectacle and de facto mass ritual such as sports stadia, outdoor and indoor, [. . .] and the use of such buildings as the Sportspalast in Berlin or the Vélodrome d'Hiver in Paris [. . .] anticipate the development of formal spaces for public mass ritual (Red Square from 1918 [in Moscow, Tiananmen Square from 1949 in Beijing]).

1983, *The Invention of Tradition*, 1–2, 303, 305

Individual artists, especially since the 1960s, have taken to inventing rituals. Anna Halprin calls some of her performances "rituals," as do many other artists (**see figure 3.19**). The impulse behind these claims is an attempt to overcome a sense of individual and social fragmentation by means of art. This need is exacerbated by the fact that artists often feel excluded by organized religion. Gay Roman Catholic artists, for example, are not able to worship openly as gay people in the church; similarly Islam, Orthodox Judaism, and many fundamentalist Protestant churches are homophobic. The need to build community is fostered by ritual. And if official rituals either do not satisfy or are egregiously exclusive, new rituals will be invented, or older rituals adapted, to meet felt needs.

Using Rituals in Theatre, Dance, and Music

Not only have rituals been invented wholesale, but older rituals have long provided grist for the artistic mill or have been used as a kind of popular entertainment. There is a long

fig 3.18. An academic procession at New York University in the 1990s. These kinds of processions are secular ritual celebrations. The music, pace of marching, kinds of robes, insignia, and hats worn by the participants indicate the school, degree, and other particulars fixed by the tradition. Photo courtesy New York University.

fig 3.19. Dancer and ritual-maker Anna Halprin takes a vehement step leading a line of performers during a workshop, 1990s. Photograph by Jay Grayam. Photograph courtesy of Anna Halprin.

history of importing "authentic rituals" and showing them at Colonial Expositions, World's Fairs, and amusement parks. Some of these presentations have had significant impact on Western theatre and dance – even when they were totally spurious. At the turn of the twentieth century, modern dance pioneer **Ruth St. Denis** (1879–1968) saw "Indian dancing" at Coney Island. The "Hindu Village" in residence there was a consequence of the great success of Little Egypt's "nautch dance" at the 1893 Chicago Exposition. What St. Denis saw was vaguely connected to Indian *sadir nac*, itself related to

ritual temple dancing – later reconstructed in India as *bharatanatyam*. Whatever she saw in Coney Island propelled St. Denis on a path that led to a revolution in modern dance. St. Denis and her partner **Ted Shawn**'s (1891–1972) students and company members included **Martha Graham** (1894–1991) and **Doris Humphrey** (1895–1958). Similarly, what French performance theorist **Antonin Artaud** (1896–1948) made of the Balinese ritual dancers he saw in Paris's 1931 Colonial Exposition changed the destiny of twentieth-century Western theatre (**see figure 3.20**).

Ruth St. Denis: (1879–1968): American dancer and choreographer who along with **Ted Shawn (1891–1972)** trained Martha Graham, Doris Humphrey, and many other modern dancers. They formed the Denishawn dance company in 1915. St Denis specialized in "oriental" dances, including the Indian *Radha* (1906), the Japanese *O-Mika* (1913), and the Chinese *Kuan Yin* (1916).

Doris Humphrey (1895–1958): American dancer and choreographer. Humphrey's major works include *Life of the Bee* (1929), *The Shakers* (1930), and *Song of the West* (1940–42).

Martha Graham (1894–1991): American modern dancer and choreographer. Graham choreographed more than 170 group and solo productions including *Primitive Mysteries* (1931), *Appalachian Spring* (1944), and *Seraphic Dialogue* (1955).

Antonin Artaud (1896–1948): French actor, director, theorist, and poet. Author of *The Theatre and its Double* (1938; Eng. 1958).

fig 3.20.

Several of the Balinese dancers Artaud saw at the Colonial Exposition of 1931 in Paris. The structure appears to be a Balinese temple, but it actually is the replica of one constructed for the Exposition. Photograph courtesy of Nicola Savarese.

The program of the performance Artaud saw. The picture is of a Balinese gamelan orchestra with the caption, "Instruments and players of the gong." The rest of the text reads, "Participation of the Netherlands in the International Colonial Exposition of Paris. Program of music and dances performed by a group of men and women dancers from the island of Bali under the direction of Tjokorde Gde Rake Soekawait. At the Pendopo (theatre) of the Holland Pavilion." Program courtesy of Nicola Savarese.

Sufi Mevlevi dancers – "whirling dervishes" – have appeared many times on concert stages. When they performed at the Brooklyn Academy of Music, spectators were admonished, "The program is a religious ceremony. You are kindly requested to refrain from applause." But it's not only in the West that such reframing occurs. I have seen Bengali and other Indian folk-ritual put on stage before "high-art" audiences in Calcutta, New Delhi, and Mumbai. Similarly, in China, Mexico, and Cuba I have witnessed rituals reframed as aesthetic performances. This kind of reframing is taking place all around the world. That is because "First World" and "Third World" people exist side-by-side in many countries. Tourist shows draw on locals as well as foreigners for audiences. The distinction is no longer mostly "East/West" or "North/South" but increasingly "center/margin," "metropolis/outlying areas," and "tourist/local."

The reshaping of ritual materials into new "original works" is also widespread. **Jerzy Grotowski** (1933–99) synthesized rituals from several cultures to make his final performance, *Action* (**see Osinski box**). Versions of *Action* are still being performed by Grotowski's designated artistic heir, **Thomas Richards** (1962–). **Philip Glass**'s (1937–) Symphony No. 5 fuses Australian Aboriginal and African music with Glass's own distinct style. The sung texts come from more than 20 different cultures and epochs, ranging over 3,000 years, from the Rig Veda, the Bible, and the Quran to Hawaiian, Zuni, and Mayan myths, Persian poetry, Chinese philosophy, and the Tibetan *Book of the Dead*. Glass's ambition was to create a "spiritual human history" from Creation to the future. Glass's intent was to make a millennial version of one of the great Masses of **Johann Sebastian Bach** (1685–1750) or **Wolfgang Amadeus Mozart** (1756–91). Glass wanted to create ritual and art simultaneously, but no longer "localized" in the Christian tradition. Using rituals to make new aesthetic performances is not a practice of European and Euro-American artists only. African-American choreographer **Ralph Lemon** (1952–), Indian theatre director **Ratan Thiyam** (1948–), and Taiwanese choreographer **Lin Hwai-min** (1949–) are three of many artists importing and/or reshaping rituals in their productions (**see figure 3.21**). The question of cultural borrowing will be examined more fully in chapter 8.

Jerzy Grotowski (1933–99): Polish theatre director, performer trainer, and theorist. Founding director of the Polish Laboratory Theater (1959–84), with which he explored environmental theatre staging, scenic and textual montage, and connections between ritual and theatre. After 1965, Grotowski investigated the links between ancient and modern rituals and the interior life of what he called the "doer," the performer. His theatre works include Stanislaw Wyspianski's *Akropolis* (1962), Christopher Marlowe's *Doctor Faustus* (1963), Calderón de la Barca's *The Constant Prince* (1965) and a work based on the New Testament, *Apocalypsis cum Figurus* (1969). Grotowski is the author of *Towards a Poor Theatre* (1968) and author/subject of *The Grotowski Sourcebook* (1997), edited by Richard Schechner and Lisa Wolford.

Thomas Richards (1962–): American actor whom Grotowski designated his "artistic heir." At present, Richards heads the Grotowski Workcenter in Pontedera, Italy, where he works closely with Mario Biagini. Author of *At Work with Grotowski on Physical Actions* (1995).

Zbigniew **Osinski**

Creating a Ritual by Means of Theatre

Every day the ritual [of *action* or *actions*] is evoked anew. Always the same and yet each time not just the same. This ritual is [. . .] not just a theatre creation, or an imitation or reconstruction of any of the familiar rituals. [. . .] Nor is it a synthesis of rituals which, in Grotowski's opinion, would be impossible in practice. [. . .] Grotowski's work [. . .] has elements related concomitantly to several traditions which are archetypal. These elements are set into a composition [. . .]. Grotowski defines the technical difference between a theatre production and a ritual in relation to "the place of montage." In the production, the spectators' minds are the place of montage. In the ritual, the montage takes place in the minds of the doers. The connection with old initiation practices is very subtle, and the basic duty of each doer is to do everything well. This should be understood in a tangible, almost physical sense. The body must respond properly and precisely, and must not pump up emotions and expression. Therefore, Grotowski would not ask anyone, "Do you believe?" but "You must do well what you do, with understanding." [. . .] The Action is evoked and accomplished each day in its totality. Sometimes it is executed every few days if the technical work on details or the search for some elements from scratch take up too much time. The theatre functions in relation to the spectators who come to see a production. Here, the logic and clarity of the Actions are essential and – through these Actions – the process of participants bringing them to life. There is no place for spectators as such.

1997, "Grotowski Blazes the Trails," 391–2

Philip Glass (1937–): American composer whose innovative compositions include collaborations with Robert Wilson, *Einstein on the Beach* (1976) and *White Raven* (1991) and David Henry Hwang, *1000 Airplanes on the Roof* (1988) and *The Voyage* (1992) as well as an opera trilogy based on the works of Jean Cocteau – *Orphée* (1993), *La Belle et la Bête* (1994), and *Les Enfants Terribles* (1996).

Johann Sebastian Bach (1685–1750): German composer, choir director, and organist. His polyphonic compositions of sacred music place him among Europe's most influential composers.

Wolfgang Amadeus Mozart (1756–91): Austrian composer and child prodigy. A vast output and range of compositions including operas, symphonies, and liturgical music.

fig 3.21. A scene from *Uttar Priyadarshi* – a "meditation on war and peace" – as performed in the USA in 2000 by the Chorus Repertory Theatre of Manipur, India, directed by Ratan Thiyam. This performance combines Buddhist ritual, Manipuri music and dance rhythms, and contemporary invention. Photograph by Ratan Thiyam. Photograph courtesy of Erin Mee.

Ralph Lemon (1952–): American dancer and choreographer, known for highly emotional dances, often involving mixed media. Dance works include *Joy* (1989), *Persephone* (1991), and *Tree* (2000).

Ratan Thiyam (1948–): Manipuri-Indian founder-director of the Chorus Repertory Theatre. Major productions include Thiyam's play *Chakravyuha* (1986) and *Uttar Priyadarshi* (1996), concerning the life of the Indian Buddhist King Ashoka (second century, BCE).

Lin Hwai-Min (1949–): Taiwanese choreographer and dancer. In 1973, he founded Cloud Gate Dance Theatre, Taiwan's foremost modern dance company.

Conclusion

Human ritual is a continuation and elaboration of animal ritual. Rituals are used to manage potential conflicts regarding status, power, space, and sex. Performing rituals helps people get through difficult periods of transition. Ritual is also a way for people to connect to a collective, even mythic past, to build social solidarity, to form a community. Some rituals are

liminal, existing between or outside daily social life. Because of their liminality, ritual performances can produce communitas, a feeling among participants of something greater than or outside of their individual selves. We have also seen how ritual plays an essential role in social dramas, helping to bring about the reintegration or schism needed to bring a community in crisis to closure. But rituals can also be very ordinary. Most everyday life situations incorporate ritualized elements. Our waking-up rituals, mealtime rituals, greeting rituals, parting rituals, and so on moderate most of our ongoing social life. Understanding these rituals can help us more successfully perform these basic human interactions.

Although the belief is widespread that the performing arts originated in or as rituals, there is no hard historical or archeological evidence to prove this assertion. More probably, from the very earliest times, the entertainment qualities of performance were as present as were the ritual elements. Instead of thinking of the binary "ritual or art," one should consider the functions of performance. To what degree does a performance entertain, give pleasure, is made so that it is beautiful; and to what degree is a performance efficacious, made in order to accomplish something, please or appeal to the gods, mark or celebrate an important event or life milestone such as birth, puberty, marriage, or death? Although specific public performances tend to emphasize either entertainment or efficacity, all performances actually are both entertaining and efficacious.

Artists of many cultures have long made art used in rituals – church music, altar pieces and devotional paintings, temple ikons, masks, religious dances and dramas, and so on. Furthermore, at first influenced by colonialism and later by globalization, artists have drawn on the rituals of many cultures for use in their own new works. Some artists have investigated not just specific rituals but the ritual process itself in order to synthesize existing rituals or invent new rituals. In the not so distant past, colonial exhibitors brought rituals from "far away" places as entertainments and exotic curiosities. This practice continues today as part of the programs of some international festivals.

Not only artists, but also governments, sports teams, schools, and other entities invent rituals. These rituals are often passed off as venerable and traditional when, in fact, they are of recent vintage. National anthems, pledges to the flag, the carrying of the Olympic torch (and many other aspects of the modern Olympic games), and sorority or fraternity initiations are some examples of invented rituals. In fact, rituals and the ritual process enact a tension between new/old, conservative/innovative. Although many rituals are long lasting and protective of the status quo, many others evolve and change. The ritual process itself encourages innovation by opening up a space and time for anti-structure. Sometimes rituals change formally through the work of councils, assemblies of ritual specialists, or state authorities. But often, in many cultures and in widely variant situations, rituals evolve by means of changes introduced by individuals at a local level.

THINGS TO THINK ABOUT

1. How is the boundary blurred between ritual and theatre? How is theatre ritualistic? How is ritual theatrical?
2. You may have experienced communitas during an event which you did not consciously perceive as a ritual (a rock concert, a sporting event, a party). Think back on that event "as" a ritual. What exactly happened to you? Not only physically, but with your feelings, with your "brain chemistry."

THINGS TO DO

1. In small groups, observe a ritual performance in a formal setting – for example, a place of worship or a courtroom. Note the demarcation of "sacred space," the use of specialized clothing, language, or objects. In what ways was the ritual you watched like/not like theatre? Was the experience liminal for any of the participants? Was there any communitas?
2. In the classroom, re-enact the key elements of a ritual you observed. How did your re-enactment preserve the essential character and function of the "original" ritual? How have you altered or adapted it?

SUGGESTED READINGS

Bell, Catherine. "Performance and Other Analogies." *Ritual Theory, Ritual Practice*. New York: Oxford University Press, 1992. 27–46.

d'Aquili, Eugene D., Charles D. Laughlin Jr., and John McManus. "The Spectrum of Ritual." *The Spectrum of Ritual*. Eds. Eugene D. d'Aquili, Charles D. Laughlin Jr. and John McManus. New York: Columbia University Press, 1979. 36–41.

Drewal, Margaret Thompson. "Gender Play." *Yoruba Ritual*. Bloomington: Indiana University Press, 1992. 174–93.

Goodall, Jane. "The Rain Dance." *In the Shadow of Man*. Boston: Houghton Mifflin, 1971. 52–54.

Turner, Victor. "Liminality and Communitas." *The Ritual Process*. Chicago: Aldine, 1969. 94–130.

4 PLAY

The Joker in the Deck

Playing – doing something that is "not for real" – is, like ritual, at the heart of performance. In fact, one definition of performance might be: ritualized behavior conditioned/permeated by play. Exactly how and why this is so is the subject of this chapter. Ritual has seriousness to it, the hammerhead of authority. Play is looser, more permissive – forgiving in precisely those areas where ritual is enforcing, flexible where ritual is rigid. To put this another way: restored behavior has a quality of not being entirely "real" or "serious." Restored behavior is conditional; it can be revised. Playing is double-edged, ambiguous, moving in several directions simultaneously. People often mix bits of play – a wisecrack, a joke, a flirtatious smile – with serious activities. "I was just kidding" makes a claim in favor of performing. This claim emphasizes those aspects of playful performing associated with the arts, with creativity, with childhood. It is not a claim that stands up well to the technical or business applications of performance.

Play is very hard to pin down or define. It is a mood, an activity, an eruption of liberty; sometimes it is rule-bound, sometimes very free. It is pervasive. It is something everyone does as well as watch others engage in – either formally

A decisive match at the Australian Open tennis tournament, Melbourne. Copyright Popperfoto.

"War Games" – during the Second World War. Notice the playful sign, "You are now crossing the Rhine River through courtesy of E Co . . ." Photograph from *After the Battle* Magazine.

in dramas, sports, on television, in films; or casually, at parties, while working, on the street, at playgrounds (**see figure 4.1**). Play can subvert the powers-that-be, as in parody or carnival, or it can be cruel, absolute power, what Shakespeare's Gloucester meant when he cried out, "As flies to wanton boys, are we to the gods, | They kill us for their sport" (*King Lear*, 4, 1: 38–39).

fig 4.1. Some of the varieties of play and playing. The actual diversity and range is endless: what is depicted here is a small sample.

A school playground in Northhamptonshire, U.K., 1988. Photograph by Brunskill. Copyright Popperfoto.

Victor Turner

The Joker in the Deck

Playfulness is a volatile, sometimes dangerously explosive essence, which cultural institutions seek to bottle or contain in the vials of games of competition, chance, and strength, in modes of simulation such as theatre, and in controlled disorientation, from roller coasters to dervish dancing. [. . .] Most definitions of play involve notions of disengagement, of free-wheeling, of being out of mesh with the serious "bread-and-butter," let alone "life-and-death" processes of production, social control, "getting and spending," and raising the next generation. [. . .] Play can be everywhere and nowhere, imitate anything, yet be identified with nothing. [. . .] Play is the supreme *bricoleur* of frail transient constructions, like a caddis worm or a magpie's nest. [. . . .] Its metamessages are composed of a potpourri of apparently incongruous elements. [. . .] Yet, although "spinning loose" as it were, the wheel of play reveals to us (as Mihaly Csikszentmihalyi has argued [1975]) the possibility of changing our goals and, therefore, the restructuring of what our culture states to be reality.

1983, "Body, Brain, and Culture," 233–34

Mihai Spariosu

Return of the Repressed

Although Plato and Aristotle convert heroic and tragic poetry into "fiction" or "literature," subordinating it to the serious and moral truth of metaphysics, the ancient agon between the poets and the philosophers comes back again and again to haunt Western thought. Whenever prerational values attempt to regain cultural supremacy, what has been repressed under the name of "literature" or "art" as mere play and illusion also reasserts its claim to knowledge and truth, that is, its claim to power. Faced with this challenge or threat, the modern philosophers may react in two ways: they either reenact the Platonic suppression of prerational values, relegating them again to the realm of "mere" art and play (the case of Kant); or they wholeheartedly embrace these values, turning literature or art into an effective weapon against their own philosophical opponents (the case of the artist-metaphysicians [Nietzsche, Heidegger, Derrida]).

1989, *Dionysus Reborn*, 162

Enlightenment: European philosophical movement peaking in the eighteenth century but continuing to the present characterized by an emphasis on rationality, empirical reasoning, and other cognitive operations.

Victor Turner called play the "joker in the deck," meaning it was both creative and untrustworthy (**see Turner box**). Indeed, in Western thought, play has been both valued and suspect (**see Spariosu box 1**). From the Enlightenment through the nineteenth century, a strong effort was made to rationalize play, to control its anarchic expressions, to channel it into numerous rule-bound, site-specific games and various official displays enacted as public, civic, military, or religious spectacle. An effort was made to assign specific places for playing and to limit playtime to after hours or Sundays (and then, when the working week shrank, to the weekend). Industrial work with its regularity and assembly line was at the top of the European and American agenda. Play had to be kept off the line as much as possible. But the best-laid plans . . . people kept playing furiously, if not always publicly. The more historians learn of Victorian Britain, for example, the more they discover secret gardens of play. Drunkenness was endemic, on the job as well as off; and the varieties of sexual gambits played havoc with official reproduction doctrine.

A change occurred at the turn of the twentieth century, and it has accelerated since then. Play returned as a category of thought. Notions of the unconscious in psychology and literature, theories of relativity and uncertainty (or indeterminacy) in physics, and game theory in mathematics and economics are all examples of play taken seriously. In the visual arts, play resumed its world-making activity with the development of cubism and then abstract expressionism. Various avant-gardes disrupted, parodied, and in other ways

Unconscious: As theorized by Sigmund Freud (1856–1939), thoughts, feelings, impulses, or memories of which we are not aware, and over which we have no control. The unconscious manifests itself in dreams and as slips of the tongue, forgetting, compulsive behavior, and the like.

playfully subverted the values of official culture. Play is intrinsically part of performing because it creates the "as if," the risky activity of make-believe. Much recent thinking on play accords it an important place in human and animal life. In Indian philosophy, play is the very ground of existence.

What is Play? What is Playing?

Is playing different than "play" — do the activities called "playing" directly correspond to the phenomenon called "play"? What do playing baseball, playing poker, playing around with your boy/girlfriend, playing a role in a play, playing the fool, letting some play into your fishing line, and playing out an idea have in common? Are fantasy, dreaming, and day dreaming kinds of interior playing? Is playing always fun? Is it always guided by rules or can it be unpredictable? Is playing prerational, rational, unrational, or irrational? How has the idea of playing figured in Western and non-Western philosophies and cosmologies? Do animals play in the same way as humans do? Do adults play in the same way as infants and children do? What are the connections between ritual and playing (**see Handelman box 1**)? Between art and playing? Between the earliest human cultures and playing? Is war a kind of playing? These questions do not exhaust what can be asked. There are more questions than can be answered — and this is a significant aspect of the whole "problem" of play and playing. The etymology of the English word "play" extends outward into the realms of law and religion and includes allusions to risk and danger (**see Huizinga box 1**).

Don **Handelman**

Complementarity of Play and Ritual

Ritual and play are shadow images of one another in the kinds of messages they transmit to the social order. They are analogous states of cognition and perception, whose messages are complementary for the resolution of the ongoing, immoral, deviant, domain of ordinary reality.

1977, "Play and Ritual: Complementary Frames of MetaCommunication," 190

If the dichotomies dividing play from work, serious business, and ritual are too rigid and culture-bound; if it is

Johan **Huizinga**

Etymology of "Play"

Etymologically the word comes from the Anglo-Saxon *plega*, *plegan* meaning primarily "play" or "to play," but also rapid movement, a gesture, a grasp of the hands, clapping, playing a musical instrument and all kinds of bodily activity. [...] The formal correspondence between the Old English *plegan* and the (Continental) Old Saxon *plegan*, the old High German *pflegan* and the Old Frisian *plega* is complete and beyond doubt. [...] The oldest meaning [of these words] is "to vouch or stand guarantee for, to take a risk, to expose oneself to danger for someone or something." [...] The German *pflegen* is also used in connection with the performance of a sacred act, the giving of advice, the administration of justice. [...] Hence the word is mainly at home in the sphere of religion, law, and ethics. [...] The difference lies in the fact that "play" moves and develops along the line of the concrete while *pflegen* does so along the line of the abstract; both, however, being semantically akin to the playsphere. We might call it the sphere of ceremonial. Among the older significations of *pflegen* occurs the "celebrating of festivals" and "the exhibition of wealth." [...] The word is also related to] the English "pledge." The oldest meaning of this is "surety," "warrant," "hostage," hence "gage" in the sense of a challenge or a "wager" ("wage" being a doublet of "gage"), and finally the ceremony of taking on the "engagement," and so "the drinking" of a pledge or of someone's health, a promise or a vow. Who can deny that in all these concepts — challenge, danger, contest, etc. — we are very close to the playsphere? Play and danger, risk, chance, feat — it is all a single field of action where something is at stake. [...] The words *play* and *pflegen* together with their derivatives are not only formally but semantically identical.

1970 [1938], *Homo Ludens*, 38–40

wrong to fence children's play off from adult play; if playing need be neither voluntary nor fun; if play is characterized both by flow — losing oneself in play — and reflexivity — the awareness that one is playing; if ethological and semiotic studies find that play's functions include learning, regulating hierarchy, exploration, creativity, and communication; if psychoanalysis links playing with fantasy, dreaming, and the expression of desires; if the "in between" and "as if" time-space of playing is the source of cultural activities including arts, sciences, and religions; if play can be irrational, unrational, and rational . . . can we ever get to the bottom of something so complex?

You might regard the writing I am doing at this moment as a game played in order to bring the multiple possibilities of play and playing under the aegis of rational thought. A principal task of scholarly writing is to find discipline within or impose it on seemingly anarchic phenomena. This tension between the orderly and the unpredictable – the rule of law (human or other) versus the throw of the dice – is irresolvable. But it is comprehensible as the struggle between two kinds of playing. The first kind of playing is rule-bound, where all players accept the rules of the game and are equal before the law. The second kind of playing is Nietzschean, where the gods can change the rules of the game at any time, and therefore, where nothing is certain.

Some Qualities of Playing

Playing is a genetically based life-long activity of humans and many (but by no means all) other animals. Adult playing is different than child's play mostly in terms of the amount of time spent playing and the shift from mostly "free" or "exploratory" play to rule-bound playing. However, some adults arrange their work so that they may continue to play in much the same ways that children do. Artists are not the only adults who are given leave to "play around." Researchers in science and industry, and even some business people, are able to integrate play into their work. Both child play and adult play involve exploration, learning, and risk and yield flow or total involvement in the activity for its own sake. Playing creates its own multiple realities with porous and slippery boundaries. Playing is full of creative world-making as well as lying, illusion, and deceit. Games – a special kind of playing – establish more fixed, solid boundaries. "You're out!" the baseball umpire shouts; "offside" draws a penalty in football.

Playing can be physically and emotionally dangerous. Because it is, players need to feel safe, seeking special play spaces and play times. The perils of playing are masked by asserting that playing is "fun," "voluntary," "ephemeral," or a "leisure activity." These are modern Western beliefs,

and hardly true. In fact, much of the fun of playing, when there is fun, is in playing with fire, in going in over one's head, engaging in what **Clifford Geertz** (1926–) calls deep play. Play is performance (when it is done openly, in public) and performative when it is more private, even secret – a strategy or reverie rather than a display. In this interiority, play is separable from ritual, which must always be enacted.

> **Clifford Geertz (1926–):** American anthropologist. Author of *The Interpretation of Cultures* (1973), *Negara: The Theatre State in Nineteenth Century Bali* (1980), *Local Knowledge* (1983), and many other works.

> **Deep play:** A concept introduced by English philosopher **Jeremy Bentham** and developed by Clifford Geertz. Deep play is the kind of play in which the risks to the player outweigh the potential rewards.

If play is a "thing," a genre, an item of culture that can be separated and described, playing is a mood, an activity, and an embodied behavior inseparable from the players. Playing takes place as play acts – distinct modules of behavior that send the message "this is play."

> **Play acts:** The basic physical units of playing and gaming. Though it is not easy to separate play from games, one can say that generally games are more overtly structured than playing. Games are rule-bound, take place in designated places (ranging from stadiums to card tables), have definite outcomes, and engage players who are clearly marked (sometimes with uniforms). Play can take place anywhere at any time engaging any number of players who may abide by or unexpectedly change the rules.

Many play acts are governed by rules that players agree to play by. Games from tennis and chess to improvisational theatre and war games are governed by rules that control moment-to-moment playing and scoring (**see figure 4.2**). But there are also many play acts with no articulated or published rules, or with rules that change during playing, as in fantasy or "kidding around." Sometimes playing is anti-structural, with the main fun being how one can get around the rules or subvert them.

fig 4.2. The musical score and printed rules for "Imitation," a children's game dating from the 1920s or earlier. From Kate F. Bremner, *A Book of Song Games and Ball Games*. New York: A.S. Barnes and Company, 1924, p. 27.

Seven Ways to Approach Play

There are at least seven interrelated ways to approach play and playing. I offer these not as a definitive list, but as strategies for organizing the inquiry into play.

1 Structure: synchronically, what are the relationships among the events constituting a play act? How, for example, how does an "at bat" fit into the structure of an

inning in baseball; and how does each inning relate to the shape of the entire game? Each play act consists of many sub-acts, distinct behavioral units that fit together into a coherent whole. A coherent sequence of play acts forms a game.

Synchronic: Happening at the same time; simultaneous.

2 Process: diachronically, over time, how are play acts generated and what are their phases of development? Again, to use baseball as an example, how do the strategies of play change as the game progresses; or how does the score, weather, injuries, and so on affect emerging strategies of play? Process and structure should be considered as a related pair.

Diachronic: Concerning changes over time.

3 Experience: what are the feelings and moods of the players and the observers? How do these affect playing? What are the different experiences of players, spectators, scholarly observers, directors, organizers, and so on? How do differing feelings and moods change over the course of play, affecting the playing itself? Are spectator sports more affected by the "home field advantage" than informal games or more intimate playing (make-believe, riding a swing or see-saw, erotic foreplay)? How does one determine whether the play has been "good" or not?

4 Function: what purposes do play acts serve? How do they affect individual and community learning, growth and creativity, distribute and express aggression, act out myths, fantasies, or values . . . or any number of other possible "uses" play has? What are the economic consequences of any particular play act or genre of play?

5 Evolutionary, species, and individual development of play. What is the relationship of human play to animal play? What is the difference, if any, between child play and adult play? What is the relationship between playing and individual creativity? What is the relationship between play and culture – especially creativity, the arts, and religion?

6 Ideology: far from being "disinterested," playing enacts, affirms, or subverts values, both individual and collective. What political, social, and personal values does any specific playing enunciate, propagate, or criticize – either knowingly or unconsciously? Are these values the same for all players, spectators, and observers? And if there are differences, how are these expressed and negotiated?

7 Frame: how do players, spectators, and so on know when play begins, is taking place, and is over? How is the message "now I am playing" broadcast and received? And what about "dark" or risky play, where the message "this is play" is intentionally omitted or disguised, such as in con games or in Augusto Boal's invisible theatre? Is "I want to stop playing" the same as "I am finished playing"?

"Invisible theatre": A performance technique developed by Brazilian director **Augusto Boal** in which events are staged in public places for an "audience" of bystanders who do not know that what they are witnessing is a theatrical performance. An invisible theatre event almost always has a political meaning.

During the rest of this chapter, I will investigate these seven aspects of play and playing. However, they cannot be separated out from each other as sharply as I have done in the list. Many of these aspects overlap each other. Therefore, the discussion will "orbit" and "touch on" these seven rather than discuss them one after the other.

Types of Playing

Sociologist **Roger Caillois** (1913–78) classifies play and games into four categories:

Roger Caillois (1913–78): French sociologist and play theorist. Author of *Man, Play, and Games* (1958, Eng. 1979).

1 Agon or competition. Games where there are winners and losers. The outcome is determined by the skills and/or strength of the players. Examples: races, weightlifting, chess.
2 Alea or chance. Games where fate, luck, or grace determines the winner. Examples: dice, roulette.
3 Mimicry or simulation. Playing within an imaginary, make-believe, or illusory world. Examples: theatre, children's make-believe play.
4 Ilinx or dizziness. Playing to induce a disorienting experience or state of mind. Examples: spinning, roller-coaster rides, getting "crazy drunk."

This division into four basic categories is useful up to a point. However, one soon discovers that actual playing and gaming more often combine categories than keep them distinct. For example, poker involves both agon and alea, with more than a touch of mimicry thrown in (the famous "poker face" worn

84

by the best players). Greek tragedies draw power and pathos from a combination of alea and agon — fate and conflict — while the stage performances of the dramas are mimicries. "Musical chairs" and "ring around the rosy" combine ilinx and agon. Carnival masquerading combines all four categories. And so on. Caillois himself recognized this, pointing out that horse racing combines agon, alea, and mimicry.

Caillois emphasized the reciprocity between any given society and the games it plays (**see Caillois box 1**). Most play theorists agree that play both expresses and drives social life. The disagreements come over what kinds of playing are preferable. Professional athletes and gamblers play for money. Business people and politicians exploit gaming techniques. Playing "mind games" in order to control other people is a social skill. Scams, stings, and con-games are endemic. Some see playing as largely a means of exercising power (**see Sutton-Smith box 1**). Caillois and others prefer the disinterested play of "gentleman amateurs," which they regard as a mark of high culture. The darker kinds of play Caillois calls "corruptions" evidencing a decline in "civilization." Caillois is imagining (or proposing) a golden age when people play by the rules. In this Utopia, violent, irruptive ecstasy is rare and strictly governed; there is little dependence on chance or fate because people live rationally. Plato was the first in the West to imagine such a world. In China, **Confucius** (551–479 BCE) proposed a similarly rational code for living.

Roger Caillois

A Society is the Games it Plays

[There is] a truly reciprocal relationship between a society and the games it likes to play. There is indeed an increasing affinity between their rules and the common characteristics and deficiencies of the members of the groups. These preferred and widely diffused games reflect, on the one hand, the tendencies, tastes, and ways of thought that are prevalent, while, at the same time, in educating and training the players in these very virtues or eccentricities, they subtly confirm them in their habits and preferences. Thus, a game that is esteemed by a people may at the same time be utilized to define the society's moral or intellectual character, provide proof of its precise meaning, and contribute to its popular acceptance by accentuating the relevant qualities.

1979 [1958], *Man, Play, and Games*, 82–83

Brian Sutton-Smith

Play and Power

Considerations of play and power come under various names, such as warfare, hegemony, conflict, competition, glory, manliness, contest, and resistance. Some of these are quite ancient terms historically, preceding the modern rhetorics of progress, the imaginary, and the self. [. . .] In modern times, however, the concept of power has also been applied in play theory to solitary play: the child plays because he enjoys the power of being a cause, or because he doesn't have power and in play is seeking empowerment as a kind of compensation or wish fulfillment. On the social play level, the general idea of the power rhetoric is that play or games or sports or athletics that have to do with some kind of contest and reflect a struggle for superiority between two groups (two people, two communities, two tribes, two social classes, two ethnic groups, two or more nations) exist because they give some kind of representation or expression to the existing real conflict between these groups. Whichever side wins the game or contest is said to bring glory to its own group, bonding the members together through their common contestive identity. Furthermore the two groups typically have in common their enthusiasm for this kind of contest, which may thus unite rather than divide them.

1997, *The Ambiguity of Play*, 75

Confucius (551–479 BCE): Chinese moral philosopher and poet. Confucianism, a code of conduct based on his teachings, was the official religion of China until 1911, and is still widely practiced.

Play Acts, Play Moods

Playing consists of actions and reactions, arousing and/or expressing differing emotions and moods. In any given play situation there may be both players and observers. The observers may be actively involved in the play — as fans or avid followers of the game; or they may be more disinterested witnesses. There are also professional watchers, the referees and judges who make sure that the playing is going by the rules or who determine who wins, who loses. It is possible to be playing from the perspective of the observers but not be playing, or at least not be in a play mood, from another point of view. The roaring Romans in the Coliseum delighted in the gladiatorial games as play, while the gladiators themselves were not playing. Modern bullfights resemble the gladiatorial games, with the odds fixed strongly in favor of the matador (**see figure 4.3**). In a bullfight, the bull is not playing, the matador is both playing and not playing, and the spectators are enjoying the blood sport. Indeed, professional sports present a particularly complex situation. A lot of hype goes into convincing fans that the players are in it "for the love of the game." Probably many players enjoy playing at a professional level. But clearly money and stardom also count for a lot. Furthermore, the players on the field are only the most visible parts of an extremely elaborate network of managers, owners, and media joined to real estate, government, and corporate interests. At what level does the play stop and something else begin? At all levels of professional sports, playing is implicated with other activities.

Hindsight can transform a "serious" event into "play." Watching home movies, for example. Or television programs like *Candid Camera*. The popularity at the turn of the millennium of "reality television," as well as access to hundreds of webcams streaming over the internet, are variations on the candid camera theme. Who is playing in these situations? And when does the playing take place? The playing is relocated to the playback; or if the program is live, the players are more like athletes engaged in a contest. With the webcams, the playing is more or less "unconscious," the delight voyeuristic. In a scam, sting, or practical joke the targets are part of a play event, but do not know it; the other participants must keep up the illusion of seriousness; the audience (friends, the police) use the event either as an occasion for amusement or as evidence. In the case of a scam, it is important to the perpetrators that there be no audience, ever.

Play acts often serve multiple, contradictory purposes simultaneously. What's fun for the cat is not for the mouse. Among the Aztecs and Mayans of Mesoamerica, ball playing fulfilled many functions. People played ball just for fun and to show off skills. The hard rubber ball, which was knocked without touching it with the hands, ranged in size from about 8 inches in diameter among the Aztecs to 18 inches in the Mayan game (**see figure 4.4**). Often there were large bets riding on a game with valuable textiles wagered (these cultures did not have money as such). Sometimes the ball game was a matter of life and death. Captives especially were forced to play – and lose both the game and their lives. Such ritual games built community solidarity and confirmed the

fig 4.3. A bullfight at Pamplona, Spain, 1997. Spanish bullfighter Pepin Liria executes a pass while on his knees – this is called a "larga cambiada." Copyright Popperfoto.

fig 4.4. A Mayan ballgame as depicted on a cylindrical vessel, 600–800 CE. The illustration is a "roll out" – the cylinder has been photographically extended into a flat plane. Note the large size of the ball. Four ball players are shown. Photograph by Justin Kerr.

superiority of ruling deities and kings, even as it brought death to those selected for sacrifice.

If play acts themselves are not necessarily "fun," neither are the processes that generate play acts always playful. Sports training and practicing often involve hours of grueling effort proving the adage, "no pain, no gain." Filming a motion picture is more tedious work involving lots of boring repetition and waiting than it is play. On the other hand, the processes involved in preparing can be more enjoyable than the outcome. Many people report that workshops and rehearsals are a lot more playful than the finished products. Thus there is no necessary relationship between process and product. Either, both, or neither may be playful.

Moods are especially labile, shifting suddenly and totally. Observe a children's playground. A kid can be laughing one minute, crying the next, angry the next, and laughing again a moment later. All of these moods are part of the playing going on. Or the playing can go over the edge, in humans as with animals. In the midst of a hotly contested match, play can suddenly turn venomous and deadly. Only in well-organized games – which constitute a minority of play acts – is the situation "under control." And even in such well-managed situations, an injury to a player or spectator, or a fight on the field or in the stands, breaks the play mood. Once the wounded player is carried from the field, or order restored, play resumes.

Though it is not easy to separate play from games, generally games are highly structured events whose rules are known by all the players. Games are played in specific designated places (stadiums, playgrounds, card tables, etc.), move toward definite outcomes, and have as players persons who are clearly marked, even uniformed. Games can range from single instances to "seasons" that take months to complete. The Olympic Games renew themselves every four years. Theorist **James P. Carse** (1932–) divides games into "finite" and "infinite" (**see Carse box**). A finite game moves toward resolution, while the goal of an infinite game is to keep on playing. Cultures are infinite games. The ultimate infinite game is the open-ended play that sustains existence.

James P. Carse (1932–): American theologian, author of *Death and Existence* (1980) and *Finite and Infinite Games* (1986).

James P. Carse

Finite and Infinite Games

There are at least two kinds of games. One could be called finite, the other infinite. A finite game is played for the purpose of winning, an infinite game for the purpose of continuing play. [. . .] The rules of a finite game are the contractual terms by which the players can agree on who has won. [. . .] The rules of an infinite game must change during the course of play. [. . .] The rules of an infinite game are changed to prevent anyone from winning the game and to bring as many persons as possible into the play. [. . .] To be serious is to press for a specified conclusion. To be playful is to allow for possibility whatever the cost to oneself. [. . .] Since culture is itself a poiesis, all of its participants are poietai – inventors, makers, artists, storytellers, mythologists. They are not, however, makers of actualities, but makers of possibilities. The creativity of culture has no outcome, no conclusion. It does not result in art works, artifacts, productions. Creativity is a continuity that engenders itself in others.

1986, *Finite and Infinite Games*, 3, 9, 19, 67

Flow, or Experiencing Playing

What about the experience of playing? There are play faces, play moods, and play experiences. The faces can be mapped from the outside; the moods can be read by someone skilled in understanding body languages, gestures, and facial displays. It is much harder to get at the player's "experience," which is an interior, private occurrence, varying enormously from one person to the next. Several people can participate in the same event, even behave identically, and yet have wildly different experiences.

In the early 1970s, **Mihaly Csikszentmihalyi** (1934–) studied the experience of playing in a wide range of people, from chess players to surgeons, rock climbers to rock dancers. The term he gave to what people felt when their consciousness of the outside world disappeared and they merged with what they were doing is "flow" (**see Csikszentmihalyi box**). By now, "flow" has entered popular language. To "go with the flow" means not only to do what everyone else is doing, but to merge with whatever activity one is engaged in. Players in flow may be aware of their actions, but not of the awareness itself. What they feel is close to being in trance (see chapter 6) and the "oceanic" experience of rituals (see chapter 3). Flow occurs when the player becomes one with the playing. "The dance danced me." At the same time, flow can be an extreme self-awareness where the player has total control over the play act. These two aspects of flow, apparently contrasting, are essentially the same. In each case, the boundary between the interior psychological self and the performed activity dissolves.

Mihaly Csikszentmihalyi (1934–): American psychologist, an expert on flow and its relation to experience and creativity. Author of *Beyond Boredom and Anxiety* (1975), *Flow* (1990), *Creativity* (1996), and *Finding Flow* (1997).

Mihaly Csikszentmihalyi

Flow

With near unanimity, respondents (even those who received extrinsic rewards for their activity: composers, chess champions, surgeons) stated that they devoted time and effort to their activity because they gained a peculiar state of experience from it, an experience that is not accessible in "everyday life." [. . .]

In the flow state, action follows upon action according to an internal logic that seems to need no conscious intervention by the actor. He experiences it as a unified flowing from one moment to the next, in which he is in control of his actions, and in which there is little distinction between self and environment, between stimulus and response, or between past, present, and future. Flow is what we have been calling "the autotelic experience."

1975, *Beyond Boredom and Anxiety*, 35–36

Flow: The feeling of losing oneself in the action so that all awareness of anything other than performing the action disappears. A gambler "on a role" or an athlete playing "in the zone" are experiencing flow.

Understanding flow tells us something important about the relationship between interpreting the meaning of a particular game and the experience of playing that game. Or being fully engaged in any activity, for that matter: acting in a play, selling automobiles, experimenting in a laboratory. Whatever the interpretation, the players themselves, if they are in flow, are focused on the immediate demands of the activity. Baseball may be interpreted as a perilous journey of a Ulysses-like hero, the batter who hits the ball in order to venture into dangerous enemy territory where he may be put out at almost any time, safe only when standing on one of three tiny islands (the bases), and successful only when he safely arrives back home. Or baseball may be seen as a romantic idealization of an open, verdant space, the "ball park," sculpted out of the brick and asphalt of a crowded city. Baseball may be any number of things on the symbolic or meaning level. But while the game is being played, baseball is about pitching, hitting, catching, and running; it is about teamwork and individual accomplishment (**see figure 4.5**).

fig 4.5. American baseball's "perilous journey" – the batter tries to get to a safe base, or even hit a home run, at Shea Stadium, New York, 2001. Photograph by Henry Bial.

Transitional Objects, Illusions, and Culture

There is another way to understand the experience of playing. Psychoanalyst **D. W. Winnicott** (1896–1971) thought that playing was a very special experience of trust that had its origins in the "potential space" between baby and mother. This space is both an actual playground and the conceptual arena where human culture originates. Experiencing this potential space starts when an infant first senses the difference between "me" and "not me." At birth, such a distinction is impossible to make. To the newborn, mother's breasts are "part of" the baby. As a baby suckles, the nipple is inside the baby's mouth; the breast gives warm, good-tasting, life-sustaining milk (**see figure 4.6**). Touching and sucking build a somatic-emotional bridge bonding mother and baby into a new liminal organism. This sucking and fondling precedes even intense mutual gazing. For a few days after birth, an infant's eyes don't focus, but the mouth works splendidly even before birth – as we know from photographs of fetuses sucking the thumb in utero. But even as the mother's breasts are "me" to the suckling infant, they are also "not me." The thumb is always there, but not the breast. The baby cries when hungry and the breast is absent. Its crying signifies something is missing. When the breast arrives, along with the familiar-smelling/feeling mother, the baby once more feels complete. Babies deprived of this early experience suffer a lack that persists into adulthood.

D.W. Winnicott (1896–1971): English psychoanalyst and developmental psychologist specializing in the relationship between mother and child as the basis for culture, art, and religion. Works include *The Child and the Family* (1957) and *Playing and Reality* (1971).

fig 4.6. An infant nursing begins the journey from self to other – hopefully establishing with mother a safe liminal "transitional space." Photograph by Richard Schechner.

The mother's breasts are, in Winnicott's term, "transitional objects" – parts of the body-person that belong solely neither to the mother nor to the baby. The mutual fondling and then gazing are "transitional phenomena." Not too long after birth, the baby begins to find or invent more transitional objects – fist, fingers, thumb; a pacifier, the corner of a "security blanket." These become players in an ever more complicated set of transitional phenomena. Soon enough there are favorite toys and other objects which the baby much values and needs. These are used to construct what Winnicott calls a "neutral space" of unchallenged illusion. Over time, as the baby begins to play in ways that adults recognize, the time spent playing increases. Almost any object, space, or span of time can be used "in play." And within this liminal play world, for the playing child, anything can become something else. The first years of life are a period of protean creativity. Toy manufacturers try to convince anxious parents that this or that product is the "right toy" for their child. Indeed, when the infant becomes a toddler, she is susceptible to advertising. But in terms of biosocial process, toys are made by the imagination, not by Mattel.

Winnicott said the origins of creativity and illusion were in playing. He said that the satisfying experience of playing was a feeling that never left a person throughout life. Winnicott also believed that this satisfying experience, grounded in illusion and playing, was inherent in art, religion, and the rest of culture. Thus Winnicott theorized that the transitional space and experiences first explored between mother and baby formed the foundation for the vast superstructure of culture (see Winnicott box). Winnicott's position was similar both to Turner's theory of liminality and the Indian philosophy of *maya–lila* (to be discussed later in the chapter).

D. W. Winnicott

Playing and the Location of Cultural Experience

Of every individual who has reached to the stage of being a unit with a limiting membrane and an outside and an inside, it can be said that there is an *inner reality* to that individual, an inner world that can be rich or poor and can be at peace or in a state of war. This helps, but is it enough?

My claim is that if there is a need for this double statement, there is also a need for a triple one: the third part of the life of a human being [. . .] is an intermediate area of *experiencing*, to which inner reality and external life both contribute. [. . .] I am here staking a claim for an intermediate state between a baby's inability and his growing ability to recognize and accept reality. I am therefore studying the substance of *illusion*, that which is allowed to the infant, and which in adult life is inherent in art and religion, and yet becomes the hallmark of madness when an adult puts too powerful a claim on the credulity of others, forcing them to acknowledge a sharing of illusion that is not their own. We can share a respect for *illusory experience*, and if we wish we may collect together and form a group on the basis of the similarity of our illusory experiences. This is a natural root of grouping among human beings. [. . .]

[W]hereas inner psychic reality has a kind of location in the mind or in the belly or in the head or somewhere within the bounds of the individual personality, and whereas what is called external reality is located outside those bounds, playing and cultural experience can be given a location if one uses the concept of the potential space between the mother and the baby. [. . .]

The place where cultural experience is located is in the *potential space* between the individual and the environment (originally the [transitional] object). The same can be said of playing. Cultural experience begins with creative living first manifest in play. [. . .]

The potential space between baby and mother, between child and family, between individual and society or the world, depends on experience which leads to trust. It can be looked on as sacred to the individual in that it is here that the individual experiences creative living.

1971, *Playing and Reality*, 2–3, 53, 100, 103

An Ethological Approach to Play

Winnicott expressed a psychoanalytic theory that was based on certain biological assumptions. This can be looked at in another way – returning to matters raised in chapter 3 with regard to ritual. Whatever the human cultural aspects of play, there are also biological aspects. Ethologically, the relationship of play and ritual is very close. Just as human ritual has roots in nonhuman animal behavior, so play has been observed in many species. Everyone has seen a dog play with a bone or stick, a cat with a ball of yarn or a mouse, the doomed rodent an unwilling playmate in a feline version of "dark play" (dark play will be discussed later in this chapter).

In fact, all mammals play in ways that are similar to human playing. And as we might expect, the play of the higher primates – chimpanzees, gorillas, and monkeys – is the closest to human play. Studying how nonhumans play provides insights not only into the evolutionary development of behavior, but also into the functions of play.

The more "freely" the members of a species play, the closer they are to humans, and the more recognizably "playful" their activities appear. Bees, ants, and fish are rich in ritual but poor in play. Only mammals, and primates especially, mix ritual and play in ways that yield new "creative" behaviors. And of the primates, only humans possess a conscious "aesthetic sense." Ritual contributes the set patterns and repetitions, the "systems" to performance; play contributes exploratory behavior, creativity, and world-making.

Ethologists identify five functions of playing in primate species, including humans:

1 Education and/or practice for the young. The young of these species need to learn because their behavior is not genetically fixed.
2 An escape from or alternative to stress.
3 A source of information about the environment.
4 A means for the young to find their place within the group's hierarchy and for adults to keep or change their places in the hierarchy.
5 Muscular exercise.

Not everyone agrees on these functions, or even with the functional approach. Play theorist **Brian Sutton-Smith** (1924–) argues that functional studies are driven by a rationalist desire to prove that "play works." However, I find the functional explanations useful.

Brian Sutton-Smith (1924–): New Zealand-born folklorist and educational theorist. Author of numerous works on play, including *Play and Learning* (1979), *Toys as Culture* (1986), and *The Ambiguity of Play* (1997).

It is also interesting to note that playing in primates — although said to be the locus of "creativity" — is unoriginal at the level of behavior. To extrapolate from the work of several ethologists, it seems that playing "borrows" behaviors from contexts where their purpose is clear — such as fighting or mating — redeploys them, makes a show of them, and uses them for no apparent purpose (**see Loizos box**). Thus a sequence of play includes "not-play" actions that are fragmented, reordered, exaggerated, and repeated. The creativity of play comes in the new ways already known behaviors are reorganized, made into new sequences. Some individual movements within a play sequence may never be completed, and this incomplete element may be repeated over and over. Seen this way, play is a very good example of "restored behavior."

In animals, a play sequence may be broken off by the introduction of different activities such as eating and then resumed later with full intensity as if the break in the action

Caroline Loizos

Primate Playing, Including Humans

One of [play's] immediately noticeable characteristics is that it is behavior that borrows or adopts patterns that appear in other contexts where they achieve immediate and obvious ends. When these patterns appear in play they seem to be divorced from their original motivation and are qualitatively distinct from the same patterns appearing in their originally motivated contexts. [. . .] The fundamental similarity [. . .] between human and animal play [. . .] lies in the exaggerated and uneconomical quality of the motor patterns involved. Regardless of its motivation or its end-product, this is what all playful activity has in common; and it is possible that it is all that it has in common, since causation and function could vary from species to species.

1969, "Play Behavior in Higher Primates: A Review," 228–29

had not occurred. This "time out" quality, as in human sports or games, is extremely important. It demonstrates how play acquires a make-believe independence. Although playing is made up of behavior taken from highly functional activities, it becomes an end in itself without direct functional consequences. The pleasure in playing is autotelic, coming not from what it "earns" but from enjoying the actions in themselves. Furthermore, playing is a way to perform safely and without consequences actions that in other contexts would determine hierarchy, mating rights, or even the right to life. Playing is "playing around." As noted, the behavior building blocks of play are structurally very close to those of ritual. Does this make play a sub-category of ritual? Or is it the other way round?

The Message, "This is Play"

How does a person signal, "I am playing"? It is easy enough when play takes the form of games played according to accepted rules. But despite the enormous popularity of rule-bound games, much playing is not formal. And even formal games are often played informally, as in "sandlot baseball," where players twist the rules to meet contingencies. More pervasive still are bursts of microplay that can erupt any-where, anytime, even in the midst of work (**see Handelman**

Don Handelman

Banana Time

So a serious discussion about the high cost of living could be suddenly transformed into horseplay or into a prank; or a worker might utter a string of "oral autisms." The expression of themes was thus temporary, somewhat idiosyncratic excursions into the reality of play; and each protagonist experimented in his own way, and to some extent at his own pace, with these transitions from the reality of work to that of expressive behavior.

1976, "Rethinking 'Banana Time,'" 442

box 2). So how do people know when someone is "just playing" or that now is the time to "pull a fast one"? Although it's not possible to answer this question definitively, we probably signal, "This is play" by overplaying or underplaying, or by culturally specific signals like a smirk or the winking of an eye (**see figure 4.7**). Anthropologist Gregory Bateson

fig 4.7. A wink is more than a blink – it's a signal, a metacommunication. Photograph of Sophia Martin Schechner by Richard Schechner.

(1904–80) theorized that an animal wanting to play "metacommunicates" that intention. A metacommunication is a signal that frames all other signals contained within it. Let me demonstrate this using "Bateson's dog" as an example. You are playing with Bateson's dog, who shows his teeth, snarls, and nips you – even exaggerating the action of nipping

you by not letting go and growling. The dog is saying, "I could really bite you, but I am not biting you. My nipping tells you the opposite of what a bite would tell you. A bite would tell you, 'I hate you; I am angry with you.' But my nip tells you, 'I love you; I am at ease with you.'" The metacommunication sends the message, "What I am doing now is playing with you. My playing refers to my 'not playing'; my 'not hurting' you refers to the fact that I could hurt you, but choose not to. My choosing not to is proof that I am playing." Within the play frame or during playtime, everything, even what would be negative or harmful, is positive and good (**see Bateson box**).

Metacommunication: A signal that tells receivers how to interpret the communication they are receiving. For example, winking an eye or holding up crossed fingers while speaking indicates to the listener that the speaker's words are not to be taken seriously.

Gregory Bateson

Playful Nips and Bites

[. . .T]he statement "This is play" looks something like this: "These actions in which we now engage do not denote what those actions *for which they stand* would denote." [. . .] Not only does the playful nip not denote what would be denoted by the bite for which it stands, but, in addition, the bite itself is fictional. Not only do the playing animals not quite mean what they are saying but, also, they are usually communicating about something which does not exist. At the human level, this leads to a vast variety of complications and inversions in the fields of play, fantasy, and art. [. . .]

Finally, in the dim region where art, magic, and religion meet and overlap, human beings have evolved the "metaphor that is meant," the flag which men will die to save, and the sacrament that is felt to be more than "an outward and visible sign, given to us." [. . .] We face then two peculiarities of play: (a) that the messages or signals exchanged in play are in a certain sense untrue or not meant; and (b) that that which is denoted by these signals is nonexistent. These two peculiarities sometimes combine strangely to reverse a conclusion reached above. It was stated that the playful nip denotes the bite, but does not denote that which would be denoted by the bite. But there are other instances where an opposite phenomenon occurs. A man experiences the full intensity of subjective terror when a spear is flung out at him out of the 3D screen or when he falls headlong from some peak created in his own mind in the intensity of nightmare. At the moment of terror there was no questioning of "reality," but still there was no spear in the movie house and no cliff in the bedroom.

1972, *Steps to an Ecology of Mind*,
180, 182–83

Extend this to the performing arts. It is easy enough to see how comedy and farce, circus and stand-up comedians, music and dance are playful. But why is tragedy playful? Why are violent video games playful? Because these arts and entertainments refer to that which, if real, would be painful. We can empathize with that pain, or pull the trigger of that video-game gun without "really doing" what we would be doing if we were not playing. This is consonant with the Stanislavskian "as if." It is also consistent with my own theory of performing as the enactment of a double negative, the "not . . . not."

The question remains: given the functions of play, does viewing tragedies or playing violent video games dull people to pain, or train them to administer it? There is a contradiction between ethological theory, which indicates play is practice and training, and Batesonian theory, which asserts play is a way around violence, a way to express aggression without doing harm. To the contrary, the Batesonian argument goes, such playing does good by clearly outlining the play frame and keeping the performance inside it. Bateson's dog "promises" not to really bite. At present, there is no resolution to this contradiction. Those who see harm in violent entertainments argue that teenagers especially are unable to keep the play frame intact; that they "actually" kill while intending to "just play." The arguments on both sides are ideologically loaded.

Bateson's *Othello*

In act 5, scene 2 of Shakespeare's *Othello*, the Moor murders Desdemona, his wife. Three actions occur simultaneously:

- Othello murders Desdemona.
- Two actors play a scene.
- Spectators experience a theatre piece.

On the first level, there is no playing. In a jealous rage, Othello commits murder. Othello does not send any message to Desdemona that he is just playing. Nor does Desdemona play at terror while pleading for her life (**see figure 4.8**).

fig 4.8 Othello, played by Willard White, murdering Desdemona, played by Imogen Stubbs, 1989. Copyright Shakespeare Centre Library.

Playing enters the scene on the second level. To play effectively, the actors have to communicate to each other that everything they do onstage is part of the play in both senses of the word: they are enacting Shakespeare's drama; they are playing with each other and not really murdering. How do they do this? They rehearse. They work out all the details. By the time of the public performance, they follow a score of restored behavior that both actors know and have practiced together. This reinforces the play frame, signalling during every performance, both to themselves and to the spectators, "We are just playing."

To use Bateson's words, "These actions in which we now engage [acting in a theatre] do not denote what those actions for which they stand would denote [murdering an innocent but presumed adulterous wife]. Not only does the playful nip not denote what would be denoted by the bite for which it stands, but, in addition, the bite itself is fictional [the murder is a stage action]." It is the fiction – not what the fiction stands for – that wins the audience's applause. Othello, Desdemona, Iago, and the rest of the characters may be condemned, admired, or pitied; what happens to them may move an audience to tears. But it is the actors who take the bows.

On the third level, what spectators experience, the nip is Shakespeare's *Othello*, and the bite is how the play resonates in each spectator's life. This is both an individual and a collective experience. Audiences share subtle but unmistakable cues. A rapt audience creates a special kind of silence and focus. Levels two and three interact. The audience receives Shakespeare's play by means of its performance. If the acting is bad, the spectators stop paying attention; there is coughing and whispering, maybe even booing. But no matter how involved or displeased, no one jumps onto the stage to stop the murder. Sometimes a play is stopped because the spectators are outraged by what they are seeing. At other times, people walk out of a performance of low quality. In these cases, the performance is rejected at levels two or three, never at level one. Some people may object to a performance at level one, believing that certain subjects or actions are not suitable for artistic representation. Two very different examples of the "unrepresentable" would be the Shoah and snuff pornography. But despite objections, probably just about everything doable or imaginable has been shown as art or as entertainment, that is, "in play."

At level three, if the actors were to depart from the score in a big way – if Othello pushed down smotheringly hard on the pillow, if Desdemona poked a finger in Othello's eye – the scene would be destroyed as play. Even less extreme, if one of the actors felt the other was no longer playing, or not playing according to the agreed-on score, the stage show would be disrupted. Many arguments erupt backstage over just that kind of thing. "You lost it; you were totally out of control!" But no matter how "out of control," no actors playing a death scene ever lost it to such a degree that they stopped playing and performed "for real." The same cannot be said for police enacting the life role of "cop."

There are "for real" performances in ordinary life and in ritual. Or are these performances playing? It is in this region

that distinctions between these two fundamental categories become very difficult to make. While in trance, performers are "being played with" rather than playing. Some force or being "possesses" them, takes them over, making them dance, sing, say, and gesture. However, even in trance, performers do not lose consciousness. In the Balinese Rangda-Barong trance drama, the dancers turn their *krisses* (8-inch long daggers) against their own breasts. They press the krisses with such force that the knife blades bend – but they never draw blood (**see figure 4.9**). The Balinese say, "If a person hurts himself, the trance is not real." Not so with the ancient Aztecs, whose ritual performances often centered on blood sacrifices. Executions in the USA must be witnessed, turning this ultimate revenge of the state into a performance. In the European middle ages, executions were elaborate shows, carefully staged and featuring final speeches by the condemned or/and long hours of painful and humiliating suffering enjoyed by hundreds of eager spectators (**see Merback box**).

What about audience participation, public meetings, Boal's Forum Theatre, or other performances whose

fig 4.9. A Balinese dancer in trance turns his kris (ceremonial knife) against his own body – but he does not hurt himself. Photograph courtesy of Eugenio Barba.

Mitchell Merback

The Spectacle of Executions in Medieval Europe

Before the execution ever took place, spectators were presented with an array of symbols communicating vital information about the criminal and his or her deeds. [. . .] In Germany the formal handing over of the convict to the executioner was treated as a spectacle: while repeating the sentence of death, the officiating judge or town clerk would hold up a wand of office, coloured white, red or black (depending on local tradition), break it with great aplomb, cast the bits down on the convict's feet and announce the condemned's now broken bond with humanity. [. . .] After sentencing a bell might toll, and then continue until the moment of death. Clothing conveyed the convict's status at a glance: nobles might wear their livery, while infamous characters were often stripped to the waist. [. . .]

What did spectators come to see? It has often been said that for ordinary people executions, though intended to be terrifying, actually offered an experience that was emotionally comforting: the reassurance that comes with seeing a bona fide sinner confess his crimes, show contrition, receive absolution, endure a painful ordeal and find redemption on the other side. If such an unfortunate wretch can be thus saved, the reasoning goes, so can a sinner like me. [. . .] Except in cases where heinous criminals, outsiders and infamous characters of various stripes became the object of intense collective hatred, the community insisted that the spectacle be edifying, not as a lesson in the majesty of the law but as a drama of Christian repentance, purification, and salvation.

1999, *The Thief, the Cross, and the Wheel*, 138, 144

Philosophies of Play

The early view of play allied it with power. Those with the most power – the gods, mythic heroes, or kings – acted with absolute freedom, creating their own rules as they went along, indulging their unconstrained desires. These beings played on a big scale. Their playing was world-making, either cosmically or socially. A basic theme of ancient Greek tragedy is the struggle between the unconstrained power of "free play" and the "rule of law," or behavior governed by rules. To whom did such unconstrained power belong – to the gods, kings, heroes, nature? There was as yet no rule of human law – a system of constraints more powerful than any individual yet not divine. This dialectical tension between power and law is strong throughout Western philosophy and history, up to the present.

About a century after the high point of ancient Greek tragic theatre, the reigning philosophers of the Western tradition, Plato and Aristotle established rationality as the dominant system of thought. Plato wanted a city, and Aristotle a science, governed by known, universal, and generally accepted rules or laws. These laws had to be obeyed by people, gods, and nature itself. Free play was replaced by rule-governed games. Free play, *paidia*, was subsumed under, or governed by, rule-bound behavior, *ludus* (**see Caillois box 2**). Caillois uses the Greek word "paidia" (related to the word for "child") to mean a spontaneous burst of play, turbulent and unconstrained. On the other hand, the Latin "ludus" means a game governed by rule-bound behavior. This useful distinction between paidia and ludus is overlooked by many theorists, who depend solely on variations of ludus – ludic, illusion, delusion, ludicrous, etc.

Roger Caillois

Paidia *and* Ludus

[. . . Play] can be placed on a continuum between two opposite poles. At one extreme an almost indivisible principle, common to diversion, turbulence, free improvisation, and carefree gaiety is dominant. It manifests a kind of uncontrolled fantasy that can be designated by the term *paidia*. At the opposite extreme, this frolicsome and impulsive exuberance is almost entirely absorbed or disciplined by a complementary,

metacommunication is that the playing includes or even demands a blurring of the boundaries separating audience and performers, stage and house? By naming participants "spect-actors," Boal signals that the Theatre of the Oppressed needs spectators to participate. Boal's message is, "This is play, and you must play with us!" During the 1960s and 1970s, signals and rules governing audience participation were often vague or ambivalent. This created confusion onstage and off.

and in some respects inverse, tendency to its anarchic and capricious nature: there is a growing tendency to bind it with arbitrary, imperative, and purposely tedious conventions [. . .]. I call this second component *ludus*.

1979 [1958], *Man, Play, and Games*, 13

Just because Plato threw the poets out of his Republic did not mean that paidia was forever banished. In the nineteenth century, themes from pre-Socratic Greek philosophy were taken up by **Friedrich Nietzsche** (1844–1900) (**see Spariosu box 2**) and further developed in the twentieth century as a scientific theory by Werner Heisenberg in the "uncertainty principle" and as a cultural theory by Jacques Derrida in the notion of "deconstruction." "Free play" in many guises – from dada to performance art, from the unconscious to indeterminacy – has regained much of its power, if not its divine status. But the question is far from settled. It probably never can be settled because the struggle is not over data or interpretation, but over basic worldviews.

Mihai I. Spariosu

Nietzsche and Prerational Play

Nietzsche's philosophical project can be seen as a return to Hellenic prerational values, and his critique of modern culture as being carried out from the point of view of these values. [. . .] If Nietzsche's doctrine of eternal return can be traced back to Heraclitus, that of the Will to Power can be traced back to the archaic principle of might makes right, and that of the *Übermensch* to the epic and tragic hero. Furthermore, Nietzsche's oracular, gnomic, and dithyrambic style bears a strong family resemblance to that of lyric and tragic poetry, suggesting a reversion to a prerational mentality. Consequently, to a predominantly rational mode of thinking Nietzsche will appear as a paradoxical, ambiguous, multi-dimensional thinker. But viewed from the prerational perspective, his philosophical project loses its para-doxical and ambiguous quality, offering instead a far-ranging critique of modern rational values.

1989, *Dionysus Reborn*, 69

Friedrich Nietzsche (1844–1900): German philosopher whose ideas and writings, including *The Birth of Tragedy* (1872), *Thus Spake Zarathustra* (1883–85), and *Beyond Good and Evil* (1886), continue to be influential.

The rationalists hold that the cosmos is an objective entity, existing wholly outside of, and without dependence on, human consciousness. This cosmos, often called "nature," is governed by entirely orderly systems that may not yet, or ever, be wholly understood by humans but which exist, as it were, "in the mind of God," or as "natural laws." The job of science is to discover these laws of nature, to confirm them through experiment and observation, and to systematize them into theories and "laws" stated in human form, principally as mathematics. Two examples of such a process are **Isaac Newton's** (1642–1727) "three laws" (of inertia, of action and reaction, and of acceleration proportional to force) and **Albert Einstein**'s (1879–1955) famous equation, $e = mc^2$ (energy equals mass times the speed of light squared).

Isaac Newton (1642–1727): English mathematician and scientist, author of the *Principia* (1687) and inventor of calculus (independently devised by Gottfried Wilhelm Leibniz, 1646–1716). Newton's "laws" of gravity and thermodynamics went unchallenged until the advent of quantum mechanics at the end of the nineteenth century.

Albert Einstein (1879–1955): German-born physicist who emigrated to the United States in 1933 as Hitler came to power. Winner in 1921 of the Nobel Prize in Physics, Einstein is best known for his special and general theories of relativity.

The opposing view holds that the cosmos is a multiverse consisting of dynamic, emergent, multiple, uncentered processes that are always changing, existing only as relational systems that can be known only probabilistically; and that these probabilities are the results of an ongoing and unfinishable negotiation between human consciousness-imagination and whatever is "out there" (if anything). There may even be billions of universes existing simultaneously (**see Waldrop box**).

If the world is a game – a metaphor not only of Western thought, but widespread in many cultures – do its rules exist outside or only within specific playfields and playtimes? Are there universal characteristics of play, as **Johan Huizinga** (1872–1945) claims, or is play culture-specific (**see Huizinga box 2**)? Does playing the game

M. Mitchell Waldrop

Multiple Universes

An analysis of localized inflation ["black holes"] suggests that empty space may be spawning universes by the billions, without us ever knowing; was our own universe created this way? What would happen if we could somehow reproduce the conditions of the Big Bang in the modern universe? More precisely, what would happen if a sample of matter were somehow compressed into a tiny region of ultrahigh density and temperature – say 10^{24}K? In one solution, for example, the outside universe simply crushes the hot region into a standard black hole. However, there is a much more interesting solution in which the hot region does indeed inflate – but in a totally different direction that is perpendicular to ordinary space and time. It becomes a kind of aneurysm bulging outward from the side of our familiar universe. In fact, it quickly pinches off and becomes a separate universe of its own. [. . .]

This newborn cosmos [could then] expand to a scale of billions of light-years, producing galaxies, stars, planets, and even life.

1987, "Do-It-Yourself Universes," 845–46

change the rules, as Heisenberg asserts? Are the consistency and universality which rationality seeks only temporary and local? This make-up-the-rules-as-you-go-along is what Nietzsche called the "will-to-power." Nietzsche believed artists and children played in this way (**see Nietzsche box**). The creation of "illusory" worlds may in fact be humankind's main preoccupation (**see Sutton-Smith box 2**).

Johan Huizinga

The Formal Characteristics of Play

Summing up the formal characteristics of play we might call it a free activity standing quite consciously outside "ordinary" life as being "not serious," but at the same time absorbing the player intensely and utterly. It is an activity connected with no material interest, and no profit can be gained by it. It proceeds within its own proper boundaries of time and space according to fixed rules and in an orderly manner. It promotes the formation of social groupings which tend to surround themselves with secrecy and to stress their difference from the common world by disguise or other means. The function of play [. . .] can largely be derived from two basic aspects under which we meet it: as a contest *for* something or a representation *of* something. These two functions can unite in such a way that the game "represents" a contest, or else becomes a contest for the best representation of something.

1970 [1938], *Homo Ludens*, 13

Johan Huizinga (1872–1945): Dutch historian and play theorist. Author of one of the most enduringly influential treatises on play, *Homo Ludens* (1938, Eng. 1944).

Friedrich Nietzsche

God's Play, Child's Play, Artists' Play

In this world only play, play as artists and children engage in it, exhibits coming-to-be and passing away, structuring and destroying, without any moral additive, in forever equal innocence. And as children and artists play, so plays the ever-living fire. It constructs and destroys, all in innocence. Such is the game that the aeon plays with itself. Transforming itself into water and earth, it builds towers of sand like a child at the seashore, piles them up and tramples them down. From time to time it starts the game anew. An instant of satiety – and again it is seized by its need, as the artist is seized by his need to create. Not hybris but the ever self-renewing impulse to play calls new worlds into being. The child throws its toys away from time to time – and starts again in innocent caprice. But when it does build, it combines and joins and forms its structures regularly, conforming to inner laws. Only aesthetic man can look thus at the world [. . .].

1962 [c. 1870], *Philosophy in the Tragic Age of the Greeks*, 62

Brian **Sutton-Smith**

Play and Human Achievement

Given that there is nothing more characteristic of human achievement than the creation of illusory cultural and theoretical worlds, as in music, dance, literature, and science, then children's and gamblers' full participation in such play worlds can be seen not as a defect, or as compensation for inadequacy, but rather as participation in a major central preoccupation of humankind. The modern computer-age habit of calling this "virtual worlds" rather than illusory worlds highlights this move toward a more positive, if narrower, epistemological attitude about their function.

1997, *The Ambiguity of Play*, 54

Heisenberg discovered that the act of observing very small particles (quanta of matter-energy) changes what is being observed. Although the mathematics is beyond me, the underlying theory and its implications can be simply stated. In the world of subatomic phenomena, ordinary common-sense causality does not function. Instead, one can only state the "probability" that a group of subatomic particles/waves will act in a certain way, be in a certain position, at a certain time (**see Heisenberg and Northrup boxes**).

matter waves [. . . which is] much nearer to the truth than the particle picture. [. . .] The two pictures are of course mutually exclusive, because a certain thing cannot at the same time be a particle (i.e., substance confined to a very small volume) and a wave (i.e., a field spread out over a large space), but the two complement each other. By playing with both pictures, by going from the one picture to the other and back again, we finally get the right impression of the strange kind of reality behind our atomic experiments. [. . .] The knowledge of the position of a particle is complementary to the knowledge of its velocity or momentum. If we know the one with high accuracy we cannot know the other with high accuracy; still we must know both for determining the behavior of the system. [. . .] A real difficulty in understanding this interpretation arises, however, when one asks the famous question: But what happens "really" in an atomic event? [. . . W]hat one deduces from an observation is a probability function, a mathematical expression that combines statements about possibilities or tendencies with statements about our knowledge of facts. So we cannot completely objectify the results of an observation, we cannot describe what "happens" between this observation and the next.

1958, *Physics and Philosophy*, 47–50

Werner **Heisenberg**

Particles, Waves, and Uncertainty

The electron may have been practically at rest before the observation. But in the act of observation at least one light quantum of the X-ray must have passed the microscope and must first have been deflected by the electron. Therefore, the electron has been pushed by the light quantum, it has changed its momentum and its velocity, and one can show that the uncertainty of this change is just big enough to guarantee the validity of the uncertainty relations. [. . .]

Actually, we need not speak of particles at all. For many experiments it is more convenient to speak of

F. S. C. **Northrup**

The Uncertainty Principle

In quantum mechanics [. . .] the very act of observing alters the object being observed when its quantum numbers are small. [. . .] The introduction of the concept of probability into the definition of state of the object of scientific knowledge in quantum mechanics rules out [. . .] *in principle* and not merely in practice due to the imperfections of human observation and instruments, the satisfying of the condition that the object of the physicist's knowledge is an isolated system. Heisenberg shows also that the including of the experimental apparatus and even of the eye of the observing scientist in the physical system which is the object of the knower's knowledge does not help, since, if quantum mechanics be correct, the states of all objects have to be defined in principle by recourse to the concept of probability.

1958, Introduction to Heisenberg, *Physics and Philosophy*, 24

It might seem that such a theory is of small consequence to everyday life, and indeed common-sense causality is not affected by the uncertainty principle. If I throw a stone at a window and the glass breaks, I can determine the instant when the stone shattered the plane of the glass. But from a philosophical point of view, the uncertainty principle was revolutionary. Heisenberg overturned classical Newtonian physics. If at a fundamental level, "nature" cannot be fixed outside of probability, then there is no physical solidity, no fundamental material substance. The "what is" of the universe is not founded on certainty but on a kind of gaming, a throw of the subatomic dice. It was this that so infuriated Einstein. He insisted that God does not play dice (**see Einstein box**).

Albert Einstein

God Does Not Play Dice

You believe in the God who plays dice, and I in complete law and order in a world which exists, and which I, in a wildly speculative way, am trying to capture. [. . .] Even the great initial success of the quantum theory does not make me believe in the fundamental dice-game [. . .].

1971, *The Born–Einstein Letters*, 180–1

Einstein (and God) aside, the uncertainty principle underlies much of contemporary thinking. When translated into philosophy, it appears as Derridean deconstruction, perhaps the most playful – if also difficult to understand – speculation ever (**see Wilson box**). According to Derrida, there is no center because the center is not a fixed place but a function (**see Derrida box**). All authority is subverted, "displaced," opening spaces for all kinds of radical free play. Derrida's writing not only inaugurates a discourse

R. Rawdon Wilson

Play and Deconstruction

[. . .] though it may not be possible adequately to define the concept, Derrida seems to make it clear that free play is limitless, unlimited by any irreducible signified or transcendental concept that cannot be further decomposed, and it manifests itself in the process of indefinite substitution. Play, considered as free play, lies beyond stable, centered structures, makes them untenable, decenters them, and deprivileges them.

1990, *In Palamedes' Shadow*, 16

Jaques Derrida

Where There is No Center, All is Playing

It was necessary to begin thinking that there was no center, that the center could not be thought in the form of a present-being, that the center had no natural site, that it was not a fixed locus but a function, a sort of nonlocus in which an infinite number of sign-substitutions came into play. This was the moment when language invaded the universal problematic, the moment when, in the absence of a center or origin, everything became discourse – provided we can agree on this word – that is to say, a system in which the central signified, the original or transcendental signified, is never absolutely present outside a system of differences. The absence of the transcendental signified extends the domain and the play of signification infinitely.

1978, *Writing and Difference*, 280

on decentering, but enacts it with plentiful word-play, punning, and double meanings. I will discuss deconstruction more fully in chapter 5.

Artists may not have followed Heisenberg literally, but they understood him metaphorically. Arts, once the home of strict choreography, precise scores, and fixed mise-en-scènes, were opened to chance processes, unpredictable eruptions from the unconscious, and improvisation. Of course, there are multiple causes bringing these operations into play during the past century. Improvisation, for example, is fundamental to African performing arts and rituals (**see Drewal box**). African cultures were becoming better known both to artists like **Pablo Picasso** (1881–1973)(who took the basics of cubism from African art) and through popular culture such as ragtime and jazz music. Freud's investigations into "dream work," the unconscious, and creativity had an enormous impact on the arts. Seen this way, Heisenberg's uncertainty principle was part of a larger movement in Western thought from the late nineteenth century onward broadening the basis of creativity and expression. A theory espoused by physicists that supported such a liberalization was eagerly taken up by artists. Among many examples of performances based on uncertainty are the chance musical compositions and lectures of John Cage, the Fluxus Group of New York artists, Happenings, and the "manifestations" of dada artists (**see figure 4.10**).

fig 4.10. Chance or indeterminate performances can take many forms, ranging from electronic music presented in a concert hall to a barely noticed "action" blending in to everyday life.

Margaret Thompson **Drewal**

Improvisation, Play, and Ritual

Whenever improvisation is a performative strategy in ritual, it places ritual squarely within the domain of play. It is indeed the playing, the improvising, that engages people, drawing them into the action, constructing their relationships, thereby generating multiple and simultaneous discourses always surging between harmony/disharmony, order/disorder, integration/opposition, and so on.

1992, *Yoruba Ritual*, 7–8

Pablo Picasso (1881–1973): Spanish visual artist, inventor of the cubist style of painting, as illustrated by *Les Demoiselles d'Avignon* (1907). Picasso's long artistic career spanned eight decades and featured innovations in a number of styles and media.

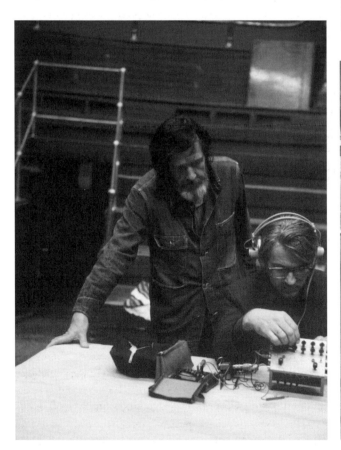

John Cage looking over the shoulder of David Tudor as they prepare a concert of "chance" music. Royal Festival Hall, 1972.

Fluxus artist Ben Vautier sweeping a street in Nice, France, 1960s. Photograph courtesy of Richard Schechner.

The Bias Against Play

The other side of the coin is the deep-seated Western bias against play. From Plato to the Puritans, the playful has been considered frivolous, unimportant, and even sinful. Playing is a major distraction tempting people away from work, which is the "real business" of living. Plato wanted to banish the players, especially poets, playwrights, and actors, from his ideal Republic. Shockingly, he almost succeeded. Adults are supposed to play only during "time off" (from work) in specially designated places and according to well-defined rules. If the playing is regarded as risky, sexual, and subversive to work-values or the authority of the state, whole neighborhoods are fenced off and designated a "red-light" district. The color symbolizes both something hot and "stop." Or special days are designated for playing – holidays, time off, and vacation. But every Mardi Gras is followed by Ash Wednesday, each binge by a confession. It is no accident that red-light districts are full of con artists, prostitutes, cross-dressers (who are fantasy-role players), actors, and musicians. In many cities, the railroad station, the theatre district, and the red-light district are cheek-by-jowl. People need efficient access to where they can play or watch others play.

In fact, the theatre has only relatively recently, and still perilously, been accorded middle-class status in the West. In Germany, the *Stadt-Theater* (municipal theatre) tradition was started by the aristocracy, but soon adopted by the increasingly wealthy and culture-hungry middle class. The German model was widely imitated throughout Europe and in the USA, where it was dubbed the "regional theatre" movement. But America's largest and most famous theatre district is New York's Broadway, located near Times Square. Commencing in the early 1990s, Times Square and West 42nd Street have undergone a transformation from an "adults-only" district into a "G-rated" neighborhood dominated by Disney, MGM, the Ford Motor Company, and other mega-corporations. Only a few blocks north of the "new Times Square," remnants of the "old Times Square" remain in place (**see figure 4.11**). How will these changes affect the performing arts?

The performing arts have traditionally behaved ambivalently with regard to reforming, with one foot in church, the other barely out of bed: from sacred music to whorehouse jazz, from magisterial displays of royalty to the strutting of Restoration epoch actresses and their rakes, from the long-legged grace of the prima ballerina to the sexually available girls of the corps de ballet displayed backstage to the men of means who could afford to purchase access to them (**see figure 4.12**).

fig 4.11. Times Square, New York – then and now, except that "then" is removed in space rather than time.

The way 42nd Street used to look before "development." This picture was taken in 2001 a few blocks away on 8th Avenue on a block not yet developed. Photograph by Richard Schechner.

The "new" 42nd Street, featuring Disney's *The Lion King*, directed by Julie Taymor. Photograph by Richard Schechner.

Other cultures have not been so ambivalent. In India, music, dance, sex, and religion were long associated with each other (until British Victorian values imposed by colonialism took hold). *Devadasis*, well-trained temple dancers whose name meant "servants of god," performed in front of the *murtis* or icons of the gods. Devadasis were available on a regulated basis for sex with priests, princes, and important patrons of the temples – who were also patrons of the arts. The children of such unions were brought up to be dancers and musicians. In most of India, the devadasis were outlawed in the 1930s

fig 4.12. Edgar Degas' *Rehearsal of the Ballet*, 1876, showing an old man supervising the young dancers while another man watches, romanticizes the availability to the gaze, and more, that men of privilege and money enjoyed. Photograph by E. G. Schemp. Copyright The Nelson-Atkinson Museum of Art, Kansas City.

after a fierce campaign against them led by both Indian reformers and the British. A few devadasis continued to dance into the 1970s. Several classical Indian dance forms — *bharatanatyam* and *odissi* among them – originated in devadasi dancing (**see figure 4.13**).

Maya–Lila

India may be more receptive to a playful mix of categories because playing is a fundamental aspect of Indian philosophy and worldview. The idea that the universe may be a cosmic dice game, that meaning is a "play of signification," that the

"will to power" and the uncertainty principle operate at all levels of natural, animal, and human life and experience has been a persistent theme in Indian philosophy and aesthetics for about 2,500–3,000 years. *Maya* and *lila* are Sanskrit words meaning "illusion" and "play." The concepts embedded in these two words are hard to pin down because — as with the Greek *mimesis*, *praxis*, and *katharsis* — key terms in Aristotle's theory of tragedy — there is an enormous library of commentary,

> **Maya–lila:** An Indian philosophical concept of life as a kind of playing where boundaries between "real" and "unreal" or "true" and "false," are continuously shifting and/or wholly permeable.

Wendy Doniger O'Flaherty

fig 4.13. Indian dancer Sanjukta Panigrahi in a classic stance of odissi, 1990s. Photograph courtesy of Eugenio Barba.

Maya and the Real Illusion

[*Maya* originally] meant *only* what was real; through its basis in the verbal root *ma* ("to make") it expressed the sense of "realizing the phenomenal world" [. . .] In the *Rg Veda*, to "measure out" the universe was to create it, to divide it into its constituent parts, to *find* it by bringing it out of chaos. [. . .] Magicians do this; artists do it; gods do it. But according to certain Indian philosophies, every one of us does it every minute of our lives.

This concept of *maya* as a kind of artistic power led gradually to its later connotation of magic, illusion, and deceit. [. . .] It often means not merely bringing something into existence [. . .] but manipulating the existent forces of nature or invoking the power to create and achieve the marvelous. Thus *maya* first meant making something that was not there before; then it came to mean making something that was there into something that was not really there. The first describes the universe in the Vedic world-view; the second, the universe in the Vedantic world-view. [. . .] In both cases *maya* can often best be translated as "transformation." [. . .] A similar cluster of meanings radiates from it [*maya*] as from the English derivatives of the Latin word for play (*ludo*) – de-lusion, il-lusion, e-lusive, and so forth – and from the word "play" itself – play as drama, as swordplay or loveplay, as the play of light that causes mirages, as the double image implicit in wordplay. [. . .] These word clusters delineate a universe full of beauty and motion that enchants us all. All Indian philosophies acknowledge that *maya* is a fact of life – *the* fact of life; but some (the *moksha*-oriented [those who seek liberation from the wheel of birth-death-rebirth] regard it as a negative fact, to be combated, while others (*samsara*-oriented [those who enjoy this world as it is] regard it as a positive fact, to be embraced.

1984, *Dreams, Illusions, and Other Realities*, 117–19

contradictory interpretations, and changing emphasis over historical time. The first meaning of maya was "real," derived from its root *ma* – "to make" (**see O'Flaherty box**). But it was not long before maya became identified with the creative force as such, both divine and artistic; and with powers of transformation – the making of something out of something else, or out of nothing.

But in India, as elsewhere, artists were suspect, slippery characters. And the gods were much like artists – sometimes to be admired, sometimes to be feared and distrusted. Therefore, maya soon began to expand its meanings to include "illusion," "not real," "false," "unsubstantial," "deceitful." It has kept these multiple meanings. "All life is maya," an Indian will say, meaning that nothing is reliable, everything is just show. But he may also mean that living is extremely unpredictable, unreliable, subject to sudden shifts, fundamentally playful, but not necessarily fun. And he may imply that all experienced reality is constructed. The ultimate absolute – the Brahman

beyond all knowing – is without shape or form, unmanifest, uncreated: the very opposite of maya.

Lila is a more ordinary word meaning "play," "sport," or "drama." In Indian terms, the gods create maya, that is, their lila: when the gods play, the world comes into existence. In north India annually a vast cycle play recounting the life of Vishnu's seventh avatar (incarnation) Rama is called "Ramlila" – the lila or play of Rama. At Ramnagar, across the sacred Ganga River from the holy city of Banaras (also called Varanasi and Kashi), the Ramlila takes 31 days to enact and draws ardently reverential crowds of up to 75,000 persons (**see figure 4.14**). At the core of the Ramlila experience is the belief that five pre-adolescent boys are actually the gods Rama, his wife Sita, and Rama's three brothers (**see figure 4.15**). The presence of the divine is a lila within a lila. The gods-as-boys/boys-as-gods is the lila of Vishnu, Rama, and Sita; the 31-day play is the specific human lila in which the divine lila takes place. If this is dizzying, that is because the relationship of maya to lila is paradoxical.

As dance and drama, lilas comprise many enormously popular sacred performances in addition to Ramlila, such as

fig 4.15. Young boys become the *swarups* or "form of the gods" during Ramlila. The swarups are garlanded, crowned, adored, and worshipped, 1997. Photograph by Sam Schechner.

Raslila and Krishnalila, enactments of the life of Krishna, another avatar of Vishnu. Ramlila, Raslila, and Krishnalila are more than make-believe dances or dramas. Different orders of reality converge in the lilas. The young boys who are the *swarups* (forms of the gods) of Rama or Krishna not only enact but also embody the gods. Like temple murtis, they do not represent the gods, but are inhabited by them. Yet at the same time the boys remain children. If a swarup giggles, forgets his lines, falls asleep, or jokes with a friend, the spectators are not taken aback. The people say: "Cannot the god play? Is not this Bala Krishna [boy Krishna], full of mischief and sleep?" Rama is more "serious," a warrior and teacher – yet inhabiting a pre-adolescent boy whose voice has not yet deepened. At Ramlila, people come to just look at him and his wife, Sita, mother of the world. Or to touch their feet, accept a lotus blossom from their hands. These devotees are face-to-face with gods, with boys, with maya–lila.

In a maya–lila world, the material universe is a playground. Everything that happens is part of Brahma's day or Vishnu's playing or Shiva's *tandava* dancing or dice game (**see Handelman and Shulman box**). Shiva's throw of the dice activates the universe – or even more: the universe is a dice game, always at risk, a play of chance, always in motion. The dice-game universe is a function of the dynamics of chance; the game, interacting with unbridled will, the god. In *The Mahabharata*, the great Sanskrit epic, the initiating action is a dice game. Shiva's tandava dance – awakening and radiating *shakti*, a combined female–male energy – brings the universe into existence. At the end of time, as Brahma sleeps, Shiva dances existence into . . . nothing. After eons, Brahma awakens, Shiva starts dancing again, and the universe is created again, the same but different. For Indians, asserting that existence is a dance, a

fig 4.14. Enormous crowds gather for some of the episodes of the 31-day long Ramlila of Ramnagar, north India, 1997. Photograph by Sam Schechner.

dream, or maya–lila is not softheaded. Did Einstein know Shiva played dice?

Don **Handelman** and David **Shulman**

Siva's Cosmic Dice Game

Siva often plays dice with the goddess – his consort, Parvati. Almost invariably, he loses to her. [. . .] Sometimes she becomes angry when he refuses to pay up, or even to acknowledge that he has lost; this stubborn stance may then lead to further conflict – aggressive acts by one or both partners, sulking, quarrels, separations, even curses hurled in rage. Or, still in a playful spirit, the goddess might cover Siva's eyes with her hands, thereby enveloping the universe itself in catastrophic darkness.

Nothing [. . .] is as rich in consequence as a game. Perhaps we should say *the* game. The dice match is in some sense equal to the cosmos, both a condensed expression of its process and a mode of activating and generating that process. If one is God, there is, finally, no other game. All the more shocking, then, is the fact that he must lose. No wonder that he is sometimes more than a little reluctant to play.

The dice throws, as is well known, correlate with the four *yugas*, the cosmic ages in their recursive, devolutionary sequence. Thus, time itself proceeds out of this divine game. Without the game, there would be no time, perhaps no space as well (for the dice also model the cardinal directions in horizontal alignment and in relation to the vertical vector of the zenith) – in short, no world as we know it: language, sexual differentiation and identity, self-knowledge – all these, too, [. . .] are part of the generative cycles of the game.

1997, *God Inside Out: Siva's Game of Dice*, 4–6

In a maya–lila world, experience and reality are multiple, a plenitude of performed, transformable, non-exclusive events or play-worlds. If all realities and experiences shape each other, are networks of flexible constructs, transformations, dreams of dreams, unsettled relationships, what then of "ordinary play" – children playing tag or make-believe, grownups knocking a golf ball across the countryside, a rapt audience listening to a Brahms symphony? These kinds of things – adjusted to suit specific cultures – happen in India, and everywhere else. But the Indians and others who have not lost their unrational abilities are more tuned to sudden, delightful, or shocking transformations, the appearance of scary or farcical demons in the midst of an all-night performance, or a glimpse of the Absolute that Krishna discloses to Arjuna at the climax of *The Bhagavad Gita* – another god who throws dice (**see Vyasa box**). It was the *Gita* that **J. Robert Oppenheimer** (1904–67), head of the scientific team that developed the atomic bomb, quoted in July, 1945, when, standing at dawn on the New Mexico desert, he witnessed the first explosion of that awesome, terrifying, yet visually spectacular weapon.

Vyasa

The Absolute Krishna

Listen [Krishna tells Arjuna] as I recount for you in essence the divine powers of myself. Endless is my extent. [. . .] I am indestructible time, the creator facing everywhere at once. [. . .] I am death the destroyer of all, the source of what will be, the feminine powers: fame, fortune, speech, memory, intelligence, resolve, patience. [. . .] I am the great ritual chant, the meter of sacred song, [. . .] the dice game of gamblers, [. . .] the epic poet Vyasa among sages.

c. 200 BCE, *The Bhagavad Gita*, 10th teaching

J. Robert Oppenheimer (1904–67): American nuclear physicist and director of the Manhattan Project, the team who developed and detonated the first atomic bomb in the New Mexico desert in 1945.

Although binary models are tricky because they split into two opposing sides a world of nuances and continua, they can also be useful if used cautiously. I offer one here, contrasting the difference between maya–lila and the Western rational understandings of play (**see figure 4.16**).

Deep Play, Dark Play

In theatrical terms, maya–lila is an interweaving of the performer and the role. Is the role "real"? And if we can safely say of aesthetic performance – of Hamlet or Shakuntala or

Contrasting Attitudes Towards Play and Playing

Maya-Lila	Rationalist
Unending cycles of creating/destroying	Single creation
Multiple realities	Single reality
How the universe is	Make-believe
Playing is on a par with religion, art	Playing is on a par with art, but not as important as religion or real as science
Creative–destructive	Creative
Everywhere	In playgrounds or other special places
Free	Rule bound
For everyone	For children mostly
All the time	After work
Fundamental	Recreational
Female–Male combined	Childlike, pre-sexual
Extremely powerful	Little power
Celebrates the erotic as the divine energy	Represses the erotic as "bad"

fig 4.16. Maya–lila is more volatile, creative-destructive, all-encompassing, and transformative than the rationalist view of play. In the West, especially since the Enlightenment, playing has been isolated, located in "after work," "recreation," or in childhood. However, in recent decades, partly because the world is more global, non-rationalist notions of playing have re-emerged in the West.

the Black Swan – that the role is not real, what of ritual performances such as the appearance of a Pope in full regalia to bless the believers or the manifestation of an Afro-Brazilian *orixa* who "mounts" the body of a dancer in deep trance? In rituals there is no "suspension of disbelief." Rather there is "deep play" as understood by Clifford Geertz's elaboration of English philosopher **Jeremy Bentham**'s (1748–1832) idea (**see Geertz box**).

Dark play: "Playing with fire," "breaking the rules," "getting away with murder." Playing which emphasizes risk, deception, and sheer thrill.

Geertz was writing about why some Balinese make ruinous bets on cockfights. Geertz's insight into deep play has broad implications. Deep play applies as well to mountain climbing, high-speed auto-racing, and many other activities of extremely high risk physically, fiscally, and psychologically. Deep play involves such high stakes that one wonders why people engage in it at all. As Geertz explains it, deep playing draws the whole person into what amounts to a life-and-death struggle expressing not only individual commitment (even to the irrational), but cultural values. Deep play is all absorbing – and closely related to what I call "dark play."

Clifford **Geertz**

Deep Play

Bentham's concept of "deep play" is found in his *The Theory of Legislation*. By it he means play in which the stakes are so high that it is, from his utilitarian standpoint, irrational for men to engage in it at all. For if a man whose fortune is a thousand pounds (or ringgits [Balinese money]) wagers five hundred of it on an even bet, the marginal utility of the pound he stands to win is clearly less than the marginal disutility of the one he stands to lose. In genuine deep play, this is the case for both parties. They are both in over their heads. Having come together in the search of pleasure they have entered into a relationship which will bring the participants, considered collectively, net pain rather than net pleasure. [. . . D]espite the force of Bentham's analysis men do engage in such play, both passionately and often, and even in the face of law's revenge. For Bentham and those who think as he does (nowadays mainly lawyers, economists, and a few psychiatrists), the explanation is [. . .] that such men are irrational – addicts, fetishists, children, fools, savages, who need only to be protected against themselves. But for the Balinese, though naturally they do not formulate it in so many words, the explanation lies in the fact that in such play, money is less a measure of utility, had or expected, than it is a symbol of moral import, perceived or imposed. [. . .] In deep ones [play], where the amounts of money are great, much more is at stake than material gain: namely, esteem, honor, dignity, respect – in a word, though in Bali a profoundly freighted word, status.

1973, *The Interpretation of Cultures*, 432–33

Jeremy Bentham (1748–1832): English philosopher, founder of utilitarianism whose basic tenet is that the aim of society ought to be to provide the greatest good to the greatest number. His most influential work, *Introduction to the Principles of Morals and Legislation* (1789), focused on the ethics of law, language, and government.

"Playing in the dark" means that some of the players don't know they are playing. It is connected to maya–lila and to the feeling of being caught in the toils of fate or chance. It involves fantasy, risk, luck, daring, invention, and deception. Dark play may be entirely private, known to the player alone. Or it can erupt suddenly, a bit of microplay, seizing the player(s) and then as quickly subsiding – a wisecrack, burst of frenzy, delirium, or deadly risk. Dark play subverts order, dissolves frames, and breaks its own rules – so much so that the playing itself is in danger of being destroyed, as in spying, double-agentry, con games, and stings. Unlike carnivals or ritual clowns whose inversions of established order is sanctioned by the authorities, dark play is truly subversive, its agendas always hidden. Dark play's goals are deceit, disruption, excess, and gratification. In my courses on play, I invite students to write examples of dark play from their own lives. Here are four responses (used with permission):

1 *Female*: When I am feeling especially depressed or angry about the world and my life, I play a form of "Russian Roulette" with New York City traffic. I cross streets without pausing to see if it is safe to do so or not. [. . .] At the time of playing there is a thrill in abandoning precautions and in toying with the value of life and death.

2 *Female*: I was on vacation with a friend who is not my boyfriend. During a bus ride I was teaching him a song when an old man turned to us, interested in where we came from, etc. Instantly the two of us made up a romance story of where we met, why we were there on vacation, and what we were planning to do – none of which was true. Since we both felt we were being approached as "a couple" we reacted to it as such, having a lot of fun doing so.

3 *Male*: When I was 15 years old, together with three friends, I spent some nights in a Youth Hostel, a 17th century castle, in a small fishing village in Holland. One night, the four of us discovered a trapdoor in the ceiling of the bathroom. We were convinced that this led to the roof of the castle. We saw many signs stating that the roof was off limits. For us, those signs were orders to get to the roof. We sneaked out of the dorm, went through the trapdoor and found some stairs. It was pitch dark, we could only find our way by touch. When we got to the roof, a very strong wind was blowing. We yelled into the storm, screamed obscenities, and cursed the Hostel managers who made us all pray before each meal. We cursed the clouds, the Virgin Mary, the village. We yelled at the fishing boats we knew were out on the sea. "Go down, go down!" one of us yelled. "Sink boats, sink!" It became a chant. "Sink, boats, sink!" Just before dawn we were back in the dorm. We felt proud as hell. At 8 a.m. we were thrown out of the Hostel. In a cafe, tired, sleepy but still excited, we drank our coffee. A local newspaper lay on the table. The headline said, "Two Fishermen Drown When Boat Sinks." One of us began to cry. I did not believe then, and do not believe now, and will never believe that we caused this accident. But it had an effect. For the next couple of days we did not play; hardly joked.

4 *Female*: I was 16 years old and on vacation at Yosemite with my father. I climbed out over the guardrail to get a better view of the waterfall. When I realized that my father was crying for me to come back, I went to the very edge and did an arabesque. I continued balancing on one leg until he got onto his knees, crying, begging for me to come back. Ten years later, in the Sierra Nevada range, I repeated the same act in front of my husband who shouted at me to think of our daughter as a motherless child. My initial inspiration for dancing on the edge was in both cases the thrill of the beauty and the danger of the dance. My father's and husband's anxiety sharpened the experience for me – the further I got away from them the closer I came to communion with some Other.

Leaving aside psychological interpretations of motives, personal gains, anxieties, desires played out, and so on, what do these examples show?

First, they subvert the metacommunicative message "this is play" that Gregory Bateson posited as necessary for play to begin, continue, and thrive. Second, in dark play, as in Boal's "invisible theatre," some of the players do not know that a game is being played. The drivers of vehicles in New York City, the old man on the bus, the fishermen caught in a storm – they didn't know that they were players in a game. These "non-knowing players" – innocents, dupes, butts, victims – are essential to the playing. In the third example, the chanting boys had no idea that their play might have an effect – and the author still believes that there was no connection between their curse and the sinking fishing boat. Still, a boy cried, the vacation was dampened, and the author still protests he has no such super-power.

The final example is complicated. This scene was played twice, ten years apart, testing first the love of a father and then of a husband. Still later, the dark-player provided me with a photograph of the re-enactment (**see figure 4.17**). The scene was played, replayed, documented, and finally made public. At each iteration it becomes more of a performance. It is a test of love, but also a mocking of love; laughing at it, taunting it. The two life roles, husband and father, were conflated and devalued. The men were manipulated into

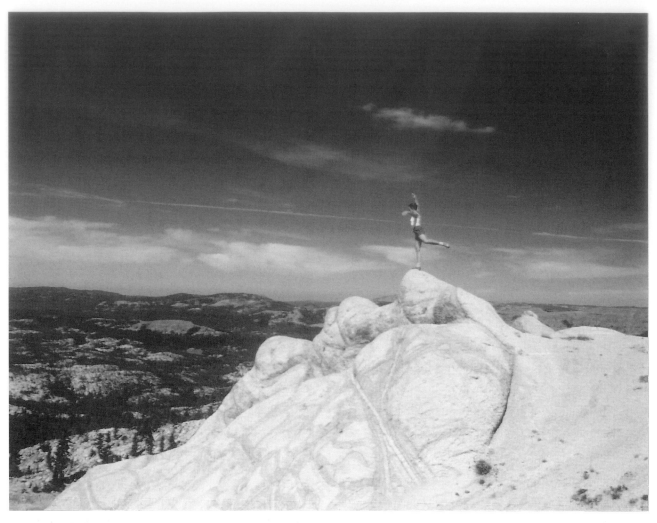

fig 4.17. An episode of dark play re-enacted on a rock at Yosemite National Park, USA. Photograph courtesy of name witheld.

begging the dancer to stop playing. The father shed tears; the husband reminded the dancer of her serious responsibilities as a mother. None of this brought the dancer back from the edge – in fact, quite the opposite: it heightened the "thrill of the beauty and the danger of the dance." The more the men were terrified, the more ecstatic the dancer. All anxiety left her and spilled into them. What was important to her was dancing on the edge. Liberated, she relished her spiritual experience. In having power over herself, she gained power over the two "patriarchal males" in her life (up to that point). And in giving me the photo for this book? A final trump card sending the message to those who know and remember, a secret few.

Why do people create and enact dark play? Are children innocent of such play? Sutton-Smith offers examples of what he calls the "masks of play" – play that conceals its purposes,

even its existence. Children no less than adults engage in this kind of play. In school, camp, prison, and church – wherever the eyes of authority gaze down on them – kids find ways around the rules. They make April Fool's jokes, play in the toilet, whisper, doodle, make faces, mock adults, and so on. They form clubs, gangs, and cliques. They even develop careful strategies in order to shoot up a school.

All these activities – the pleasant, the provocative, and the terrifying – can be understood as playing, as ways of establishing autonomous social orders and hierarchies, of exploring or exploding the limits of power, of resisting the adult world that apparently so dominates them. Some of these children grow up to be spies, police, colonels, conmen, and crooks – all with sensible reasons for making dark play. But why do others engage in it? Assuming a new or alternative identity, even briefly, is very important. Masking, cloaking one's ordinary self just to get away from the humdrum, is also important. Much of the role-playing over the internet is this kind of dark play. Sometimes a person puts herself at risk to test her luck, to prove her value, to enact a special destiny. In life-risk play such as crossing the street without looking, one's "immortality" is tested. In dancing on the edge, one leaves behind the mundane, hears it screaming and begging, and soars into a realm of spirituality. In disguise-play such as fooling the old man on the bus, alternative selves are given license. The gratification and thrill of dark play involves everything from physical risk-taking to inventing new selves to engaging one's inner self to communion with the Other. There is something excitingly liberating about this kind of playing.

In dark play sometimes even the conscious players are not certain if they are playing or not. What begins as a game, as a gesture of bravado, can quickly get out of hand. More than a few have died on a dare. Survivors may claim they were "just fooling around." On the other hand, actions that were not play when they were performed become play retroactively when the events are retold. What happened does not change, but when a person recounts a "narrow escape," for example, what was deadly serious in the doing becomes playful in the retelling.

Conclusion

In this chapter, I've examined play "as" performance, and play "is" performance. When animals and humans play, they exaggerate and show off in order to impress playmates as well as non-players who are watching (this is true of chimpanzees, gorillas, and monkeys as well as of humans). In most kinds of play, in order to play successfully, all the players must agree to play. Players send metacommunicative messages that say, "We are playing." In some ways, play is very much like ritual and theatre. Play is often an orderly sequence of actions performed in specified places for known durations of time. Much playing is narrational, with winners and losers, conflict, and the arousal and display of emotion. But there is also playing that is less formal-bursts of microplay that can lessen the tensions in a room or relieve the boredom of routinized work. Some play is "dark," making fun of people, deceiving them, or leading them on. One group of play theorists sees playing as the foundation of human culture, art and religion especially. Others regard play as an ambivalent activity both supporting and subverting social structures and arrangements. However one looks at it, play and playing are fundamentally performative.

THINGS TO THINK ABOUT

1. Have you ever engaged in "dark play"? What examples can you think of from your own life? What is the relationship between your own experience of "dark play" and the theories of Geertz and Bateson?

2. What is the relationship between flow, discussed in this chapter, and communitas, discussed in chapter 2?

THINGS TO DO

1. Teach a group from the class how to play a game you used to play as a child. Don't theorize, but rather attempt to convey only what's required to play the game. After playing, discuss the structure of the game. Does it have a beginning, middle, and end? How do you know when to stop? Are the rules stable? Or are they obscure and subject to change? What signals are used to send the message "This is play"? Did the group find the game enjoyable? Why or why not?

2. In a small group, using Augusto Boal's "Invisible Theatre technique," prepare a brief scene: an argument, an unexpected meeting of two people who have not seen each other for years, the discovery that your purse or wallet is missing . . . anything at all. Perform your scene in a public place without letting on that it is "theatre." Have a designated observer or observers note how the scene is received by people. Afterwards, discuss the reactions. Was what you performed theatre? If not, why not? What was it if not theatre?

SUGGESTED READINGS

Bateson, Gregory. "A Theory of Play and Fantasy." *Steps to an Ecology of Mind*. New York: Ballantine Books, 1972. 177–93.

Csikszentmihalyi, Mihaly. "A Theoretical Model for Enjoyment." *Beyond Boredom and Anxiety*. San Francisco: Jossey-Bass, 1975. 35–54.

Handelman, Don. "Play and Ritual: Complementary Frames of Meta-Communication." *It's a Funny Thing, Humour*. Eds. H. J. Chapman and H. Fout. London: Pergamon Press, 1977. 185–92.

Huizinga, Johan. "The Nature and Significance of Play as a Cultural Phenomenon." *Homo Ludens*. Boston: Beacon Press, 1970. 1–28.

Sutton-Smith, Brian. *The Ambiguity of Play*. Cambridge: Harvard University Press, 1997. 1–17, 214–31.

5 PERFORMATIVITY

A Term Hard to Pin Down

Performativity is everywhere – in daily behavior, in the professions, on the internet and media, in the arts, and in language. It is a term very difficult to pin down. The words "performative" and "performativity" have a wide range of meanings. Sometimes these words are used precisely. But more often they are used loosely to indicate something that is "like a performance" without actually being a performance in the orthodox or formal sense. "Performative" is both a noun and an adjective. The noun indicates a word or sentence that does something (I will explain this shortly). The adjective inflects what it modifies with performance-like qualities, such as "performative writing" (**see Phelan box**). "Performativity" is an even broader term, covering a whole panoply of possibilities opened up by a world in which differences between media and live events, originals and digital or biological clones, performing onstage and in ordinary life are collapsing. Increasingly, social, political, economic, personal, and artistic realities take on the qualities of performance. In this sense, performativity is similar to what I called "as" performance in chapter 2.

In performance studies, performativity points to a variety of topics, among them the construction of social reality including gender and race, the restored behavior quality of performances, and the complex relationship of performance practice to performance theory. Some of these topics are covered in other chapters; some will be dealt with here. In fact, performativity is a major underlying theme of this book taken as a whole. Understanding performativity can be helped by examining certain key terms, theories, and artistic practices:

- Austin's performatives
- Searle's speech acts
- postmodernism
- simulations
- poststructuralism
- constructions of gender
- constructions of race
- connections between performativity and performance art.

Peggy Phelan

Performative Writing

Performative writing is different from personal criticism or autobiographical essay, although it owes a lot to both genres. Performative writing is an attempt to find a form for "what philosophy wishes all the same to say." Rather than describing the performance event in "direct signification," a task I believe to be impossible and not terrifically interesting, I want this writing to enact the affective force of the performance event again, as it plays itself out in an ongoing temporality made vivid by the psychic process of distortion (repression, fantasy, and the general hubbub of the individual and collective unconscious), and made marrow by the muscular force of political repression in all its mutative violence. [. . .]

Performative writing is solicitous of affect even while it is nervous and tentative about the consequences of that solicitation. Alternately bold and coy, manipulative and unconscious, this writing points both to itself and to the "scenes" that motivate it.

1997, *Mourning Sex*, 11–12

Performatives and Speech Acts

The concept of the performative was explained by linguistic philosopher J. L. Austin in lectures delivered in 1955 at Harvard University (posthumously edited and published as *How to Do Things with Words*). Austin coined the word "performative" to describe utterances such as, "I take this woman to be my lawful wedded wife" or "I name this ship the *Queen Elizabeth*" or "I bet you ten dollars it will rain tomorrow" (**see Austin box 1**). In these cases, as Austin notes, "To *say* something is to *do* something." In uttering certain sentences people perform acts. Promises, bets, curses, contracts, and judgments do not describe or represent actions: they are actions. Performatives are an active part of "real life." Even when the heart says "no," if the tongue says "yes" a performative occurs. If the tongue says "I do" at the wedding or "I bet $100" at the poker table, the act sticks. Many performatives combine physical acts and words – pushing chips onto the table, signing the wedding contract, etc. A performative is "infelicitous" (to use Austin's word) if uttered in inappropriate circumstances. Saying "I name you *The Richard*" and smashing a champagne bottle against the bow of a ship I have no business christening does not make it so. The utterances of characters on a stage are also infelicitous.

J. L. **Austin**

The Performative

The term [. . .] "performative" is derived, of course, from "perform" [. . .]: it indicates that the issuing of the utterance is the performing of an action. [. . .] The uttering of the words is, indeed, usually a, or even *the*, leading incident in the performance of the act [. . .].

1962, *How To Do Things With Words*, 6–8

Characters swear, bet, and marry, but the actors do not. The performative utterances of actors speaking as characters are, according to Austin, "parasitic [. . .] etiolations of language" (**see Austin box 2**). In his own way, Austin, like Plato, bans the poets. But within a generation, Jacques Derrida brings them back by pointing out that all utterances are infelicitous. To Derrida, speech in the theatre is a "determined modification" of a "general iterability" (**see Derrida box 1**). By 1972, when Derrida wrote this, the uses of Austin's "performative" had expanded exponentially. Given the collapse of categories that marks the postmodern period, it is not surprising that Austin's term took off on its own in a protean manner (**see Parker and Sedgwick box**).

One of those first to expand Austin's performatives was **John R. Searle** (1932–), who in the 1960s asserted that the basic unit of communication was the "speech act" (**see Searle box**). Yet, like Austin before him, Searle separates "normal real world talk" from "parasitic forms of discourse such as fiction, play acting, etc." Searle and Austin take this position because they don't recognize that art can be a model for rather than a mirror of life. But many people have been for quite

J. L. **Austin**

Theatre the Parasite

[. . .] a performative utterance will [. . .] be *in a peculiar way* hollow or void if said by an actor on the stage, or if introduced in a poem, or spoken in soliloquy. [. . .] Language in such circumstances is in special ways – intelligibly – used not seriously, but in ways *parasitic* upon its normal use – ways which fall under the doctrine of *etiolations* of language. All this we are *excluding* from consideration. Our performative utterances [. . .] are to be understood as issued in ordinary circumstances.

1962, *How To Do Things With Words*, 22

Jacques **Derrida**

Successful Performatives are Impure

For, ultimately, isn't it true that what Austin excludes as anomaly, exception, "non-serious," *citation* (on stage, in a poem, or a soliloquy) is the determined modification of a general citationality – or rather, a general iterability – without which there would not even be a "successful" performative? So that – a paradoxical but unavoidable conclusion – a successful performative is necessarily an "impure" performative [. . .]?

1988 [1972], "Signature, Event, Context," in *Limited Inc.*, 17

some time very aware of the collapsing differences between "fiction" and the "real." This is not only, or even mostly, a matter of theory, but a practice in performance art, media, film, the internet, experimental theatre, and the visual arts. In fact, notions of performativity permeate culture.

Popular films of the late 1990s, such as *Wag the Dog*, *The Truman Show*, *Ed TV*, and *The Blair Witch Project* explore the very porous membrane separating the "real" from the "staged." The movies are fictions about dissolving the differences between the real and the fictional. Reality television goes much further. Shows such as *Survivor* strive to erase the distinctions between the real and the staged. *Survivor* contestants were drawn from the public (not stars) and

Andrew Parker and
Eve Kosofsky Sedgwick

Defining "Performative"

[. . .W]hile philosophy and theatre now share "performative" as a common lexical item, the term has hardly come to mean "the same thing" for each. Indeed, the stretch between theatrical and deconstructive meanings of "performative" seems to span the polarities of, at either extreme, the *extroversion* of the actor, the *introversion* of the signifier. [. . .I]n another range of usages, a text like [Jean-François] Lyotard's *The Postmodern Condition* uses "performativity" to mean an extreme of something like *efficiency* – while, again, the deconstructive "performativity" of Paul de Man or J. Hillis Miller seems to be characterized by the *dis*linkage precisely of cause and effect between the signifier and the world. At the same time, it's worth keeping in mind that even in deconstruction, more can be said of performative speech acts than that they are ontologically dislinked or introversively nonreferential. [. . .The performative is marked by] the torsion, the mutual perversion, as one might say, of reference and performativity.

1995, *Introduction to Performativity and Performance*, 2–3

John R. Searle (1932–): American philosopher who was a student of J. L. Austin at Oxford University in the 1950s. Searle developed Austin's ideas in *Speech Acts* (1969) and *Expression and Meaning* (1979). His more recent work concerns theories of consciousness and artificial intelligence.

marooned on a desert island. Each week the group voted on who to throw out until there was only one person left, The Survivor – winner of a million-dollar prize. By August, 2000, more than 30 million viewers tuned in.

What were they getting? The thrill of the real, sexiness, type-casting, unpredictability, and the amateur status of the contestants – the "That could be me!" factor? Cameras were always rolling, even if manned by the contestants. The film was edited in the network studio facilities to ensure a high level of drama and the expurgation of "inappropriate" material. Contestants knew that if a real emergency arose, they would be evacuated. Because their own votes would

John R. Searle

Speech Acts

The unit of linguistic communication is not, as has generally been supposed, the symbol, word or sentence, or even the token of the symbol, word or sentence, but rather the production or issuance of the symbol or word or sentence in the performance of the speech act. To take the token as a message is to take it as a produced or issued token. More precisely, the production or issuance of a sentence token under certain conditions is a speech act, and speech acts [. . .] are the basic or minimal units of linguistic communication.

1969, *Speech Acts*, 16

determine who the final survivors would be, tensions rose as the weeks went by. What *Survivor* contestants were enacting was not improvised theatre, exactly; nor was it real life, exactly.

In the midst of all this a "really real" life drama exploded on the scene. Dr. **Ronald S. Shemenski** (1942–), the only doctor stationed at the Rothera Research Station, Antarctica, diagnosed himself with a serious gall-bladder problem. A made-to-order media event was at hand. Brave pilots volunteered to fly from southern Chile to Antarctica in wintery darkness, land on snow, rest briefly, and evacuate the ailing medic. (He later had his gall bladder removed and his heart arteries unclogged.) Millions watched this "real-life" survivor narrative. Shemenski himself told CBS news hours after arriving in Chile, "If I had my druthers, I'd be at the Pole. But the window of opportunity to get me out was now. I couldn't sit around and wait." Because Shemenski-type opportunities come only once in a blue moon, media producers will cook up new *Survivor* look-alikes until public interest in the genre diminishes. By that time, some other kind of performance will emerge into the spotlight.

Ronald S. Shemenski (1942–): American physician whose rescue from Antarctica made headlines in early 2001.

Sponsoring "real-life" adventures to gain market share and increase revenues is not new. The genre developed hand-in-glove with the growth of newspapers, magazines, and other media that sprang up to create and then satisfy an appetite for vicarious excitement. In the nineteenth century there was the additional thrill of participating in the "fruits" of colonialism. Take, for example, the manufactured expedition into central Africa of British adventurer **Henry Morgan Stanley** (1841–1904), assigned by *The New York Herald* to find "missing" explorer **David Livingstone** (1813–73). After months of looking, Stanley located Livingstone in 1871 at Ujiji on Lake Tanganyika. At the moment of first meeting, Stanley tells us he spoke the famous one-liner, "Dr. Livingstone, I presume." But did he, actually? We have only Stanley's word for it. Stanley's expedition was cooked up and exploited by *The Herald*, who owned and published Stanley's account. The colonial practice of entering the "exotic," "primitive," or "unknown" (to the West) continues to this day under the auspices of such organizations as the National Geographic Society. Because treating human societies in the manner of the nineteenth- to mid-twentieth-century adventurers is no longer appropriate, attention has refocused on wildlife and the challenges of "nature" – the life-cycle of a pride of lions on the Serengeti, the perils of scaling Mt. Everest, or the challenge of raising unbroken dinnerware from the *Titanic*. The impulse remains the same, while vastly improved technology allows for better "on-the-scene" participation by distant viewers.

Henry Morgan Stanley (1841–1904): English travel writer and explorer who conducted a highly publicized (and successful) search through Central Africa in 1870–71 to find fellow English explorer **David Livingstone (1813–73).**

The news programs about the Shemenski rescue had a lot in common with the Stanley–Livingstone story and with entertainment programs. The Shemenski story suited our times: condensed, episodic, and visual. News came via airplane and satellite, rather than through trekking and hand-delivered manuscripts. There was the "human interest" side of things, controlled reports of dangers and progress, a growing tension about the outcome, and a happy ending. *Survivor* had all this plus the thrill of a sports-like elimination contest. Not "real sports," but rather more like professional wrestling with its over-stuffed heroes and villains cheered and jeered by deliriously excited fans. Over time, *Survivor* viewers picked their favorites to love, pity, admire, and hate. Is the contest real or rigged? We know that the outcome of a stage drama is settled before the curtain rises. The public expects sports to be untampered with – although the cricket scandal of 2001 and the ongoing mess around steroid-use throw into doubt the legitimacy of all sports.

The fact is, the tons of money in play on television, and the fierce struggle among networks for viewer share, have eroded the walls once separating "entertainment," "news," and "sports." It's all entertainment now – ironically, that's where "reality" is located. What is true of TV is doubly so on the internet, where 24-hour webcams broadcast a continuous stream of "reality" (**see figure 5.1**). Here there are fewer

fig 5.1. The view one day in 2001 from an always-broadcasting Amsterdam webcam. The image changes every 30 seconds. Take a look yourself at www.xs4all.nl/ ~shs/webcam.html. Of course, there are hundreds of other webcams to choose from.

taboos than on television. Sex and nakedness are big attractions. But almost anything will do. The prototype of this genre of entertainment was the months' long broadcast of the ongoing lives of the Loud family of southern California in 1971. People asked then, and the question remains salient, does the presence of the camera change behavior or convert someone's home from a "real-life" venue into a "theatre"? It is a sociological application of Heisenberg's indeterminacy principle where the observation affects the outcome. The Louds and *Survivor* are managed by the networks. But the little guy is in on the action too. Starting in the mid-1990s there arose a profusion of internet sites such as "JenniCam" (**see figure 5.2**). Although Jenni says she is not an actress or entertainer, on her site she advertises the *JenniShow*, a bi-weekly video webcast hosted by Jenni herself (**see Ringley box**). Viewers can send emails to Jenni, who reads them during the show. Many of these "real-life" sites are "subscriber only" – you have to pay to watch – converting "just living life" into a business. Sometimes others are paid to watch us, even if we do not want to be watched, using surveillance cameras installed by corporations and police. The panopticon was first a means for guards to surveil prisons. Does the ubiquity of the looking eye make the world into one vast prison (as Hamlet believed Denmark to be)? Viewing the output of these cameras – sometimes even broadcasting footage on television or over the internet – converts ordinary or illicit actions into "performances for the camera." Almost anyone can avail themselves of a "photo op" once reserved for stars and politicians. Where will the line separating private from public be drawn? Can it be drawn anywhere? The line is disappearing, if it has not already vanished. These are situations addressed, but by no means resolved, by theories of performativity.

fig 5.2. Jenni makes a face for the camera – her webcams are always turned on. Check Jenni out at www.jennicam.org. But to see the pictures at a faster rate you have to join. As Jenni says on her homepage, "JenniCam is not suitable for children."

Postmodernism

Performativity as understood by performance studies exists as part of, or in close relation to, the postmodern. One of the decisive qualities of postmodernism is the application of the "performance principle" to all aspects of social and artistic life. Performance is no longer confined to the stage, to the arts, and to ritual. Performativity is everywhere linked to the interdependence of power and knowledge. An early authority on postmodernism, Jean-François Lyotard, argues that power depends on the optimization of performance (in the business and technical senses), a kind of performativity that is self-legitimating (**see Lyotard box**). Theorist **Linda Hutcheon** (1947–) takes the opposite position. Focusing not on business, government, or technology but on postmodern art, Hutcheon sees artists continuing the subversive project of the historical avant-garde by undermining the basic principles of bourgeois liberalism (**see Hutcheon box**). **Fredric Jameson** (1934–) believes that in postmodern times "the market has become a substitute for itself and fully as much a commodity as any of the items it includes within itself" (**see Jameson box**). These views are not easily reconcilable with each other – but this ability to embrace contradiction and eclecticism is a hallmark of the postmodern.

Jean-François Lyotard

Jennifer Ringley

JenniCam

JenniCam is, to put it simply, a sort of window into a virtual human zoo. My name is Jennifer Ringley, and I am not an actor, or dancer, or entertainer. I am a computer geek with the good fortune to be able to work from home. I design, code, and administer this website and manage the company that keeps the site alive. [. . .] The "JenniCam" is a series of cameras located throughout the house Dex and I live in, cameras that take images of my house all day long, every day. [. . .] So feel free to watch, or not, as you desire. I am here to be loved or hated. I am here simply to be me.

2001, from www.jennicam.org

Performativity and Power

This is how legitimation by power takes shape. Power is not only good performativity, but also effective verification and good verdicts. It legitimates science and the law on the basis of their efficiency, and legitimates this efficiency on the basis of science and law. It is self-legitimating, in the same way a system organized around performance maximization seems to be. Now it is precisely this kind of context control that a generalized computerization of society may bring. The performativity of an utterance, be it denotative or prescriptive, increases proportionally to the amount of information about its referent one has at one's disposal. Thus the growth of power, and its self-legitimation, are now taking the route of data storage and accessibility, and the operativity of information.

The relationship between science and technology is reversed. [. . .] Research funds are allocated by States, corporations, and nationalized companies in accordance with this logic of power growth. Research sectors that are unable to argue that they contribute even indirectly to the optimization of the system's performance are abandoned by the flow of capital and doomed to senescence. The criterion of performance is explicitly invoked by the authorities to justify their refusal to subsidize certain research centers.

1984, *The Postmodern Condition*, 47

Linda Hutcheon (1947–): Canadian literary critic, cultural theorist, and professor of English at the University of Toronto. Author of *Narcissistic Narrative* (1980), *A Theory of Parody* (1985), and *A Poetics of Postmodernism* (1988).

Linda **Hutcheon**

Postmodern Human-made Truths

Postmodern art similarly asserts and then deliberately undermines such principles as value, order, meaning, control, and identity that have been the basic premises of bourgeois liberalism. Those humanistic principles are still operative in our culture, but for many they are no longer seen as eternal and unchallengeable. The contradictions of both postmodern theory and practice are positioned within the system and yet work to allow its premises to be seen as fictions or as ideological structures. This does not necessarily destroy their "truth" value, but it does define the conditions of that "truth." Such a process reveals rather than conceals the tracks of the signifying systems that constitute our world – that is, systems constructed by us in answer to our needs. However important the systems are, they are not natural, given, or universal. The very limitations imposed by the post-modern view are also perhaps ways of opening new doors: perhaps now we can better study the interrelations of social, aesthetic, philosophical, and ideological constructs. In order to do so, postmodernist critique must acknowledge its own position as an ideological one.

1988, *A Poetics of Postmodernism*, 13

Fredric Jameson (1934–): Marxist cultural critic and professor of Comparative Literature at Duke University. Author of *The Political Unconscious* (1981) and *Postmodernism or the Cultural Logic of Late Capitalism* (1991).

Fredric **Jameson**

What is Postmodernism?

So, in postmodern culture, "culture" has become a product in its own right; the market has become a substitute for itself and fully as much a commodity as any of the items it includes within itself: modernism was still minimally and intentionally the critique of the commodity and the effort to make it transcend itself. Postmodernism is the consumption of sheer commodification as a process. [. . .] Culturally, the precondition [of postmodernism] is to be found [. . .] in the enormous social and psychological transformations of the 1960s. [. . . The] economic preparation of postmodernism or late capitalism began in the 1950s, after the wartime shortages of consumer goods and spare parts had been made up, and new products and new technologies (not least those of the media) could be pioneered. On the other hand, the psychic *habitus* of the new age demands the absolute break, strengthened by a generational rupture, achieved more properly in the 1960s.

[. . .] As the word itself suggests, this break is most often related to notions of the waning or extinction of the hundred-year-old modern movement (or to its ideological or aesthetic repudiation). Thus abstract expressionism in painting, existentialism in philosophy, the final forms of representation in the novel, the films of the great *auteurs*, or the modernist school of poetry [. . .] all are now seen as the final, extraordinary flowering of a high-modernist impulse which is spent and exhausted with them.

[. . . The] fundamental feature of [. . .] post-modernism [is] the effacement [. . .] of the older (essentially high-modernist) frontier between high culture and so-called mass or commercial culture, and the emergence of new kinds of texts infused with the forms, categories, and contents of that very culture industry so passionately denounced by all the ideologues of the modern [. . .].

> Nor should the break in question be thought of as a purely cultural affair: indeed, theories of the postmodern – whether celebratory or couched in the language of moral revulsion and denunciation – bear a family resemblance to all those more ambitious sociological generalizations which, at much the same time, bring us the news of the arrival and inauguration of a whole new type of society, most famously baptized "postindustrial society" [. . .] but often also designated consumer society, media society, information society, electronic society or high tech, and the like.
>
> 1991, *Postmodernism, Or, The Cultural Logic of Late Capitalism*, x, xx, 1, 2–3

Therefore, it is not easy to summarize postmodernism because it means one thing to dancers, several other things to cultural critics and philosophers, and still something else to architects. Defining and theorizing the postmodern began in the turbulent 1960s with attacks on the "master narratives" of modernism: the nation-state, natural law, rational logic, patriarchal authority, mandatory coherence, and beginning-middle-and-end stories. But after the deconstruction of the master narratives, then what? Fragmentation, pastiche, relativism, local truths, delight in contradictions?

On the one hand, the media rush in with a host of "temporary master narratives." Pundits galore make sense out of the day's events, especially political and economic news. Anchors intone, and feature reporters dramatize, the presentation of ordinary life. The arts themselves take a back seat because ordinary life is framed so "artistically." Authored dramas are relegated to public networks or less-viewed specialty channels. Widely watched news channels propagate tug-the-heart human-interest stories even as they make the ups and downs of the stock market into a soap-opera cliffhanger. Instead of this resulting in a single narration or even a coherent bundle of narrations, the media offer hundreds of fragmented stories and compressed dramas. Television commercials are 15- or 30-second mini-dramas, exquisite from the technical point of view, emotional and convincing – but ultimately empty except in stimulating the urge to buy. Surfing the internet brings viewers into contact with multiple texts and links, most sporting hyperactive banner ads blinking or beeping for interaction.

Recognizing, analyzing, and theorizing the convergence and collapse of clearly demarcated realities, hierarchies, and categories is at the heart of postmodernism. Such a convergence or collapse is a profound departure from traditional Western performance theory. From Plato and Aristotle forward, theorists have agreed that theatre "imitates," "reflects," "represents," or "expresses" individual actions and social life. As Hamlet told the Players, the purpose of theatre is "to hold the mirror up to nature." Representational art of all kinds is based on the assumption that "art" and "life" are not only separate but of different orders of reality: life is primary, art secondary. But developments in photography, film, and digital media overturned traditional theories. Questions arose concerning exactly what was an "original" – even if there could be such a thing as an original.

Before photography, there was "nature" and there was "painting." Copies could be made of paintings, but these constituted either authorized reproductions or forgeries. With the advent of photography came the negative (which was not the photo but that from which the "positive" or photograph was made). How could either a negative or a positive made from the negative be an original? And if a particular positive was *an* original, which one – the first made from the negative, the best from a technical point of view? A question that was relatively easy with regard to painting became very troubled in photography. **Walter Benjamin** (1892–1940), writing about "the work of art in the age of mechanical reproduction," took up this problem. If there were no original, there could be no "presence," no "unique existence," and no "aura" surrounding the art work (**see Benjamin box**). This demystification of art – and by implication of all cultural products, including the state and religion – was not at all bad. It created the possibility for a transfer of power from elites to the masses.

Walter Benjamin (1892–1940): German leftist essayist and intellectual who committed suicide while fleeing from the Nazis. His writings – including *Illuminations* (1968), *Understanding Brecht* (1973), and *Reflections* (1986) – were collected well after his death.

But Benjamin had no sense of the further complications introduced by digital media and bio-technology. If reproduction threatens the "authority of the object," think how much greater the threat to that authority when there is no original at all. Digital images are not present, emit no aura, and cannot be authenticated. That is because these images are actually binary codes capable of generating any number of identical images or anything else specified by the program. Cloning is roughly the same idea applied to biology. In all these cases – the painting, photo, digital image, clone – "nature" still exists as separate from, or at least prior to,

Walter Benjamin

Authenticity, Presence, Aura

In principle, a work of art has always been reproducible. Manmade artifacts can always be imitated by man. Replicas were made by pupils in practice of their craft, by masters for diffusing their works, and finally, by third parties in the pursuit of gain. Mechanical reproduction of a work of art, however, represents something new. [. . .]

Even the most perfect reproduction of a work of art is lacking in one element: its presence in time and space, its unique existence at the place where it happens to be. This unique existence of the work of art determined the history to which it was subject throughout the time of its existence. This includes the changes which it may have suffered in physical condition over the years as well as the various changes in its ownership. [. . .]

The authenticity of a thing is the essence of all that is transmissible from its beginning, ranging from its substantive duration to its testimony to the history which it has experienced. Since the historical testimony rests on the authenticity, the former, too, is jeopardized by reproduction [. . .]. And what is really jeopardized when the historical testimony is affected is the authority of the object.

One might subsume the eliminated element in the term "aura" and go on to say: that which withers in the age of mechanical reproduction is the aura of the work of art. This is a symptomatic process whose significance points beyond the realm of art. One might generalize by saying: the technique of reproduction detaches the reproduced object from the domain of tradition. By making many reproductions it substitutes a plurality of copies for a unique existence.

1969 [1936] *Illuminations*, 218, 220–1

production" are owned and controlled by a very few — a true corporate-military-government complex. It is not easy to tell whether experimental artists are resisting or aiding the corporations. Some of the most creative performance artists are pushing the conflation further, experimenting with "cyborg" bodies (amalgams of the biological, the mechanical, and the digital). I will discuss some of these experiments at the end of this chapter.

Simulation

What Benjamin was leaning toward, but what he did not possess the theoretical tools to explore, was "simulation." With simulation representation ends, and reproduction (cloning, digital and biological) takes over. Jean Baudrillard foresaw this in the early 1980s (**see Baudrillard box 1**). Simulation as the concept continues to evolve in the twenty-first century is closely related to "reality" television and

Jean Baudrillard

The Phases of Imaging

These are the successive phases of the image:

– it is the reflection of a basic reality
– it masks and perverts a basic reality
– it masks the *absence* of a basic reality
it bears no relation to any reality whatever: it is its own pure simulacrum.

In the first case, the image is a *good* appearance – the representation is of the order of sacrament. In the second, it is an *evil* appearance – of the order of a spell. In the third, it *plays at being* an appearance – it is of the order of sorcery. In the fourth, it is no longer in the order of appearance at all, but of simulation.

1983, *Simulations*, 11–12

whatever comes after. But these classic distinctions between "nature" and "art" are getting more difficult to make. It is not only changes in philosophical theories that blur the boundaries. "Integration" is a powerful movement at the highest levels of centralized power. Big business long ago moved in to control the means of information production. On the margins dissident individuals can put up what they want on their own websites. But the "means of digital

internet sites. A simulation is neither a pretense nor an imitation. It is a replication of . . . itself as another. That makes simulations perfect performatives. A cloned sheep or a U-2 song distributed digitally over the internet is not a "copy" but an "original" in a theoretically infinite series. Or it is a "copy" in a theoretically infinite series. There is no difference between "copy" and "original." The decision about whether to call the digitized data an original or a copy is a matter of ideology, not of any difference between the so-called original and the so-called copy. One can determine the "first" in chronological and even legal terms, as the courts have done; but this determination depends on knowledge outside the simulation. There is nothing in it that tells whether it was first, fifth, or . . . nth.

A simulation is not the enactment of a fiction, as when an actress plays Ophelia. It is not even a scam over the internet where thousands are convinced of the existence of a little girl dying of leukemia who really didn't exist or of a CBS billboard seen by tens of millions which also didn't exist (**see Kuczynski box and Hafner box 1**). These are hoaxes. A simulation is not a hoax but something in which the appearance in itself is the actuality. It is possible, of course, to progress from pretending to acting to performing to simulating. As Baudrillard points out, a person pretending to be sick knows she is not really sick, but someone simulating sickness actually produces the symptoms of the illness and in so doing "is" sick (**see Baudrillard box 2**). Once the symptoms appear there is no way to tell someone who is "sick" from someone who is sick. The quotation marks can be added only extrinsically (by knowing that a simulation is taking place). Phenomenologically, the distinction between real and feigned disappears — but in a peculiar way. In the simulated illness, and like cases, the imaginary causes the actual. As I will point out in the next chapter, this is not so different from what shamans undergo. The shaman does not feign the illness she suffers in sympathy with the patient — the shaman simulates the illness with such thoroughness that she gets sick herself.

Alex Kuczynski

Simulated Billboard Advertising

Inserting digital images has become increasingly common in sports and entertainment programming — usually to insert advertising and corporate logos and first down markers in football [. . .]. News show logos that appear real are being inserted on the sides of structures, like the General Motors building, on the back of horse-drawn carriages in Central Park, in the fountain outside of the Plaza Hotel, and [. . .] in the center of Wollman [ice-skating] Rink.

In some instances, the logo clearly resembles a large billboard advertising CBS news. "We were looking for some way to brand the neighborhood with the CBS logo," said Steve Friedman, the executive producer of "The Early Show." [. . .] "It's a great way to do things without ruining the neighborhood. Every day we have a different way of using it, whether it's logos or outlines. And we haven't even scratched the surface of its uses yet." Mr. Friedman said that the practice did not press the boundaries of ethical guidelines for CBS News.

2000, "On CBS News, Some of What You
See Isn't There", 1–2

Katie Hafner

Death and Life on the Internet

On May 14 [2001], Kaycee Nicole Swenson, an effervescent 19-year-old, died from complications surrounding leukemia, which she had been battling for nearly two years. From her home in Kansas, Kaycee, an unyieldingly optimistic high school basketball star, had chronicled her remissions and relapses in her online diary, or Weblog, which she had dubbed "Living Colours."

For nearly a year thousands of people went to the site to follow her travails. Many came to feel as if they knew her, and a few talked with her regularly on the phone. Some sent her gifts. Others with cancer spoke of her as an inspiration. [. . .]

Hundreds of people [. . .] were crushed by the news of her death. "So many people reached out to this beautiful girl who was so positive in the face of adversity," said Saundra Mitchell, a screenwriter in Indianapolis.

But Ms. Mitchell was one of the first to cast doubt on what turned out to be an intricately detailed fabrication. A few days after the death announcement, Debbie Swenson, a 40-year-old homemaker, confessed to having invented the life and death of Kaycee. Ms. Swenson, who has two teenage children and lives in Peabody, Kan., a small town about 50 miles northeast of Wichita, had posed as Kaycee's mother. [. . .]

Ms. Swenson's fabrication was constructed so expertly and made so emotionally compelling that even when faced with evidence that it was not true, many people who were sophisticated Internet veterans set aside their skepticism and continued to believe it. Others put their online expertise to work to ferret out the truth about the fictitious Kaycee. [. . .]

Ms. Swenson said that she believed the Kaycee character had been more helpful than harmful. "A lot of people have problems," she said. "I know I helped a lot of people in a lot of different ways." She could be right. So compelling was Ms. Swenson's creation that powerful online connections were made among those who believed in the Kaycee persona and among those who pulled it apart.

[John Halcyon] Styn, whose gifts to the fictitious Kaycee had included a care package filled with hats to cover her head during periods of baldness, said that he refused to become cynical in the incident's unsettling wake. [. . .] "The fact that she wasn't really there doesn't mean that thousands of people weren't able to trust and give love to a stranger. The fact that the Internet is a medium where people can feel those things is encouraging."

2001, "A Beautiful Life, an Early Death, a Fraud Exposed," 1–2, 5

Jean Baudrillard

Feigning To Have What One Doesn't

To dissimulate is to pretend not to have what one has. To simulate is to feign to have what one hasn't. One implies a presence, the other an absence. But the matter is more complicated, since to simulate is not simply to feign: "Someone who feigns an illness can simply go to bed and make believe he is ill. Someone who simulates an illness produces in himself some of the symptoms" (Littre). Thus, feigning or dissimulating leaves the reality principle intact: the difference is always clear, it is only masked; whereas simulation threatens the difference between the "true" and "false," "real" and "imaginary." Since the simulator produces "true" symptoms, is he ill or not? He cannot be treated objectively either as ill, or as not ill.

1983, *Simulations*, 5

This process can be outlined as:

real life ⟶ pretending ⟶ acting on stage ⟶ simulating ⟶ real life

On the page, the progression moves from left to right, but actually the system loops back into itself with the extreme right, "real life," equal to the extreme left, "real life." The shaman — or any performer similarly self-convinced — performs with such intensity and conviction that she transcends the pretense that first characterizes her performance. One pretends, then acts, then simulates, then arrives back at real life. A kind of experiential mobius strip is performed. Is this second real life "real life" and not real life? How can one tell? This can be a legal-ethical question as much as a philosophical one, as can be seen in a child pornography case argued before the US Supreme Court in 2001 (**see Liptak box**).

These individualized simulations are not the only kind. Other simulations include elaborately designed entertainment environments such as Disney World with its

119

Adam Liptak

Is Simulated Sex Too Real?

In the science-fiction thriller *The Matrix*, Keanu Reeves confronts a future in which computer-generated virtual reality is not only indistinguishable from ordinary experience but also has powerful real-world consequences. Last Monday [22 January 2001], the Supreme Court announced that it would follow Mr. Reeves into the virtual realm by agreeing to hear a case concerning whether uncannily realistic digital simulations of children involved in sexual activity should have real-world consequences of up to 30 years in prison.

The federal law in question criminalizes the creation or possession of fake but sometimes startlingly exact images of children in sexual settings. The Supreme Court will decide whether the law is constitutional and whether, as the American Civil Liberties Union put it in a friend-of-the-court brief, "there is a real difference between touching children sexually and touching computer keys to create images."

The question is a variation on one that has often been before the courts in the digital era: do perfect replicas require different rules? So far, in contexts like the controversy over Napster and the banning of computer code allowing decryption of DVD's, the courts have tended to answer yes. In other words, the better the simulation, the more likely it is to be illegal. [. . .]

Neither the courts nor the experts foresaw the quality of modern digital simulations and the ease with which they can be distributed over the World Wide Web. These developments have caused courts to shut down file-sharing services like Napster and to forbid Internet publications from even linking to Web sites containing code allowing DVD's to be copied.

These technical advances also caused Congress to ban simulated child pornography, based on the indirect real-world consequences of the simulations. The sponsors of the 1996 law said real children are hurt by fake pornography because simulated images may be used to entice real children into participating in sexual activity. They also argued that simulated images may be traded for real ones, thereby driving the market for child pornography generally, and that virtual pornography whets the sexual appetites of pedophiles. [. . .]

Scholars question whether the justifications offered for the law are real or a pretext for suppressing troubling speech. "The fundamental problem," said Prof. Eric M. Freedman, a First Amendment specialist at Hofstra Law School, "is that the statute goes beyond regulating the use of real children in the production of pornography and attempts to suppress the idea of juvenile sexuality. It proceeds on the premise that the underlying idea is so pathological that it should be banned from public discourse."

Joan E. Bertin, the executive director of the National Coalition Against Censorship, agreed. It is implicit in the law, she said, that: "'If you're a viewer, you're a doer.' We don't subscribe to the notion that by looking at or considering an idea that you necessarily endorse it."

2001, "When is a Fake Too Real? It's Virtually Uncertain," 1–2

simulated Mexico, China, Italy, and so on (**see figure 5.3 and Baudrillard box 3**). However, Disney and like theme parks are not much more than stage or movie sets reconfigured to satisfy consumers. So much so that some of the most popular sites are simulations of movie sets, or even working movie sets, as at Universal Studios in Orlando, Florida. Here entrepreneurs designed a simulating machine that simulates a simulating machine. But who's fooled? At a somewhat more sophisticated level of simulation are restored villages such as Colonial Williamsburg or Plimoth Plantation that not only claim to look like what the sites once "really were," but employ trained "interpreters" to replicate

historical persons who once lived there (**see figure 5.4**). Here the purpose is to trade on a national nostalgia in the garb of education. But only children are fooled – and even they not for long.

Where twenty-first century simulations are most effective is at the level of corporate operations, military war games, and scientific experiments. Here simulations are replacing actual events because simulations are cheaper and more reliable than real life, while either yielding reliable information about real life or having known effects on real life. Of course, in movies simulated settings, effects, and characters are commonplace. Some of these, as in video

fig 5.3. Disneyworld in Florida features very sanitized, and commercialized, versions of Mexico, China, Italy, and other nations. The structures are mostly facades, suitable for photographing, leading to interiors that contain restaurants and stores.

Mexico

China

Italy

Jean **Baudrillard**

Disneyland is Simulated

Disneyland is a perfect model of all the entangled orders of simulation. To begin with it is a play of illusions and phantasms: Pirates, the Frontier, Future World, etc. This imaginary world is supposed to be what makes the operation successful. But what draws the crowds is undoubtedly much more the social microcosm, the miniaturized and *religious* reveling in real America, in its delights and drawbacks. [. . .]

The objective profile of America, then, may be traced throughout Disneyland, even down to the morphology of individuals and the crowd. All its values are exalted here, in miniature and comic strip form. Embalmed and pacified. [. . .] Disneyland is there to conceal the fact that it is the "real" country, all of the "real" America, which *is* Disneyland [. . .]. Disneyland is presented as imaginary in order to make us believe that the rest is real, when in fact all of Los Angeles and the America surrounding it are no longer real, but of the order of the hyperreal and of simulation. It is no longer a question of a false representation of reality (ideology), but of concealing the fact that the real is no longer real [. . .].

1983, *Simulations*, 23–25

fig 5.4. A view of Plimoth Plantation, where "it is always 1627" (as the Plantation's website announces). Plimoth is a reconstruction of the Pilgrim settlement in Massachusetts. A reconstruction rather than restoration because none of the original structures survive and the Plantation is near but not exactly at the spot where the Pilgrims lived in the 17th century. Photograph from the 1980s by Richard Schechner.

games, announce their unreality; but many present themselves as actual. As in the child pornography case before the US Supreme Court, it is not possible for a viewer to detect a difference between a "picture of . . . X" and a "picture that is simulated." In these situations the performative is primary.

Japan, barred by its post-Second World War constitution from fielding an army, wages simulated war instead. In an exercise conducted on Mt. Fuji in 2000, 300 Japanese soldiers engaged 100 invading enemy. Commanders watched the battle over closed-circuit television, monitoring every move and exchange of fire. The soldiers were actually on the mountain, but everything else – small arms, artillery, mines, and mortars – was controlled by the computer program. "This was one of the most overwhelming exercises of my career," an officer said. "When you see your soldiers being killed and injured one right after the other, it adds a sense of realism to the drill." The US Army also uses simulations extensively. Hundreds of soldiers in different locations can engage in a tank battle on the same virtual battlefield under very realistic conditions. The army is also working with experts from computer science and Hollywood to perfect simulations of emotionally stressful situations in order to train soldiers to deal with peace-keeping operations and terrorist threats (**see Hafner box 2**). If the simulated can seem real, the opposite is also true – the real can appear to be simulated. Many commentators noted that real war – as fought by the US against Iraq in 1992, or the bombing of Yugoslavia in 1999 – is like a videogame, with "smart bombs," missiles launched from distances of hundreds of miles, and damages "assessed" (scored) by satellite observation.

Katie Hafner

Emotional Simulations for the Military

ARINA DEL REY, Calif. – On a quiet street in a village in the Balkans, an accident suddenly puts an American peacekeeping force to the test. A Humvee has hit a car, and a child who has been injured in the collision lies unmoving on the ground. A medic leans over him. The child's mother cries out. A crowd of local residents gathers in the background. How they will react is anyone's guess. A lieutenant arrives at the scene and is confronted by a number of variables. In addition to the chaos unfolding in the village, a nearby unit is radioing for help. Emotions – not only the lieutenant's own and those of his sergeant, but also those of the panicked mother and the restive townspeople – will clearly play a role in any decision he makes.

This seven-minute situation is a simulation, generated on a large computer screen with sophisticated animation, voice synthesis and voice recognition technology. It is the product of about six months of work here by three research groups at the University of Southern California: the Institute for Creative Technologies, largely financed by the Army to promote collaboration among the military, Hollywood, and computer researchers; the Information Sciences Institute; and the Integrated Media Systems Center. The only human player is the lieutenant. The rest of the characters, including the sergeant who has been conferring with the lieutenant, have been generated by the computer. [. . .]

Such simulations are still experimental. But when they are ready, they will be used at bases around the country to train soldiers and officers alike to make decisions under stress. The University of Southern California exercise illustrates the latest challenge among researchers: to focus on the more unpredictable side of the human psyche, simulating emotions and the unexpected effects that panic, stress, anxiety and fear can have on actions and decisions when an officer or a soldier is deep in the fog of war.

"How does a hand-grenade explosion a few feet away from you motivate you if you've just been marching 16 hours in tremendous heat?" asked Dr. Barry G. Silverman, an engineering professor at the University of Pennsylvania. Of course, video and computer games are the closest most people come to experiencing situations like that. In fact, Dr. Silverman said one of his students had recently asked him why he even bothered with his research when there are games like "Age of Empires," Microsoft's popular warfare strategy series. The similarities, Dr. Paul S. Rosenbloom, a computer scientist who is deputy director of the Intelligence Systems Division at the Information Sciences Institute, acknowledged, are obvious. "You're in an environment and interacting with characters trying to accomplish something," he said. "The difference is in the underlying technology."

But there are also important distinctions. Simulations like those he works on, he said, are more concerned with trying to understand how people really react in a variety of circumstances. "It can react appropriately to you under a wide range of things you might do and essentially intelligently adapt its behavior," he said. "There are no computer games that have anywhere near that flexibility. There aren't characters who have a deep understanding of a situation." [. . .]

The growing interest among researchers in these kinds of simulations comes with the rise in computer processing power and the growing sophistication of psychological theories. [. . .] Dr. Silverman said that not only have new theories emerged on the role of emotions in decision-making, but computer processing has also become fast and inexpensive enough that computers are able to do the complex calculations necessary to model behavior. "The agents can now think in real time and react and have emotions in real time," he said. But the degree to which emotions can be simulated depends on the type of behavior being modeled. The effect of stress or sleep deprivation, for instance, is better understood than, say, panic, fear or anxiety. [. . .]

The exercise simulating the Balkans mission is one step toward introducing emotional individuals into a situation so people can be trained for complex tasks like peacekeeping duties. [. . .] To enhance the realism, the Institute for Creative Technologies, with a $45 million grant from the Army, has built a theatre here with a screen that wraps around roughly half the room. Three projectors and a sound system make the theater so realistic and directional that it can trick the listener into believing that a sound's source is coming from anywhere in the room.

After completing the exercise, a trainee receives an evaluation, said Dr. Bill Swartout, the institute's director of technology. "Depending on the path you took, a particular tape is played," he said. Because there are only a few possible paths in this version of the simulation, he said, it is possible to record the evaluations in advance. As the simulation becomes more sophisticated, there will be more choices for the lieutenant, and software will put the story together on the fly. [. . .]

In one project Dr. Silverman is working on, the human player is the leader of a squad guarding a checkpoint at a bridge. All the other participants are simulations. In the exercise, a school bus approaches, filled with women and children. The bus also holds armed terrorists who are planning an attack. "Throughout the ages," Dr. Silverman said, "we have been taught that emotions are the opposite of rationality and that cold logic is devoid of emotions." But new research shows that most decisions are guided by emotions, he said. "It's ironic, but to build realistic, clever software agents, we are giving them emotions and the capability of emotionally reacting to events and actions."

Dr. Silverman is optimistic about how quickly the new direction in research will prove effective. "It's definitely coming together," he said. "We're at the early stage, and there's a lot more theory than data. It's very easy to program a theory, but much harder to ground that in data and say this actually duplicates how people behave. But the field is moving rapidly forward."

But Dr. Richard W. Pew, a principal scientist at BBN Technologies in Cambridge, Mass., and an expert on military simulations, is less optimistic: "I'm not sanguine that in the next five years we'll be there. People are complicated. You never do exactly the same thing twice. Every situation you face is always a little bit different, so trying to build a model that can reflect the importance of that context is where the challenges are." To make further advances, Dr. Pew said, will require closer cooperation between psychologists and computer scientists. "If we want to be more successful with computer models, we need to go deeper into the psychology of how people perform," he said. "Because many of the models are ginned up by computer scientists who don't know anything about human behavior."

2001, "Get Hold of Yourself Lieutenant," *The New York Times*, 21 June.
From *NY Times* website.

The most extensive use of simulations is in science. During 1999 and 2000, *Science*, the journal of the American Association for the Advancement of Science, published 138 articles reporting research based on simulations used across the whole range of scientific inquiry from genetics, climatology, and molecular biology to astrophysics, medicine, earthquake prediction, and lots more. In fact, simulation has become the most important single tool in scientific research, prediction, and teaching. The rise of simulation is tightly joined to the increasing speed, reduced size, visual abilities, and number-crunching power of computers – computers that "perform better." The result is a conjunction of commercial, military, scientific, and academic operations where the "performance principle" is a concatenation of theatre, power, and knowledge. The leading players include corporate executives, university officials, military brass, and government bureaucrats. The workers – those crunching data into information, developing new simulations, participating in experiments and training – are professors, soldiers, scientists, and a few artists.

Poststructuralism/Deconstruction

Postmodernism and poststructuralism are the bases for academic theories of performativity. These are at odds with the uses of performativity in business, science, and the military. The scholars who developed Austin's ideas were vehemently anti-authoritarian. They wanted to use notions of performativity to subvert established authority. But what's happened is that the techniques of performativity – simulation especially – have been eagerly taken up by the most powerful groups in society and used to enhance their power and control over knowledge. At the same time, academics today still use notions of performativity to subvert authority. How this contradiction will be resolved is not certain.

Postmodernism and poststructuralism must be understood in relation to each other. Postmodernism is a practice in the visual arts, architecture, and performance art. Poststructuralism, a.k.a. "deconstruction," is the academic response to postmodernism. Poststructuralism, a discourse in cultural, linguistic, and philosophical circles, began in France in the 1960s both as a revolt against "structuralism" and in sympathy with the radical student movement that culminated in the strikes and insurrections of 1968. Poststructuralism has never totally lost touch with its radical beginnings, though (as we will see) this has also proven to be a burden as the rest of the world moves on.

Structuralism, closely associated with the "structural linguistics" of **Ferdinand de Saussure** (1857–1913) and **Roman Jakobson** (1896–1982), and led in the 1960s and 1970s by **Claude Lévi-Strauss** (1908–), took as its main program the discovery of universal unconscious structures of language, mind, and culture (**see Lévi-Strauss and Ehrmann boxes**). The structuralists often worked by analyzing cultural practices both "diachronically" (over time) and "synchronically" (as a single structural unit). A favorite device of the structuralists was the use of "binary opposites" to characterize the dialectical tensions of a social system. The poststructuralists deplored the desire to universalize and the use of binary opposites. Both of these, they believed, reduced complex situations to over-simplified models. Furthermore, the poststructuralists felt that structuralism buttressed the status quo socially, politically, and philosophically. Poststructuralists opposed all notions of universals, originals, or firsts. To poststructuralists, every act, every idea, is a performative.

Poststructuralists regard each phenomenon as part of an endless stream of repetitions with no "first voice" of ultimate authority (**see Foucault box 1**). In their insistence on process, poststructuralists are Heraclitean and Nietzschean

---

Ferdinand de Saussure (1857–1913): Swiss linguist, whose posthumously published *Course in General Linguistics* (1916, Eng. 1959) lays the foundation of structural linguistics, as well as of structuralism more generally.

Roman Jakobson (1896–1982): Russian-born linguist. Author of *Fundamentals of Language* (1956), *Studies in Verbal Art* (1971), and *Main Trends in the Science of Language* (1973).

Claude Lévi-Strauss (1908–): French anthropologist, a key figure in the development of structuralism. His works include *The Elementary Structures of Kinship* (1949, Eng. 1969), *Structural Anthropology* (1958, Eng. 1963), *The Savage Mind* (1962, Eng. 1966), and *The Raw and the Cooked* (1964, Eng. 1969).

Claude Lévi-Strauss

The Universal of Structuralism

If, as we believe to be the case, the unconscious activity of the mind consists in imposing forms upon content, and if these forms are fundamentally the same for all minds – ancient and modern, primitive and civilized (as the study of the symbolic function, expressed in language, so strikingly indicates) – it is necessary and sufficient to grasp the unconscious structure underlying each institution and each custom, in order to obtain a principle of interpretation valid for other institutions and other customs, provided of course that the analysis is carried far enough.

1963, *Structural Anthropology*, 21

Jacques Erhmann

What is Structuralism?

What is structuralism? Before being a philosophy, as some tend to see it, it is a method of analysis. Even as such its many facets and different uses make it a subject of various interpretations, debate, even polemics. No simple or single definition applies to it except in very general terms. One could say a structure is a combination and relation of formal elements which reveal their logical coherence within given objects of analysis. Although structuralism can hardly be subsumed in some overall formula, or be given any label which will identify it for public consumption, we can say it is first of all, when applied to the sciences of man, a certain way of studying language problems and the problems of languages.

1966, Introduction to special issue of *Yale French Studies* on Structuralism, 7

– everything is in flux. The flux of experience and history is the battleground for an ongoing power struggle. Who has the authority to speak in the "father's voice" – except there is no father. Just as the Wizard of Oz proves to be an illusion, a magic show manipulated by an ordinary man, so do the great icons of societal power. (An insight that **Jean Genet** [1910–86] expressed as early as 1956 in *The Balcony*.) Unstable "iteration" – repetition, but not quite exactly – replaces stable representation. But by the turn of the new millennium, this idea ran smack into the practice of digital and biological cloning. Thus, on the one hand, postmodern repetition and recombination; on the other, poststructuralist *différance* (to be discussed soon).

Although their discourse is principally about language and takes the form of essays and books, poststructuralists have a very broad view of what constitutes language. "There is

Michel Foucault

A Secret Origin, an Already-Said

We must renounce two linked, but opposite themes. The first involves a wish that it should never be possible to assign, in the order of discourse, the irruption of a real event; that beyond any apparent beginning, there is always a secret origin – so secret and so fundamental that it can never be quite grasped in itself. Thus one is led inevitably [. . .] towards an ever-receding point that is never itself present in any history; this point is merely its own void; and from that point all beginnings can never be more than recommencements or occultation (in one and the same gesture, this *and* that). To this theme is connected another according to which all manifest discourse is secretly based on an 'already-said'; and that this 'already-said' is not merely a phrase that has already been spoken, or a text that has already been written, but a 'never-said,' an incorporeal discourse, a voice as silent as a breath, a writing that is merely the hollow of its own mark. It is supposed therefore that everything that is formulated in discourse was already articulated in that semi-silence that precedes it, which continues to run obstinately beneath it, but which it covers and silences. The manifest discourse, therefore, is really no more than the repressive presence of what it does not say; and this 'not-said' is a hollow that undermines from within all that is said. The first theme sees the historical analysis of discourse as the quest for and the repetition of an origin that eludes all historical determination; the second sees it as the interpretation of 'hearing' an 'already-said' that is at the same time a 'not-said.' We must renounce all those themes whose function is to ensure the infinite continuity of discourse and its secret presence to itself in the interplay of a constantly recurring absence. We must be ready to receive every moment of discourse in its sudden irruption; in that punctuality in which it appears, and in that temporal dispersion that enables it to be repeated, known, forgotten, transformed, utterly erased, and hidden, far from all view, in the dust of books. Discourse must not be referred to the distant presence of the origin, but treated as and when it occurs.

1972, *The Archeology of Knowledge*, 25

Jean Genet (1910–86): French playwright and novelist whose works include *The Maids* (1948, Eng. 1954), *Our Lady of Flowers* (1948, Eng. 1949), *The Thief's Journal* (1949, Eng. 1959), *The Balcony* (1956, Eng. 1958), and *The Blacks* (1958, Eng. 1960).

nothing outside the text," Derrida wrote. But the "text" in Derrida's theory is all of human culture. "Writing," as Derrida has it, comprises an all-inclusive array of cultural expressions and social practices. By "writing" Derrida means more than graphic inscription and literature. He means the entire system of "inscribed" power: laws, rituals, traditions, politics, economic relations, science, the military, and the arts (**see Derrida box** 2). Derrida views cultures as constructed sets of relations, historically founded and always contested. Inscribed power performs its privileges by means of established authorities – police, courts, the military, priesthood, scientists, teachers, and critics. It's no accident that the word "authority" includes the word "author." The

writing produced by the authorities is not "transparent" – a windowpane through which one sees the "true," the "real," or the "natural." All writing enacts agendas of power. Writing doesn't serve power, but the other way around: who writes performs authority. Yet all authority, whatever its proclamation of eternity and universality, is temporary: "inalienable rights," "the 1,000-year Reich," "all roads lead to Rome" – no "writing" is either first or final.

Jacques Derrida

"Writing" and "Deconstruction"

If we take the notion of writing in its currently accepted sense – one which should not – and that is essential – be considered innocent, primitive, or natural, it can only be seen as a *means of communication* [. . .] *extending* enormously, if not infinitely, the domain of oral or gestural communication. [. . .]

Once men are already in the state of "communicating their thoughts," and of doing it by means of sounds [. . .], the birth and progress of writing will follow a line that is direct, simple, and continuous. [. . .]

The representational character of the written communication – writing as picture, reproduction, imitation of its content – will be the invariant trait of all progress to come. [. . .] Representation, of course, will become more complex, will develop supplementary ramifications and degrees [. . .].

A written sign is proffered in the absence of the receiver. How to style this absence? [. . .T]his distance, divergence, delay, this deferral [*différance*] must be capable of being carried to a certain absoluteness of absence if the structure of writing, assuming that writing exists, is to constitute itself. [. . .] My communication must be repeatable – iterable – in the absolute absence of the receiver [. . .]. Such iterability – (*iter*, again, probably comes from *itara, other* in Sanskrit, and everything that follows can be read as the working out of the logic that ties repetition to alterity) structures the mark of writing itself, no matter what particular type of writing is involved [. . .]. A writing that is not structurally readable – iterable – beyond the death of the addressee would not be writing. [. . .]

The possibility of repeating and thus of identifying the marks is implicit in every code, making it into a network that is communicable, transmittable, decipherable, iterable for a third, and hence for every possible user in general. To be what it is, all writing must, therefore, be capable of functioning in the radical absence of every empirically determined receiver in general. And this absence is not a continuous modification of presence, it is a rupture in presence. [. . .] What holds for the receiver holds also, for the same reason, for the sender or producer. To write is to produce a mark that will constitute a sort of machine which is productive in turn, and which my future disappearance will not, in principle, hinder in its functioning, offering things and itself to be read and to be rewritten. [. . .]

[T]he traits that can be recognized in the classical, narrowly defined concept of writing are generalizable. They are valid not only for all orders of "signs" and for all languages in general but moreover, beyond semio-linguistic communication, for the entire field of what philosophy would call experience, even the experience of being: the above-mentioned "presence." [. . .]

Every sign, linguistic or nonlinguistic, spoken or written (in the current sense of this opposition), in small or large units, can be *cited*, put between quotation marks; in so doing it can break with every given context, engendering an infinity of new contexts in a manner which is absolutely illimitable. This does not imply that the mark is valid outside of a context, but on the contrary that there are only contexts without any center or absolute anchoring. [. . .]

We are witnessing not an end of writing that would restore [. . .] a transparency or an immediacy to social relations; but rather the increasingly powerful historical expansion of a general writing, of which the system of speech, consciousness, meaning, presence, truth, etc., would be only an effect, and should be analyzed as such. [. . .]

> Deconstruction cannot be restricted or immediately pass to a neutralization: it must, through a double gesture, a double science, a double writing — put into practice a *reversal* of the classical opposition *and* a general *displacement* of the system. [. . .] Deconstruction does not consist in moving from one concept to another, but in reversing and displacing a conceptual order as well as the nonconceptual order with which it is articulated.
>
> 1988, *Limited Inc.*, 3, 5, 7–9, 12, 21

That is because behind every writing are other writings. New writing tries to erase or co-opt what came before, but is never wholly successful. To Derrida, cultures are palimpsests of official and counter-hegemonic graffiti. Every writing is a power struggle (**see Derrida box 3**). Even simple binaries such as "day/night," "white/black," "man/woman" inscribe power. In Western languages, by reading the term on the left first we perform its authority over the term on the right. To reverse terms is to perform a new power relation: "black/white" is different than "white/black." From this perspective, history is not a story of "what happened" but an ongoing struggle to "write," or claim ownership, over historical narratives. Yet every narrative, no matter how elegant or seemingly total, is full of holes, what Derrida calls "aporia" — open spaces, absences, and contradictions. Nothing can be totally erased. These aporias leak various pasts and alternatives into the present order of things.

Palimpsest: A document or art work that has been repeatedly written or drawn on, then partly erased, then written or drawn on again, so that the previous writings leave a still visible trace on the writing surface. Thus a palimpsest contains and expresses its own history of being inscribed on

Hegemonic: Exerting dominance or control, usually by or on behalf of the state, religious body, corporation, or other established power.

The authorities — "those who author" — attempt to make the present take on the appearance of being the outcome of an inevitable process (fate, destiny, historical necessity). But this smooth continuity — a knowable past that determines a stable present leading to an inevitable future — is a fiction. The past is full of holes; the present is provisional, the future not known. All historical narratives are haunted by what/who is erased, threatened by what/who demands representation. The struggle to write history, to represent events, is an ongoing performative process.

Jacques Derrida

Writing and Power Never Work Separately

Fostering the belief that writing *fosters* power (one can, in general, and one can write if occasioned to), that it can ally itself to power, can prolong it by complementing it, or can serve it, the question suggests that writing can *come* [*arriver*] to power or power to writing. It excludes in advance the identification of writing as power or the recognition of power from the onset of writing. It auxiliarizes and hence aims to conceal the fact that writing and power never work separately, however complex the laws, the system, or the links of their collusion may be. [. . .]

Writing does not come to power. It is there beforehand, it partakes of and is made of it. [. . .] Hence, *struggles* for *powers* set *various* writings up against one another [*les* luttes pour *les* pouvoirs opposent *des* écritures].

1998 [1979], from *Scribble (writing-power)*, in *The Derrida Reader*, 50

In order to show the unstable, performative quality of writing, Derrida coined the word *différance* (French), meaning "difference" + "deferral" — otherness plus a lack of fixed or decided meaning. Because writing is always contested, a system of erasing as well as composing, meaning cannot "be" once-and-for-all. Meaning is always performed: always in rehearsal, its finality forever deferred, its actuality only provisional, played out in specific circumstances. This "playing out" is related to Nietzsche's "will-to-power" (see chapter 4). As play acts, performatives are not "true" or "false," "right" or "wrong." They happen. Furthermore, writing in the poststructuralist sense consists of "iterations" — quotations, repetitions, and citations. Derrida emphasizes that language in general and speech acts in particular depend on an active estrangement, an encounter with "otherness." This is very close to Brecht's *Verfremdungseffekt* (alienation effect). In Brechtian theatre, the actor stands beside herself and beside the events enacted – doing and showing at the same time (**see figure 5.5**). The Brechtian performer is not lost in the role,

Différance: A noun coined by Jacques Derrida emphasizing the double meaning of the French verb *différer* – "to differ" and "to defer." "Différance" – a difference and a deferral – marks the slippage between a word as such and what the word refers to. *Différance* has entered English and is used without quotation marks.

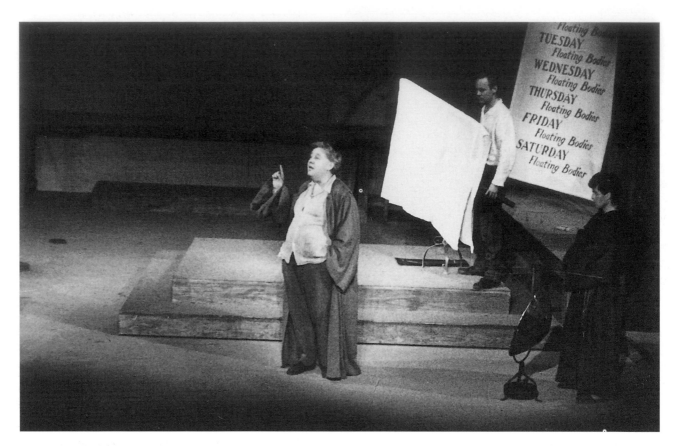

fig 5.5. Charles Laughton, an actor Bertolt Brecht admired, performing in Brecht's *The Life of Galileo* in the Beverly Hills Coronet Theatre, 1947. Photograph by Ruth Berlau. Copyright the Bertolt Brecht Archive, Berlin.

or entirely empathetic with the situation (I will discuss this kind of acting more thoroughly in the next chapter). Brecht argued that art is not a mirror held up to nature but a hammer with which to shape it.

The Diffusion of Poststructuralism

From the 1980s onward, poststructuralism spread far beyond France. For English speakers, the most influential French poststructuralists are Michel Foucault, Jacques Derrida, Giles Deleuze (1925–95), and Félix Guattari. Very important as well, though not strictly speaking poststructuralists, are Jean

Baudrillard, Guy Debord, and Jacques Lacan. In the UK and North America poststructuralism drew on and soon enough merged with theories of the performative conceived by Austin and richly elaborated by **Judith Butler** (1956–) – whose ideas I will have more to say about later in this chapter. Many adherents of the poststructuralist approach were also drawn to the **Frankfurt School** of critical studies and their intellectual allies, men such as **Theador Adorno** (1903–69), **Max Horkheimer** (1895–1973), **Jürgen Habermas** (1929–), **Herbert Marcuse** (1898–1979), Walter Benjamin, and Bertolt Brecht. This set up a fruitful convergence of poststructuralist, Marxist, and Freudian thought – which fed a wide range of theories and "studies" –

gender, cultural, postcolonial, race, queer, and performance. What unites this diverse and even sometimes self-contradictory collection is both an identification with the subaltern, the marginalized, and the discriminated against and a desire to sabotage, if not directly overthrow, the existing order of things.

Judith Butler (1956–): American philosopher and queer theorist whose work has concentrated on developing a theory of gender performativity. Her books include *Gender Trouble* (1990), *Bodies that Matter* (1993), and *Excitable Speech* (1997).

The Frankfurt School of social science and cultural studies emerged in Germany during the 1920s and 1930s. Its members included **Theodor Adorno (1903–69)**, **Max Horkheimer (1895–1973)**, **Herbert Marcuse (1898–1979)**, **Walter Benjamin (1892–1940)**, and, later, **Jürgen Habermas (1929–)**. Despite its name, the Frankfurt School was neither a school nor limited to Frankfurt. The term is used to designate a group of cultural critics who applied Marxist thought to the arts and popular culture. With the rise of the Nazis, many adherents of the Frankfurt School emigrated to England and the United States. Their ideas deeply influenced the radical social movements of the 1960s and beyond.

Subaltern: Literally, subordinate, of low rank. Often used to indicate the oppressed or marginalized status of persons or groups in the Third World.

The core operation of poststructuralism is "decentering," an attack on every kind of hegemony, authority, and fixed system – philosophical, sexual, political, artistic, economic, artistic. Poststructuralists subvert the First Performative of Western and Islamic cultures, God's Utterances in *Genesis*, "God said . . . and there was!" (Derrida, though French, grew up Jewish in Arab Algeria. His early cultural experiences are Semitic, European, and colonial.) Poststructuralists also undercut Aristotle's notion of a First Cause. On these originary Spoken Presences, Derrida pours acidic puns and ironies. Derrida's attacks are consonant with Foucault's renunciation of the "secret origin" and the "already-said." Foucault wanted to undermine the idea that history proceeded as a continuous stream of causal events. He proposed instead seeking the "ruptures" and "transformations" that continually throw up "new foundations" (**see Foucault box 2**). The poststructuralists challenge not so-called facts, but how knowledge itself is manufactured, performed, and

written (in the Derridean sense). As a consequence, the term "performative" now includes everything from doable acts of the body, to imaging of all kinds, and writing as such.

Michel Foucault

Threshold, Rupture, Break, Mutation, Transformation

And the great problem [. . .] is not how continuities are established, how a single pattern is formed and preserved, how for so many different, successive minds there is a single horizon, what mode of action and what substructure is implied by the interplay of transmissions, resumptions, disappearances, and repetitions, how the origin may extend its sway well beyond itself to that conclusion that is never given – the problem is no longer one of tradition, of tracing a line, but one of division, of limits; it is no longer one of lasting foundations, but one of transformations that serve as new foundations, the rebuilding of foundations. What one is seeing, then, is the emergence of a whole field of questions, some of which are already familiar, by which this new form of history is trying to develop its own theory: how is one to specify the different concepts that enable us to conceive of discontinuity (threshold, rupture, break, mutation, transformation)? By what criteria is one to isolate the unities with which one is dealing; what is *a* science, what is an *œuvre* [work]? What is *a* theory? What is *a* concept? What is *a* text? How is one to diversify the levels at which one may place oneself, each of which possesses its own divisions and form of analysis? [. . .] In short, the history of thought, of knowledge, of philosophy, of literature seems to be seeking, and discovering, more and more discontinuities [. . .].

1972, *The Archeology of Knowledge*, 5–6

Problems with Poststructuralism

Despite its highly developed political consciousness and its analysis of, and sympathy with, the plight of the marginalized and disempowered, poststructuralism is not a mass movement with a direct impact on the vast majority of people. Poststructuralists are mostly sequestered in the ivory tower, the "tenured radical" phenomenon. The authorities both within academia and outside it don't worry much about poststructuralists disrupting the status quo. In fact, an ironclad status quo has developed within poststructuralism. Ironically, poststructuralism is ruled by the works of (mostly dead) authors. The relatively few writings and ideas that constitute the poststructuralist canon are continually recycled inside a closed hermeneutical system.

The causes of this situation are not difficult to locate. Once the "disturbances" of the 1960s were snuffed out, many defeated radicals took refuge in academia, where they won in theory what was not accomplished in the streets. Addressing other poststructuralists and their students, poststructuralist writing grew complex and arcane, cleaving a bigger and bigger space between the movement and the larger public. Even as the range of subjects studied expanded – including all aspects of popular culture – direct contact with the people decreased. Upon graduation, most students left poststructuralism behind. The few who continued to hold the torch became young professors. What had started as an effort to change society ended as an academic "tradition" dependent on the aforementioned canon of anti-canonical authors.

Neither the corporations, government, nor university officials messed with what was happening. Why bother? Unlike the disruptions of the 1960s, the new radicals kept their activities confined to "discourse" – writings, seminars, petitions, art works, well-regulated protests, and so on. These were all cultural products that made the universities appear "liberal" and open to the widest diversity of opinion. An increasingly totalizing global system could easily tolerate or even exult in displaying the products of this liberalism. In fact, the more liberal the academic system was, the better it could control any radical impulses that might arise. At the level of governance, power was increasingly centralized in deans, presidents, and boards of trustees. The universities – public as well as private – corporatized bigtime in management style. The whole relation to "campus radicals" took on a quality of play – performative play. Absorbed into academia with its own strict rules of tenure, promotion, and administrative control, the revolution in thinking and society envisioned by the poststructuralists was largely reduced to and transformed into game playing.

Yet I wonder how much of the poststructuralist program has been accomplished. Isn't there much more acceptance of diversity in European and North American cultures? Haven't women, people of color, and Jews gotten further in these societies than ever before? Aren't unpopular opinions heard more often? Haven't school curriculums been thoroughly revised and expanded? What about the street demonstrations against the World Trade Organization? Or AIDS walks and the many other manifestations of minoritarian values and desires? Community-based performance gives voice to those who were not previously heard. Much of this can be credited to the long-term impact of poststructuralism. But be careful about confusing "tolerance" and "good management" with actual change. In the United States, at least, the diversity of behavior and opinion has not yet been tested against a serious economic recession or depression. Not to mention large-scale war. It's easy to be "generous" when times are good. It takes hard times to bring out the need for scapegoats. Time will tell.

Constructions of Gender

If history is an open project, and social reality the interplay of conflicting performatives, how does this affect circumstances thought to be fixed biologically or by unshakable traditions, gender and race, for example? Is a person "woman" or "man," "of color" or "white" because genetics says so or because of social arrangements? This is not a question of how people are treated or how much power they have. A revolution, or other engine of change, could result in women or people of color taking power without shaking the supposedly inherent differences between the sexes and the races. The "performative inquiry" includes but also seeks beyond changes wrought by social action. The performative inquiry asks, what constitutes individual identity and social reality; are these constructed or given; and if constructed, out of what? The questions are begged, of course: once one deems gender and race (plus all other social realities) "performative," the answer is that these consist not of naturally determined operations but of something built and enforced by means of "performance" in the senses I used to describe that word in chapter 2. Even "nature" is not natural, or prior, but a humanly constructed concept designed (consciously or unconsciously) to accomplish human ends. This argument could be, and has been, applied to many areas of human activity. Here I will explore it as it pertains to gender and race.

Judith Butler develops the assertion of French existential writer **Simone de Beauvoir** (1908–86) that "One is not born, but, rather, *becomes* a woman" (**see Butler box 1**). That is, one's biological sex ("female" or "male") is raw material to be shaped through practice into the socially constructed performance that is gender ("woman" or "man"). Of course, these binaries are much too simple, but for the moment let us stick with them. Each individual from an early age learns to perform gender-specific vocal inflections, facial displays, gestures, walks, and erotic behavior as well as how to select, modify, and use scents, body shapes and adornments, clothing, and all other gender markings of a given society. These differ widely from period to period and culture to culture – indicating strongly that gender is constructed (**see Acting the part of a woman box**). To perform these "successfully" give a person a secure place within a given social world. To refuse to perform one's assigned gender is to rebel against . . . "nature."

Simone de Beauvoir (1908–86): French feminist, existentialist philosopher, and novelist. Her best-known non-fiction text is *The Second Sex* (1949, Eng. 1953), which called for an end to the myth of "the eternal feminine." Other works include *The Mandarins* (1954, Eng. 1960) and *Force of Circumstance* (1963, Eng. 1965).

Judith Butler

Gender is Performative

[. . .T]he body *is* a historical situation, as Beauvoir has claimed, and is a manner of doing, dramatizing, and *reproducing* a historical situation. [. . .]

The act that gender is, the act that embodied agents *are* inasmuch as they dramatically and actively embody and, indeed, *wear* certain cultural significations, is clearly not one's act alone. Surely, there are nuanced and individual ways of doing one's gender, but *that* one does it, and that one does it *in accord with* certain sanctions and proscriptions, is clearly not a fully individual matter. [. . .] The act that one does, the act that one performs, is, in a sense, an act that has been going on before one arrived on the scene. Hence, gender is an act which has been rehearsed, much as a script survives the particular actors who make use of it, but which requires individual actors in order to be actualized and reproduced as reality once again. [. . .]

Gender reality is performative, which means, quite simply, that it is real only to the extent that it is performed. [. . .] If gender attributes [. . .] are not expressive but performative, then these attributes effectively constitute the identity they are said to express or reveal. The distinction between expression and performativeness is quite crucial, for if gender attributes and acts, the various ways a body shows or produces its cultural signification, are performative, then there is no preexisting identity by which an act or attribute might be measured; there would be no true or false, real or distorted acts of gender, and the postulation of a true gender identity would be revealed as a regulatory fiction. That gender reality is created through sustained social performances means that the very notions of an essential sex, a true or abiding masculinity or femininity, are also constituted as part of the strategy by which the performative aspect of gender is concealed. [. . .]

Gender reality is performative, which means, quite simply, that it is real only to the extent that it is performed.

1988, "Performative Acts and Gender Constitution," 521, 524–28

Acting the Part of a Woman

1860, Anonymous

Some ladies walk so as to turn up their dresses behind, and I have seen a well-dressed woman made to look very awkward by elevating her shoulders slightly and pushing her elbows too far behind her. Some hold their hands up to the waist, and press their arms against themselves as tightly as if they were glued there. Others swing them backward and forward as a businessman walking along the street. Too short steps detract from dignity very much, forming a mincing pace; too long steps are masculine.

1860, *Complete Rules of Etiquette and Usages of Society*, 3–4

2001, Cara Birnbaum in Cosmopolitan

How do you work everything from tone of voice to body language to dazzle anyone instantly – from a hot stud to a cold-as-ice job interviewer? [. . .] It's crucial that your nonverbal cues, including gestures and posture, work overtime to put you in the best possible light. [. . .] To score some guy candy: Subtly tilt your head and pivot your body whenever he does. If he pauses to loosen his tie, stop for a second to moisten your lips. It's all about showing him you're enchanted enough to be tracking his every move. [. . .] Start by adjusting your voice so that it matches his energy level. If his tones are enthusiastic, enthuse back. If he sounds mellow, you should too. It will only take a few minutes for a man to make up his mind that you're just like him. Once you've established that, you can be yourself.

June, 2001, "How to Wow Anyone you Meet," 148–49

As Butler points out, there are "nuanced" and "individual ways" of playing one's gender, but whatever these are, a person performs her or his gender in accordance with already inscribed performatives. Butler very specifically compares gender roles to rehearsed theatrical performances that follow known scripts which survive the particular actors of the moment. In this Butler is applying the "all the world's a stage" metaphor enunciated by Shakespeare and explored in our own time by Erving Goffman and his many followers. Where Butler makes her own contribution is in her application of notions drawn from poststructuralism's theory of performatives. Butler argues that gender as performed in contemporary Western societies enacts a normative heterosexuality that is a major tool for enforcing a patriarchal, phallocentric social order (**see Butler box 2**). Thus Butler politicizes non-heterosexual (queer, gay, lesbian, drag, etc.) sexuality and positions these behaviors in opposition to the hegemonic male-dominated/defined social order. In other words, to become gay is to enact a radical politics along the order of "the personal is the political."

Judith Butler

Compulsory Heterosexuality

To guarantee the reproduction of a given culture, various requirements, well established in the anthropological literature of kinship, have instated sexual reproduction within the confines of a heterosexually-based system of marriage which requires the reproduction of human beings in certain gendered modes which, in effect, guarantee the eventual reproduction of that kinship system. As Foucault and others have pointed out, the association of a natural sex with a discrete gender and with an ostensibly natural "attraction" to the opposing sex/gender is an unnatural conjunction of cultural constructs in the service of reproductive interests. Feminist cultural anthropology and kinship studies have shown how cultures are governed by conventions that not only regulate and guarantee the production, exchange, and consumption of material goods, but also reproduce the bonds of kinship itself, which require taboos and a punitive regulation of reproduction to effect that end. [. . .] My point is simply that one way in which this system of compulsory heterosexuality is reproduced and concealed is through the cultivation of bodies into discrete sexes with "natural" appearances and "natural" heterosexual dispositions. [. . .] The contention that sex, gender, and heterosexuality are historical productions which become conjoined and reified as natural over time has received a good deal of critical attention not only from Michel Foucault, but Monique Wittig, gay historians, and various cultural anthropologists and social psychologists in recent years. [. . .]

The transformation of social relations becomes a matter, then, of transforming hegemonic social conditions rather than individual acts that are spawned by these conditions. [. . .] Just as within feminist theory the very category of the personal is expanded to include political structures, so there is a theatrically-based and, indeed, less individually-oriented view of acts that goes some of the way in defusing the criticism of act theory as "too existentialist."

1988, "Performative Acts and Gender Constitution," 524–25

Which leads to those who refuse to perform their assigned heterosexual gender roles. It is to be at the least an "oddball," maybe an actor or dancer. Or, if the refusal is more radical, to be "queer," or "butch" or "femme," a "drag queen," bisexual or transsexual – or any other gender possibility that is outside hetero-orthodoxy. Butler and others who adhere to her point of view believe that gender is "real" only insofar and in the specific ways it is performed. She also makes the very important distinction between performing against the dominant code in a theatre and doing so in the street. Much more is permitted onstage than off. Offstage there are no conventions of the theatre to protect a drag queen from ridicule or worse (**see figure 5.6**). Even remaining in the closet, being "quietly gay," as it were, is no protection against attacks ranging from stares and verbal abuse to murder. Unorthodox gender performatives are not merely affronts to patriarchy; they challenge long-standing Western philosophical distinctions between appearance

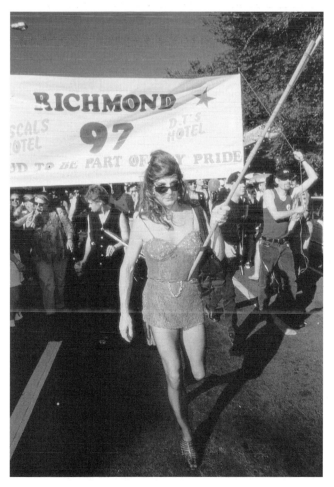

fig 5.6. A drag queen at the annual Gay Pride March, Melbourne. Photograph by Robert Francis. Copyright Hutchison Library.

and reality. If one wears and can to some degree change what one "really is," then what about the existence of a settled identity or an indwelling eternally abiding soul?

Constructions of Race

If gender is performed, what about race? Does one "become" black, white, brown, red, or yellow in the same way that one becomes a woman or man? Does skin color, a set of facial features, hair, or any single attribute, or combination of attributes, indicate that a person belongs to one race or another? Are there any dependable markers of race? Skin color and all other "racial features" are extremely variable across populations.

Race is akin to ethnicity, a human cultural feature. As a cultural feature, race matters. But the importance of race as a cultural category cannot be sustained by its often purported basis in "nature." Visible marks of race are unreliable. To take "blacks" and "whites" as an instance, many so-called "whites" have darker skin than many so-called "blacks." Other visible markers such as hair texture, eye and nose shape, and so on are also unreliable – not only in relation to "black" and "white" but also with regard to other groups. Jews have sometimes been designated as a race with specific facial characteristics (big noses, thick lips, dark eyes), sometimes as a religious group with no particular racial markers. But what about under the skin? Biologists and anthropologists agree that race has no basis in genetics or biology (**see Marshall box**).

Because race is a cultural construct, racial identifications change in reaction to culture-specific historical forces. For example, throughout much of US history, people were placed in, and placed themselves in, very definite racial categories. But with the numbers of multiracial and multicultural children growing, and the influx of millions of people from Latin America and Asia, the categories began to collapse. In the 2000 US census, more people than ever before identified themselves as "multicultural" or refused to categorize themselves racially. Even the shift in nomenclature is important. As late as the 1970s words such as "black," "Negro," or "colored" were in general use. But today one speaks mostly of "African Americans," pointing to culture and geography rather than color. Other groups that formerly were identified by color are also now marked by nationality or ethnicity ("Chinese" or "Japanese," not "yellow," "Native American," not "red," "Indian" or "South Asian," not brown). Despite this, racial categories tied to visible markers persist and have very important effects. Ironically, even after color

Eliot Marshall

There is No Such Thing as "Race"

Genetic diversity appears to be a continuum, with no clear breaks delineating racial groups. Last year, the U.S. Office of Management and Budget (OMB) completed a contentious 4-year review of the racial and ethnic categories that will be used to define the U.S. population in federal reports, including the 2000 census. It finally settled on seven groupings: American Indian or Alaska Native; Asian; Black or African American; Native Hawaiian (added after OMB received 7000 postcards from Hawaiians) or Other Pacific Islander; White; Hispanic or Latino; and Not Hispanic or Latino. The categories could have enormous implications – from the distribution of government resources to political districting to demographic research. But as far as geneticists are concerned, they're meaningless.

"Ridiculous" is the word cultural anthropologist John Moore of the University of Florida, Gainesville, uses to describe such racial typing. This view is based on a growing body of data that indicates, as Moore says, that "there aren't any boundaries between races." Geneticist Kenneth Kidd of Yale University says the DNA samples he's examined show that there is "a virtual continuum of genetic variation" around the world. "There's no place where you can draw a line and say there's a major difference on one side of the line from what's on the other side." If one is talking about a distinct, discrete, identifiable population, Kidd adds, "there's no such thing as race in [modern] Homo sapiens." Indeed, the American Anthropological Association urged the government last year to do away with racial categories and, in political matters, let people define their own ethnicity. [. . .]

Anthropologists have long objected to the stereotypes that are used to classify human populations into racial groups. But the most potent challenge to such groupings has come from genetic studies of human origins. The field was "transformed" in the late 1980s, says anthropologist Kenneth Weiss of Pennsylvania State University in University Park, by an analysis of variations in mitochondrial DNA (mtDNA) begun by Rebecca Cann of the University of Hawaii, Manoa, Mark Stoneking of Penn State, and the late Allan Wilson of the University of California, Berkeley. These researchers reported that diversity in mtDNA genes was two to three times greater in Africa than in Europe or the rest of the world. Assuming that the rate of change in mtDNA was fairly constant, they concluded that Africans' mtDNA was older than that of non-Africans, and that modern humans originated from a small population that emerged from Africa and migrated around the globe.

1998, "DNA Studies Challenge the Meaning of Race," 654

as a racial marker has been dispensed with, the general term "people of color" continues to be widely used. Race may not be real scientifically, but it is strongly operative culturally.

In addition, specific stereotyped looks and behaviors are associated with certain groups. The stereotypes often disparage "the Other" as inferior or, oppositely, too powerful. Sometimes, particularly in relation to Jews, the hated group is felt to be both inferior and too powerful. Frequently, stereotypes jumble race, ethnicity, religion, and nationality. Stereotypes abound, aimed at just about every group, including "WASPs," white Anglo-Saxon Protestants. Nor is being victimized an inoculation against disparaging others. Targeted groups turn around and target other groups. The whole matter is further complicated when certain stereotypes are embraced by those they are meant to stigmatize, transforming the would-be attack into a positive cultural expression. For example, many African Americans enjoy the humor of **Eddie Murphy** (1961–), buy tickets to Blaxploitation movies, and help make rapsters into superstars. With regard to rap and hip-hop, there are strong feelings both for and against. For some, rap and hip-hop are energetic manifestations of youthful African American men's culture. For others, the music is violent, sexist, and gynophobic. This division of opinion is not wholly along racial or gender lines. And if this were not enough of a complication, there's also a lot of crossing over. **Eminem** (1976–) is visibly white, but his music and presentation of self are black. In fact, "black style" dominates mainstream American pop music and is a strong influence on other areas of American culture. But this does not inhibit African Americans from adopting elements of "white culture." There is in the US no dominant racial "way to be" comparable to what Butler terms "compulsory heterosexuality." Instead, there is an enormous amount of cultural-racial mixing.

Eddie Murphy (1961–): American actor and comedian. Films include *48 hrs* (1982), *Beverly Hills Cop* (1984), *The Nutty Professor* (1996), and its sequels.

Eminem (1976–): American rap artist, born Marshall Mathers. Hit songs include 'The Real Slim Shady' (2000) and 'Way I Am' (2000).

Adrian Piper (1948–): Conceptual artist and philosopher whose work in numerous media, including live performance, focuses on issues of race, racism, and racial stereotyping. *Adrian Piper: A Retrospective* (1999) is a comprehensive overview of her art works. Many of Piper's writings are published in the two-volume collection *Out of Order, Out of Sight: Selected Writings in Meta-Art and Art Criticism 1967–1992* (1996).

Immanuel Kant (1724–1804): German philosopher, author of the *Critique of Pure Reason* (1781/87), *Critique of Practical Reason* (1788), and *Critique of Judgment* (1790) as well as numerous other seminal works in critical philosophy.

Adrian Piper (1948–) theorizes race both in her writings and in performance. Piper, a philosopher specializing in **Immanuel Kant** (1724–1804), is also a conceptual artist whose performance art and installations focus on racism, racial stereotyping, and xenophobia. One of her best-known works is *Cornered* (1988), a video installation that begins with Piper, dressed in dark clothes, a string of pearls around her neck, seated in the corner of a room at a table, hands folded, looking directly at the camera (**see figure 5.7**). The TV set on which Piper's image appears is itself placed in the corner of the gallery with an overturned table in front of it. The set up suggests both being cornered (that is, trapped) and some kind of violent overturn. After a pause, the light-skinned Piper begins. "I'm black. Now let's deal with this social fact and the fact of my stating it, together." Piper's inaugural challenge is a "speech act," a performative. She goes on. "If I don't tell you who I am, then I have to pass for white. And why should I have to do that? The problem with passing for white is that it is not only that it is based on sick values, which it is. It's also that it creates a degrading situation in which I may have to listen to insulting remarks about blacks made by whites who mistakenly believe there are no blacks present. That's asking a bit much. I'm sure you'll agree." Assuming a white spectator, for the next 30 minutes Piper, earnestly but with cutting irony, dissects the emotional impact, social practices, and legalities of racism in America.

Piper never raises her voice. She develops her points with impeccable logic. She does not speak directly of enslavement, lynchings, and segregation or give graphic examples of American racism. Her anger is understated. Presenting herself in a manner that confounds stereotyping, Piper dissects what constitutes racial identity. She asserts that according to commonly accepted beliefs that race is "in the blood," everyone in the USA has between 5 and 20 percent black ancestry. "Most purportedly white Americans are in fact black. [. . .] The chances are really quite good that you are, in fact, black. What are you going to do about it?" Sarcastically, Piper invites the viewer to tell friends and employers that s/he is black. Or, Piper suggests, why not take

fig 5.7. *Cornered*, a video installation, 1988. Photograph courtesy of Adrian Piper.

advantage of "affirmative action" programs designed to assist blacks? Or stay silent or discredit the research or dismiss *Cornered* as just another "art experience." Piper corners the viewer, concluding the 20-minute piece with the challenge, "Now that you have this information about your black ancestry, whatever you do counts as a choice. [. . .] So, what are you going to do?" In *Cornered* and many other of her works, Piper probes the shifting ground that barely supports socially constructed racial categories. Take, for example, the Angry Art "calling card" Piper gives to people who make racist remarks or let them pass unchallenged when made by others (**see figure 5.8**). When someone who "looks" black "acts" white, or vice versa, the person may be accused of "passing" – pretending or performing a self that one has no legitimate claim to given the racist constructions of contemporary Euro-American society (**see Piper box**). But as Piper points out, the very concept of racial classification is an instrument of racism. Race, like gender, is constructed.

Dear Friend,
I am black.
I am sure you did not realize this when you made/laughed at/agreed with that racist remark. In the past, I have attempted to alert white people to my racial identity in advance. Unfortunately, this invariably causes them to react to me as pushy, manipulative, or socially inappropriate. Therefore, my policy is to assume that white people do not make these remarks, even when they believe there are no black people present, and to distribute this card when they do.
I regret any discomfort my presence is causing you, just as I am sure you regret the discomfort your racism is causing me.

fig 5.8. An "Angry Art" card Adrian Piper gives to people who make racist remarks or do not intervene when others do so, 1986. Card courtesy of Adrian Piper.

Adrian Piper

On Passing and Not Passing

It was the New Graduate Student Reception for my class, the first social event of my first semester in the best graduate department in my field in the country. I was full of myself, as we all were, full of pride at having made the final cut [. . .]. I was a bit late, and noticed that many turned to look at – no scrutinize – me as I entered the room. I congratulated myself on having selected for wear my black velvet, bell-bottomed pantsuit (yes, it was that long ago) with the cream silk blouse and crimson vest. [. . .] The most famous and highly respected member of the faculty observed me for a while from a distance and then came forward. Without introduction or preamble, he said to me with a triumphant smirk, "Miss Piper, you're about as black as I am."

One of the benefits of automatic pilot in social situations is that insults take longer to make themselves felt. [. . .] What I felt was numb, and then shocked and terrified, disoriented, as though I'd been awakened from a sweet dream of unconditional support and approval and plunged into a nightmare of jeering contempt. [. . .] Finally, there was the groundless shame of the inadvertent impostor, exposed to public ridicule or accusation. For this kind of shame, you don't actually need to have done anything wrong. All you need to do is care about others' image of you, and fail in your actions to reinforce their positive image of themselves. Their ridicule and accusations then function to both disown and degrade you from their status, to make you as not having *done* wrong but as *being* wrong. [. . .]

And I experienced [then, and at other times] that same groundless shame, not only in response to those who accused me of passing for black but also in response to those who accused me of passing for white. This was the shame caused by people who conveyed to me that I was underhanded or manipulative, trying to hide something, pretending to be something I was not, by telling them I was black, like the art critic in the early 1970s who had treated me with the respect she gave emerging white women artists in the early days of second-wave feminism, until my work turned to issues of racial identity; she then called me to verify that I was black, reproached me for not telling her, and finally disappeared from my professional life altogether. [. . .]

But I've learned that there is no "right" way of managing the issue of my racial identity, no way that will not offend or alienate someone, because my designated racial identity itself exposes the very concept of racial classification as the offensive and irrational instrument of racism that it is. We see this in the history of classifying terms variously used to designate those brought as slaves to this country and their offspring: first "blacks," then "darkies," then "Negroes," then "colored people," then "blacks" again, then "Afro-Americans," then "people of color," now "African-Americans." Why is it that we can't seem to get it right, once and for all? The reason, I think, is that it doesn't really matter what term we use to designate those who have inferior and disadvantaged status, because whatever term is used will eventually turn into a term of derision and disparagement in virtue of its reference to those who are derided and disparaged, and so will need to be discarded for an unsullied one.

1992, "Passing for White, Passing for Black," in *Out of Order, Out of Sight*, vol. 1, 275–76, 96

Performance Art

Piper's pieces are performance art, a grab-bag category of works that do not fit neatly into theatre, dance, music, or visual art (**see Brentano box**). Much performance art puts into practice theories of performativity. This is especially true of performance art that deals with the construction of identity and in so doing enacts the slogan, "the personal is the political," a program that originated with feminist performance artists in the 1970s (**see Roth box**). This formulation is only possible in light of the theoretical proposition of performativity as developed by the post-structuralists. Only by recognizing that identity is constructed, not given, contested, not settled, historically and politically evolving, not fixed in "nature," can the practice of personal art, be regarded as political. There are many examples of "the personal is the political" art but none more striking than **Carolee Schneemann**'s (1939–) 1975 performance, *Interior Scroll* (**see figure 5.9**). Naked, Schneemann reaches into her vulva and pulls out a long scroll from which she reads her text:

[. . .] there are certain films
we cannot look at
the personal clutter
the persistence of feelings
the hand-touch sensibility
the diaristic indulgence
the painterly mess
the dense gestalt
the primitive techniques.

Robyn Brentano

Performance Art

The term "performance art" first appeared around 1970 to describe the ephemeral, time-based, and process-oriented work of conceptual ("body") and feminist artists that was emerging at the time. It was also applied retrospectively to Happenings, Fluxus events, and other intermedia performances from the 1960s. Over the past thirty-five years, many styles and modes of performance have evolved, from private, introspective investigations to ordinary routines of everyday life, cathartic rituals and trials of endurance, site-specific environmental transformations, technically sophisticated multimedia productions, autobiographically-based cabaret-style performance, and large-scale, community-based projects designed to serve as a source of social and political empowerment. [. . .] What has come to be called performance art [. . .] has taken myriad forms, a result of its interdisciplinary nature (drawing from painting, sculpture, dance, theater, music, poetry, cinema, and video) and disparate influences, including [. . .] the Futurists, Dadaists, Constructivists, Surrealists, Abstract Expressionism, performance and art traditions of Native American and non-European cultures, feminism, new communications technologies, and popular forms such as cabaret, the music hall, vaudeville, the circus, athletic events, puppetry, parades, and public spectacles.

1994, *Outside the Frame*, 31–32

Moira Roth

The Personal is the Political

Performance art began in the late 1960s at the same time as the women's movement. In the general context of a highly charged and theatrical decade, radical feminists employed theatre in such events as the 1969 disruption of the Miss America Pageant in Atlantic City and the nationwide WITCH (Women's International Terrorist Conspiracy from Hell) demonstrations at the same time. In feminist art circles, theatrical means – raw eggs and sanitary napkins littering pristine museum spaces – were used to protest the low percentage of women in the 1970 Whitney Museum's Biennial in New York. [. . .]

At the same time as women plunged into public battles, they also took on, within themselves, private ones. Through consciousness-raising groups, harsh feminist manifestos, poetic evocations in literature and scholarly studies, women – including many early performers – individually explored and collectively validated the substance of their lives. They re-examined and redefined the models on which they had based their self-images. As early feminists recognized that what had previously been designated (and, accordingly, often dismissed) as merely individual experience was, in actuality, an experience shared by many others, they developed the concept that "the personal is the political." It was this fresh and passionate investigation of self and of identification with other women that created the fervent supportive alliance between the first women performers and their audiences. And it was this bonding with the often all-women audiences, as much as the new personal content in the art, that accounted for the power of the early work.

1983, *The Amazing Decade*, 16–17

Carolee Schneemann (1939–): American visual and performance artist. Works include *Meat Joy* (1964), *Interior Scroll* (1975), *Catscan* and *Vulva's School* (1995). She is the author of *More Than Meat Joy* (2nd edn, 1995).

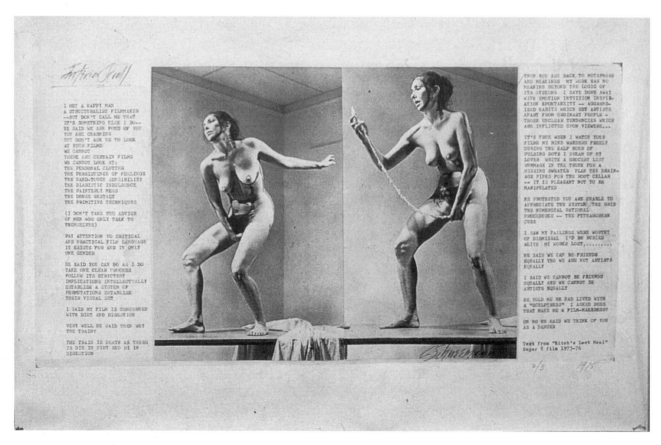

fig 5.9. Carolee Schneemann performing *Interior Scroll*, 1975. Photograph courtesy of Carolee Schneemann.

These were words Schneemann attributed to a "structuralist filmmaker" who refused even to look at Schneemann's films. Ironic, angry, and – given the taboos of that time – shocking, Schneemann's piece was personal, political, and avant-garde. She did not reject the filmmaker's estimation that her work was personal, full of touch, indulgent, messy, primitive. She rejected his rejection, arguing on the contrary that the very qualities the male filmmaker felt disqualified Schneemann's work from even being looked at were what made her work important and new. History proved her right.

In the early days of performance art, much of the audience consisted of fellow artists who freely borrowed from each other. What took place was an extremely fertile convergence of ideas, techniques, and audiences. Some artists sought out specific audiences of women or gays or political activists of a given kind. No longer was art seen as converging on the grand places and occasions of official culture, Lincoln Center or Broadway. Performance art took place in venues not previously used for performance – roofs, beaches, swimming pools, galleries, street corners, storefronts (and many more). Performance art evolved to some degree from painting (**see Kaprow box 1**). Therefore, unlike theatre, dance, and music much performance art was and is the work of individual artists using their own selves – bodies, psyches, notebooks, experiences – as material. The work was not shaped for large general audiences, but kept particularity and edge. It was a fine equivalent to the quirky, difficult, and stimulating thought of people like Derrida.

Allan Kaprow

Happenings

With the breakdown of the classical harmonies following the introduction of "irrational" or nonharmonic juxtapositions, the Cubists tacitly opened up a path to infinity. Once foreign matter was introduced into the picture in the form of paper [collage], it was only a matter of time before everything else foreign to paint and canvas would be allowed to get into the creative act, including real space. Simplifying the history of the ensuing evolution into a flashback, this is what happened: the pieces of paper curled up off the canvas, were removed from the surface to exist on their own, became more solid as they grew into other materials and, reaching out further into the room, finally filled it entirely. [. . .] Inasmuch as people visiting such Environments are moving, colored shapes too, and were counted "in," mechanically moving parts could be added, and parts of the created surroundings could then be rearranged like furniture at the artist's and visitors' discretion. And, logically since the visitor could and did speak, sound and speech, mechanical and recorded, were also soon to be in order. Odors followed.

1966, *Assemblage, Environments, and Happenings*, 165–66

Performance art is part of a line of the avant-garde reaching back to the turn of the twentieth century – symbolism, futurism, dada, surrealism, and so on. The immediate source of performance art was a convergence of Happenings, postmodern dance, and pop art (**see figures 5.10 and 11**). Allan Kaprow coined the word "Happenings" to describe art events that simply happened without picture frames, plots, or any marks of orthodox visual arts, theatre, dance, or music. In 1966, Kaprow outlined the seven qualities of Happenings (**see Kaprow box 2**). In his own way, he was laying the basis for "the personal is the political." Kaprow, like **Marcel Duchamp** (1887–1968) and Andy Warhol, wanted to demystify art, debunk the establishment that controlled museums, and make arts that could be performed by anyone. Kaprow proclaimed what he called "lifelike art" – not naturalism or any other kind of mimesis, but art that conformed to the processes of ordinary life. During the same period, many postmodern dancers rejected the strict codifications of both ballet and modern dance. They favored "pedestrian," or everyday, movement, let dancers speak about their own lives as they danced, and got involved in political actions (**see Banes box**).

Marcel Duchamp (1887–1968): Extremely influential French dada artist. Among his many works are the painting *Nude Descending a Staircase* (1912), the construction *The Bride Stripped Bare by her Bachelors, Even* (also known as the *Large Glass*) (1915–23), and his "readymades" – ordinary objects displayed as art. Duchamp's most notorious readymade is *Fountain* (1917), a urinal. Duchamp lived for many years in New York, becoming an American citizen in 1955.

Allan Kaprow

The Seven Qualities of Happenings

1. The line between art and life is fluid, even indistinct.
2. The themes, materials, and actions of happenings are taken from anywhere but the arts.
3. Happenings should be performed in several widely spaced locales.
4. Time, which follows closely on spatial considerations should be variable and discontinuous.
5. Happenings should be performed only once.
6. Audiences should be eliminated entirely – everyone at a Happening participates in it.
7. The composition/sequence of events is not rational or narrational, but based on associations among various parts; or by chance.

1966, *Assemblage, Environments, and Happenings*, 88–98

fig 5.10. Marilyn Monroe Diptych by Andy Warhol, 1962. Copyright Tate, London. Copyright Andy Warhol Foundation for the Visual Arts, Inc./ARS, NY and DACS London.

fig 5.11. The dance collective Grand Union in performance at Judson Church, 1960s. Photograph by Michael Kirby. Photograph courtesy of Richard Schechner.

Mimesis: Greek word meaning "imitation." In the *Poetics* Aristotle argues that a tragedy is a "mimesis of a praxis" (an action) of great enough magnitude to have a beginning, a middle, and an end. Exactly what Aristotle meant by mimesis has been the subject of much debate over the centuries. Currently, most commentators agree that Aristotle did not mean mimesis literally but as a specific artistic process of representation.

Sally **Banes**

Postmodern Dance

Originally reacting against the expressionism of modern dance, which anchored movement to a literary idea or musical form, the post-modernists propose [. . .] that the formal qualities of dance might be reason enough for choreography, and that the purpose of making dances might be simply to make a framework within which we look at movement for its own sake. But there are other purposes post-modernism claims for dance. One is that a dance can formulate or illustrate a theory of dance [. . .]. Another purpose, partly inspired by phenomenological philosophers and writers, is to embody different perspectives on space, time, or orientation to gravity [. . .]. The breakdown of the distinction between art and life [. . .], the clarification of individual, discrete movements, the isolation of the essential characteristics of dance, have all become valid purposes for making a dance. So has the option of making a dance for the pleasure of the dancer, whether or not the spectator finds it pleasing, or even accessible. The very question of what it means to create a dance can generate choreography: Is writing a score [. . .] an act of choreography? Is dance making an act of construction and craft or a process of decision making? In post-modern dance, the choreographer becomes a critic, educating spectators in ways to look at dance, challenging the expectations the audience brings to the performance, framing parts of the dance for closer inspection, commenting on the dance as it progresses.

1980, *Terpsichore in Sneakers*, 15–16

What the Gravedigger Knew about the Performative

Discussing whether or not Ophelia's suicide bars her from heaven, the more theoretical of two Gravediggers asserts, "An act hath three branches – it is to do, to act, to perform" (*Hamlet*, 5.1: 11). The Gravedigger divides an action into its physical attributes ("do"), its social aspects ("act"), and its theatrical qualities ("perform"). But why does he use the word "act" twice – first as an overall category and then as a subset of itself?

Any action consciously performed refers to itself, is part of itself. Its "origin" is its repetition. Every consciously performed action is an instance of restored behavior. Restored behavior enacted not on a stage but in "real life" is what poststructuralists call a "performative." It is their contention that all social identities, gender, for example, are performatives. The Gravedigger is not so much repeating himself as he is proposing a situation where the smaller ("to act") contains the larger ("an act"). He is also connecting "an act" as something accomplished in everyday life with "to act," something played on the stage. The ultimate example of "to act" is "to perform" – to be reflexive about one's acting. Shakespeare did not have Austin, Derrida, or Butler in mind when he wrote *Hamlet*. But the Gravedigger's brief disquisition shows that the notion of performativity has been around a long time.

Conclusion

Theories of performativity insist that all social realities are constructed. The construction of gender, race, and identity are but three examples of an all-encompassing theory. Social life as behaved is performed in the sense that I outlined in chapter 2: every social activity can be understood as a showing of a doing. I write "as behaved" to underline the "liveness" of certain aspects of social life – and to circumscribe the particular region that is most important to performance studies. This broad definition of liveness includes film, television, recorded musics, telephony, and the internet. These cannot be regarded as mere reproductions; because of how they are produced and received they participate in "liveness." Other parts of social life are not behaved, or at least not obviously so, such as laws, architecture, written literature, and the like. However, poststructuralist theories of performativity indicate that even these aspects of social life can be best understood "as performance." Austin's performative concerned utterances only. But those who built on Austin's ideas were soon discovering a wide range of "speech acts" and applying the theory of performativity to all areas of social life. Derrida's insistence that all human codes and cultural expressions are "writing" is a powerful example of this kind of thinking.

These theories of the performative inhabit performance art, especially works dealing with gender, race, and the assertion that the personal is the political. And just as theorists found the performative in all areas of personal and social life, so performance artists broke free from orthodox venues and styles of performance. Some performance art may take only a few seconds, while other events can take a year or more to complete. Some works occur on street corners or in store-front windows; others are dispersed to locations all around the world. In other words, just as there are no theoretical limits to performativity, so there are no practical limits to performance art.

What are the relationships between performativity, the performative, and performance proper – between what goes on at the Metropolitan Opera and what the post-structuralists posit? By far, performativity is the larger category. Many performances are clearly marked and delimited, such as formal presentations in theatres or episodes of public ceremony. Other performances are less clearly marked. Even non-performance – sitting in a chair, crossing the street, sleeping – can be made into a performance by framing these ordinary actions "as performance." If I look at what happens on the street, or at the rolling ocean, and see these "as performance," then in that circumstance they are such. This is what John Cage meant when he answered my question, "What is theatre?" with, "Just look and listen." Indeed, performances belong mostly to the eye and ear. Performatives also come in two types – the clearly marked and the more diffuse. A performative may be a specific speech act such as a promise, bet, or contract. Or it may be something difficult to pin down – a "concept" (as in conceptual art), the "idea of" performance suffusing an act or activity. In this sense, there is an "as if" of performativity analogous to the "as if" of theatre. In theatre, the "as if" consists of characters, places, actions, and narratives – all of which exist only as they are performed. In performativity, the "as if" consists of constructed social realities – gender, race, what-have-you – all of which are provisional, are "made up." At another level, performativity is a pervasive mood or feeling – belonging not so much to the visual-aural realm (as performances do) but to the senses of smell, taste, and touch. "I smell something funny going on," or "that's to my taste," or "I was touched by what happened" are ways of apprehending the performative.

THINGS TO THINK ABOUT

1. The "performative" began as a theory about utterances. It has developed into something much broader than that. Do you think that this expansion of the term makes it "unusable" or "useless"? Or do you feel that indeed much of postmodern life is lived "as a performative"? Defend your position.
2. What are some of the political and social implications of conceiving race, gender, and other identity formations as "performative"?

THINGS TO DO

1. Cross dress, then go out for a "night on the town." Note how people react to you, how you feel about yourself. Come home and write two pages on the subject "Gender is a social construction: true or false?"
2. Compose a piece of "performative writing" that draws on your own personal experiences in relation to some of the theoretical issues raised in this chapter.

SUGGESTED READINGS

Austin, J. L. "Lecture II." *How to Do Things with Words*. Cambridge, Mass.: Harvard University Press, 1962. 12–24.

Butler, Judith. "Performative Acts and Gender Constitution." *Theatre Journal* 40, no. 4 (1988): 519–31.

Derrida, Jacques. "The Theatre of Cruelty and the Closure of Representation." *Writing and Difference*. Tr. Alan Bass. Chicago: University of Chicago Press, 1978. 232–50.

Parker, Andrew, and Eve Kosofsky Sedgwick. "Performativity and Performance." *Performativity and Performance*. Eds. Andrew Parker and Eve Kosofsky Sedgwick. London: Routledge, 1995. 1–9.

Searle, John. "Why Study Speech Acts?" *Speech Acts: An Essay in the Philosophy of Language*. Cambridge: Cambridge University Press, 1969. 16–19.

6 PERFORMING

The Broad Spectrum of Performing

Performing onstage, performing in special social situations (public ceremonies, for example), and performing in everyday life are a continuum. These various kinds of performing occur in widely divergent circumstances, from private solo shows before the mirror to large-scale public events and rituals, from shaman healing rituals to identity-changing trances, from theatre and dance to the great and small roles of everyday life (**see figure 6.1**). This broad spectrum of performing can be depicted as a continuum with each category leading to, and blending into, the next (**see figure 6.2**). There are no clear boundaries separating everyday life from family and social roles or social roles from

fig 6.1. An array of the many different kinds of performing.

Mrs. Agnes Smith, a forewoman at an English shipbuilding yard and a mother of 10, during World War Two, 1941. Copyright Imperial War Museum, London.

Lord Justice Tucker.
Photograph Bassano, Camera Press, London.

A splendidly garbed Havana dancer at a party. Courtesy of Moira Taylor.

A tourist performance by Maasai warriors in Kenya. Photograph Bertrand Arthus. Copyright Ardea London Ltd.

Older persons gather in a Polish village to exchange stories, songs, and other "cultural material" as part of the work of the Gardzienice Theatre Association, 1980s. Photograph courtesy of Wlodzimierz Staniewski.

Ram Chakyar as the demoness Surpanikha in Kutiyattam, Sanskrit theatre performed in Kerala, India, 1976. Photograph by Richard Schechner.

A realistic European drama on a conventional proscenium stage, late 19th or early 20th century. Photograph courtesy of Richard Schechner.

Ron Vawter as Irma in Jean Genet's *The Balcony* gazes in the mirror at himself as a woman. The Performance Group, 1979, production directed by Richard Schechner. Photograph by David Behl. Photograph courtesy of Richard Schechner.

Magna Carta procession at Runnymead, 1986, U.K. Photograph courtesy of Moira Taylor.

PERFORMING IN EVERDAY LIFE—FAMILY AND SOCIAL ROLES—JOB ROLES—SPECTATOR SPORTS AND OTHER

fig 6.2. The broad spectrum of performing. Although the chart shows distinct categories, several of these categories blend into one or more of the others. There are no fixed boundaries separating, for example, "family and social roles" from "job roles" or "secular and sacred rituals" from "shamanism" or "trance."

Displaying the newborn in a neonatal unit of the Christchurch, New Zealand Woman's Hospital, 1970. Photograph courtesy of Moira Taylor.

A Korean shaman performing a ritual to bring peace for persons who drowned in a boat accident, 1981. Photograph by Du-Hyun Lee. Photograph courtesy of Richard Schechner

An earnest Prime Minister Tony Blair presents himself to the camera – with a tie, but sans jacket. He performs both his seriousness and his informality. Photograph courtesy of the Labour Party Office, London.

POPULAR ENTERTAINMENTS—PERFORMING ARTS—SECULAR AND SACRED RITUALS—SHAMANISM—TRANCE

job roles, church ritual from trance, acting onstage from acting offstage, and so on. I separate them for teaching purposes. Furthermore, a person can "jump" from one category into another – from daily life into trance, from ritual into entertainment, from one everyday life role into another. Sudden changes are common. Usually, a person knows when she is playing a role and when she is "being herself." To "be myself" is to behave in a relaxed and unguarded manner. To "perform myself" means to take on the appearance (clothes, demeanor, etc.), voice, and actions of Mother or Friend, Plumber or Doctor, and so on. Some people work very hard to enact one of society's "great roles" such as Judge, Senator, or Movie Star. Others have a great role thrust on them, such as Survivor of Catastrophe, Grieving Parent, Lottery Winner, or even King. Most people, most of the time, know the difference between enacting a social role and playing a role onstage – wearing the clothes, making the gestures, uttering the words, and maybe even feeling the emotions of characters in a drama.

All of this is complicated both by the media and by panoptic surveillance systems. Network, cable, and satellite television are joined by the internet and thousands of surveillance cameras whose eyes are ever open, gazing down on people in stores, streets, elevators, and who knows where else. Some cameras bring us the news of the day as it happens wherever it is happening. Other cameras are deployed supposedly for our "safety" both to protect us and, failing that, to "catch criminals in the act." Some eyes in the sky spy on military deployments and industrial outputs. Other satellites are able to pinpoint the location of any given individual anyplace on the planet – if that person (or car, boat, or plane) is so equipped. The always open lens adds a disturbing sense not only of being watched but of requiring us to be always "on," to play for the cameras knowing that our performances are being studied by people we do not know and whom we have not given permission to look. Then there are actors, athletes, politicians, and more than a few clerics – paid performers all seeking attention, adulation, re-election, and money. These types play not only for local audiences in arenas, stadiums, churches, and public halls but for the many millions tuned in around the globe. Across this very wide spectrum of performing are varying degrees of self-consciousness and consciousness of the others with whom and for whom we play. The more self-conscious a person is, the more one constructs behavior for those watching and/or listening, the more such behavior is "performing." There are exceptions. In trance performing, the possessed are sometimes unaware of their own performances.

Acting

Acting is a sub-category of performing comprising a very broad range of behaviors. At one extreme is the "minimal-acting" of some performance art (**see figure 6.3**). At the other extreme is the "total acting" of shamans and the trance-possessed (**see figure 6.4**). Acting consists of focused, clearly

fig 6.3. Performance artist Spalding Gray delivering one of his monologues. His whole presentation is studied and stable from one monologue to the next: a plaid or box-pattern shirt, simple wood table, water glass, and microphone. Photograph by Donna An McAdams. Photograph courtesy of Spalding Gray.

fig 6.4. A Balinese sanghyang dedari performer in trance. Photograph courtesy of Richard Schechner.

marked, and tightly framed behaviors specifically designed for showing. At the "not-acting end of the spectrum, there is no portrayal of another or of a "character." The minimalist actor simply performs certain actions that are received as acting by spectators because of context. By contrast, in total acting, the "other" is so powerful that it takes over or possesses the performer.

Performance theorist **Michael Kirby** (1931–97) proposed a continuum of acting passing through five nodal points (**see Michael Kirby box**, **see figure 6.5**):

- nonmatrixed performing
- symbolized matrix
- received acting
- simple acting
- complex acting

Nonmatrixed performance is doing something onstage other than playing a character – such as the work of the *koken* (stagehands) of Japanese kabuki theatre who, while the performance continues and in full view of the audience, move props and assist in onstage costume changes. Symbolized matrix performing is someone performing actions that can be understood by spectators as "belonging to" a character even

> **Michael Kirby (1931–97):** American performance historian and theorist, director, and actor. Editor of *The Drama Review* (1971–85). Author of *Happenings* (1965) and *A Formalist Theatre* (1987).

though the performer always behaves "as herself." Received acting is what "extras" do – they are in costume, they may speak fragments of lines, and the audience reads them as part of the situation of a scene. But extras do very little "character acting." Simple acting involves simulation and impersonation. The performer generates a character with feelings. Some emotional work is required. In complex acting, the whole being of the performer – physical, mental, emotional – is called on at a high level of commitment. Acting becomes increasingly complex the more elements are used in constructing the characterization. The difference between simple and complex acting is one of degree but not a matter of genre. Performing realistically takes training and effort, just as does performing in a marked style such as *jingju* (Beijing "opera"). Realistic acting seems "easier," that is, more familiar, because it draws its basic vocabulary from everyday life. But to simulate or recreate everyday life onstage is a difficult task (**see Stanislavsky box**).

Michael Kirby

Not Acting and Acting

To act means to feign, to simulate, to represent, to impersonate. As Happenings demonstrated, not all performing is acting. [. . .] The performers in Happenings generally tended to "be" nobody or nothing other than themselves. [. . .]

There are numerous performances that do not use acting. Many, but by no means all, dance pieces would fall into this category. Several Far Eastern theatres make use of stage attendants such as the Kurombo and Koken of Kabuki. These attendants move props into position and remove them, help with on-stage costume changes, and even serve tea to the actors. Their dress distinguishes them from the actors, and they are not included in the informational structure of the narrative. [. . .]

Extras, who do nothing but walk and stand in costume, are seen as "actors." Anyone merely walking across a stage containing a realistic setting might come to represent a person in that place – and, perhaps, time – without doing anything we could distinguish as acting. [. . .] "Received actor" is only an honorary title.

If the performer does something to simulate, represent, impersonate, and so forth, he or she is acting. [. . .] Acting may be said to exist in the smallest and simplest action that involves pretense. [. . .]

Acting becomes more complex as more and more elements [including the emotions] are incorporated into the pretense.

It must be emphasized that the acting/not-acting scale is not intended to establish or suggest values. Objectively, all points on the scale are equally "good." It is only personal taste that prefers complex acting to simple acting or nonmatrixed performing to acting. The various degrees of representation and personification are "colors," so to speak, in the spectrum of human performance; artists may use whichever colors they prefer.

1987, A Formalist Theatre, 3, 6–7, 10, 20

NOT-ACTING				**ACTING**
Nonmatrixed performing ⟷	**Symbolized matrix** ⟷	**Received acting** ⟷	**Simple acting** ⟷	**Complex acting**

fig 6.5. Figure from Michael Kirby's *A Formalist Theatre*, p 10.

nonmatrixed performing: A term coined by **Michael Kirby** to indicate actions performed onstage which do not involve role-playing.

symbolized matrix performing: Onstage actions which the spectator recognizes as "belonging to" a character, even though the performer continues to behave "as herself."

received acting: Onstage behavior in which the performer makes no attempt to impersonate a character, but is nonetheless viewed by the audience as part of the situation of a scene. "Extras" practice received acting.

simple acting: When a performer simulates the speech and behavior of a character.

complex acting: When the performer's entire physical, mental, and emotional capability is involved in the portrayal of a character.

Another way to understand acting, one not so dependent on notions of impersonation, is to divide acting into five kinds according to the congruence to daily life, the kind of actions presented, the state of mind of the performer, and the importance of performing objects:

1 realistic
2 Brechtian
3 codified
4 trance
5 performing objects – masks and puppets.

These terms are somewhat arbitrary. Certainly, a single genre or actor may employ more than one kind of acting (**see Harding box**). But the terms are a useful way to begin examining similarities and differences in performing across a range of genres and cultures.

Frances Harding

Konstantin Stanislavsky

How Hard It is to act "Naturally"

In every branch of art there are first hundreds of people who wish to study it. Many come in response to the bait of "learning creatively," but having realized how much of their time they have to devote to it; how difficult it is to achieve the complete freedom of the body and all its parts; how long it takes to control then develop one's attention and to learn to transfer it entirely – at one blow – and instantly from one group of muscles to another before you even get to the psychological problems; how difficult it is to develop the sense of rhythm in oneself and change it in the most extraordinary way to the rhythm of the music before you even start on your exercises for collecting your energy and distributing it in different directions – having grasped all that, the majority of those who come to study the art of acting will leave the studio. Many of those who stay behind will also very soon leave, for the temptation to earn money by slipshod work is very great.

1961, *Stanislavsky on the Art of the Stage*, 161–62

Acting and Not-Acting in Africa

[In Africa] the audience–performer relationship [is one] in which the interaction between them is a suspension of the *ordinary* rather than a suspension of *reality* and thus constitutes more of a *heightening* of reality in which it is recognized that ordinary people can become extra-ordinary for a period of time. [Following from this] is a preference for multilayered performances whereby any one performer may, within a single performance, be at one point "acting" and at another point "presenting the self." Neither the audience nor the performer experiences any difficulty in accommodating a movement between the two. A sustained, uninterrupted representation is not required in order to convince the spectators of the presence of an "other." It is more a case of recognizing that some people have – albeit temporarily (i.e., for the duration of the performance) – the power to move betwen the presentation of self and the presentation of an "other."

1999, "Presenting and Re-Presenting the Self: From Not-Acting to Acting in African Performance," 119

Realistic acting

In realistic acting, the behavior onstage is based on that in ordinary life. This kind of acting was considered avant-garde when it was introduced in Europe in the last decades of the nineteenth century. Soon it became dominant (**see figure 6.6**). Realistic acting remains the dominant style of Western acting in everything from soap operas to movies and television. Even when the story, action, and settings are fantastic – as in *Star Wars* or *Crouching Tiger, Hidden Dragon* – the acting is realistic. Realistic acting assumes that the emotions of the characters are like those of "real people" even if the characters are dancing across treetops or living in a distant galaxy. They may fight in a way no real humans ever could or pilot spaceships through a time warp across billions of light years – but when they speak, they speak ordinary language in the ordinary way. They fall in love, argue, joke, feel sad, and explode in rage in ways that are easily recognizable. Spectators need no special knowledge of a theatrical code to understand what is going on. Codified forms, from ballet to noh, and many rituals, operate from a different assumption (which I will discuss later in the chapter).

Along with realistic acting came realist playwriting, set design, and staging. Realist theatre reached many parts of the world on the wings of colonialism and the spread of Western culture. In Japan, realistic theatre was called *shingeki* (new theatre), in China, *huaju* (spoken theatre) (**see figure 6.7**). In many places, the realist theatre was known simply as "modern theatre," akin to the rest of modernism – railroads and automobiles, telephones, and new kinds of political and economic relations. Realist theatre was regarded as progressive, while traditional forms represented outmoded social systems and beliefs. Most traditional theatres around the world consist of the conjunction of drama, dance, song, and music. They are frequently codified. For a time, these theatres were rejected. Many revolutionaries wanted cultural as well as technical, political, and economic modernization. They wanted to bring traditional forms into line with new views of what the social order ought to be (**see Mao box**).

Of course, realistic acting changes as social life changes. What was "natural" in 1902 is not natural in 2002; and 2002 behavior will look unnatural when regarded by those living

fig 6.6. Act 4 of Anton Chekhov's *Three Sisters*, directed by Konstantin Stanislavsky at the Moscow Art Theatre, 1903. Olga Knipper as Masha, M. G. Savitskaya as Olga, and N. N. Litovtseva as Irina. Copyright SCR Photograph Archive, London.

fig 6.7. A huaju or spoken drama play, Sun Huizu's *Mingri Jiuyao Chu San* (Tomorrow He'll Be Out of the Mountains) in a production at the Shanghai Peoples Art Theatre, directed by Richard Schechner, 1989.

Mao Zedong

The Cultural Army Serves the People

In our struggle for the liberation of the Chinese people there are various fronts, among which there are the fronts of the pen and of the gun, the cultural and the military fronts. To defeat the enemy we must rely primarily on the army with guns. But this army alone is not enough, we must also have a cultural army. [. . .] The first problem is: literature and art for whom?

This problem was solved long ago by Marxists, especially by Lenin. As far back as 1905 Lenin pointed out emphatically that our literature and art should "serve [. . .] the millions and tens of millions of working people." [. . .]

Indeed literature and art exist which are for the exploiters and oppressors. Literature and art for the landlord class are feudal literature and art. Literature and art for the bourgeoisie are bourgeois literature and art. [. . .] Then literature and art exist which serve the imperialists. [. . .] With us, literature and art are for the people, not for any of the above groups. We have said that China's new culture at the present stage is an anti-imperialist, anti-feudal culture of the masses of the people under the leadership of the proletariat. [. . .]

In the last analysis, what is the source of all literature and art? Works of literature and art, as ideological forms, are products of the reflection in the human brain of the life of a given society. [. . .] The life of the people is always a mine of raw materials for literature and art, materials in their natural form, materials that are crude, but most vital, rich, and fundamental; they make all literature and art seem pallid by comparison; they provide literature and art with an inexhaustible source, their only source. [. . .] Some may ask, is there not another source in books, in the literature and art of ancient times and of foreign countries? In fact the literary and artistic works of the past are not a source but a stream; they were created by our predecessors and the foreigners out of the literary and artistic raw materials they found in the life of the people of their time and place. We must take over all the fine things in our literary and artistic heritage, critically assimilate whatever is beneficial, and use them as examples when we create works out of the literary and artistic raw materials in the life of the people of our own time and place. [. . .]

Our specialists in literature should pay attention to the wall newspapers of the masses and to the reportage written in the army in the villages. Our specialists in drama should pay attention to the small troops in the army and the villages. Our specialists in music should pay attention to the songs of the masses. Our specialists in the fine arts should pay attention to the fine arts of the masses. [. . .] On the one hand, they should help and guide the popularizers, and on the other, they should learn from these comrades and, through them, draw nourishment from the masses to replenish and enrich themselves so that their specialties do not become "ivory towers," detached from the masses and from reality, devoid of content or life. [. . .] Only by speaking for the masses can a specialist educate them and only by being their pupil can he be their teacher.

1967 (1942), *Mao Tse-Tung on Literature and Art*, 1, 10–11, 18, 22–23 in 2102. This can be demonstrated if one looks at old movies made in a realist style. The acting often appears stilted and "unreal." This is both because realist acting, like all acting, is stylized (abstracted and shaped from what happens in ordinary life) and because the daily behaviors upon which realist acting is modeled change over time. Old newsreels, documentaries, and movies provide evidence of how the behavior of daily life changes from one historical period to another. One notes also, however, that certain behaviors — those of religious, judicial, and secular rituals, for example — tend to conserve themselves. This kind of acting will be discussed in the section on "codified acting."

In realistic acting, the actor "disappears into the role" (**see figure 6.8**). Audiences experience the characters as real, living persons. When an actor performs realistically, she is probably following basic principles laid down by **Konstantin Stanislavsky** (1863–1938) at the turn of the twentieth century and reinforced many times since. The Russian actor and director developed techniques such as the "magic if" and "emotional recall" to help an actor identify deeply with the character — to such a degree that the actor's own self is fused with the self of the character. The goal of actor training in realistic acting is twofold. First, to help the actor find situations in her own life that are analogous (emotionally, if not actually) to what happens to the character. Second, to be able to show these feelings in a sincere way to spectators. This last is particularly difficult, because revealing "real feelings" tends to happen only among intimates, not before several hundred strangers. Actor Studio founder **Lee Strasberg** (1901–82) recognized this difficulty and devised the "private moment" exercise to deal with it (**see Strasberg box 1**).

Lee Strasberg

"The Private Moment"

Another recent exercise – which is very valuable, even for staging – is what I call "The Private Moment." It came from a rereading of that Stanislavsky book in which he uses the famous phrase about being "private and public." The most difficult thing for the actor is to be private in public, which means he must seem to be in a real situation while he knows full well that he is on a stage. In order to deal with this directly, I experimented with some of the people I had difficulty with. There was a great deal of inner emotion, a lot taking place which wasn't coming out because of the tension created by the audience. But how to deal with it – after all, the audience is there and you can't wipe it out. If you can concentrate, fine, but if somehow it doesn't work for you, what do you do? And then I said: you must have a moment in life when you're alone, when you behave in a way which, if anyone comes in, if you hear the door opening, you immediately stop. In other words, it is not a moment when you are simply alone, it is a moment when you are *private*. I thought by making use of the strong impulse and impetus of something that happens only in private, and yet placing it in public before an audience – making the actor do that – we could lick this problem of the actor's being inhibited by the audience. And it worked. [. . .]

We also found wonderful theatrical material. [. . .] We found that people have wonderfully theatrical behavior when they're private, much more so than when they are simply alone. They speak to themselves with such vividness, they argue, they tell people off. They carry on in a way which they immediately inhibit when somebody is there. So, in addition to the training effect of the Private Moment, we found that it had within itself enormous possibilities as a guide to staging certain moments – soliloquies, monologues, opera moments, moments when a person is left alone on the stage – what Stanislavsky calls the Star Pause.

1964, "Working With Live Material," 125–26

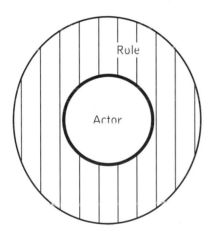

fig 6.8. In realistic acting, the actor is enclosed within the role.

Konstantin Stanislavsky (1863–1938): Russian actor, director, and acting teacher. Co-founder in 1898 with Vladimir Nemirovich-Danchenko of the Moscow Art Theatre. In the early part of the twentieth century, Stanislavsky developed principles of actor training that continue to be extremely influential. Author of *My Life in Art* (1924), *An Actor Prepares* (1936), and other books on acting.

Lee Strasberg

Lee Strasberg (1901–82): American acting teacher, actor and director. Co-founder of the Group Theatre (1931). Strasberg taught at the Actors Studio in New York from 1949 until his death. There he developed "the Method," a system based on Stanislavsky's but which emphasized how actors could use their own personal emotional lives as the basis for developing roles.

Realistic acting works best with realist or naturalist dramas – such as **Henrik Ibsen**'s *Hedda Gabler*, **Arthur Miller**'s *Death of a Salesman*, or **David Mamet**'s *American Buffalo*. Realistic acting is well suited to film, where close-ups and microphoning add immeasurably to the illusion of intimacy. Realistic acting does not work as well with poetic drama such as the plays of Shakespeare, **Kalidasa** (5th century CE), or **Federico García Lorca**. But for all its apparent "naturalness," realistic acting is a style – it is not "real life itself." If it were, no actor training would be necessary to master this style. The existence of many schools of acting indicates clearly that realist acting is a style. Even Strasberg emphasized that realism was a style, not "life itself." He felt it was necessary for the actor to rise to the level of the play. It was a mistake to bring the play down to the experiences of the actor (**see Strasberg box 2**).

Henrik Ibsen (1828–1906): Norwegian playwright noted for his pioneering realistic dramas dealing with the personal social interactions of middle-class characters. Among his many plays are *Peer Gynt* (1867), *A Doll's House* (1879), *Ghosts* (1881), *Hedda Gabler* (1890), and *The Master Builder* (1891).

Arthur Miller (1915–): American playwright. Among his many plays are *All my Sons* (1947), *Death of a Salesman* (1949), *The Crucible* (1953), *A View from the Bridge* (1955), *After the Fall* (1964), *The Price* (1968), *The Ride Down Mt. Morgan* (1991, revised 1999), and *Broken Glass* (1994).

David Mamet (1947–): American playwright, screenwriter, and director. Among his many plays are *American Buffalo* (1975), *Glengarry Glen Ross* (1983), *Oleanna* (1992), and *The Old Neighborhood* (1997). His films include *House of Games* (1987), *The Spanish Prisoner* (1998), and *Wag the Dog* (1998).

Federico García Lorca (1898–1936): Spanish poet and dramatist, killed by the fascist rebels led by **Francisco Franco** (1875–1972) at the outset of the Spanish Civil War. Lorca's plays include *Blood Wedding* (1933), *Yerma* (1934), and *The House of Bernarda Alba* (1936).

Lee Strasberg

Raising the Actor to the Level of the Character

First, you must define the essential ingredient in a part. In other words: what would have to happen to me so that I would be Lady Macbeth? We don't say, "I'm Lady Macbeth," and then begin work.

There is a formulation here which I would like to emphasize because it's one of the few things worth putting theoretically. [. . .] Generally speaking it is true that Stanislavsky would say, "Now, if you were Lady Macbeth, how would you do this? How would you behave?" And in doing this, he often made the aesthetic mistake of taking the role down to the actor.[. . .] On the other hand, [Yevgeni] Vakhtangov [1883–1922] says, "If you had to do such and such a thing [. . .], what would have to happen to you, what would motivate you to do that?" In other words he places the aesthetic intention first and then uses the technique as a way of carrying out the aesthetic intention. When that is not done, often, even in Stanislavsky's productions, the work makes the reality descend to the level of the actor, rather than helping the actor to ascend to the level of the character. You see, work on a part helps create the reality and so we must be careful to bring the actor to the reality of the play by motivating him to act as the character acts.

1964, "Working With Live Material," 129

Brechtian Acting

Brechtian acting is not so much "opposed" to realistic acting as supplemental to it. Brecht was both a playwright and a director. In staging his own plays, he emphasized both the meaning of the drama and the individual agency of the actor. Brecht did not want the actor to disappear into the role. He wanted the actor to engage the role actively, to enter into a dialectical relationship with the role (**see figure 6.9**). Brecht called this *Verfremdungseffekt*, a word difficult to translate into English, but roughly meaning "alienation" or "estrangement" effect (**see Willet box**). It is best to think of the V-effekt as a way to drive a wedge between the actor, the character, the staging (including blocking, design, music, and any other

fig 6.9. Elizabeth LeCompte as Yvette and Jim Griffiths as the Colonel in a scene from The Performance Group's production of Bertolt Brecht's *Mother Courage and Her Children*, directed by Richard Schechner, New York, 1975. Here both LeCompte and Griffiths stand "next to" as well as "inside" the roles they play.

John Willet

Verfremdungseffekt *in Brecht*

With "Verfremdung" went the "Verfremdungseffekt," where "Effekt" corresponded to our own stage use of the word "effects": a *means* by which an effect of estrangement could be got. Both these new words have a single object: to show everything in a fresh and unfamiliar light, so that the spectator is brought to look critically even at what he has so far taken for granted. [. . .] "Verfremdung", in fact, is not simply the breaking of illusion (though that is one means to the end); and it does not mean "alienating" the spectator in the sense of making him hostile to the play. It is a matter of detachment, of reorientation: exactly what [Percy Bysshe] Shelley (1792–1822) meant when he wrote that poetry "makes familiar objects to be as if they were not familiar," or [Arthur] Schopenhauer (1788–1860) when he claimed that art must show "common objects of experience in a light that is at once clear and unfamiliar."

1960, *The Theatre of Bertolt Brecht*, 179

production element) so that each is able to bounce off of, and comment upon, the others.

Brecht's idea of the V-effekt, modeled on the Russian formalist notion of *priem ostranennia* (way to make strange), was powerfully reinforced when Brecht, while in Moscow in 1935 (apparently oblivious to the Stalinist terror then in full bloom), saw the great Chinese actor **Mei Lanfang** (1894–1961) perform. At a formal banquet in his honor, in a tuxedo, and without lights, scenery, or makeup, Mei showed a *dan* (woman) role from *jingju* (**see Brecht box**). Mei's performance disrupted the equation "theatre = reality." Mei confirmed for Brecht the superiority of non-illusionistic theatre. Mei exemplified exactly those qualities Brecht was

Mei Lanfang (1894–1961): Chinese performer of *jingju* and *kunju* (classical sung theatre or "opera"), specializing in *dan* roles (women). Mei's international tours and demonstrations helped bring Chinese theatre to the attention of non-Chinese theatre practitioners and scholars.

looking for: a distance separating actor from role; a disregard for the fourth wall; a quoting of the character played rather than any complete conversion into the character.

In Brechtian acting, the actor does not hide behind the attributes of the role or disappear into the role. The actor — and the playwright and director, too — takes a position to some degree outside what is being performed (**see figure 6.10**). From this more objective place, the artist can offer opinions — both directly and by means of a specific gesture (a "gestus," Brecht called it) — concerning the dilemma facing the character, the social context of the drama, and the relationship of the play to the situation of the audience. The important thing is to create an art where history is not already given, a theatre not controlled by fate or destiny, but open to historical intervention and actual social change. This insistence on the ability to interrogate, intervene, and change forms the basis of Augusto Boal's "Theatre of the Oppressed" — a neo-Brechtian community-based theatre of social change enacted by spectators turned into actors, "spect-actors," as Boal calls them (**see Boal box**).

Brechtian acting interrogates the character's actions, proposes alternative actions, and demystifies events that

Bertolt Brecht

"Alienation Effects in Chinese Acting"

[. . .] the Chinese artist never acts as if there were a fourth wall [. . .]. He expresses his awareness of being watched. This immediately removes one of the European stage's characteristic illusions. The audience can no longer have the illusion of being the unseen spectator at an event which is really taking place. [. . .] The artist's object is to appear strange and even surprising to the audience. He achieves this by looking strangely at himself and his work. As a result everything put forward by him has a touch of the amazing. Everyday things are thereby raised above the level of the obvious and automatic. [. . .] The Chinese artist's performance often strikes the Western actor as cold. That does not mean that the Chinese theatre rejects all representation of feelings. The performer portrays incidents of utmost passion, but without his delivery becoming heated. [. . .] The Chinese performer [. . .] rejects complete conversion. He limits himself from the start to simply quoting the character played. But with what art he does this!

1964 (1936), *Brecht on Theatre*, 91–94

Augusto Boal

The Spect-Actor Rehearsing the Revolution

In order to understand the poetics of the oppressed one must keep in mind its main objective: to change the people – "spectators," passive beings in the theatrical phenomenon – into subjects, into actors, transformers of the dramatic action. [. . .] The spectator delegates no power to the character (or actor) either to act or to think in his place; on the contrary, he himself assumes the protagonist role, changes the dramatic action, tries out solutions, discusses plans for change – in short, trains himself for real action. In this case, perhaps the theatre is not revolutionary in itself, but it is surely a rehearsal for the revolution. [. . .] It is not the place of the theatre to show the correct path, but only to offer the means by which all possible paths may be examined.

1985 (1974) *Theatre of the Oppressed*, 122, 138

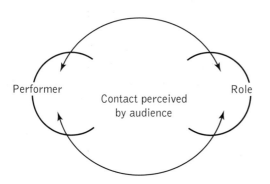

fig 6.10. In Brechtian acting, the actor takes a position to some degree outside the role, engaging the role and even criticizing the character. The audience is aware of the tension that both draws the actor to the role and separates her from the role.

contradictions, tests variations, tries out events from several points of view. Brecht's theatre was profoundly social. (Brecht was himself criticized for putting his name alone on works that belonged to the "committee," for taking too much individual credit for collective work – especially in relation to the women he so depended on, **Ruth Berlau** (1906–74), **Margarete Steffin** (1908–41), and **Helene Weigel** (1900–71).

Ruth Berlau (1906–74): Danish novelist, actress, and theatre director. Collaborated with **Bertolt Brecht** on the writing of *The Caucasian Chalk Circle* (1943–5) and *The Good Person of Szechwan* (1938–41).

Margarete Steffin (1908–41): German author who collaborated with Brecht on the writing of several of his plays including *The Round Heads and the Pointed Heads* (1931–4), *The Terror and Misery of the Third Reich* (1935–8), *Señora Carrar's Rifles* (1937), *Galileo* (1937–9), *The Good Person of Szechwan* (1938–41), and *The Resistible Rise of Arturu Ui* (1941).

might otherwise appear to be "inevitable." If Stanislavsky stressed the actor's "work on oneself," urging an intense personal study and preparation, Brecht worked "in committee," collaborating with a dedicated group of colleagues. The creative team stops, reflects, uncovers

Helene Weigel (1900–71): Austrian-born actor and wife-partner of Brecht. Weigel played leading roles in a number of Brecht's plays including *The Mother* (1932) and *Mother Courage and her Children* (1949). After Brecht's death in 1956, Weigel became leader of the Berliner Ensemble.

Codified Acting

For Brecht, Mei might have been demonstrating the V-effekt, but according to his own culture, Mei was engaged in the highly formalized, centuries-old acting characteristic of jingju. This style of codified acting employs meaningful gestures, movements, songs, costumes, and makeup set by tradition and passed down from teacher to student by means of a rigorous training that takes years (**see Mei box**). Codified acting is a semiotic system of references. Although some of the actions in a codified system may be derived or abstracted from everyday behavior, a codified system as a whole is not directly analogous to everyday behavior. It is more like a spoken or written language. One has to know the specific vocabulary and grammar of a codified system of acting in order to fully understand what is being expressed. Unless you know the vocabulary and grammar of jingju, you can't really understand Mei's performing.

Mei Lanfang

The Aesthetic Basis of Chinese "Opera"

Like all other arts, the Chinese classical opera has its own aesthetic basis. The Chinese classical operas based on singing and dance movements must follow the cadence of the music to form a certain pattern. The beautiful dance movements created by past artists are all based on gestures in real life, synthesized and accentuated to become art. And so the performing artist has a twofold task: apart from acting his role according to the development of the story, he must also remember that his job is to express himself through beautiful dance movements. [. . .]

The teacher gives us our basic training. In the beginning, naturally we have no artistic perception or judgment, we can only imitate his every sound, every gesture. After we reach a certain level, we have to concentrate on the teacher's special technique. [. . .] For example, at the time I studied the *kun qu* opera *The Peony Pavilion* under veteran kun qu artist, Jiao Huilan. Jiao had already long since given up the stage. My impression of him was that of a wizened old man. But when he started demonstrating gestures, I felt that the aged man wearing an old fur coat had ceased to exist. I could see only the exquisite movements of the heroine in the play.

When you develop perception, not only can you emulate your teachers — you discover things worth noticing everywhere. For instance, you observe the expression of a man sitting leisurely, those of a person who has lost his child on the road, the way a good calligraphist holds his pen, the adept movements of a woman washing clothes, and so on. [. . .] All unusual expressions or highly rhythmic movements can be grasped by a person with a sharp sense of perception, then translated into art and adapted for the stage. [. . .]

Sometimes the artist intends to absorb useful material from life, but because he cannot distinguish the good from the bad, the beautiful from the ugly, and has not studied properly the experience of past artists [. . .] he does not know what things can be adapted to the stage and what cannot.

Take for instance the character of the Monkey King. When played by a good actor, the audience feels that he is a hero, a god; on stage he looks splendid. His makeup and movements convey his heroic spirit, while at the same time he displays the characteristic agility of the monkey. That is how the character should be depicted. However, some actors playing this role do not convey the same feeling. They try hard to imitate a real monkey, bringing to the stage a lot of unbecoming gestures. Such an indiscriminate adherence to nature is a very bad tendency. Of course, an artist should be inventive in his stage art, but this originality must come through study. If he has not studied widely, if he has not properly digested past experiences, he will not be able to find the right means of expression.

1981 (1956), "Reflections in my Stage Life," 35–36, 44–45

Codified acting: Performing based on semiotically constructed gestures, movements, songs, costumes, and makeup set by tradition and passed down from teacher to student by means of rigourous training.

Codified acting is widespread throughout the world. There are hundreds, if not thousands, of codified systems of acting. Ballet, kathakali, gelede, jingju, and noh are codified. In fact, the notion of devising new movements, songs, costumes, and stage designs for each production is a relatively recent phenomenon, closely associated with realistic and Brechtian acting. In Asia, codified acting has been practiced and theorized for more than 2,000 years. The *Natyasastra* of **Bharata Muni** (approximately second century BCE–second century CE), a Sanskrit manual of theatre, dance, and music conceived of as a single art, details with great precision how hand and eye movements, body gestures, dance steps, music, and costumes express and communicate specific emotions, dramatic situations, and character types (**see Bharata Muni box**). In Chinese jingju, when an actor is led on to the stage by a stagehand carrying a "wind flag" the character is understood to be caught in a windstorm. If a character exits walking on his knees, spectators understand that he is brought down by grief or terror. If an actor walks around the stage in a circle, he is presumed to have traveled many miles; if he carries a riding whip, he has made the trip on horseback (**see figure 6.11**). Most often, the gestures of codified acting carry specific meaning. But sometimes the codified behavior has no specific meaning. It simply is itself. This is true of much modern dance, where movements may evoke emotions in the spectators but are not directly translatable into words or situations, as in jingju or bharatanatyam.

Although I am discussing codified acting in terms of the performing arts, most rituals – secular as well as sacred – some popular entertainments, and sports employ codified movements. To perform a marriage, execute a ballroom dance, or shoot a basketball requires mastering codified behavior (**see figure 6.12**). Sports matches are incomprehensible to those who don't know the codified movements of the game. Sports owe their particular power to engage players and spectators to the combination of codified and improvised behavior. The basic moves are codified, and knowing these moves allows people to get what's going on, to appreciate fine play and disparage poor play. At the same time, individual moves are brief and flexible enough to allow variations and new combinations. A "great player" is one who knows the moves and can riff on them as an accomplished jazz musician knows a particular progression of music and is able to improvise on it.

Bharata Muni

Acting with a Single Hand; with the Chest

Abhinaya [acting] done by a single hand are 24. [. . .] 1. *Pataka*: With thumb bent and other fingers stretched out. To convey striking, driving, joy, pride, etc. With both hands and fingers moving, it suggests rain, showering of flowers, etc. [. . .] 5. *Arala*: The thumb is bent, the other fingers are spread out from each other, the second finger bent like a bow. This *mudra* [hand gesture] is used for blessing in the case of males, and for collecting the hair in the case of women; courage, dignity of men and self-admiration by women are also suggested. [. . .] 21. *Sandamsa*: This *mudra* is Arala (no. 5) but with the change that the tips of the thumb and the second finger touch and the palm is downwards. It is of three kinds – (i) Agraja, when taking out a thorn or picking delicate flowers, (ii) Mukhaja, when flowers are picked from the stalks or when brushes (for putting collyrium on the eyes) are used, and (iii) Parsvaja, when pearls are pierced, etc. [. . .] These, says Bharata, are all *mudras* shown by one hand. [. . .]

Movements of the chest are of five kinds. [. . .]. 1. *Abhugna*: both the shoulders are drooping down and (arms) loosely held, while the back is arched outwards. It conveys or suggests agitation, fear, sorrow, touch of cold, rain falling, etc. 2. *Nirbhugna*: is when the breath is drawn in, the chest expands and lifts, and the back curves in. This suggests speaking truth, bragging, haughtiness, deep breath, affected indifference (by women). [. . .]

1996, *The Natyasastra*, 83, 84, 86, 87

Bharata Muni (*c.* second century BCE–*c.* second century CE): Indian sage, the putative author of *The Natyasastra*, the earliest and still very influential theoretical and practical treatise on all aspects of traditional Indian theatre, dance, playwriting, and to a lesser extent, music.

It is important to note the differences among scored, codified, and improvised performances. Any performance – even the most naturalistic – can be "scored," all its details set and invariable. But scoring a production does not mean it is codified. Codified acting is present only when there is a

fig 6.11. In various traditional Chinese sung theatre genres, actions are conveyed to the audience by means of codified gestures, movements, and vocal patterns. This scene from *bangzi*, a north China genre, shows a group traveling by boat. The action is conveyed by the Boatman's oar and the alignment and movement of the three actors to the Boatman's left. Photograph by Isabelle Duchesne.

fig 6.12. Some examples of codified performances outside of the theatre.

A rabbi performing the marriage of Christine Dotterweich to Henry Bial, 1998. Photograph courtesy Henry Bial.

A basketball player at the 1996 Atlanta Olympics takes aim. Copyright Colorsport.

Ballroom dancing as shown in the Australian movie, *Strictly Ballroom*, with Paul Mercurio and Gia Carides, 1992. Copyright Kobal Collection, London.

semiotic system of meaning separate from everyday behavior. Of course, everyday behavior can be analyzed semiotically – all behavior "means something." In codified acting, the actors have consciously mastered a system separate from ordinary behavior. One can improvise either with new materials or with codified behavior. Improvising means working without a set score. The bits a performer uses to build an improvisation can be from everyday behavior or from codified behavior.

Mastering codified performing takes years of training. Each genre has its own vocabulary. In kathakali, young actors have their bodies massaged into "kathakali shape" (**see figure 6.13**) and practice rigorous exercises to train each part of their bodies, including the eyes (**see figure 6.14**). When he was a boy, Mei was told his eyes were too dull and inexpressive for jingju. To correct this, Mei practiced staring at a point of incense burning in a dark room, following kites as they flew high in the sky, and tracing with his eyes the soaring and wheeling of birds. Mei succeeded in earning the

bright eyes for which he was renowned. Training that actually reforms the body is used in sports too. Weight lifting, pole-vaulting, and acrobatics are codified forms demanding specifically trained and re-formed bodies. One can begin to learn realistic or Brechtian acting relatively late in life because people have "practiced" daily behavior all their lives. Training in realist performance is focused on gaining conscious control over what one already knows how to do. But to master a codified form, one must begin very young when both mind and body are flexible. Acquiring a "second body" and a "focused mind" is not easy. Each form has its own demands, whether ballet or kathakali, piano or violin, the opera or acrobatics, sprint racing or marathon running, power forward or football lineman. To some degree, a person is born with the disposition toward a specific body. But for those who reach world-class levels of performance, an enormous effort and determination goes into conforming to the demands of the codified behavior of a specific genre or sport (**see Barba box**).

fig 6.13. A kathakali student at the Kalamandalam, Kerala, India, receives a massage that helps shape his body to the needs of this exacting genre, 1976. Photographs by Richard Schechner.

fig 6.14. TRYPTICH. a–c
Some examples of the exercises used at the kathakali Kalamandalam, Kerala, India for training the eyes, 1976. Photograph by Richard Schechner.

Eugenio Barba

Lokadharmi *Versus* Natyadharmi

"We have two words," the Indian dancer Sanjukta Panigrahi said to me, "to describe man's behavior: *lokadharmi* stands for behavior (*dharmi*) in daily life (*loka*); *natyadharmi* for behavior in dance (*natya*)." [. . .] Certain Oriental and Occidental performers possess a quality of presence which immediately strikes the spectator and engages his attention. This occurs even when these performers are giving a cold, technical demonstration. [. . .] The way we use our daily bodies in daily life is substantially different from the way we use them in performance. We are not conscious of our daily techniques: we move, we sit, we carry things, we kiss, we agree and disagree with gestures which we believe to be natural but which are in fact culturally determined. [. . .] The first step in discovering what the principles governing a performer scenic *bios*, or life, might be, lies in understanding that the body's daily techniques can be replaced by extra daily techniques, that is, techniques which do not respect the habitual conditioning of the body. Performers use these extra daily techniques.

1991, *A Dictionary of Theatre Anthropology: The Secret Art of the Performer*, 9

The codified actor "steps into" or "puts on" a role much as it has been performed by earlier masters. The novice does not learn abstractly but directly from a teacher passing down a specific line of a tradition. In Bali, the dance teacher is behind the student literally manipulating the young dancer, putting the dance directly into the body (**see figure 6.15**). The results of this kind of specific learning are traditions rich in subtle variations. In noh theatre there are five families. To an outsider, a performance by the Kanze family may look just like one by the Kongo family. But connoisseurs are able to detect and appreciate differences in tempo, intensity, singing, use of the noh masks, and so on. Similarly, "ballet" is a general term for a traditional genre of dancing developed in Europe from the eighteenth century forward. But there are different styles of ballet, tied to specific choreographers and dancers. Each of these is codified. Individual dancers interpret but do not change the movement. New ballets are composed using the basic vocabulary which is codified.

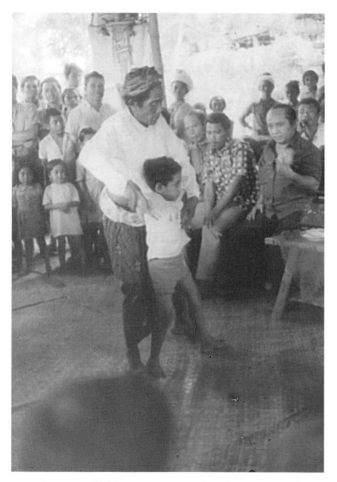

fig 6.15. A Balinese dance teacher stands behind his young pupil manipulating the student's body – literally putting the dance into the body, 1972. Photograph by Richard Schechner

In realistic or Brechtian acting there are as many ways to play a role as there are actors and directors ready to interpret it. This is true even if the drama is not realistic, as with Shakespeare. Any text can be played realistically, in Brechtian style, or according to a codified system of acting. Some might worry that codified acting is mechanical and dull. However, this is not so. As attested to by many performers and spectators, deep feelings can be expressed and shared within the strict confines of a codified form.

Codified Acting and the Avant-garde

Of course, the avant-garde delights in stretching all envelopes, including that of codified acting. In 1995, for example, British choreographer **Matthew Bourne** (1960–) opened his all-male *Swan Lake* (**see Lyall box**). It is important to note that the dancing followed the rules of ballet. It was only the casting and the interpretation of the story that caused a stir. What critics and audiences alike admired was Bourne's ability to work within the strictures of ballet and come up with something exhilarating and new. Bourne's approach is not the only one. For many years, the Trocadero Ballet de Monte Carlo has also presented an all-male *Swan Lake* – but as parody. However, even the parody demands ballet dancers with a reasonably high level of skill (**see websites box**).

No one has done more experiments with codified forms than **Eugenio Barba** (1936–)and his colleagues at the International School of Theatre Anthropology. In a 1987 ISTA session in Italy, Barba spent a week investigating how **Johan Wolfgang von Goethe**'s (1749–1832) and **Christopher Marlowe**'s (1564–93) versions of *Faust* could be interpreted by non-Western performers employing their own codified means of expression. Indian odissi dancer **Sanjukta Panigrahi** (1932–97) and Japanese buyo dancer **Azuma Katsuko** (1943–96) improvised scenes from *Faust* using their own specific genres of performance (**see figure 6.16**). The intention was to "destabilize" the codified forms – to stretch their limits of expressivity. The result was an intercultural clash, simultaneously invigorating and confusing (**see Pavis box**). In chapter 8, I will discuss intercultural performance in more detail.

Matthew Bourne (1960–): English dancer and choreographer. Winner in 1996 of the Olivier and Tony Awards for his all-male *Swan Lake*.

Sarah Lyall

Matthew Bourne's All-Male **Swan Lake**

When it opened at Sadler's Wells last year [1995], Matthew Bourne's provocative version of the most classic of classic ballets was immediately labeled the "gay Swan Lake." It was not surprising: Mr. Bourne's swans were not dainty dancers in tutus, but fierce, bare-chested men in feathery pantaloons. The result could have been a disastrous parody, a fiasco destined to make Mr. Bourne a laughingstock in London's unforgiving ballet world. But audiences and critics alike have lavished praise on the production. [. . .]

Mr. Bourne studied the swans in St. James Park [in London] and showed his dancers a slow-motion videotape of an angry swan attacking a fishing boat. "Swans are not always beautiful, and they're not always gliding," he said. He strove, he said, to evoke the swannish ungainliness the birds show when, for example, they land on the water and shift their weight backward. "It's an odd, almost ugly thing, and it's very undancerly," he said.

1996, "A 'Swan Lake' with Male Swans is a Hit in London," 1–3

Websites

Trocadero Ballet de Monte Carlo

The beefcake ballerinas, otherwise known as Les Ballets Trokadero de Monte Carlo or The Trocks, are approaching the quarter century mark. It is perhaps a surprising age for an all-male ensemble that dances en pointe and in drag elevating the classical ballet repertoire to heights of hilarity unknown before. Founded by Peter Anastos and friends in 1974, The Trocks quickly achieved success not just because of their gut-rupturing humor and physical appearance, but because they also demonstrate superlative dance skills in their performances.

2001, Gaywave.com/arts

"Trocadero Ballet De Monte Carlo" – a drag ballet . . . tall, striking, sometimes handsome butch men in tu-tus and dancing on point. Could have descended into totally (merely) hilarious camp, except for the fact that all the dancers were superbly trained – and thus gave a performance that was enjoyed at many levels. The juxtaposition of muscular, strapping ballerinas with hairy armpits dancing with fey, wimpy princes (in the Swan Lake piece) is an image that will keep you chortling long after the two encores.

2001, Inkpot.com/theatre/London

Eugenio Barba (1936–): Italian-born director and theorist, founder in 1964 of the Odin Theatre of Holstebro, Denmark. The Odin features ensemble devised pieces, intensive actor training, workshops, and touring. In 1980 Barba convened the first session of ISTA – the International School of Theatre Anthropology, an ongoing intercultural investigation into performing. Barba's books include *The Floating Islands* (1979), *Beyond the Floating Islands* (1986, with Nicola Savarese), *A Dictionary of Theatre Anthropology: The Secret Art of the Performer* (1991, with Savarese), *The Paper Canoe* (1995), and *Land of Ashes and Diamonds* (1999).

Johann Wolfgang von Goethe (1749–1832): Prolific and influential German poet, novelist and playwright – first a Romantic and then a classicist. Among his many works are *The Sorrows of Young Werther* (1774), *Iphigenia in Taurus* (1787), *Torquato Tasso* (1789), *The Apprenticeship of Wilhelm Meister* (1796), and *Faust* (part I, 1808, part II, published posthumously, 1833).

Christopher Marlowe (1564–93): English playwright whose works include *The Jew of Malta* (c. 1589), *Edward II* (c. 1592), and *Dr. Faustus* (c. 1593).

Sanjukta Panigrahi (1932–97): Indian dancer widely regarded as the leading exponent of odissi dance. Panigrahi also collaborated with **Eugenio Barba** at the International School of Theatre Anthropology (ISTA) on many experiments exploring the relationship between Asian and Western performing.

Azuma Katsuko (1943–96): Japanese buyo dancer. Azuma collaborated with **Eugenio Barba** for a number of years at the International School of Theatre Anthropology (ISTA).

Patrice Pavis

fig 6.16. Azuma Kazuko, left, and Sanjukta Panigrahi improvise a scene from the Faust plays and legend as part of Eugenio Barba's work at the International School of Theatre Anthropology, 1987. Photograph by Tony d'Urso. Photograph courtesy of Eugenio Barba.

Improvising with Codified Acting

The Japanese dancer Katsuko Azuma and the Indian dancer Sanjukta Panigrahi belong to two totally different cultural and theatrical/choreographic worlds. [...] Getting these performers to work together is not self-evident, since the contrast in their presence, dynamic, and gestural representations is striking. [...] It is not easy to measure the distance between canonical odissi or buyo and the improvisations created by these dancers. Deviation from the codified traditional gestures does not seem to be a threat, but rather a consciously assumed risk. The director's role [...] is to destabilize the dancer, to unbalance her in the sense of imposing a gesture or series of gestures, an attitude foreign to the original codification. For example, Barba puts a glass bottle in Panigrahi's hands and asks her to do drunken – and therefore rhythmically distorted – mudras, to show the character's drunkenness. This process of voluntary *de-formation* is immediately followed by *re-formation*, by moving to another type of codification. The dance of the drunken mudras becomes a parody of popular dance in which one dancer imitates the movements of the other, a joyful dance of two drunkards who end up synchronizing their drunkenness. This *de-formation* is not an elimination of the codified traditional form, but a *re-formation* into another kind of gesture, inspired by the tradition and which prepares for the next stages of the reelaboration.

1989, "Dancing with *Faust*," 39–40

Codified Acting and Ritual

Strictly speaking, performing rituals is not "acting" at all in the theatrical sense. The doer is performing but not acting. It is not acting because most rituals involve no impersonation. (Some rituals, such as shamanizing, include impersonation; this kind of performing will be dealt with later in the chapter.) Persons performing rituals do prescribed actions, wear designated costumes, and in other ways enact highly codified behaviors. A Roman Catholic priest celebrating the Mass follows a strictly prescribed scenario that dictates what clothes he wears, where he stands in the church, and what he says and does. His performance is understood by those who know what the vestments, gestures, utterances, chalice, wafer, and church architecture mean. The Mass is similar to liturgies in other religions – not in specific detail, but in basic structure and process. Liturgies consist of sequences of publicly performed symbolic behavior expressing meanings shared by both the performers and the receivers (**see Rappaport box**). Liturgies are codified performing.

Roy A. Rappaport

The Codified Liturgical Order

Without performance there is no ritual, no liturgical order. [. . .] A liturgical order is an ordering of *acts or utterances*, and as such it is enlivened, realized, or established *only when* those acts are performed and those utterances voiced. [. . .] Since to perform a liturgical order, which is by definition a relatively *invariant* sequence of acts and utterances *encoded by someone other* than the performer himself, is to *conform* to it, authority or directive is *intrinsic* to liturgical order. [. . .] This is to say that by *performing a liturgical order the performer accepts, and indicates to himself and to others that he accepts, whatever is encoded in the canons of the liturgical order in which he is participating* [italics Rappaport's].

1979, *Ecology, Meaning, and Religion*, 192–3

Some secular rituals such as the coronation of a British monarch or the inauguration of an American President are as codified as the Mass. Other secular rituals such as the signing of leases and other contracts, the christening of a ship at launch, and courtroom trials combine codified and improvised behavior. The overall shape of the event is set. Some of the core actions are performed exactly and invariably – breaking a bottle on the bow of the ship, witnessing legal documents, rising when the judge enters a courtroom. But other parts of the performance are open – even in unexpected and startling ways, as with surprise testimony in a trial.

Rituals are theatre-like, but they are not theatre itself. They differ in at least two ways. First, those performing rituals are not impersonating others. The ritualist is himself in his designated ritual role. Second, the virtuosity of the performer as a stage presence is not highly prized in itself as it is in theatre. The first of these differences leads to the second. The ritualist must actually be who she is designated as being, even if she cannot perform the ritual with theatrical

flair. How excellently a ballet dancer elevates herself on toe, how rich a vocal range of interpretation a jingju actor displays, and so on, are at the very core of codified acting on stage. Codified art forms are to a large degree about how well the artist is able to perform – and to a lesser degree about what the performance means. But in rituals, the meaning and consequence of the ritual action as authenticated by the presence of the actual person enabled to enact the ritual are what count. This is so even if this person is feeble in voice and unsteady in gesture. In fact, sometimes the lack of theatrical virtuosity adds to the power of a ritual performance by underlining the importance of the action and of the social-sacred role of the ritual performer. John Paul II celebrating the Mass is all the more affecting in his weakened old age, carrying in his frail physical being the millennia-long authority of the Roman Catholic Church.

At the personal level, "private rituals" (toilet habits, erotic foreplay, ways of preparing food and eating it, etc.) are also to a large degree codified. This behavior is variously termed habit, routine, ritual, or even compulsion, depending on how one wants to regard the performer and the action. What all these terms share is their pointing to a fixed sequence of behavior.

Trance Acting

In trance acting, performers are taken over by non-human beings – gods, spirits, demons, animals, or objects (**see figure 6.17**). Trance performers enact actions not of their

fig 6.17. Photograph by Maya Deren from *Divine Horsemen: The Living Gods of Haiti*, © 1952 Maya Deren. All rights reserved. Courtesy of McPherson & Company, Publishers.

own devising. After the trance is over, an actor may or may not remember what she said and did. Whether the performer remembers or not differs from culture to culture, genre to genre, even instance to instance. Trance acting is very widespread, occurring in a variety of cultures and contexts ranging from Siberian and Korean shamans to Afro-Brazilian candomble, from fundamentalist Christians "falling out" and "speaking in tongues" to Balinese *sanghyang dedari* pre-adolescent girls.

Trance acting is the opposite of Brechtian acting. Brecht asked actors to maintain a critical distance from their roles. He wanted actors at one moment to be in character and at the next to step outside the role and comment on the social situation of the character and the action. For Brecht, the ability to choose, to control history in its small details, was very decisive. He wanted actors and audiences to practice a consciously politically engaged relationship to the drama. In trance acting, the actor has little or no agency. The trancer is "taken over" – sometimes willingly, sometimes forcibly – by beings and/or forces more powerful than the performer. Trance performing is so widespread and popular because it provides actors and spectators alike an extraordinarily powerful "total theatre" experience. People enjoy giving over, surrendering to all-powerful forces, melding into the community, congregation, or crowd.

We need to examine trance possession from several vantage points, starting with how it feels to be "in trance." There is no single answer. The "experience" of being in trance depends on cultural circumstances. What it feels like to be in trance in Bali is different from how it feels to "fall out" in an African-American church, or to be on a Native American "vision quest." In the 1930s, **Jane Belo** (1904–68) investigated the question of what it felt like to be in trance in Bali. In one Balinese village, the sanghyang (trance) performers were possessed by the most ordinary beings – small animals, local spirits, and even brooms, pot lids, and potatoes. Belo was struck by how ordinary trance was to these villagers, a routine, enjoyable event that both entertained people and drew the community close together (**see Belo box**). Trance dancing in Bali, and probably everywhere else, does not occur accidentally. Balinese trance dancers are trained – if not in the formal way that *topeng* or *gambuh* dancers are, then in a method of osmosis whereby they absorb what they are to do and systematically led step-by-step into the kind of behavior expected of them. The ecstasy of trance as we see it today in many parts of the world is not very different from what might have been practiced by the ancient Greeks dancing to Dionysus (**see Dodds box**). This consistency of behavior and experience in many different cultures and historical periods can be explained neurobiologically.

Trance acting: Occurs when performers are taken over, or "possessed," by non-human beings – gods, spirits, demons, animals, or objects.

Jane Belo (1904–68): American anthropologist and ethnographic filmmaker who worked with Margaret Mead in Bali. Author of *Trance in Bali* (1960).

Jane Belo

Trance in a Balinese Mountain Village

A quite distinct type of trance manifestation was the group of *sanghyangs* performed in the mountain district around Selat, in the eastern section of Bali. These were folk plays, crude, earthy performances given without any elaborate and gilded costuming and paraphernalia but using the simple homely objects to be found around the house. [. . .] No-high-flown jargon relating to the gods [. . .] was invoked to explain why Darja suddenly would go into trance and wallow in the mud like a pig, why Darma suddenly would climb the bamboo pole and sway from it like a monkey. [. . .]

The crowd that gathered was alert and attentive, the whole spirit like that for a game in which everyone would take part. Everyone would join in the singing which directed the trancers' performance. People would call out jibes to the performers, urging them on, taunting them with phrases known to infuriate them. The crowd enjoyed this very much indeed. When the time came to bring the act to an end, a whole group would fall upon the trancer, who struggled fiercely in convulsions precipitated by the attack. Amid great excitement, everyone would fall over everyone else in a headlong rough-and-tumble. Then they would set themselves to nursing the trancer back to normal consciousness. All would then be just as intent and caring for the man who was coming back to himself as they had been a few moments before in taunting and exciting the creature he had "become."

[. . .]

[Belo's Balinese assistant "GM" talked to those who went into trance.]

GM: What is your feeling when you are first smoked [put into trance]?

DARJA: Somehow or other suddenly I lose consciousness. The people singing I hear. If people call out, calling me "*Tjit – tah!*" [pig call], like that, I hear it too. If people talk of other things, I don't hear it.

GM: When you're a *sanghyang* pig, and people insult you, do you hear it?

DARJA: I hear it. If anyone insults me I am furious.

GM: When you've finished playing, how do you feel, tired or not?

DARJA: When it's just over, I don't feel tired yet. But the next day, or the day after that, my body is sick.

[. . .]

GM: If you're a *sanghyang puppy*, what do you feel?

DARJA: I just feel like a puppy. I feel happy to run along the ground. I am very pleased, just like a puppy running on the ground. [. . .]

GM: And if you're a *sanghyang* broom, what's it like, and what do you feel?

DARMA: Like sweeping the filth in the middle of the ground. Like sweeping filth in the street, in the Village, I feel I'm being carried off by the broom, led on to sweep.

[. . .]

GM: And who enters *sanghyangs*, god or demons?

GOJA: Those three cannot be separated – god, demon, man – they cannot be broken off from each other.

1960, *Trance in Bali*, 201–202, 220–22

E. R. Dodds

Dionysian Ecstasy, Illusion, and Trance

The joys of Dionysus had an extremely wide range [in ancient Greece], from the simple pleasures of the country bumpkin, dancing a jig on greased wineskins, to the [. . .] ecstatic bacchanal. At both levels, and at all levels between, he is Lusios, "the Liberator" – the god who [. . .] enables you for a short time to *stop being yourself*, and thereby sets you free. [. . .] For Dionysus was the master of Magical Illusions, who could make a vine grow out of a ship's plank, and in general enable his votaries to see the world as the world's not. [. . .] The aim of his cult was *ecstasis* – which again could mean anything from "taking you out of yourself" to a profound alteration of personality.

1951, *The Greeks and the Irrational*, 76–77

From a neurobiological perspective, trance is the outcome of the simultaneous stimulation of both hemispheres (frontal lobes) of the brain (**see Lex box**). In brief, the left lobe guides logical thought and speech; it is the seat of the "ergotropic" (energy) system. Stimulating the left lobe makes one energized, aroused, and alert. The right lobe guides spatial and tonal perceptions; it is the seat of the "trophotropic" (relaxation) system. Stimulating the right hemisphere loosens a person's ego, dissolving boundaries between self and other, inner and outer. By means of repetitive rhythms, psychotropic drugs, incense, sleep and food deprivation, meditation, and so on, both hemispheres are stimulated simultaneously (**see Lewis box**). This results in changes in both the nervous system and the body. When the ergotropic system is engaged, heart rate, blood pressure, and sweat increase. The pupils of the eyes dilate. Brainwaves are desynchronized, muscles become tense or even rigid. Hormones such as epinephrine, norepinephrine, cortisol, and thyroxine are pumped into the blood. When the trophotropic system is engaged, heart rate, blood pressure, and sweat decrease. The pupils constrict, brainwaves are synchronized, muscle tone relaxes, and secretions of insulin, estrogen, and androgen increase.

Ordinarily, one or the other hemisphere is dominant. At slightly aroused levels, this dominance continues. A person usually can't be tranquil and anxious at the same time. But

Barbara Lex

The Neurobiology of Ritual Trance

Ritual trance may constitute a hitherto neglected cultural universal. [. . .] Near-universality of these experiences suggests a human biological substrate or propensity; this interpretation is confirmed by observable changes in motor behavior, speech patterns, and response to external stimuli in trance states reported both by laymen and by scientifically trained observers. [. . .] Exposure to manifold, intense, repetitive, emotion-evoking stimuli ensures uniformity of behavior in ritual participants. Further, attainment of ritual trance is both an inward and outward manifestation of desired emotional states. [. . .]

Briefly stated, in most human beings the left cerebral hemisphere functions in the production of speech, as well as in linear analytic thought, and also assesses the duration of temporal units, processing information sequentially. In contrast, the specializations of the right hemisphere comprise spatial and tonal perceptions, recognition of patterns – including those constituting emotion and other states in the internal milieu – and holistic, synthetic thought, but linguistic capability is limited and the temporal capacity is believed absent. [. . .]

Ergotropic response consists of augmented sympathetic discharges, increased muscle tonus, and excitation in the cerebral cortex manifested as "desynchronized" resting rhythms; the *trophotropic* pattern includes heightened parasympathetic discharges, relaxed skeletal muscles, and synchronized cortical rhythms. [. . .]

Techniques to facilitate ritual trance generally employ trophotropic tuning [. . .]. Stiff, jerky limb and trunk movements [. . .] and facial contortions, as well as twitches, all involve increased muscle tonus and are aspects of ergotropic activation, which, if intensified or sustained, can result in trophotropic rebound. Among other consequences, trophotropic tuning produces increased sensitivity to hyperventilation and hence chanting and singing augment trophotropic responses [. . .] in addition to providing repetitive proprioceptive and exteroceptive stimulation. Trophotropic tuning also reduces sensitivity to pain [. . .].

The *raison d'être* for rituals is the readjustment of dyphasic biological and social rhythms by manipulation of neurophysiological structures under controlled conditions. Rituals properly executed promote a feeling of well-being and relief, not only because prolonged or intense stresses are alleviated, but also because the driving techniques employed in rituals are designed to sensitize or "tune" the nervous system and thereby lessen inhibition of the right hemisphere and permit temporary right-hemisphere dominance, as well as mixed trophotropic-ergotropic excitation, to achieve synchronization of cortical rhythms [. . .].

1979, "The Neurobiology of Ritual Trance," 118, 120, 125, 139, 144–45

I. M. Lewis

Getting into Trance

As is well known, trance states can be readily induced in most normal people by a wide range of stimuli, applied either separately or in combination. Time-honoured techniques include the use of alcoholic spirits, hypnotic suggestion, rapid over-breathing, the inhalation of smoke and vapours, music, and dancing; and the ingestion of such drugs as mescaline or lysergic acid and other psychotropic alkaloids. Even without these aids, much the same effect can be produced, although usually [. . .] more slowly, by such self-inflicted or externally imposed mortifications and privations as fasting and ascetic contemplation.

1971, *Ecstatic Religion*, 39

when one side is fully in play, it "rebounds," bringing the other side fully into play also (**see Fischer box**). This complex brain–body scenario progresses in three phases. In the first phase, either the ergotropic or the trophotropic system prevails; in the second phase the rebound produces a balance or "tuning" of the two systems; in the third phase both systems operate simultaneously — resulting in intense and varied experiences such as sexual orgasm, yogic or zen meditation, and trance (**see figure 6.18**). A person feels both profoundly excited and deeply calm. Although "opposites," shamanic ecstasy and yogic *samadhi* produce the same feeling state.

In this state of maximum bi-hemispheric arousal, people feel weightless, or outside of their bodies, or "oceanic." You feel "one with the universe" or "one with the community," totally without any personal self. Extreme experiences may be rare, but "light trance" is common. Victor Turner called this state of unboundedness "spontaneous communitas." This kind of feeling occurs during trancing, ritualizing, and meditating, but also when one is taken over by the "crowd spirit" at a sports match (or, more terrifyingly, during a riot or lynching), or you lose yourself in hours of disco dancing driven by the music, drink, drugs, and camaraderie. Shamans are masters at creating and drawing people into this kind of experience.

Roland Fischer

Ergotropic and Trophotropic in Synchrony

In spite of the mutually exclusive relation between the ergotropic and trophotropic systems, however, there is a phenomenon called "rebound to superactivity" or trophotropic rebound which occurs in response to intense sympathetic excitation, that is, at ecstasy, the peak of ergotropic arousal. [. . .] Meaning is "meaningful" only at that level of arousal at which it is experienced, and every experience has its state-bound meaning. During the "Self"-state of highest levels of hyper or hypo arousal, this meaning can no longer be expressed in dualistic terms, since the experience of unity is born from the integration of interpretive (cortical) and interpreted (subcortical) structures. Since this intense meaning is devoid of specificities, the only way to communicate its intensity is the metaphor; hence, only through the transformation of objective signs into subjective symbol in art, literature, and religion can the increasing integration of cortical and subcortical activity be communicated.

1971, "A Cartography of the Ecstatic and Meditative States," 902

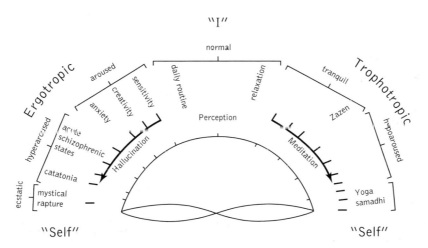

fig 6.18. Fischer's cartography of the ecstatic and meditative states. Varieties of conscious states [are] mapped on the perception-hallucination continuum of increased ergotropic arousal (left) and a perception-mediation continuum of increasing trophotropic arousal (right). These levels of hyper and hypoarousal are interpreted by man [sic] as normal, creative, psychotic, and ecstatic states (left) and Zazen and samadhi (right). The loop connecting ecstasy and samadhi represents the rebound from ecstasy to samadhi, which is observed in response to intense ergotropic excitation. Fischer 1971: 898. Reproduced by permission of the American Association for the Advancement of Science. Copyright 1971 by the AAAS.

Trance Acting and Shamanism

E. T. Kirby

Shamans cure, prophesy, avenge, exorcise, and entertain by means of trance possession, story-telling, dancing, singing, magic, masks, and costumes (**see figure 6.19**). They heal the sick, hex enemies, tell the future, locate game, settle quarrels, ease childbirth, and a lot more. The exact work of a shaman will vary from culture to culture. Shamans enact and retain a community's knowledge. Shamans are able to separate their souls from their bodies and, aided by their animal or spirit helpers, undertake magical journeys to nonhuman worlds in pursuit of demons or in search of cures. Often, shamans perform while in trance. They may even induce trance in spectators.

fig 6.19. For three hours in 1981, Korean shaman Yu-son Kim performed the *peridegi* – a dramatic combination of singing, story-telling, dance, and enactment. The goal of the peridegi is to obtain curing water from the other-world. Yu-son Kim performed for three hours without a break. Photograph by Du-Hyun Lee. Photograph courtesy of Richard Schechner.

Shamanistic Origins of Popular Entertainments

[. . .] shamanistic ritual was the "great unitarian artwork" that fragmented into a number of performance arts. [. . .] Shamanist ritual occurs or has occurred virtually the world over, among the most different and distantly separated peoples or cultures, and can be traced back to prehistoric times. [. . .] At their origin, popular entertainments [ventriloquism, acrobatics, magic tricks, playing with fire, sword-swallowing, rope tricks, clowning, etc.] are associated with trance and derive from the practices of trance [. . .]. They do not seek to imitate, reproduce, or record the forms of existent social reality. Rather, the performing arts that develop from shamanist trance may be characterized as the manifestation, or conjuring, of an immediately present reality of a different order, kind, or quality, from reality itself. Shamanist illusionism, with its ventriloquism and escape acts, seeks to break the surface of reality, as it were, to cause the appearance of the super-reality that is quote "more real" than the ordinary.

1974, "The Shamanistic Origins of Popular Entertainments," 6, 14

Shamanism: An ancient kind of performance practiced by specialists in healing and trance, employing music, dance, masks, and objects. Although the word is of central Asian origin, shamanism in its many varieties is practiced all over the world.

The word "shaman" is of Tungus (Siberian) origin. It can be argued that in a strict sense, shamanism belongs to North Central Asia. But shamanism occurs all over the world – in the Americas, Africa, Australia, Europe, Asia, Polynesia, and Micronesia. Because it is so widespread, some scholars believe that shamanism is the "original" theatre (**see E. T. Kirby box**). The vast spread of shamanism is not coincidental. Archeological remains, evidence of migrations, and similarities in performance styles link the shamanism of North Central Asia to practices in Korea, the Americas, India, Sri Lanka, China, Tibet, and Bali. Elements of shamanism are visible in ancient Greek rituals and Japanese noh. Shamanism indicates that the earliest human performances were both entertaining and sacred; the radical separation between "secular" and "sacred" is not inherent in performance practice.

Shamans are expert performers and story-tellers – masters at throwing their voices, dancing, singing, manipulating objects, and constructing spectacular costumes and masks. The shamanic ceremonies of the Kwakiutl, Bella Bella, and Haida who live along the Gulf of Alaska were once complex dance theatre performances employing spectacular "transformation masks" (**see figure 6.20**). At a climactic moment of a performance, the outer male mask sprang open and the interior female mask was revealed. An example of this kind of event is the *hamatsa* performance, which in recent years has been revived (**see Huntsman box**). Participants and spectators are entertained as well as cleansed and ritually renewed.

fig 6.20. A transformation mask from the Haida, Pacific coast of North America. At a climactic moment in the performance, the outer male mask springs open revealing a female mask behind, 1884–93. Photograph courtesy of the Center for Inter American Relations.

Many shamans did not intend to be shamans. They were drawn into shaman-work by an irresistible force (**see Rothenberg box**). Korean shamans, called *mansins*, are expected at first to resist the call and often suffer severe illness as a result (**see Kendall box**). But once a mansin is initiated, she begins a long period of rigorous training which in many ways is very like what is demanded of any person preparing to perform a highly codified performance genre. Thus, paradoxically, even though a Korean shaman performs in a trance, the songs, gestures, and other details of her performance are codified and learned through apprenticeship. The training gives the shaman her dancing and singing. The trance gives her the necessary psychic strength to undertake the perilous journey and battle the malevolent forces (the shaman's narrative). Together these comprise the core of the shaman's performance.

Jeffrey F. Huntsman

The Hamatsa Shaman Drama

The most important drama of the northern end of the Northwest Coast is the [. . .] *hamatsa*, which is the centerpiece of the Winter Ceremonial. The drama is the reenactment of a long and complex myth in which four young hunters come upon the dwelling of BaxbakualanuXsiwae, the Cannibal-at-the-North-End-of-the-World. Hideous, whistling eerily from dozens of open, bloody mouths over his body, BaxbakualanuXsiwae flies through the air driven by a ravenous hunger for human flesh. [. . .] The courageous incoming hunters kill BaxbakualanuXsiwae and his numerous man-eating servants, then return triumphant to their village. As in many other Native American dramas, the victorious hunters bring back with them the masks, whistles, and sacred cedar bark garments that are the accoutrements of the re-enactment and the songs and dances that are its script. Performed in a typically magnificent great lodge of the Kwakiutl, the *hamatsa* drama is a masterpiece of Native American dramatic art.

2000, "Native American Theatre," 94–95

Jerome Rothenberg

Isaac Tens Heeds the Call to be a Shaman

Then my heart started to beat fast, & I began to tremble, just as has happened before. [. . .] My flesh seemed to be boiling. [. . .] My body was quivering. While I remained in this state, I began to sing. A chant was coming out of me without my being able to do anything to stop it. Many things appeared to me presently: huge birds & other animals. [. . .] These were visible only to me, not to the others in my house. Such visions happen when a man is about to become a shaman; they occur of their own accord. The songs force themselves out completely without any attempt to compose them. But I learned & memorized those songs by repeating them.

1968, *Technicians of the Sacred*, 51–52

Shamans are in fact very much like stage actors. In a single performance, a shaman may enact many characters who sometimes are in conflict with each other. Although these roles are given by tradition, the shaman's performance is full of creativity. The mark of a successful shaman is the degree to which he imbues his performance with his own singular style. While he is possessed, in a state where the shaman is very deeply taken by his roles, his ordinary daily self is effaced or replaced. Then follows a transformation of voice, movements, gestures, and even thoughts and feelings. This transformation is strengthened by careful use of makeup, masks, costumes, props, and audience participation.

Laurel Kendall

The "God-Descended" Shamans of Korea

A *mansin* [shaman] engages in a battle of wills with the gods from the very beginning of her career. A woman is expected to resist her calling and struggle against the inevitable, but village women say that those who resist the will of the gods to the very end die raving lunatics. [. . .] According to Yongsu's Mother,

> It's very difficult for them. They're sick and they stay sick, even though they take medicine. And there are people who get better even without taking medicine. There are some who can't eat the least bit of food; they just go hungry. There are some who sleep with their eyes open, and some who can't sleep at all. They're very weak but they get well as soon as the gods descend in the initiation *kut* [shaman ceremony]. For some people the gods descend gently, but for others the gods don't descend gently at all. So they run around like crazy women.

> 1987, *Shamans, Housewives, and Other Restless Spirits*, 57

Shamanic narratives most often center on a life-and-death struggle against powerful opponents: a disease, or a spell that is threatening an individual or the well-being of a patient or an entire community. In this drama, the shaman is the main but not only performer. Shamans-in-training or assistant shamans help. In some cases, there are animal sacrifices. Always there is audience participation. In shamanic healing, the one afflicted by disease is passive, sometimes barely conscious. The immediate stage of the struggle is the body of the patient. But the bad demons may emerge into the performance space and the site of the battle may expand across a wide arena. This titanic struggle is played out by the shaman, who enacts, tells, dances, and sings what is happening, drawing the audience deeper and deeper into the reality of the performance (**see Anisimov box**).

The shaman is a link, a connector, a hero whose perilous journeys to the under and over worlds bring into simultaneous play several contending, overlapping, and dynamic domains: that of the individual and community the shaman serves, that of the disease or curse which is expelled but never entirely extirpated or exterminated (it may return, to the same or another patient, or to the whole tribe or community); that of the spirit-helpers; and that of the various

A. F. Anisimov

Shaman's Performance, Siberia 1931

In the middle of the tent a small fire burned. The tent was in semi-darkness. Along the sides sat the clansmen, talking softly. A pervasive feeling of expectation of something extraordinary [. . .]. Opposite the entrance the shaman sat. His pinched nervous face pale; he, silent, alert, irritable, moved his shoulders, gently swaying side to side. His face twitched, his hands trembled. [. . .]

In an improvised song of summons to the spirits, the shaman addressed his spirit helpers, calling them to his aid in the struggle against the spirit of the disease. [. . .] The shaman sent the *khargi* [the shaman's chief helper, his animal-double] to the lower world to learn the cause of the clansman's illness. The sound of the drum became thunderous, the shaman's song more agitated. [. . .]

The journey of the khargi to the other world is described in the shaman's songs in such fantastic form, so deftly accompanied by motions, imitations of spirit-voices, comic and dramatic dialogues, wild screams, snorts, noises, and the like that it startled and amazed even this far from superstitious onlooker. The tempo of the song became faster and faster, the shaman's voice more and more excited, the drum sounded ever more thunderously. The moment came when the song reached its highest intensity and feeling of anxiety. The drum moaned, dying out in peels and rolls in the swift, nervous hands of the shaman. One or two deafening beats were heard and the shaman leaped from his place. Swaying from side to side, bending in a half-circle to the ground and smoothly straightening up again, the shaman let loose such torrent of sounds that it seemed everything hummed, beginning with the poles of the tent, and ending with the buttons on the clothing. Screaming the last parting words to the spirits, the shaman went further and further into a state of ecstasy, and finally, throwing the drum into the hands of his assistant, seized with his hands the thongs connected to the tent pole then began the shamanistic dance – a pantomime illustrating how the khargi, accompanied by the group of spirits, rushed on his dangerous journey fulfilling the shaman's commands. [. . . .]

Under the hypnotic influence of the shamanistic ecstasy, those present fell into a state of mystical hallucination, feeling themselves active participants in the shaman's performance.

> 1963, "The Shaman's Tent of the Evenks," 100–102

regions the shaman and/or the helpers journey to. Shamanic performances are, or within recent memory were, very powerful total theatre experiences (**see Shirokogoroff box**).

s. m. Shirokogoroff

The Intensity of Shamanic Performing

The rhythmic music and singing, and later the dancing of the shaman, gradually involve every participant more and more in a collective action. When the audience begins to repeat the refrains together with the assistants, only those who are defective fail to join the chorus. The tempo of the action increases, the shaman with a spirit is no more an ordinary man or relative, but is a "placing" (i.e. incarnation) of the spirit; the spirit acts together with the audience, and this is felt by everyone. The state of many participants is now near to that of the shaman himself, and only a strong belief that when the shaman is there the spirit may only enter him, restrains the participants from being possessed in mass by the spirit. [. . .] When the shaman feels that the audience is with him and follows him he becomes still more active and this effect is transmitted to his audience. After shamanizing, the audience recollects various moments of the performance, their great psychophysiological emotion and the hallucinations of sight and hearing which they have experienced. They then have a deep satisfaction — much greater than that from emotions produced by theatrical and musical performances, literature, and general artistic phenomena of the European complex, because in shamanizing the audience at the same time acts and participates.

1935, *Psychomental Complex of the Tungus*, as quoted in I. M. Lewis, *Ecstatic Religion*, 53

In shamanic performance, entertainment holds a high place. Shamanic entertainment is incidental but fundamental to the healing. For the healing to succeed, the community's attention must be grabbed and focused; energies must be enlisted and directed. Entertainment is an attention-getter, a crowd-gatherer. The whole event is a panoply of happenings that add up to proving the efficacy of the shaman's journey, struggle, and triumph. Persons who have grown up with electric lights, televisions, and movies may find it hard to empathize or even imagine societies submerged in frightening nightly darkness or, in the far North, months of wintery gloom. Shamanic performances combined the competition of sports, the terror of blood sacrifice, the suspense of life-and-death struggle, and the narrativity of drama and story-telling — all thrillingly incorporated into music, song, dance, costumes, and masks.

Masks, Puppets, and Other Performing Objects

What happens when actors are not people at all, but masks and puppets? A mask is more than a way to cloak the identity of the masker. A puppet is more than dead wood or flat leather animated by human actors. Masks and puppets actually constitute second beings who interact with the human actors. These performing objects are suffused with a life force capable of transforming those who play with and through them. In Japan, a noh actor will sometimes sleep next to the mask of a role he is to play so that the mask will meld with him. A Balinese performer assesses each new mask, looking for ways to let its life enter into his body (**see Emigh box**). The *chapayeka* masks of the Yaquis of Mexico and the United States are the many faces of Judas who pursue Jesus during the annual six-week long Waehma (Passion Play). Chapayeka masks possess such strong negative force that at the end of Waehma they are burned as their wearers rush into the church to renew communion with the tribe and with God (**see figure 6.21**). Because new masks are made each year, the visible aspect of Judas changes over time.

The *dhalang* of Javanese *wayang kulit* (leather puppets) is both shaman and puppeteer. He alone manipulates and gives voice to the myriad puppet characters of dramas that last for eight hours without pause. The narratives of wayang kulit are all-inclusive, spanning the mythic and the modern, the gods, demons, and humans. Improvised banter attacking local and national excesses is interwoven with set dialogues. The puppets vary also, keeping up with the times without losing touch with tradition. Puppets depict boys on motorbikes, fat divine clowns, the heroes of the *Mahabharata*, and many more (**see figure 6.22**). Dhalangs are spiritually powerful people, even if they (like actors almost everywhere) are often also wanderers and outcasts. They draw their authority from the performance knowledge they embody and from the puppets. In Japanese *bunraku*, three persons manipulate each puppet — one controls the head and right arm, one the left arm, and one the feet. A chanter accompanied by a *samisen* (stringed instrument) narrates the story. But bunraku acting is not

John Emigh

The Living Mask

When a Balinese actor holds a new mask in his right hand, gazing upon it, turning it this way and that, making it move to a silent music, he is assessing the potential life of the mask and searching for the meeting place between himself and the life inherent in its otherness. If he is successful, then a bonding takes place that will allow him to let the potential life flow through his own body. If he finds that place of congruence between his physical and spiritual resources and the potential life of the mask, then a living amalgam is created: a character, a persona. This amalgam is at best unstable – based as it must be upon paradox, ambiguity, and illusion – but "it" moves, "it" speaks, "it" breathes, "it" is perceived – by the performer and by the audience – as having an organic integrity. If the performer fails to find such a meeting place within this field of paradox, ambiguity, and illusion, then the mask will retain its separateness: whatever its worth as an object, a "work" of art, it will at best function as a decoration, a costume element. The process begins with a respect for the mask's potential life as a separate entity and proceeds by narrowing the gap between self and other through a process of imaginative play.

1996, *Masked Performance*, 275

fig 6.21. At the end of the Yaqui Waehma, a Native People-Christian syncretic Lent-to-Easter performance, the Chapayekas are defeated, their masks burned. Photograph by Western Ways. Photograph courtesy of Richard Schechner.

fig 6.22. Wayang kulit, Javanese shadow puppet theatre.

The view from in front of the screen watching the shadows cast by the puppets. Photograph by Richard Schechner.

The view from behind the screen watching the dhalang manipulate the puppets. Photograph by Richard Schechner.

dispersed. Everything is focused on the puppets. Their presence unifies the performance.

In the political and criminal vein, masks can be used both to hide identities and shape public opinion. For example, in March 2001, leaders of the Zapatista movement of Mexican indigenous peoples traveled from Chiapas to Mexico City to present their grievances and hopes to the Mexican Congress. At one and the same time, the Zapatistas were heroes and outlaws, rebels and citizens. Their leader, who operates under the pseudonym Subcommander Marcos, was not present. The 23-member group was led by Commander Esther, a Mayan woman. The whole delegation wore black ski masks which they said symbolized the "facelessness of indigenous people in Mexico."

> **Anna Deavere Smith (1950–):** American actor, performance artist, and writer best known for her one-woman shows – *Fires in the Mirror* (1992) and *Twilight LA* (1993) – in which she embodied individual responses to the violent crises that shook their communities. Author of *Talk to Me: Listening Between the Lines* (2000).

Hybrid Acting

Many actors do not strictly adhere to the categories I have discussed. In one and the same performance, an actor may perform realistically, use a mask, combine codified behavior with improvisation, and in other ways jump or elide the boundaries between kinds of acting. But the question remains whether hybrid acting is a melding or a quilt. For the most part, it is a quilt, moving from one kind of acting to another. It is difficult to imagine how to blend codified acting with realistic acting, or trance with realistic acting. By definition, Brechtian acting does not blend in with other kinds of acting but can be used side-by-side with any kind.

But sometimes a performer is able to create a unity that draws on several kinds of acting. For example, Anna Deavere Smith in her celebrated one-woman performances *Fires in the Mirror* and *Twilight L.A.* enacts many points of view of different persons who were involved in momentous, violent events that millions of people know through the media (**see figure 6.23**). *Fires* deals with the confrontation among African-Americans, Jews, and the police in Brooklyn in 1991; *Twilight* with the riots in Los Angeles that followed the acquittal of the policemen who beat **Rodney King** (1966–). Smith develops her performances out of in-depth interviews she makes with many who were involved in the events. Smith studies the body language, gestures, and vocal patterns of ordinary people in the street, victims, accused, community and political leaders, and academic pundits. The result is something more than imitation or impersonation. Smith's own body spirit becomes a site for the playing out of many of the conflicts troubling American society, especially those about race, ethnicity, and neighborhood. Smith is actually very like a dhalang. Like a dhalang, Smith takes into herself the

fig 6.23. Anna Deavere Smith embodying three of the many persons in her *Twilight Los Angeles*, film version, 2001.

As Cornel West. Photograph by Adger W. Cowans. Photograph courtesy of Anna Deavere Smith.

As Gina Rae, also known as Queen Malkah. Photograph by Adger W. Cowans. Photograph courtesy Anna Deavere Smith.

As Katie Miller. Photograph Adger W. Cowans. Photograph courtesy of Anna Deavere Smith.

events of the community. She gives back to the community both the "facts" and her own inimitable interpretation. We witness her struggling to "take it all in" and make sense of it all. Sometimes she "fails" to make a smooth performance. Smith is to some degree possessed by those she represents. By carefully juxtaposing one character, one incorporation, to another, she opens Brechtian spaces for humor, irony, and social dialogue.

Rodney King (1966–): African-American motorist whose beating in 1991 by a group of Los Angeles policemen was recorded on videotape and seen repeatedly on television. Despite this evidence, in 1992, these policemen were acquitted of any crime. The verdict ignited the Los Angeles riots of 1992.

Performing in Everyday Life

How different is performing in "real life" from acting in a play? Sometimes performing in everyday life is casual, almost unnoticeable, as when a person slightly adjusts an aspect of the presentation of self or personality – a change of clothes, a tone of voice – to "impress" someone else. If this is carried to an extreme, one might say, "Sally is showing off." Some everyday life performances are so subtle and informal that you don't even know that you are performing – for example, when a parent "talks down" to a small child or the child raises the pitch of his voice in order to ask for ice cream. Many everyday life performers, when playing their assigned social roles, are clearly marked by wearing special clothes and insignia, using prescribed tones of voice and professional vocabularies, and exercising authority – such roles include clergy, nurses, and police (**see figure 6.24**). Other performances in everyday life are very like stage dramas. The actions of prosecutor, defense, judge, and jury at a high-visibility criminal trial, the behavior of doctors at work when a life is at risk, or the public appearances of a head of state during a national crisis. All are inherently dramatic because the stakes are high and the behavior of the participants is so well established that it is as if a script is being enacted. That is why these situations are favored subjects from *Oedipus* to *ER*. *Oedipus* combines the plight of a head of state in crisis, a detective story, and a trial.

In chapter 5, I discussed performing in everyday life as it relates to performativity, especially the constructions of gender and race. Here I will elaborate on the subject not from the perspective of speech acts or poststructuralism, but from the vantage of Erving Goffman's work (**see Brissett and**

fig 6.24. A British policeman leads a young boy away from a demonstration where things are turning violent. Photograph by Homer Sykes. Copyright Camera Press, 1982, London.

Edgley box). The theorists discussed in chapter 5 begin with language. Even when dealing with behavior they take a language-centric position. For them, behavior – indeed all culture – is to be "read" as complex, interacting texts. Goffman, on the other hand, approaches social life as theatre, an interplay of behaviors where players with different motives rehearse their actions, maneuver to present themselves advantageously, and often perform at cross purposes with one another. Where the adherents of the two approaches agree is in the assertion that people are performing all the time whether or not they are aware of it (**see Goffman box 1**).

All actors are performers, but not all performers are actors. In theory, one can specify the difference between actors and performers. But in practice these differences are in the process of collapsing. Stage actors enact roles composed by others, repeat these roles on a regular basis before audiences who know that the actors are pretending

Dennis Brissett and Charles Edgley

Goffman's Reality

Goffman's insistence that social life can be understood as a series of performances was tied to an understanding that still strikes many people as strange and contradictory: that the most revealing insights to be gleaned about human beings lie simply in a close look at what is right on the surface. Appearance is real. [. . .] Appearance can never be destroyed by "reality," but only be replaced by other appearances. [. . .] So Goffman wrote about guises, semblances, veneers, surfaces, illusions, images, shells, and acts. He was not, as most scholars pompously try to bill themselves, about substances, things, facts, truth, and depths. But more importantly, Goffman's argument dissolves the very distinction between the merely apparent and the fundamentally real in social life. Life to him appeared to consist of various levels of understanding and awareness, not of layers covering a fundamental core which could be duly revealed by proper scientific work. As a result, he appeared to reverse the order of everything. The theatre of performances is not in people's heads, it is in their public acts. People encounter each other's minds only by interacting, the quality and character of these interactions comes to constitute the consequential reality of everyday life. In everyday life things really are as they seem to be; but "how they seem to be" is ever changing.

1990, "The Dramaturgical Perspective", 36–37

Erving Goffman

Performances of Everyday Life

The legitimate performances of everyday life are not "acted" or "put on" in the sense that the performer knows in advance just what he is going to do, and does this solely because of the effect it is likely to have. The expression it is felt he is giving off will be especially "inaccessible" to him. But as in the case of less legitimate performers, the incapacity of the ordinary individual to formulate in advance the movements of his eyes and body does not mean that he will not express himself through these devices in a way that is dramatized and pre-formed in his repertoire of actions. In short, we act better than we know how.

1959, *The Presentation of Self in Everyday Life*, 73–74

to be who they enact. In spectator sports, the situation is complicated. Athletes are not pretending, but they are performing. They focus on accomplishing tasks specific to particular sports ("ball play," "fighting," "racing," "jumping," "weight lifting," etc.) at the same time as they display themselves publicly. The build-up to a big game is part of the whole event. And although athletes are not pretending to be anyone, the more famous an athlete becomes, the more her actions in certain ways approach those of the stage actor. The exercise of skills remains the core performance, but the bigger the star, the more the presentation of self becomes character acting.

Performing in everyday life involves people in a wide range of activities from solo or intimate performances behind closed doors to small group activities to interacting as part of a crowd. Sometimes performing in everyday life uses consciously enacted conventional behaviors, as at a formal dinner party or a funeral; sometimes the scenario of every-day life is loose, as when you are walking down the street in casual conversation with a friend. Most of daily living is taken up by performing job, professional, family, and social roles. Each of these, in every culture, comes equipped with ways of behaving and interacting. Everyone masters to some degree or another the social codes of daily life. Rebels intentionally break the rules; revolutionaries want to change them permanently.

To what degree is human social life an unending stream of performances? According to the Roman historian

Suetonius (*c.* 70–130), Emperor **Caesar Augustus** (63 BCE–14 CE) on the day he died called for a mirror, instructed servants to comb his hair and fix in place his slackened jaw, and then assembled his courtiers. "Have I played the comedy of life well?" Augustus asked. He didn't wait for their answer, but replied himself. "Since I've played my part well, all clap your hands and dismiss me from the stage with applause." Shortly after, Augustus died. The emperor's deathbed scene is not as extraordinary as it may at first appear. Before the era of nursing homes and mechanically extended lives, carefully staged deathbed scenes were common. In some cultures they still are. But even at less momentous times, theatre haunts everyday life. "You acted bravely," a mother might say in praise to her daughter who stood up to a bullying aunt. This same mother at supper might rebuke her daughter, "Don't stuff your mouth, act more grownup!" Both the praise and the admonition refer to behaviors that are decided and definite, that have a clear shape. We can easily picture such actions in our mind's eye. The words "act" and "action" are citations of not-so-hidden social scripts. Such social scripts permeate daily life. Although social scripts vary from culture to culture and epoch to epoch, there are no cultures or historical periods bereft of social scripts.

Suetonius (*c.* 70–*c.*130): Roman historian, author of *The Lives of the Caesars* (*c.* 110).

Caesar Augustus (63 BCE–14 CE): First emperor of Rome. Presided over the expansion of the Roman Empire across Europe and northern Africa.

In mid-nineteenth-century America, as women were demanding their rights in the first wave of feminism, manuals such as **Emily Thornwell**'s mid-nineteenth century *The Lady's Guide to Perfect Gentility* instructed "young ladies" on how to "behave properly" (**see Thornwell box**). Thornwell's book was a reaction against the "unruly" behavior that feminists were proposing as alternative scripts for women. As noted in chapter 5, one can analyze Thornwell's manual, and much of today's "advice" on how women (or men) should behave, from the point of view of the construction of gender. But why stop with scenarios of etiquette? Most social behavior is constructed. The matter is complicated because the assertion, "Now I am performing" is often met by another equally insistent assertion, "The role I am playing is myself." So where or who is the "real me"? In all societies, this multiplying of personae is obvious with regard to more or less fixed roles such as "mother," "doctor," "teacher," "child," and so on. The specific gestures, tones of voice, costume, and so on appropriate to social roles are well known. These vary from place to place, circumstance to circumstance. For example, the roles of "bus driver" or "automobile mechanic" may be well known in one society and all but unknown in another. But whatever the roles, disrupting accepted codes of behavior can meet with reprimands ranging from "Go to your room!" to "You are in contempt of court." More serious violations can get a person excommunicated, ostracized, jailed, or killed. Role-specific and situation-specific conventions govern all social interactions. In all circumstances, there are conventions, rules, and laws: social behavior is never free and unbound.

Emily Thornwell

How a Lady Ought to Behave in Public

Propriety of movement and general demeanor in company. To look steadily at any one, especially if you are a lady and are speaking to a gentleman; to turn the head frequently on one side and the other during conversation; to balance yourself upon your chair; to bend forward; to strike your hands upon your knees; to hold one of your knees between your hands locked together; to cross your legs; to extend your feet on the andirons; to admire yourself with complacency in a glass; [. . .] to laugh immoderately; to place your hand upon the person with whom you are conversing; to take him by the buttons, the collar of his cloak, the cuffs, the waist, and so forth; to seize any person by the waist or arm, or to touch their person; [. . .] to rub your face or your hands; wink your eyes; shrug up your shoulders; stamp with your feet, and so forth; – all these bad habits, of which we cannot speak to people, are in the highest degree displeasing.

1856, *The Lady's Guide to Perfect Gentility*, 87–88

Emily Thornwell (mid-nineteenth century): American author of *The Lady's Guide to Perfect Gentility* (1856), which instructed women on "proper behavior" in all manner of social situations.

But what happens in less guarded moments, when people are "off duty" – when the judge is not judging, the teacher not teaching, the parent not parenting? During these times, the performance aspect of ordinary behavior is less obvious, but not absent. One sets aside formal enactments to play roles that allow more leeway in behavior, that are less like scripted dramas and more like loose improvisations. People become "just friends," the judge shows that he is "an ordinary Joe like me," the house-cleaner sits down with the house-owner for a cup of tea. But "friend" and "ordinary Joe" are also roles – ones that blend into the background of ongoing social life rather than stand out as highly marked. Goffman felt that all social encounters were theatre-like because "life itself is a dramatically enacted thing" (**see Goffman box 2**).

Erving Goffman

All the World's a Stage?

It does take deep skill, long training, and psychological capacity to become a good stage actor. But this fact should not blind us to another one: that almost anyone can quickly learn a script well enough to give a charitable audience some sense of realness in what is being contrived before them. And it seems this is so because ordinary social intercourse is itself put together as a scene is put together, by the exchange of dramatically inflated actions, counteractions, and terminating replies. Scripts even in the hands of unpracticed players can come to life because life itself is a dramatically enacted thing. All the world is not, of course, a stage, but the crucial ways in which it isn't are not easy to specify.

1959, *The Presentation of Self in Everyday Life*, 71–72

One might say that the more public and "larger than life" the social role, the more it is like theatre. The American President adheres to a tightly scripted schedule, reads speeches written for him, and follows strictly enforced protocol. He even memorizes the apparently impromptu answers given to reporters or the adlibs shouted to the crowds who greet him as he travels around the country. Of course, the Monarch of England has long been more a theatrical role than an actual decision-maker. But the pomp-and-circumstance, the stuff of royal ritual, has a big effect on political and social life. The membrane separating what "appears" and what "is" is a very thin one.

In the theatre, the actor and the audience both know that the actor is "not" who she is playing. But in "real life" a person is simultaneously performing herself and being herself. The matter is, of course, nicely complicated because in some methods of realistic acting, actors are taught how to use their own selves to construct theatrical roles. This technique of "pretending to be really myself" or "building the character from myself" has permeated society, and not only in the West. Through the media and more recently by means of the internet, people in everyday life play many roles, have access to numerous Avatars. Advertising encourages people to believe that by means of cosmetics, surgery, mood-altering drugs, exercise, diet, hairstyle, and clothes one can radically change personality. Who "I am" is no longer a given, if it ever was. As the number of available "new selves" increases weekly, the media emphasize that no self need be permanent. Continuous alteration is possible. This promise of mutability entices people into playing more and more roles, discovering as many variations of themselves as possible. As never before, people are performing their multiple selves all day, every day.

Trials and Executions as Performance

As noted, jury trials are inherently dramatic (**see Harbinger box**). Prosecution and defense construct contradictory narratives from the evidence. The "crime drama" nested inside the "courtroom drama" consists in molding the forensic evidence and witness testimony into two mutually contradictory narratives forcing the jury to decide which story is "the truth." In the process, each side tries to undermine the opponent's narrative. Truth in a trial is not so much what "really happened" as it is a test of which side is more adept at using the law and shaping the data – at "building a case." The judge serves as referee keeping attorneys in line, interpreting the law to the jury, and maintaining order in court. High-visibility trials of famous persons or depicting horrendous crimes attract several audiences surrounding the trial in concentric circles. The courtroom itself is crowded with spectators and press. The proceedings may be televised.

The first trial broadcast on television was that of Nazi Adolph Eichmann, who in 1961, for his leading role in the Holocaust, was tried and condemned to death by an Israeli court in Jerusalem. During the trial, Eichmann was kept in a bullet-proof glass box where he could be safe from harm, displayed, and morally quarantined (**see figure 6.25**).

Richard Harbinger

Trial by Drama

An adversary trial is a dramatic thing put to legal use. [. . .] When one observes an adversary trial, he sees a play; when he observes a while longer, he perceives a play within the play. This is the essential, ineluctable form of the adversary trial: a "play without" and a "play within." And from this form all else naturally proceeds: double plots, double casts, double settings, double audiences, and double effects. [. . .]

A "play within a play" is [. . .] a crime drama within a courtroom drama. [. . .] *People v X* is the archetype of a million murder trials – past, present, and future. [. . .] The courtroom drama ("the play without") stages the legal combat between the prosecuting attorney and the defense attorney. [. . .] The "play within" tells the story of the alleged killing by the defendant. [. . .] A courtroom drama stars the prosecuting attorney and the defense attorney, and the title page of the transcript gives them top billing. The starring attorneys get most of the dialogue and the action and they do most of the emoting and agonizing. It is only in a legal sense that the people win or lose; in a dramatic sense the attorneys win or lose. The crime drama, on the other hand, stars the defendant, and sometimes the victim. [. . .] The drama of the courtroom takes place in the courtroom, while the drama of the crime takes place elsewhere.

1971, "Trial by Drama," 122–24

fig 6.25. Adolph Eichmann, the Nazi overseer of the Holocaust, on display in a glass box during his trial in Jerusalem, 1961. Eichmann was executed in 1962. Photograph reproduced on the internet at http//remember.org/eichmann/eich1.htm.

The 1995 murder trial of former football and movie star **O. J. Simpson** (1947–) was watched live by millions. Winning acquittal for his client made defense attorney **Johnny Cochran** (1937–) into a star in his own right. Because of the enormity of his crime, and the newness of using television in this way, Eichmann's trial was treated with respect. But by the time of Simpson's trial, there had been a plethora of TV pseudo-trials such as "The People's Court" and "Judge Judy." The confluence of Hollywood, big-time sports, miscegenation, jealousy, and murder was too much to resist. Although he played innocent (and was acquitted), Simpson was widely regarded as guilty – an inarticulate Othello. There was something bigger than life about the trial that fascinated Americans. Simpson's story, like that of the great theatrical murderers – Oedipus, Hamlet, Clytemnestra, Othello – could not be resolved by the jury's verdict of innocent. The "whole truth" may never be known, cannot be reduced to the "facts." But, finally, rather than rising to Shakespearean heights, the Simpson trial was soap-opera melodrama. Soon after the trial ended, a four-videotape documentary made from the trial was on sale. More videos followed. It's not the search for truth that holds the audiences for such trials. The Simpson trial was about much more than who murdered Nicole Brown Simpson and Ronald Goldman. It was about race relations in the US, the lifestyle of the rich and famous, sex and jealousy, and the kind of justice money can buy. And what does it say about the public imagination that a Google internet search made in June, 2001 came up with 1,910 sites for "Adolph Eichmann" versus 124,000 for "O.J. Simpson"?

O. J. Simpson (1947–): American football star and then movie actor, television commentator and pitchman who was tried in 1995 for the murders of his former wife Nicole Brown Simpson and her companion Ron Goldman. Simpson was acquitted, but later Nicole's family won a large award in civil court.

After a guilty verdict comes the punishment. The execution of convicts has long been a theatrical spectacle (**see Chute box**). Even Christ's Crucifixion was seen as a theatricalized execution (**see Herrick box**). In medieval and Renaissance Europe, both the condemned and spectators prepared for the big event. Before mounting the scaffold, the condemned delivered orations while spectators picnicked. In modern times, from the busy guillotine of the French Revolution to the Moscow trials of the 1930s, or the more recent trials in Iran and China, political trials and executions have been called "show trials" because their import goes beyond the fate of the accused. Such trials and executions are designed to demonstrate the power of the state and terrify the public. "Killing a chicken to scare the monkeys," goes the old Chinese proverb. In many parts of the world, the death penalty has been outlawed. But where it persists people pay attention. The condemned's "last meal" and "final words" are reported. In the U.S., executions must be witnessed. In June, 2001 the Oklahoma City bomber **Timothy McVeigh** (1968–2001) was executed by lethal injection. Nearly 300 persons – relatives of some of the 168 persons killed in the bombing – watched the execution via closed-circuit television. There was a call to broadcast McVeigh's death on public television or over the internet, but the government denied requests. Persons gathered near the prison where McVeigh died, some to celebrate the death of a mass murderer and others to protest capital punishment.

Marchette **Chute**

Performing Public Executions in Elizabethan London

Another source of public entertainments was executions, and the criminals knew what was expected of them by the public. They went to their death like actors, delivering final speeches from the scaffolds, and a hanging at Wapping was made especially impressive because the chief performer wore breeches of crimson taffeta. When there was an important mass execution, like that which followed the Babington Conspiracy in 1586, the government made the scaffold high and railed off the place to keep horsemen away so "the people might plainly see the execution." The idea of the government was to imprint on the popular mind the horrors of treason and the ghastly death to which it led, but the Londoners treated the occasion like an especially interesting day at the theatre. "There was no lane, street, alley or house in London [. . .] out of which there issued not some of each age and sex, insomuch that the ways were pestered with people so multiplied, as they thronged and overran one another for haste, contending to the place of death for the advantage of the ground where to stand, see and hear."

1949, *Shakespeare of London*, 67–68

Robert **Herrick**

Jesus Christ, Actor

Put off Thy Robe of *Purple*, then go on
To the sad place of execution:
Thine houre is come; and the Tormentor stands
Ready, to pierce Thy tender Feet and Hands.
[. . .]
The *Crosse* shall be Thy *Stage*; and Thou shalt there
The spacious field have for thy *Theater*.
Thou art that *Roscius*, and that markt-out man,
That must this day act the Tragedian,
To wonder and affrightment: Thou art He,
Whom all the flux of Nations comes to see;
Not those poor Theeves that act their parts with Thee.
[. . .]
Why then begin, great King! ascend Thy Throne,
And thence proceed, to act Thy Passion
To such an height, to such a period rais'd,
As Hell, and Earth, and Heav'n may stand amaz'd.

1956 (1647), *Noble Numbers* in *Poetical Works*, 398–99

Surgery as Performance

Trials put lives at risk and executions take lives. Medical practice – from shamanism to surgery – saves lives. I wrote about shamanism earlier in this chapter. I will now discuss aspects of allopathic medicine. The body-in-medicine has long been a biological, performative, and artistic subject.

An experienced doctor performs his anatomical and diagnostic knowledge when dissecting a cadaver or diagnosing a patient before an audience of fellow doctors or medical students (**see figure 6.26**).

fig 6.26. Medical procedures, then and now.

Above, medical students examining a patient under the eyes of a supervising physician in a contemporary teaching hospital. Photograph Homer Sykes. Copyright Camera Press.

An amputation being performed in the operating theatre of old St. Thomas's Hospital, London, in 1875–76. Note the observers in the gallery. Copyright St. Thomas's Hospital Archive.

Consider also a surgeon performing in the operating theatre. Surgery in a teaching hospital brings into play the concept of "performance" in at least two of its meanings: a showing of a doing and an activity demanding the coordinated efforts of a team working together at an extremely high level of skills. Nurses hover about performing necessary tasks. The anesthesiologist monitors the patient's breathing and life-signs. Let us suppose that also present are interns in training to become surgeons. The surgeon performs on the patient, with her team, and for these interns. A star surgeon points out what she is doing and why. In addition to its meliorative function, the surgery is a medical performance used for

teaching. In some hospitals, a spectators' gallery overlooks the operating room. Some pioneering operations are broadcast over closed-circuit television so that doctors in remote locations can watch. This kind of medical performance is nothing new, even if the techniques of dissemination have been enhanced.

Furthermore, isn't the operating theatre similar to the aesthetic theatre in its architecture, roles, costumes, and scripts? The operating room is flanked by backstage areas and dressing rooms where both the patient and the medical team prepare. Different roles are marked by distinctive costumes separating doctors from nurses from patient. Guiding the procedure are sets of known gestures and rituals. A successful operation is one where there is little need for improvisation. But when unpredictable occurrences call for improvised responses, these are based on bits of rehearsed behavior because mistakes can be fatal. What role does the patient play in all this? For the patient, the surgery is a performance in which he is not present at the level of ability to interact consciously. Is the patient a star or a prop? Even before being put under anesthesia, the patient is stripped of key elements of his daily self. He is wrapped in hospital garb, the site of the surgery tightly framed and well lit, discolored by antiseptic, and drawn on with indelible ink. The patient is reduced to the object of the surgical procedure at hand. The real star of the performance is the surgeon.

Belief in the Role One is Playing

To what degree does a person believe her own performance? Goffman noted that self-belief spans a continuum with the tendency to accept ourselves "as performed" (**see Goffman box 3**). Long before Goffman, Nietzsche made a more radical suggestion – that "great deceivers" are so entrancing as performers that they convince themselves of the truth of what they perform. Only then, when they are saturated with

the self-confidence resulting from the power of their own performing, are they able to draw others into their magic circle (**see Nietzsche box**). Nietzsche says this is so of the founders of religions, as surely it is of Hitlerian dictators, Churchillian prime ministers, and master hucksters of every kind. We may ask, if the deception is complete, if everyone believes it, is it a lie? Theoretically, if no one stands outside the magic circle, there is no way to measure the veracity of what is declaimed.

It was this kind of monstrous "total theatre" that the Nazis staged inside Germany. **Adolph Hitler**'s (1889–1945) frenetic yet well-prepared orations, the pageantry of mass rallies, and the parades of the armed forces were as important as the terror of the Gestapo. The massive Nuremberg rallies of the 1920s and 1930s solidified the party faithful. In 1936, 100,000 Nazi officers assembled in the outdoor site, flanked by a "cathedral of light" made by powerful anti-aircraft search-lights aimed directly up into the night sky (**see figure 6.27**). At Nuremberg, and in other Nazi shows, theatre went beyond the theatre. **Albert Speer**'s (1905–81) lights, the massed military cohorts carrying thousands of flags and other Nazi paraphernalia, the Hitler-adoring roars of "Heil!" and the Führer's cadenced, shrill oratory combined to enact a fantasy of the "thousand-year Reich" played by "pure-Aryan German *Volk*" (folk, people, community). The Gestapo terror

Erving Goffman

Believing the Role One Plays

At one extreme, one finds that the performer can be fully taken in by his own act; he can be sincerely convinced that the impression of reality which he stages is the real reality. When his audience is also convinced in this way about the show he puts on – and this seems to be the typical case – then for the moment at least, only the sociologist or the socially disgruntled will have any doubts bout the "realness" of what is presented.

At the other extreme, we find that the performer may not be taken in at all by his own routine. This possibility is understandable, since no one is in quite as good an observational position to see through the act as the person who puts it on. [. . .] When the individual has no belief in his own act and no ultimate concern with the beliefs of his audience, we may call him cynical. [. . .] It should be understood that the cynic [. . .] may obtain [. . .] pleasures from his masquerade, experiencing a kind of gleeful spiritual aggression from the fact that he can toy at will with something his audience must take seriously. [. . .] Perhaps the real crime of the confidence man is not that he takes money from his victims but that he robs all of us of the belief that middle-class manners and appearance can be sustained only by middle-class people. [. . .]

These extremes are something a little more than just the ends of a continuum. Each provides the individual with a position which has its own particular securities and defenses, so there will be a tendency for those who have traveled close to one of these poles to complete the voyage.

1959, *The Presentation of Self in Everyday Life*, 17–19

Friedrich Nietzsche

The Power of Believing in the Self One is Performing

Even when in the deepest distress, the actor ultimately cannot cease to think of the impression he and the whole scenic effect is making, even for example, at the burial of his own child; he will weep over his own distress and the ways in which it expresses itself, as his own audience. [. . .]

If someone obstinately and for a long time wants to *appear* something it is in the end hard for him to *be* anything else. [. . .] With all great deceivers there is a noteworthy occurrence to which they owe their power. In the actual act of deception, with all its preparations, its enthralling voice, expression, and gesture, in the midst of the scenery designed to give it effect, they are overcome by *belief in themselves*: it is this which then speaks so miraculously and compellingly to those who surround them. The founders of religions are distinguished from these great deceivers by the fact that they never emerge from this state of self-deception: or very rarely they experience for once that moment of clarity when doubt overcomes them; usually, however, they comfort themselves by ascribing these moments of clarity to the evil antagonist. Self-deception has to exist if a grand *effect* is to be produced. For men believe in the truth of that which is plainly strongly believed.

1986 [1878], *Human, All Too Human*, 39–40

eliminated Hitler's enemies, while the pageantry solidified his popular support. This total theatre drew on the "movement choirs" of **Rudolf von Laban** (1879–1958), who staged displays for the 1936 Berlin Olympics and the lighting, and architectural designs of Speer (**see Speer box**). The ideas of Laban and Speer were to some degree derived from the work of two important performance personages, theatre design visionary **Adolphe Appia** (1862–1928) and the founder of eurhythmics, **Emile Jacques-Dalcroze** (1865–1950). Appia and Dalcroze worked with each other before the First World War and Laban was one of Dalcroze's students. In other words, it's not possible to sift out "art" from "politics." The two were profoundly intermeshed then and now — as the mobilization of public opinion (directly or via media) constitutes a decisive base of political, military, state, and economic power.

fig 6.27. A night-time rally of Nazis in Nuremberg, 1936. Note the "cathedral of light" formed by aiming hundreds of anti-aircraft search lights straight up. Spectacle and invented rituals helped the Nazis arouse and control their adherents. The photograph is from an official Nazi publication, *Der Parteitag der Ehre, vom 8. bis 14. September 1936*. The photograph is reproduced on the internet at http//www.calvin.edu/academic/cas/gpa/pt36p.htm.

Adolph Hitler (1889–1945): Nazi dictator of Germany from 1933 to 1945.

On a more quotidian level, a person's sense of self is very much tied to her ability to believe in the roles she plays. The matter is complicated because the roles are not played by a single, stable self. The self is created by the roles even as it plays them — a psychological mobius strip keeps turning outside into inside and inside into outside. Nor are all social roles played equally well. How well a person plays a social role usually depends on how much the person believes in the role. In ordinary life, a person plays to two audiences at the same time: oneself, and the social audience. "Insincerity" as an experience is the interior mode of "hypocrisy" as a social fact. The question remains, to what audience ought a person pay more attention? Should we, as **Henry David Thoreau** (1817–62) advised, listen to our own internal drumbeat; or ought we tune ourselves to the demands of social life? There is no correct answer. There are only varying degrees of response. History offers plenty of examples on both sides of the case, ranging from martyrs who died for their beliefs to monarchs who adapted in order to save their crowns.

Rudolf von Laban (1879–1958): German dance pioneer whose work included movement choirs, expressionist dance, and the development of a system of movement notation still widely used today. Laban for a time willingly worked for the Nazis until he was "dismissed" in 1936 because of his "decadent choreography."

Albert Speer

The 1934 Nuremberg Rally of the Nazi Party

Every year a rally was held at the Zeppelin field for the assemblage of middle and minor party functionaries [. . .]. I explained my plan to the organization leaders of the Party Rally. The thousands of flags belonging to all the local groups in Germany were to be held in readiness behind the high fences surrounding the field. The flag bearers were to divide into ten columns, forming lanes in which the Amtsverwalter [party officials] would march up. Since all this was to take place at evening, bright spotlights would be cast on these banners and the great eagle crowning them all. That alone would have a dramatic effect. But even this did not seem sufficient to me. I had occasionally seen our new anti-aircraft searchlights blazing miles into the sky. I asked Hitler to let me have a hundred and thirty of these. [. . .]

The actual effect far surpassed anything I had imagined. The hundred and thirty sharply defined beams, placed around the field at intervals of forty feet, were visible to a height of twenty to twenty-five thousand feet, after which they merged into a general glow. The feeling was of a vast room, with the beams serving as mighty pillars of infinitely high outer walls. Now and then the clouds move through this wreath of lights, bringing an element of surprise to the mirage. I imagine that this "cathedral of light" was the first luminescent architecture of this type, and for me it remains not only my most beautiful architectural concept but, after its fashion, the only one which survived the passage of time.

1997 [1970] *Inside the Third Reich*, 58–59

Albert Speer (1905–81): Hitler's architect and later director of war industries during the 1940s. For the Nazi Nuremberg Rally of 1936, Speer designed a "cathedral of light" by aiming batteries of anti-aircraft searchlights directly up. Convicted of war crimes, Speer served 20 years and was released in 1966.

Adolphe Appia (1862–1928): Swiss visionary opera and stage designer who was particularly fascinated by the possiblities of "living light." He also advocated abstract rather than romantic or naturalistic stage settings. His practical work and theories have had a deep impact on modern theatre lighting and stage design. Many of his important ideas are contained in *Adolphe Appia: Texts on Theatre* (1993).

Emile Jacques-Dalcroze (1865–1950): Swiss educator and originator of "eurhythmics," a system combining music, rhythm, and movement. The goal of Dalcroze's method is to integrate all the senses in the service of aesthetics. Dalcroze's method continues to be widely practiced and influential.

Henry David Thoreau (1817–62): American writer who championed peaceful "civil disobedience" as a way to protest oppressive or illegal acts by the government. He also cherished the "simple life" as detailed in his best-known work, *Walden* (1854).

How Realistic is Realistic Acting?

Ever since **Charles Darwin**'s (1809–82), *The Expression of Emotions in Man and Animals* 1872, scientists have proposed behavior as part of the evolutionary development of the human species. Ethology, sociobiology, and kinesics are based on the assumption that behavior has evolved in a way analogous to the evolution of human anatomy. Behavior is very complex, ranging from simple motor activities like grasping, running, and jumping to the expression of emotions and intentions by means of facial displays, body gestures, tone of voice, and so on. The term "body language" refers to these expressions. **Paul Ekman** (1934–) proposes that the facial displays of six "target emotions" (happiness, sadness, anger, fear, disgust, and surprise) are recognizably similar in all cultures. Long before Darwin, actors knew that emotional expression could be codified. As noted earlier in this chapter, two millennia ago, Bharata Muni in the *Natyasastra* set down the details of a codified system of emotional expression

Paul Ekman (1934–): American psychologist. Leading authority on the expression of emotions by the human face. Ekman has tried to prove that these emotional expressions are universal. His writings include *Unmasking the Face* (1975, with Wallace V. Friesen), *Emotion in the Human Face* (1982), *Telling Lies* (1985), and *The Nature of Emotion* (1994, with P. Davidson).

strikingly similar to Ekman's (**see figure 6.28**). In the West, in 1839, **François Delsarte** (1811–71) began his *cours d'esthétique appliqué* (course in applied aesthetics), a system coordinating gestures, voice, and emotional expression (**see Stebbins box**).

François Delsarte (1811–71): French teacher of acting and singing. Originator of a complex system coordinating facial displays, hand gestures, movements, and voice to express specific emotions. His ideas are summarized in Genevieve Stebbins' *Delsarte System of Expression* (1977 [1902]).

What is the relationship between the "natural" displays studied by Darwin and Ekman and the codified aesthetic systems proposed by Bharata-muni and Delsarte? All we can be sure of is that both ordinary behavior and aesthetic behavior are codified. Ordinary behavior does not appear to be codified because people perform ordinary behavior day in, day out — it's as "natural" to them as speaking their mother tongue. Are ordinary behaviors as culturally distinct as spoken languages? The answer is both yes and no. Whole suites of gestures, signs, inflections, and emphases are culture-specific. At the same time, even when persons can't converse in a spoken language, gesturing gets meanings across. Some expressions — the happy smile, lifting the nose in disgust, the wide eyes of surprise, for example — occur in all human cultures. Perhaps the physical displays are universal, while meanings vary from culture to culture and even circumstance to circumstance. Not all happy smiles signify happiness. As Goffman was quick to point out, people are always putting on shows, hiding feelings, dissembling.

fig 6.28. A comparison of performances of the "basic emotions" as described in the *Natyasastra* and identified "universally" by Paul Ekman. Ekman photographs courtesy of Paul Ekman and Wallace V. Freisen. Rasa photographs courtesy of Phillip Zarrilli.

Natyasastra

Sringara: love, happiness

Ekman

Happiness

Hasya: mirth, but also impudence

Natyasastra

Ekman

Karuna: sadness

Sadness

Natyasastra

Ekman

Bibhasta: disgust

Disgust

Raudra: anger, violence

Anger

Adbhuta: surprise, excitement

Surprise

Vira: vigor, heroic

Bhayanaka: fear, guilt

Fear

Shanta: peace, meditation

Genevieve Stebbins

The Delsarte System

A perfect reproduction of the outer manifestation of some passion, the giving of the outer sign, will cause a reflex feeling within. [. . .] Certain attitudes, by extending or contracting the muscles, by compelling the breath to come and go more rapidly, by increasing the heart-beats, cause physical interior sensations which are the correspondences of emotion. [. . .] In emotion, if the hand seeks the chin, vital instincts predominate: namely, appetites, passions; while if the hand seeks the forehead, the mental instincts predominate; if the hand touches the cheeks, the moral instincts; that is, the affections, predominate. [. . .] Excitement or passion tends to expand the gesture; thought or reflection tends to contract gesture; love or affection tends to moderate gesture. Thus, passion tends to extreme expansion of the muscles; thought tends to extreme contraction of the muscles; affection tends to a happy medium of activity of the muscles. [. . .]

1977 [1902], *Delsarte System of Expression*, 141, 217–18, 258–59

In any case, even realistic acting is codified. Realistic acting appears natural because it is based on behaviors people learn from infancy. Realistic acting may not look realistic to a person from another culture. Japanese realistic acting may appear understated and codified to an Italian, while Italian realistic acting might appear bombastic and codified to a Japanese. What about the codified acting of kabuki or Delsarte's exercises? Because this behavior is "natural" to no one, whoever sees it will recognize it as codified. But a person who knows kabuki or any other codified genre well will follow the action easily and not regard it as strange or "foreign."

Conclusion

An actor on the stage, a shaman, or someone in trance stands for or is taken over by someone else or something else. This "else" may be a character in a drama, a demon, a god, or a pot. On the other hand, a performer in everyday life is not necessarily playing anyone one but herself. Paradoxically, this self can be known only as it is enacted. The non-stage roles of ordinary life are many, ranging from the highly formalized performances of government and religious leaders to the semi-fixed roles of the professions, to the more easy-going improvisations of informal interactions.

The two kinds of performing encounter each other when an actor studies a person in ordinary life in order to prepare a role for the stage. But this mimesis is actually not of "real-life" but of a performance. There is no such thing as

unperformed or naturally occurring real life. The object of the actor's "real life study" is also performing, though she may not be fully aware that her behavior is codified. All behavior is "twice-behaved," made up of new combinations of previously enacted doings. A wholly conscious performer, if such a person exists, is one who "twice-performs" twice-behaved behaviors.

THINGS TO THINK ABOUT

1. What is meant by saying that the "performances of everyday life are as codified as ballet"? And if this is so, what about ballet? Can some of the concepts explained in earlier chapters – such as "restoration of behavior" – help?
2. What are the most salient differences between the performing of a shaman in trance, the acting of a realistic movie actor such as Robert De Niro, and a mother chiding her daughter for really bad behavior?

THINGS TO DO

1. Stage a scene from a realistic play – Ibsen, Mamet, or Miller – in a totally non-realistic manner. Is your scene "successful"? Discuss how the text of a drama does or does not determine the style of acting.
2. Make a Happening. Be certain that all the performing in it is "nonmatrixed."

SUGGESTED READINGS

Anisimov, A. F. "The Shaman's Tent of the Evenks." *Studies in Siberian Shamanism*. Ed. Henry M. Michael. Toronto: University of Toronto Press, 1963. 84–96.

Belo, Jane. *Trance in Bali*. New York: Columbia University Press, 1960. 216–222.

Brecht, Bertolt. "A Dialogue about Acting." John Willett, ed. and tr. *Brecht on Theatre*. New York: Hill and Wang, 1964. 26–29.

Grotowski, Jerzy. "The Actor's Technique." *Towards a Poor Theatre*. New York: Simon and Schuster, 1968. 173–83.

Kirby, Michael. "Acting and Non-Acting." *A Formalist Theatre*. Philadelphia: University of Pennsylvania Press, 1987. 1–20.

7 PERFORMANCE PROCESSES

The Earliest Performances?

Events that can be designated "performance" – dance, music, and/or theatre – occur among all the world's peoples and date back as far as archaeologists, anthropologists, and historians can go (**see Wilford box**). These words or their equivalents are not universal, but the behaviors are. Of course, such behaviors differ from place to place, culture to culture, and epoch to epoch. Surviving cave art and prehistoric artifacts indicate that dancing, singing, music-making, wearing masks and/or costumes, impersonating other humans, animals, or supernaturals, acting out stories,

representing past events, experiences, memories, dreams, or fantasies are coexistent with the human condition. Nor can anyone answer the chicken-or-egg question, "Which came first, ritual or entertainment?" Most probably the earliest performances were both ritual and entertainment. For many centuries, in many cultures, religious rituals have entertained vast numbers of participating believers. Conversely, in today's world, more than a few aesthetic performances, popular entertainments, and sports events have been ritualized.

John Noble Wilford

Prehistoric Dancing

No one will ever know when someone first raised arms into the air, pivoted and took a few steps this way and that – and danced. [. . .] Archeologists are at a loss to know the origins of dancing in prehistory because they lack direct evidence, nothing comparable to the art of Altamira or Lascaux. [. . .] An Israeli archeologist now thinks he has pieced together a significant body of evidence for dancing, if not at its beginning, at least at a decisive and poorly understood transitional stage of human culture.

Examining more than 400 examples of carved stone and painted scenes on pottery from 140 sites in the Balkans and the Middle East, Dr. Josef Garfinkel of Hebrew University in Jerusalem has established what he says is an illustrated record of dancing from 9,000 to 2,500 years ago. This record, apparently the earliest of its kind, coincides with the place in time hunters of wild game and gatherers of wild plant food first settled into villages and became pastoralists and farmers.

Some show only stick figures with triangular heads, and some headless, in highly schematic scenes that appear to be dances. Others include figures in a dynamic posture, usually with bent arms and legs. Several scenes depict people in a line or completely circling an illustrated vessel, their hands linked. There is some resemblance here to current folk dancing or even a Broadway chorus line. [. . .]

The prevalence of what appear to be dancing scenes in the earliest art from the ancient Middle East, Dr. Garfinkel said in a recent interview, suggests the importance of the dance in these preliterate agricultural communities. "Dancing was a means of social communication in prestate societies," he said. "It was part of the ritual for coordinating the community's activities." [. . .]

In his research, Dr. Garfinkel found the earliest examples of the dancing motif in art from two 9,000-year-old sites in the Middle East. Engraved on a stone basin, excavated at Nevali Cori in southeastern Turkey, were three human figures in a line, faces forward, legs wide and arms bent upward. The two outer figures are larger than the central one, suggesting a scene of two dancing men flanking the woman. Only in a few cases, mainly in art from early Egypt, Dr. Garfinkel said, are both sexes seen dancing together. At Dhuweila, a small campsite in Jordan, rock carvings depict a row of four human figures holding hands. They have elongated necks and heads that appear to be nonhuman. Dr. Garfinkel thinks they're wearing masks, evidence for which has been found at other sites.

In later millenniums, most of the dance art has been found painted on pottery, usually small vessels for eating and drinking. As Dr. Garfinkel observed, the scenes emphasize dancing as a community activity. The focus is on a line or circle of identical figures moving in the same direction, indicating the importance of the group over the individual. "Dance is thus an activity through which society instills collective discipline in its members," he concluded.

The dances also appear to take place in the open; in the few examples where some architectural elements are visible, the dance seems to be outside them. And since most of the dancing figures appear as silhouettes, it is possible the dance is being performed at night. Dr. Garfinkel expressed surprise that no musical instruments are seen in the motifs.

2001, "In Dawn of Society, Dance Was Center Stage," *The New York Times*, 27 February.
From *NY Times* website

Exactly how we in the twenty-first century can relate to what took place as long ago as paleolithic times – 20,000–30,000 years before the present – is not obvious. We do not even know if the works preserved in the caves of southwest France and northern Spain are unique. Similar, if less sophisticated, prehistoric "art" has been found in Africa, Asia, the Americas, and Australia. Because works are often hidden in caves difficult to access (the discovery of the European materials was accidental), there is no saying if or not other similar troves exist. Performing itself is ephemeral, leaving no direct traces, but surviving paintings, sculptings, and objects point to rich prehistoric performance traditions. The sophistication of the surviving art works makes it logical to assume that the associated performances were not spontaneous but consisting of traditional gestures, utterances, and musics that were the result of forethought and preparation requiring training and rehearsing. Exactly what constitutes training and rehearsing is one of the subjects of this chapter.

As for precisely what was going on at these sites, we know next to nothing. Scientists are not even in agreement concerning when our species "began," with dates ranging from several hundred thousand years to 2 million years ago. Within this time scheme, the "cave art" of paleolithic Europe, dating from 15,000 to 30,000 years ago, is "recent." But this art is very distant when measured against historical traces of "civilizations" that go back only to 5,000 to 10,000 years ago. The origins of theatre and dance in China can be dated to about 4,000 years ago; in Greece to about 2,600 years ago. That the peoples of Africa, Native America, and elsewhere were performing is evident – but exactly what these performances were like, we are not likely ever to know with any finality.

Nevertheless, it seems clear that the paleolithic cave art of France and Spain was not meant to be viewed as in a museum, but to surround or be part of performing (**see figure 7.1**). Perhaps the images were a kind of "action painting/sculpting" nested within encompassing ceremonial activities. The acts of making the paintings and sculptings may in themselves have been performances. Residues of ashes and, in one case, footprints in a circular pattern indicate long-burning fires and dancing. It is unlikely that the people danced in silence, so singing and other kinds of music are inferred. These earliest of theatres are hidden deep in the earth. Most of the "galleries" are difficult to get to. Today flashlights and even electricity illuminate the cave walls. But in the period when the art was being made – and evidence indicates continuous usage over a period of centuries and in some cases millennia – torches or fires would have provided the only

fig 7.1. The cave-theatre of Lascaux, southwest France. In paleolithic times the only light in the caves came from fires or torches. Under the warm colors and flickering flames, the images and sculptings would appear to move. Photograph courtesy Commissariat General au Tourisme, France.

light. Moving, singing, and dancing – not viewing – would be the best explanation of how the caves were used.

Because so many of the paintings and sculptings are of animals, the performances probably concerned hunting and/or fertility. It is clear why the two are associated. Until recently, among the Kung! hunter-gatherers of the Kalahari Desert in southern Africa, for example, when an animal was killed, a ritual entreated the gods for replenishment of the life taken. But it was not only animal fertility that stone-age humans celebrated. Figures, carvings, paintings, and symbols depict human fertility as well. The most ancient sculptures are those of women with enlarged vulvas, milk-laden breasts, and massive thighs and buttocks – such as the "Venus" of Willendorf, dated at about 24,000 years before the present (**see figure 7.2**). Somewhat later come phallic symbols, cylindrical rocks worn smooth by touching. Many centuries

later are the sculptures in the eleventh- to twelfth-century Khajaraho temples of India where erotic poses are also dance steps frozen in stone (**see 7.3**).

fig 7.3. At the 11th–12th century temple complex of Khajaraho in India, the sculptings are often both erotic and dance like. This is one example from the Lakshman Temple as reproduced on the internet at http//www.cmp. caltech.edu/~mcc/ India/PictureShow/ Khajaraho_map. html.

fig 7.2. One of a number of female figures from paleolithic times, this "Venus" of Willendorf is perhaps the best known. This photograph appeared on the internet at
http// www.aeiou.at/aeiou.encyclop.data.image.v/ v136200a.jpg.

What actually went on in the paleolithic caves, or in above-ground human sites, we may never know with any assurance. But is it not logical to assume that there were performances associated with the paleolithic sexual art, as there are with Khajaraho? Before writing in the alphabetic sense, performances were ways of enacting, reliving, remembering, and passing beliefs and knowledge through time. Some caves were in use over a period of millennia, indicating that whatever was going on in them was traditional, linking generation to generation. And if there were performances, they were not isolated but woven into a complex of activities. If the art on the walls was trans-personal and abiding, belonging to communities rather than to individuals, the ceremonies, gestures, incantations, and dance steps also were trans-personal. The means of transmitting such collective performance knowledge was body-to-body learning. In other words, these prehistoric performances were part of a larger, inclusive process that included training, performing, remembering, and starting the process over again.

Performance Process as a Time-Space Sequence

The performance process is a time-space sequence composed of proto-performance, performance, and aftermath. This three–phase sequence may be further divided into ten parts:

Proto-performance
1 training
2 workshop
3 rehearsal

Performance
4 warm up
5 public performance
6 events/contexts sustaining the public performance
7 cooldown

Aftermath
8 critical responses
9 archives
10 memories.

This process applies to all kinds of performances – the performing arts, sports and other popular entertainments, rituals, and the performances of everyday life. Understanding this time-space sequence means grasping how performances are generated, how they are staged in a focused manner, how they are nested within larger events, and what their long-term effects are. The model is not prescriptive. I intend it to be an aid to understanding, not a straitjacket.

Performances have both a short-term impact and a longer after effect, leaving traces in the bodies of the performers and participants-spectators, in archives, and in traditions. Performance processes can be studied from the point of view of actions enacted, of the spaces in which a performance takes place, of the temporal structure of a performance, and as events surrounding and succeeding the performance, both affected by it and affecting it.

Performance processes can also be studied as interactions among four types of players:

1 sourcers (authors, choreographers, composers, dramaturgs, etc.)
2 producers (directors, designers, technicians, business staff, etc.)
3 performers
4 partakers (spectators, fans, congregations, juries, the public, etc.).

Sourcers find, compose, or invent the actions to be performed. Producers work with the performers and sourcers to transform the sources into publicly performed events. Performers play the actions. Partakers receive the actions and sometimes participate in them. The first three types of players – sourcers, producers, and performers – often work together. Producers and performers almost always work together. Partakers usually take part in the process after much of the prepatory work has already been done. A person can simultaneously belong to more than one of these categories. A group may collectively devise or enact all of these processes.

Let me now present this system in more detail.

Proto-Performance

The proto-performance (or "proto-p") is what precedes and/or gives rise to a performance. A proto-p is a starting point or, more commonly, a bunch of starting points. Very few performances start from a single source or impulse. A proto-p may be a legal code, liturgy, scenario, script, drama, dance notation, music score, oral tradition, and so on. It may even be a certain way that a performer makes her body into something "not ordinary," something special for performing – what Eugenio Barba calls the "pre-expressive" (**see Barba box and figure 7.4**). Many proto-p's exist outside the written realm altogether – as plans, drawings, paintings, diagrams, manifestoes, or ideas. A proto-p may be a group of people who want to stage a performance. A proto-p may be an upcoming date that requires a performance – a birthday, Christmas party, or initiation rite – the list of date-driven proto-p's is very long. A proto-p may also be a prior performance, revived, revised, or reconstructed or simply used as a model or starting point for a performance-to-be. The performances of classics as well as the enactment of rituals are always more or less driven by prior performances.

> **Proto-performance (proto-p):** A source or impulse that gives rise to a performance; a starting point. A performance can (and usually does) have more than one proto-p.

Eugenio Barba

Pre-Expressivity

Widely known and practiced throughout Asia, martial arts use concrete physiological processes to destroy the automatisms of daily life and to create another quality of energy in the body. It is this very aspect of martial arts, that is, their use of acculturation technique, which has inspired codified theatre forms. The legs slightly bent, the arms contracted: the basic position of all Asiatic martial arts shows a *decided body* ready to leap and to act. This attitude, which could be compared to the *plié* in classical ballet, can be found in the basic positions of both Oriental and Occidental performers. It is nothing more than a codification, in the form of extra-daily technique, of the position of an animal ready to attack or defend itself.

1991, *A Dictionary of Theatre Anthropology: The Secret Art of the Performer*, 197

fig 7.4. An actor in Jerzy Grotowski's Polish Laboratory Theatre in the early 1960s doing "the cat," an exercise designed to help performers train their pre-expressive skills. Photograph courtesy of Eugenio Barba.

One may think of the proto-p as a "pretext," something that not only comes before the performance, but is also a strategy of concealing from the audience significant portions of the performance process. Rehearsals and preparations are usually closed. Even during the performance itself, the audience is let in on only some of what's happening. Not only are backstage activities hidden, but the master performer reveals only some of what she is able to do. The sense that

there is much more in reserve adds immeasurably to a performance's impact. Just as an iceberg is three-fourths submerged, so a strong performance is largely concealed. This the Japanese noh master **Zeami Motokiyo** (1363–1443) knew well, advising actors to show audiences only 20 percent of what they knew, holding the other 80 percent in reserve.

> **Zeami Motokiyo (1363–1443):** Japanese actor and playwright, the foremost figure in the history of noh theatre. His plays still form the core of the noh repertory; and his ideas on acting remain extremely influential. His treatises on acting, which at one time were secret, have now been published – see *On the Art of the No Drama: The Major Treatises of Zeami* (1984).

What is this hidden portion of a performance? It is what the performer has learned, not only about the specific role being enacted – the particular pretext that informs a given performance – but also about the whole craft, the years of knowledge standing behind each enactment. Being confident of a base of knowledge applies not only to the performing arts but across a wide range of professions. It is also related in each particular performance to what Stanislavsky called the "subtext" – the ongoing driving life force of a scene that exists behind the spoken words and the visible gestures. In this way, pretexts operate secretly concealed deep within the performance.

In the performing arts, rituals, sports, and in many trades and professions such as lawyer, doctor, carpenter, teacher, the proto-p is worked out in three phases: training, workshop, and rehearsals. Obviously, not all arts, rituals, sports, trades, and professions employ all three of these proto-p's. Identifying what is emphasized and what is omitted is important to understanding both the performance process and the social world which contains and is also shaped by particular performances.

A Note on "Text"

Before discussing performance processes in more detail, a note on the notion of "text." Poststructuralists such as Derrida and interpretive anthropologists such as Geertz consider culture itself as a text that can be read. This approach has permeated cultural studies and performance studies. *Reading Dance*, **Susan Foster**'s (1949–) influential book, is but one example of very many that examine performances and proto-performances as texts. Terms such as "dramatic text" and "performance text" are commonly used. In earlier writings I also used these terms. I choose not to use them here because although "text" can be understood dynamically, as an action, it remains linked to writing both in a specific literary sense and in its extended Derridean meaning.

Susan Foster (1949–): American dancer, choreographer, and scholar. Author of *Reading Dance* (1986), *Choreographing History*, and *Corporalities* (1996).

Performance text: Everything that takes place on stage that a spectator experiences, from the movements and speech of the dancers and/or actors to the lighting, sets, and other technical or multimedia effects. The performance text is distinguished from the **dramatic text**. The dramatic text is the play, script, music score, or dance notation that exists prior to being staged.

Pinning down the "real meaning" of "text" is not easy. In everyday usage, people think of a text as words inked or printed on paper or pixeled on a computer screen. But etymologically "text" is related to "textile" and "texture," connoting fabric and feel. "Text" enters English via French from the Latin *texere*, which means to weave or to compose. The Latin is related to the Greek *techne*, meaning skill and artfulness (thus the group of words including "technique" and "technical"), and *tekton*, carpenter or builder. The Indo-European root is *tekb*, to plait, wind, or twist several into one. Thus in its earliest and most active meanings, a text is the product of a skilled joining of different materials to make single, supple, whole, and strong stuff. Those who make texts are both artists and crafts persons. In fact, in early usage there is scant distinction between art and craft. Although today text implies writing, the earlier meanings continue to operate – behind the scenes, as it were. Texts are synthetic, constructed, crafted, made up, invented: sites of interpretation and disagreement, not fixed canons.

Texts can be inscriptions on stone, inked on vellum, printed on paper, or etched on silicon chips. Texts can also be neural engrams or a dancer's body memory, a painting or architectural plan – and many other techniques of remembering, describing, representing, initiating, or repeating events. Texts can be "read" as coherent systems of communication – writing, visual art, music, theatre. Even a city or a historical epoch may be read as a coherent text. Semioticians argue for a very broad definition of text (**see De Marinis box**). In fact, during the past half-century the concept of text has been greatly expanded. For all that expansion, today's notions of text reinvoke the earliest meanings of the word.

Marco De Marinis

What is "Text"?

From a semiotic standpoint, the term /text/ designates not only coherent and complete series of linguistic statements, whether oral or written, but also every unit of discourse, whether verbal, nonverbal, or mixed, that results from the coexistence of several codes (and other factors too [. . .]) and possesses the constitutive prerequisites of completeness and coherence. According to this understanding of textuality, an image, or group of images, is, or can be, a text. A sculpture, a film, a musical passage, or a sequence of sound effects constitute texts also, or rather *they can be considered as such*. Clearly, therefore, even the units known as performances can be considered as texts, and can thus become the object of textual analysis [. . .].

1993, *The Semiotics of Performance*, 47

Understood performatively, texts are transformable and pliable sign and/or symbol systems. Every text invites being remade into new texts. This proves to be the case, especially with regard to texts used in or as performances. For example, Shakespeare's *Hamlet* has been the pretext for any number of productions. *Hamlet* has even been deconstructed into new playtexts such as **Heiner Müller**'s (1929–95) *Hamletmachine*, itself a gloss on Shakespeare's play, a playtext in its own right, and a proto-p for many widely stylistically variant productions.

Heiner Müller (1929–95): German playwright and director. Works include *Hamletmachine* (1979) and *Quartet* (1982). Director of the Berliner Ensemble from 1992 until his death.

Training

Training is logically if not always experientially the first step of the proto-performance. Training is the acquisition of particular skills. Training may be either informal or formal (**see Okpewho box**). In informal training, the novice acquires skills over time by absorbing what is going on. Mistakes are corrected as part of daily life. Such training can be very effective. This is the way infants learn to speak.

This is how most people learn how to "fit in" to their families and social groups. In much of the world, training for a wide variety of occupations was or is informal, and extremely effective. Much of childplay is a kind of training for both social and technical skills that will be useful later in life. A lot of performance training is informal. Many persons who have never taken a class are excellent social dancers. In Bali, trance dancers who have never been formally trained perform simple, precise movements (**see Covarrubias box**).

exclusively through apprenticeship are now taught in school. The school approach to learning assumes a systematic progression through different "grades" of knowledge and the division of knowledge into "subjects." Informal training is more holistic.

Informal training is deemed successful when the trainee begins to practice on his own. Formal training often concludes with an initiation rite – graduation ceremonies where diplomas are conferred amidst festivities that bring family and friends together. Some great artists have been

Isidore Okpewho

Formal and Informal Training

[. . .] Two kinds of training are involved in the development of the African oral artist: informal and formal. Informal training entails a kind of loose attachment whereby the future artist happens to live or move in an environment in which a particular kind of oral art is practiced and simply absorbs the skill in it as time goes on. [. . .] It is reasonably clear what goes on in informal training. First, the future artist must be a person blessed with a considerable amount of natural genius who possesses an interest in the kind of oral literature that is practiced around him or her. Second, since no formal coaching is involved, these novices must look and listen closely and in this way absorb the ideas, the idioms, and the techniques peculiar to the art. [. . .] And finally, the process of learning entails that the novices use their imagination to select the relevant materials from the large amount they may have acquired and to increase their store of knowledge as time goes on. Very much the same things happen in the formal kind of training, except that the process is better organized and the relationship between the trainee and the teacher properly established. [. . .]

Formal training is particularly useful for the more complex kinds of oral literature – e.g., some forms of ritual poetry and performances involving the accompaniment of music – on which the future artist could depend as a major source of livelihood. [. . .] The state may recognize both the cultural value and the popularity (especially with foreigners) of a category of oral traditions and so set up a "school" where young men can be taught the skills of that art – not only to preserve the culture but also to promote the tourist economy.

1992, *African Oral Literature*, 21–25

Training: The phase of the performance process where specific skills are learned and practiced.

Formal training comes in a variety of methods. Classroom schooling is the prevalent kind of formal training in the world today. But there is also apprenticeship and one-on-one teaching. Formal training became increasingly necessary with the advent of industrialization, which displaced work from the home, farm, and village to factories and cities. The increasingly technical quality of life – from science and economics to law, medicine, and computers – demands formal training. Some performing arts – such as filmmaking, and interactive telecommunications – require formal technical training. But even arts that at one time were taught

trained informally, others formally. Frequently, formal and informal training co-exist. In medicine, for example, once school is over, the neophyte doctor becomes a hospital intern under the supervision of resident and senior physicians. Specialist designations take even more training.

In the arts and sports especially, one continues training as long as one performs, even over a whole lifetime. At this level, training comprises "keeping in shape" perhaps even more than acquiring new skills. In the physical arts – dancing and sports – the older one gets, the more one needs to sustain her or his training. Although acting is not as physically demanding, many successful actors feel the need to take classes.

Sometimes apprenticeship training is combined with classroom training. At the Kathakali Kalamandalam in Kerala, southwest India, some boys begin training at 8 years

Miguel Covarrubias

Training for Trance Dancing in Bali

Two little girls, trained to go into a trance, are chosen from all the girls of the village for their psychic aptitudes by the temple priest. [. . .] Choruses of men and women are formed and the training begins. Every night, for weeks, they all go to the temple, where the women sing traditional songs while the men chant strange rhythms and harmonies made up of meaningless syllables, producing a syncopated accompaniment for the dance that the little girls, the *sanghyangs*, will perform. By degrees the little girls become more and more subject to the ecstasy produced by the intoxicating songs, by the incense, and by the hypnotic power of the *pemanku* [priest]. The training goes on until the girls are able to fall into a deep trance, and a formal performance can be given. It is extraordinary that although the little girls have never received dancing lessons, once in a trance they are able to dance in any style, all of which would require ordinary dancers months and years of training to learn. But the Balinese ask, how it could be otherwise, since it is the goddesses who dance in the bodies of the little girls.

1937, *Island of Bali*, 335–36

fig 7.5. Three young students in the 1980s at the Kalamandalam, Kerala, India, in kathakali's basic stance, knees akimbo, back arched, the weight on the outside of the foot. This position is the first thing students learn. Photograph courtesy of Eugenio Barba.

of age. No one over the age of 14 is accepted. (That is, no Indian over that age. Some adult foreigners are admitted – but I know of no case where a foreigner has undergone the full 7–8 years of continuous training that the Indians undertake.) Trainees rise before dawn during the rainy season of July–August for eight hours of intense psychophysical training embedded in a 13-hour day that also includes text analysis and lessons in Indian philosophy (**see figure 7.5**). The prerequisite for more detailed training of the hands, eyes,

feet, and torso is a demanding program of physical exercise (**see figure 7.6**). The flexibility and turnout needed to perform kathakali is molded into the young bodies of the trainees by means of massage administered by older students or their teachers.

In their performance classes, the trainees practice gestures and movements identical to, or based on, what they will actually use later on when performing kathakali. Learning is by immersion and imitation. There is no improvisation

fig 7.6. A kathakali student makes a stupendous leap as part of his basic training at the Kalamandalam, Kerala, India 1976. Note the glistening of the bodies – this is because they are thoroughly oiled to make the muscles more limber. Photograph by Richard Schechner.

or what in the West might be called "free, creative work." Over time, the training goes into their bodies – the trainees are transformed both physically and mentally into kathakali performers. Later in life, some performers – recognized by their peers and by connoisseurs of kathakali as "masters" – will improvise – not in rehearsals but in public performances – making changes in the scores they learned as students or after. These changes, if appreciated by knowing spectators, will become part of a particular performer's style. He will then pass them on to his students, who will imitate the master (who once himself was a student learning by imitation). In this way, kathakali both maintains and develops its performing tradition.

But the kathakali training system is not the only way to acquire performance knowledge. Learning how to perform the ritual dances of the Yoruba of southwest Nigeria is done in a different manner (**see figure 7.7**). After a long period of training that involves rote learning, intense concentration, and practice, the Yoruban performer is set free to improvise. The same pattern occurs elsewhere in West Africa (**see figure 7.8**). Training includes not only instruction in how to perform in public, but also the memorizing and interpreting of sacred oral texts. These texts are learned from a ritual

fig 7.7. Diviner Kolawole Oshitola drums while four neophytes in ritual dress and Oshitola's three apprentices complete the liminal stage of the Itefa ritual that establishes the personal destiny of each initiate into Ifa divination practice and initiates them as "new men." Yoruban region, Nigeria, 1986. The ritual performance is at once an initiation and a training ground. Photograph by Henry and Margaret Drewal, courtesy of the Henry Drewal and Margaret Thompson Drewal Collection.

specialist to whom the neophyte is apprenticed. Specific techniques are passed down, but the Yorubans believe that performances need always to be changing, adjusting to new circumstances and realities if the traditions are to remain meaningful (**see Margaret Thompson Drewal box**). Thus the Yorubans train their performers to be alert for opportunities to improvise, to apply the traditional knowledge to immediate contingent circumstances, to make performances that are both old and new at the same time. Given the successive impact of colonialism, modernization, and globalization on many Third World cultures, this ability to integrate the new with the given, to improvise creatively, has proven invaluable. In Africa and in the African diaspora, the penchant for combining rigor with improvisation is expressed in a total and precisely embodied performance knowledge (**see Thompson box**).

fig 7.8. Two identical female Gelede dancers facing each other as they interpret the rhythms of the drums. The crowd controller in the foreground with a long stick keeps the dance space open. Much of the actual performing is improvised. Benin, 1971. Photograph by Henry and Margaret Drewal, courtesy of the Henry Drewal and Margaret Thompson Drewal Collection.

Margaret Thompson Drewal

Training a Ritual Specialist in Nigeria

Acquiring techniques for producing ritual action is mostly a rote exercise demanding sustained effort and concentration. Oshitola [a ritual specialist] described to me how his grandfather used to make him sit attentively for hours at a time studying the oral texts of divination and ritual processes in action. Some techniques require more effort than others to master. To acquire such techniques — in other words, to know how something is accomplished, particularly if it can be picked up easily — without simultaneously learning the values and ethics operating behind that knowledge can lead to misuse and even abuse. This is particularly critical in rituals performed to effect change, as in rites of passage, divination, and healing. [. . .] What distinguishes ritual specialists from each other, and from charlatans, are their particularized ritual roles, which they have often inherited and for which they have been specifically selected and trained. It is the transformative power of this kind of sustained experience that is essential, which is why Oshitola often voiced to me his concern that "you can't learn everything in a day," in response to my persistent questioning. The fact is nobody can witness a Yoruba performance in its entirety, not even ritual specialists themselves. This is true not only because of the exclusivity of many ritual segments, but because of the simultaneity of ritual action generally. [. . .] If I could observe every aspect of a ritual firsthand, or any other kind of performance for that matter, I would have observed undoubtedly more than any other participant.

1992, Yoruba Ritual, 24–25

197

Robert Farris **Thompson**

The Vital Aliveness of African Dance

African dance is seen in the eyes of its performers as an instrument of strong expression. The dancer must be strong. He must shake his being with vigor, creating a vision "terrible to watch" in the words of a Bangwa hunter. Vital aliveness, high intensity, speed, drive — these are some of the facets of artful muscularity and depth of feeling that characterize the dances of this continent. The concept of vital aliveness leads to the interpretation of the parts of the body as independent instruments of percussive force. [. . .] The dancer must impart equal life, equal autonomy, to every dancing portion of his frame. [. . .] Thus one Yoruba talked about *making* the shoulders, with forcefully marked activations, a Banyang mentioned his father *playing* his toes, and an Ejagham remarked on dancing "with the things where they *make 'em*," i.e., the transformation of upper and lower parts of the body into zones of independently enlivened motion.

1974, *African Art in Motion*, 9

Imitation as a Way of Acquiring Performance Knowledge

What about learning by imitation in the West? At the end of the nineteenth century, Stanislavsky was struggling against mechanical and declamatory acting. He, along with others, found in realism an access to the "truth" and "spontaneity" of everyday life which they wanted to bring into the theatre. Today's people recognize that realism and naturalism are styles as much as kathakali or Yoruban dancing are. Realism is no more "true" than any other performance mode. As we have seen in previous chapters, even everyday life consists of "twice-behaved behaviors." It is also true that only a few masters will be able to formulate in words the grammar of whatever performance genre they practice, be it kathakali, ballet, rock music, baseball, noh, or shamanism. Most performers will not be able to articulate precisely what they do, even if over time they get better and better at doing it. The proper use of imitation and repetition in training is in directly transmitting performance knowledge without

the need for a verbal explanation or theorizing. Such "talking about" may be very helpful at a certain stage of acquiring performance knowledge, but it can hinder such acquisition if used too early or too frequently. It is better usually to get the performance knowledge into the body on its own terms, as movement, gesture, tone of voice — whatever the techniques of a particular genre are. By means of imitation, learners acquire through practice an organic mastery of the craft that underlies every art. It is only after making various performance scores "second nature" in the sense of giving a person new ways of standing, walking, gesturing, speaking, and singing that the maturing artist earns the right to experiment and improvise within the vocabulary of the genre.

When I followed well-trained kathakali actors through rehearsals into performance, I witnessed artists who were "controlled" in all their actions from the most gross to the twitching of an eye, the bending of a small finger, and the turning-up of the toes. These actors felt "free" because in performance their "second body" was perfectly "natural." Performers trained this way embody their training so thoroughly that they no more think of it than a native speaker thinks while speaking of the grammar of the language he is uttering. During performances these artists are not in trance, but they may as well be in terms of total conformity to the rules of their genre. They express both their individual creativity — the variations mature performers are expected to introduce into their scores — and the specific cultural meanings embedded in the roles they embody.

Workshop

Workshop is the active research phase of the performance process. Some artists use workshops to explore processes that will be useful in rehearsals and in making performances. For example, in workshops I led in the 1990s at New York University, I developed an exercise roughly based on the eight fundamental emotions described in the *Natyasastra*, the ancient Sanskrit manual for performers, directors, playwrights, and theatre architects. The rasaboxes exercise takes place inside a rectangle of nine boxes, each of which is the "place" of a basic emotion. As performers move from one box to the next, they must instantly change their emotional expression from, say, *karuna* (sadness or compassion) to *bibhasta* (disgust), or *raudra* (rage), or *sringara* (love) (**see figure 7.9**). But these words are not the key — each rasa is an entire range of feelings clustered around an emotional core; a flavoring and savoring of emotions, rather than anything

fig 7.9. The "rasaboxes" exercise devised by Richard Schechner and developed by Michele Minnick and Paula Murray Cole.

Cole on the left and Minnick practicing opposing "rasas" in two of the boxes. Photograph courtesy of Richard Schechner.

Cole demonstrating the raudra (rage) rasa. Photograph courtesy of Richard Schechner.

Workshop: The phase of the performance process where materials are found, invented, and played with.

fixed or "texted." The ultimate aim of the exercise is to help performers compose, control, embody, and express emotions as nimbly as athletes are able to rest on the sidelines and then, when asked to play, plunge into the game with full intensity. Antonin Artaud once called for actors to be "athletes of the emotions," and this is what the rasaboxes exercise trains them to become.

But this kind of exploration and training is not the only thing workshops are good for. Workshops may be used to dig up materials from personal, historical, or other sources and then find ways to express these in actions and interactions. These materials may find their way into actual aesthetic or therapeutic performances. Or they may remain inside the workshop, a means of exploration only. In New Age venues such as Esalen or Naropa institutes, workshops focus on meditation, whole-body healing, and the integration of many different religious and philosophical systems. In the performing arts, workshops cover a very broad range of activities. Some workshops bring together persons from different cultures and/or genres to exchange techniques, ideas, and approaches. Other workshops introduce people to particular skills or techniques. Probably the most prevalent kind of workshop is used to "open people up" to new

experiences, helping them recognize and develop their own possibilities. Workshops have become popular in business and as recreation. Some workshops, often sponsored by businesses, help people acquire certain social skills such as learning how to be at ease in public or how to assert oneself without being overly aggressive, and so on. Plainly, the difference between training and workshop is blurry. Generally, workshops look toward "the new" both personally and artistically.

Many activities are "workshopped" before they are produced. To workshop something is to produce a prototype or experimental model. This is true not only in the arts but across a wide range of activities. For example, in auto manufacturing, new car models built in prototype by teams pooling resources in an atmosphere of workshop. Designers and engineers play around with new ideas leading to the making of a single prototype. The prototype is built not on the assembly line, but on an individual basis. Of course, such a "new car" is not really wholly new. A prototype combines already proven engineering and design along with what is really new. But sometimes, auto companies go far out, trying to imagine what a "car of the future" would be. Such a vehicle is called a "concept car." Sometimes it is not even really finished. It may have a very advanced exterior design but no comparable motor. But by means of concept cars auto manufacturers can familiarize themselves and their customers with possibilities. Often elements

199

from a concept car will find their way into the proto-type, which, in turn, serves as the basis for what comes off the assembly line. The process goes from workshop (concept car) to rehearsal (prototype) to production (performance). Similarly, in the performing arts, the workshop phase is where possibilities that may never be performed in public are explored. Only when a project achieves a certain level of solidity is it moved out of the workshop and into rehearsals.

Architects **Lawrence Halprin** (1916–) and **Jim Burns** (1926–94), working closely with Lawrence's wife, choreographer **Anna Halprin** (1920–), developed a collective creative workshop process they called the "RSVP Cycles" (**see Halprin and Burns box, see figure 7.11**). The RSVP Cycles are both a theory of the workshop process and a very useful technique:

Resources — all the subjective and objective material used in the creative process. These include space, people, money, things, etc.; and objectives, feelings, fantasies, open and hidden agendas, etc.

Scores — what I have termed the proto-performance: scenarios, instructions, plans. Scores can be either open or closed. A closed score controls the action; an open score allows for a variety of options.

Valuation — where the group considers feedback about the ongoing creative process. Scores are revised on the basis of the feedback. Halprin and Burns coined the term "valuaction" to emphasize the action aspect of the feedback. Scores are revised not just by talking about what happened but by means of new actions.

Performance — the most optimal outcome possible using the scores within the given circumstances.

Lawrence Halprin (1916–): American architect who, with his wife, dancer **Anna Halprin** (1920–), and fellow architect **Jim Burns** (1926–94), developed a set of workshop processes known as the RSVP Cycles.

Lawrence Halprin and Jim Burns

The RSVP Cycles

The RSVP Cycles is a model of creativity that organizes and makes visible methods for people to work together in groups. The model is participatory and cyclical rather than hierarchical and linear; it emphasizes ongoingness and process, not sequence and goal attainment. It focuses on people as participants, not as mechanisms, tools, or inert recipients of products. For this reason, one step does not lead to the next. Instead, access to the cycle can occur at any point and influence the direction of change and growth.

Our concept of creativity in groups is based on the premise that people have creative potential and that, when they interact in groups, this creativity can be unleashed and enhanced. [. . .] When each facet comes into play, it is not blocked by the other three and the freedom to act remains open rather than inhibited as it usually is.

RSVP is a framework for process. It enables the process to move and action to be taken – it provides a way for many people to work together in groups productively rather than chaotically and to be aware of the process *while* they are involved in it. Since it is cyclical, it accepts input and change from each person rather than rejecting it if it does not fit. [. . .]

Using the RSVP Cycles permits and encourages each person to influence profoundly what happens as well as how it happens. Groups of people working with the cycles do not act out someone else's ideas or carry up pre-established intentions – they do not have a preformed goal (which is the what of things) to which they simply add their own ideas of how it should be done.

The RSVP Cycles allow people to determine what should happen, the program and objectives of actions, as significantly as how it should be accomplished. The cycles make possible the shifting and reevaluation of objectives during the process as they are influenced by events, without invalidating the process or stopping its flow. In this way process and objectives become linked and intertwined, and what happens in a group situation is affected by how it happens.

1974, *Taking Part: A Workshop Approach to Collective Creativity*, 27–29

The RSVP Cycles

fig 7.10. An active, schematic rendition of the RSVP Cycles of Lawrence Halprin and Jim Burns. The drawing itself shows the dynamic quality of the RSVP system. Drawing courtesy of Lawrence Halprin.

RSVP Cycles: A workshop technique developed by **Anna Halprin, Lawrence Halprin**, and **Jim Burns**. RSVP is an acronym for **R**esources, **S**cores, **V**aluation, **P**erformance.

In the Halprin–Burns method, the RSVP cycle is repeated several times during workshops. There is no right place to start. The group may enter the cycle at any of its nodes. Nor is the performance phase necessarily a public performance. Often the performance is for members of the workshop only. At some point, a public may or may not be invited to experience the results of the workshop. This kind of workshop is not designed primarily to find materials out of which public performances are made. The primary objective of this kind of workshop is self-discovery and/or the building and solidifying of a creative group or team.

Insofar as workshops are where new ways of doing things are explored and resistances to new knowledge are identified and dealt with, they are similar to initiation rites. As discussed in chapter 3, van Gennep called initiations "rites of passage" because by means of an initiation rite a person passes from one social identity to another. According to van Gennep's theory, initiation rites consist of three phases: separation, the liminal or "in between" phase, and reintegration. During initiations, persons leave their ordinary lives behind (separation), undergo ordeals by means of which old behaviors are erased and new behaviors and knowledge learned (liminal phase), and emerge reborn as new or at least profoundly changed beings ready to rejoin their society but at a new level of responsibility (reintegration). Workshop participants follow a similar path by isolating themselves from their ordinary

lives, putting aside old habits, delving into themselves, and learning new ways of doing things. As in many initiations, the journey is not undertaken alone. A group sustains individual efforts just as individual contributions strengthen the group.

If a workshop is successful, participants re-emerge as changed beings. Sometimes these changes are minor, sometimes fundamental. For a workshop to succeed, the participants must do the hard work of not only mastering new skills (training) but opening themselves up to others and to new ideas and practices. This is not easy. But once participants are able to be receptive and vulnerable, they are ready to grow and change. Workshop and training may overlap in function, but they are experienced very differently. Training is a long, slow, repetitive, immersive process. Workshops are relatively brief, intense, and suddenly transformative. Some workshops use "ordeals" as a way of breaking down resistance to learning and as a way of incorporating new knowledge into the body. Fasting, long hours, strict discipline, and difficult psychophysical exercises are just some of the techniques used to push people beyond their ordinary limits.

Rehearsal

Rehearsals operate differently and at a different level than workshops. Workshops are a way of breaking down, digging deep, and opening up. Resources are identified and explored. During the workshop phase, possibilities abound. Rehearsals organize the materials found in workshops. Rehearsals build on, and fill in, the foundations laid down in training and explored in workshops. During rehearsals, actions are separated into what can be used and what must be discarded or put aside for another project. Often effective actions and meaningful insights are simply not useful for the project at hand. These are not wasted but set aside or warehoused for future use. For long stretches, rehearsals may be mostly tedious repetition and revision, a slow building-up process. But then, surprisingly and suddenly, things fall into place – an interaction, a scene, or even a whole act "makes sense" onstage for the first time (**see figure 7.11**). Or everyone experiences a "creative moment" simultaneously, adding immeasurably to the work. Even master directors such as Peter Brook are hard-pressed to understand how these moments occur or how they can be brought about (**see Selbourne box**).

Rehearsal: The phase of the performance process where the specific details of a performance are shaped, repeated, and made ready for a public showing.

David Selbourne

Creative Moments During Rehearsal

We [Peter Brook and Selbourne] also spoke of the nature of the "creative moments" in rehearsal, when a so-far fleeting sense of discovery and illumination suddenly raises the spirits, and — however briefly — suggests the ultimate possibility of exhilaration in performance. Was everyone aware simultaneously of such moments? He thought they were. For these moments, when feelings, words, and movements came together and fused into new life, depended on the "running of a current," an opening to which all present contribute. I asked him whether he thought that these and other experiences of rehearsal could be described, captured in words. "Not at all. Of course not," he replied with some asperity.

1982, *The Making of A Midsummer Night's Dream*, 39

fig 7.11. A sharp-eyed director, himself a master performer, leads a rehearsal of kathakali at the Kalamandalam, Kerala, India, in 1976. Photograph by Richard Schechner.

Rehearsing is the process of building up specific blocks of proto-performance materials into larger and larger sequences of actions that are assembled into a whole, finished performance. Rehearsals are always tailored to the specific needs of the performance-at-hand, whether a wedding or a production of *As You Like It*. Rehearsals reduce the "noise" in a system, creating a graceful "finished product" (**see Birdwhistell box**). Commenting on Ray Birdwhistell's

observation that grace and beauty equals simplicity, ethologist Konrad Lorenz noted that when noise is eliminated from any system, the signal is less ambiguous (**see Lorenz box**). This increases the chances that whatever message is being sent will be correctly received and interpreted. If Lorenz is right, then "aesthetics," whatever other values it may have, and wherever it may occur – in all areas of human life – serves an evolutionary purpose.

Both Birdwhistell and Lorenz argue for efficiency and simplicity – the "grace" of an accomplished dance. The model is like that of performance from the business perspective – the removal of "extraneous" movements, time-and-effort efficiency and productivity. But many art works, not to mention daily social interactions, are extremely complex, lumpy, ambivalent, and "inefficient." Many great works of art are anything but simple. The plays of Shakespeare, the spectacles of Robert Wilson, the paintings of Breughel, Yoruba Gelede masked dances, etc. are no less artistic than the plays of Beckett, the paintings of Mondrian, or haiku poetry. The "inefficient" art works would not be any the better if made simpler and clearer. Some persons have attempted to rewrite Shakespeare to remove some contradictions, to make the flow of the action more logical. These efforts diminish rather than improve the plays. Clearly, a normative, single standard for making and evaluating art is

Ray Birdwhistell

Graceful Behavior

We have been running trajectories on dancing and other acts described as graceful behavior.

Note B and A are trajectories of an arm or leg or body. A is a smooth curve; B is the zigzag line. The sizes of the zigzags are unimportant. It is the shape of the movement with which I'm concerned. A and B express the same trajectory. However, ultimately trajectory A shows minimal variation or adjustment within the scope of the trajectory. In A there is a minimum of messages being reacted to in process. This is "grace." In B multiple messages are being introduced into the system and there is the zigzag. The things we call graceful are always multi-message acts in which the secondary messages are minimized, and there the role of the whole is maximized.

1959, *Transactions of the Conference on Group Processes of 1957*, 101–102

Konrad Lorenz

Eliminating "Noise," Creating Dance

[. . .] with the elimination of the noise in the movement, when the movement becomes graceful, and becomes more unambiguous as a signal [. . .] the easier it is for it to be taken up unambiguously by the receptor. Therefore, there is a strong selection pressure working in the direction of making all signal movements [. . .] more graceful, and that is also what reminds us [in animal behavior] of a dance.

1959, *Transactions of the Conference on Group Processes of 1957*, 202–203

insupportable. One must always respect cultural, historical, and individual differences. These differences give works their particular heft, tone, and flavors.

The problem of "productivity" is tractable if we relocate the simplifying process from finished works to rehearsals. The question then becomes not how simple or complex a finished work is, but what happens during rehearsals. How does the production team determine which of all the things thought of and/or tried will survive into the public performance? Comparing the many possibilities that arise during rehearsals to the relatively few actions actually performed in the finished work reveals how many adjustments take place during rehearsals. The goal of rehearsing is to bring the finished product into harmony with the process that produced it. The result may be simple or complex, logical or arational, easy to follow or annoyingly difficult. But in every successful work (however that is determined), the rehearsal process will have sifted out what does not belong – will have simplified in the sense of keeping "the least rejected of all the things tried" (as Brecht once said). A number of supposedly unrehearsed activities – some Happenings, many common behaviors in ordinary life – are not really spontaneous and unedited. Investigating how they came to be what they are reveals extensive editing and rehearsing (either actual or in the imagination).

Furthermore, the social nature of the performing arts, sports, and rituals makes them special. Although all behavior is in some sense rehearsed and then performed, only the arts, sports, and rituals almost always rehearse in groups and present their products to a group. The performing arts are rarely a one-on-one experience. Some experimental performances have featured one-on-one interactions, but these constitute the exceptions, not the rule. Even solo performances involve more than one person during rehearsals; and of course the public performance occurs before a gathering of people. A principal task of rehearsals is to coordinate the various skills, opinions, and desires of the production team. This is true of rituals as well as other genres of performance. Among Australian First Peoples, for example, the elders will spend hours discussing, arguing, and arranging for what results in a 10-minute performance that is part of a much longer initiation rite. In sports, rehearsals are called "practice." A coach may use a chalkboard in the locker room to show how a play ought to be run, but soon enough the players are on the field and practice playing. In law, too, moot courts serve as rehearsals for future lawyers where the performance aspects of the moot court are emphasized (see **UCLA Moot Court Handbook box**).

UCLA Moot Court Handbook

Performing Your Brief

The advocate should use his eyes, his hands, and his voice to maintain the attention of the court and strengthen the persuasive effect of his arguments. The advocate should not hesitate to use the unique advantages of his personal presence during oral argument. Good eye contact, effective gestures, and an interesting voice pattern may substantially augment the persuasive quality of a legal argument. [. . .] Looking at each member of the panel squarely in the eyes is a particularly valuable means of capturing and maintaining the undivided attention of the court. [. . .] Certain distracting habits reoccur in student arguments frequently enough to justify the following lists of Do's and Don'ts:

1. Stand straight; do not lean on the podium, slouch, or move back and forth.
2. Keep your hands at your sides or resting (not leaning) on the podium [. . .].
3. Speak in a clear audible voice; do not shout, mumble, or whisper.
4. Do not neglect to address the court. Use, "If it please the Court," "Your Honors," or "This Court;" do not address the court as "you."
5. Use affirmative language [. . .].
6. Sit up straight and listen attentively while opposing counsel or co-counsel is speaking. [. . .]
7. Dress appropriately for the occasion.
8. Introduce yourself before you speak.

A well-delivered presentation adds immeasurably to the persuasiveness of the case. It gives an air of polish and distinction to the argument.

n.d., Anonymous, *Handbook of Appellate Advocacy*, 48–49

During rehearsals proto-performances are researched, interpreted, absorbed, recomposed, and rewritten. Each proto-p enters rehearsals belonging to a single person – the author, choreographer, composer, designer, or performer. Everyone brings their own agendas into rehearsals. The job of rehearsals is to sort through and transcend all this stuff – to weave disparate or not entirely understood proto-performances into a coherent public performance.

Warm-up

On any Sunday morning at the Institutional Church of God in Christ in Brooklyn, New York, before the service really gets going, four or five children ranging in age from about 8 to 12 begin playing the drums, an electric guitar, and the keyboard. Only five or six members of the congregation are in the church at that time. About 20 minutes later, as the congregation gathers, the young instrumentalists accompany the Youth Choir, who belt out a few rousing songs. Then both the Youth Choir and their backup retire in favor of more mature musicians. Those in attendance number 50 or more. Soon enough, deacons make announcements, Scripture is

read, a member or two of the congregation offer testimony. More people keep entering the sanctuary. Finally, more than an hour after the children started banging the drums, the Radio Choir makes its dramatic entrance marching down the center aisle, preceded by Bishop Carl E. Williams, Sr., other preachers, and a visiting dignitary or two. The service proper is ready to begin. What went on before was warm-up.

> **Warm-up:** The phase of the performance process immediately before the public performance.

Every performance is immediately preceded by a warm-up, some lengthy as at the Institutional Church, some brief and hardly noticeable, as when odissi dancer Sanjukta Panigrahi made a few solemn gestures to the statue of the god Jagganath – which she made certain was onstage when she danced. "I dance for Jagganath," she told me; "the rest of the world can watch if it wishes." Many actors concentrate their minds prior to stepping onstage. Singers run scales or in some other way warm-up the voice. A fully costumed and masked noh actor contemplates his image in a mirror mask just before going onstage (**see figure 7.12**). A public speaker goes over

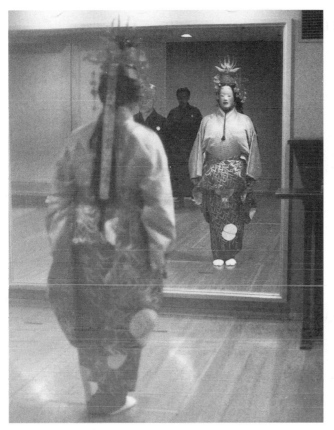

fig 7.12. Noh *shite* ("doer," the main performer) Izumi Yoshio as the heavenly maiden in *Hagoromo* by Zeami regarding his image in the mirror just before going on stage. Photograph by Monica Bethe.

formers prepare to make the leap from "readiness" to "performance." This leap is decisive, a jump over a void of time-space. On one side of the void is ordinary-life, on the other, performance. The warm-up takes place on the ordinary-life side, preparing the performer for the leap, giving the performer the courage to jump into performance.

In organized, ritually determined performances – the performing arts, law, medicine, religion, and so on – warm-ups are often ritualized, involving specific costumes and well-known performance "faces" (attitudes, demeanors). In such cases, there may be a "pre-warm-up" where the individual performer follows her own private routine – because the ritualized warm-up is already a performance in its own right. In other words, every performance, every entry into the enactment of a known and necessary score, demands a "time before" when the performer can ready herself for putting on the role. Shakespeare knew all about this when he penned, "The readiness is all." (Hamlet, 5.2: 236–37).

Public performance

Training and workshops give performers the necessary skills and help them acquire courage and confidence. Rehearsals construct a particular performance score. The warm-up readies the performer for the leap-into-performing. Most of this book deals with what happens next, the vast range of public performances. Therefore, I will not linger here on what constitutes a public performance. Even in theatre there are so many different kinds of performances that at best one can refer only to a few (**see figure 7.13**). Add to theatre the untold other kinds of performances – and one comes up with what is, for all practical purposes, an endless list. But what is a "public performance"? A "public performance" is no easier to specify than was "is" performance in chapter 2. I note only that a performance is whatever takes place between a marked beginning and a marked end. This marking, or framing, varies from culture to culture, epoch to epoch, and genre to genre. In the performing arts in mainstream Western genres, lowering the houselights and bringing the stage lights up, raising or opening curtains, and other procedures mark the start of a performance or portion of a performance. The closing or dropping of a curtain, the dimming of stage lights, the applause of spectators, and the actors taking bows mark the end of mainstream performances. At American sports events, the singing of the national anthem precedes the start of a game. For every genre, in every culture, there are usually very clear markers signaling the start and finish of a public performance.

her notes, looks at herself in the mirror. Stanislavsky advised actors to prepare at length during the day of a performance. A judge will review case dockets, put on robes, and enter the courtroom on cue when the clerk announces her. A doctor will review patient records and perhaps confer with nurses or colleagues before an examination. Surgeons enact complex rituals concerning their instruments, scrubbing, and other procedures before making the first incision. Athletes stretch and meditate, preparing both body and mind for the contest. Even during a game warm-ups continue. For example, a baseball pitcher will throw a few balls before each inning, or go through more extensive warm-up in the bullpen. A batter in the batting circle will swing his bat a few times before approaching the plate. A mother getting ready to scold a child may rehearse in her mind exactly what she will say and do.

The list can go on and on. There are many different kinds of warm-ups, each suiting a particular performer and performance. There is before every kind of performance – aesthetic, social, athletic, ritual, political, personal – a liminal time, sometimes brief, sometimes extended, when per-

fig 7.13. An array of different kinds of performances. This selection by no means exhausts the possibilities.

Mick Jagger singing at Woodstock, 1968. Photograph by Ken Regan.

Spalding Gray as The Bishop and Joan Evans as The Penitent in The Performance Group's production of Jean Genet's *The Balcony*, directed by Richard Schechner, 1979. Photograph courtesy Richard Schechner.

Kate Valk as the Narrator in The Wooster Group's production of *Brace Up!* based on Anton Chekhov's *Three Sisters*, 1991. Photograph by Mary Gearheart. Copyright The Wooster Group.

Sarah Bernhardt, right, as Hamlet, 1899. Most probably Ophelia is at the spinning wheel – perhaps this is the "Get thee to a nunnery" scene, act 3, scene 1. Bernhardt (1844–1923) played several male roles during her illustrious career. Photograph courtesy of Richard Schechner.

Kabuki actor Ichikawa Ennosuke in the *aragoto* pose. Photograph courtesy of Eugenio Barba.

But even these apparently definite conventions can be played with – throwing into doubt exactly what constitutes a performance. A famous example is John Cage's *4'33"* (1952). This concert consisted of pianist **David Tudor** (1926–96) walking onto stage, sitting down at a grand piano, and . . . not playing any music. At the start of each movement as indicated on Cage's score, Tudor shut the cover of the piano keyboard. He opened it again after a certain interval. Otherwise, Tudor sat at the keyboard, attentive but unmoving. The music Cage wanted his audience to listen to was the ambient sounds in the room over the duration of four minutes and thirty-three seconds. The theorist-composer wanted to show that there was no such thing as silence. He insisted that any period of properly marked listening was music. As the title, *4'33"*, indicates, time was measured (as music is marked by measures); what people heard within that time frame was designated by Cage as his musical composition.

> **David Tudor (1926–96):** American pianist and composer who frequently collaborated with **John Cage** and **Merce Cunningham**.

Cage, of course, was not the only artist to challenge accepted conventions. The definition of "performance" – in the arts and beyond – has been vastly enlarged partly because of the insistence of experimental artists who actively explored new venues, new ways of performing, and new ways of receiving performances as audiences, spectators, and participants (**see figure 7.14**). Today we have an enormous range of aesthetic, ritual, secular, civic, sportive, and other kinds of performances. Some are virtuosic, demanding well-trained persons; others are more ordinary, or occur within the framework of daily life and pass almost unnoticed (except by performance theorists). Some performances are polished and finished; others are intentionally "open" or unfinished.

fig 7.14. An unusual "found space" "site specific" setting for Grzegorz Kwiecinski's *Faustus* of his Theatre of Fire and Paper, 1984. Photograph courtesy Richard Schechner.

Most audiences wait until a performance is finished or nearly so before witnessing it. But many artists and groups invite people to open rehearsals. Previews followed by revisions are a necessity in commercial theatre and even with some films. The Wooster Group continues to work on its productions throughout the entire time a work remains in the repertory. There is no formal opening of a Wooster piece. And even after a work has been reviewed, many changes will be made in it on a continuing basis. Revising works or changing how one performs is of course more the fact with regard to aesthetic or sports performances than with regard to rituals. But even in everyday life, after a failed event, people revise their behavior. And in business one might say that the debut of a new product or service constitutes an "opening." Prior to the opening, test markets are used for rehearsals, with new products being changed on the basis of test market results.

Not all performances are successful. A performance can fail in two ways: if it does not please its public or if it does not accomplish most of what those making the performance intend. But even these indications of success and failure can be mistaken. Some artists are never satisfied – even with works that the public loves. Then there are those performances that more than fail to please the public or critics – shows that outrage the public. At its 1896 première in Paris, **Alfred Jarry**'s (1873–1907) proto-surrealist *Ubu Roi* was greeted by a riot (**see Melzer box**). In 1999 and 2001, New York Mayor **Rudolph Giuliani** (1944–) was so upset by paintings exhibited at the Brooklyn Museum of Art that he tried to take away the Museum's funding – and later convened a "decency panel" to recommend ways to monitor New York City's art (**see Giuliani box**). But history has its way of rectifying things. Naturalism, once deemed outrageous, became film and theatre's dominant style. *Ubu* is still frequently performed without any disruption. What future generations will make of Giuliani's puritanical efforts remains to be seen. Often, new generations find it hard to grasp what the fuss was all about.

Alfred Jarry (1873–1907): French "pataphysicist," a term he coined. Jarry was a forerunner of the theatre of the absurd and other avant-garde movements. Best known for his "Ubu plays" – grotesque dark comedies about the petty and foolish King Ubu. The most famous of these is *Ubu Roi* (King Ubu, 1896).

Annabelle Melzer

Ubu Roi *Opens, Audience Riots*

When the curtain opened [before an audience of 2,500, actors [Firmin] Gemier and [Louise] Marie France were already on stage, Gemier sporting a huge belly and wearing a heavy mask which had been designed by Jarry. [. . .] Gemier opened with the play's infamous "Merdre" ["shitr!"]. The resulting pandemonium has been chronicled by many critics. Laughter, hisses, cries of anger and applause vied with each other for prominence. [. . .] Tristan Bernard and Jules Renard screamed and whistled, enjoying themselves enormously in the confusion, while monocled and restrained Edmond Rostand smiled indulgently. In an effort to calm the crowd, Ferdinand Herold, in the wings (where he was responsible for the lighting), switched on the house lights. This brought only a momentary lull as members of the audience suddenly saw each other with hands raised and mouths agape. [. . .] In the days that followed the critics continued to stoke the smouldering fire of outrage. The general conclusion was unanimous, "A scandal . . . no other word will do."

1994, *Dada and Surrealist Performance*, 116–17

Rudolph Giuliani (1944–): American politician who was Mayor of New York City, 1993–2001.

Rudolph Giuliani's "Decency Commission"

NEW YORK (AP) – A city "decency commission," created to judge the morality of publicly funded art, will include three artists, three clergy members, Guardian Angels founder Curtis Sliwa and the mayor's own divorce lawyer.

Mayor Rudolph Giuliani, who named the panel's 20 members on Tuesday, said he had hoped they could issue a report on decency standards within three months, but they said it would likely take longer. [. . .]

The panel was created after Giuliani became incensed two months ago by a photograph at the city-funded Brooklyn Museum of Art. The 5-foot-tall photo, called "Yo Mama's Last Supper," shows a nude, black woman portraying Jesus surrounded by disciples.

Giuliani called the work "disgusting" and "anti-Catholic." The mayor used similar language in 1999 to denounce another artwork at the Brooklyn Museum: a painting of the Virgin Mary dappled with elephant dung. Giuliani halted city funding of the museum, but a federal court later ordered the city to resume it.

On Tuesday, Sliwa – who at 47 is one of the younger commission members – acknowledged that he knew little about art but believes he can contribute. "I know the difference between a Michelob and a Michelangelo," said Sliwa, who wore his trademark red beret and satin jacket. [. . .] Other members include Giuliani's attorney, Raoul Felder, and Alfred Curtis Jr., president of the United Nations Development Corp., as well as a rabbi, a bishop and an imam, a humanities professor and a free-lance news producer. The artist Peter Max declined to join after other artists criticized the panel and several news organizations reported that Max had been convicted of income tax evasion.

2001, Associated Press, "NYC Names Decency Panel," 4 April

Larger Events and Contexts

Every focused public performance is nested in one or more larger events or contexts. These events and contexts define the limits of a performance. It may not be easy to say exactly when or where a given larger event or context ends and ordinary life begins. The focused performance is usually clearly marked at its start and its conclusion; not so the larger contexts in which a given performance is nested. Despite this blurriness, it is important to understand the larger events and contexts because these give the focused performance at least some of its meanings, channeling people, resources, and energies both to, through, and away from the performance. The larger event may be ritual, political, commercial, or social – or more than one of these simultaneously.

At the simplest level, the larger event includes everything taking place at the performance venue – the performance itself, the behavior of the audience, the backstage life, etc. – from the time a particular performance begins until it is over. This includes arriving at the performance venue, setting up, the activities in the dressing room, the box office, the lobby, and so on. It also includes shutting down the performance venue after the show is over.

Every public performance operates within or as part of a network of technical, economic, and social activities. Take an ordinary theatre, dance, or music performance. Long before the first spectator arrives, the technical staff has prepared the theatre – from cleaning the dressing rooms to making sure that all the props are ready and the stage equipment works. The box office staff is prepared to honor reservations and sell tickets. The "actual performance" is nested within both technical and economic situations that extend in time, space, and kind beyond what is going to happen onstage. At home also preparations are being made by those who will attend the performance. For some, it is a "time out," perhaps even a very special celebration. Others are part of a theatre party or group. "Going to the theatre" may be part of a larger social occasion such as a birthday celebration, a school project, or any number of other circumstances. Sports events are very much like the performing arts in this regard – activities heavily implicated in larger technical and economic networks. Furthermore, big-time sports – whether professional or at the college level – are enmeshed in the media, television especially, but also the internet.

What is so of aesthetic performances is even truer of social, ritual, and political performances. One can perhaps speak of "art for art's sake," but not of politics, ritual, or social events for their own sakes. These are always in the service of larger systems; and the performances always affect these larger systems. For example, a political rally brings a candidate in contact with her supporters. The whole event is staged – school children are bussed in, the media are contacted, and flags, lapel pins, and other paraphernalia are distributed. At a precise and pre-arranged moment, the Candidate Herself "appears," as if spontaneously. More spontaneous-but-carefully-scripted actions take place. Hand shaking, baby-kissing, waving to the crowd. A speech, sometimes the often-repeated "stump speech," more rarely something distinct and new, is offered to the expectant and receptive crowd. Off camera, one can see the candidate's handlers telling the crowd exactly when to cheer. The whole event is packaged for television – and, if it is successful from the candidate's point of view, 30 seconds of the rally will be seen on a number of different channels during the day, and especially on the widely watched early evening news. Now where does such an event take place? Who are its authors? Who is served by the performance?

The expanded event nesting a performance is in a positive feedback loop to the performance. What goes on "at the center" affects all of the outer activities. And the needs and tone of these outer activities contain, shape, and infiltrate the core event. There is a dynamic interaction among the claims of the media, the demand of producers for a profit, performers wanting good roles, the pressures of allies, enemies, friends, and family that certain ideological, political, aesthetic, professional, and/or religious values be expressed or embodied – and so on down through a long and culture-specific and event-specific list. No performance is an island. Even the most apparently marginal or independent experimental performance is actually embedded in several outlying circles. At the very least, there is the circle of friends and artistic associates. But just as important is an "imaginary circle" of desires for a receptive audience, for new contacts, for recognition. Emerging artists work the phones, hoping to grab the interest of critics and producers. Sports events are haunted by agents. Political upstarts seek just the right photo-op. The event-in-itself is systematically linked to a complex panoply of larger events.

Cooldown

Whatever the performance, at some point it is over. The curtain comes down, the audience leaves, the inauguration is over, the bride and groom have left the party, the dancers are in their dressing rooms changing into street clothes (**see figure 7.15**). As the performers unwind, the spectators gather their belongings, chat about what they have just

fig 7.15. The Lady-Boys of Bangkok cooling down in their dressing room after performing. Photograph by Geraint Evans. Copyright *The Independent*.

seen or participated in, and go out for a bite or home to rest. Things return to "normal." This transition between the show and the show-is-over is an often overlooked but extremely interesting and important phase. If warm-ups prepare people for the leap into performance, cooldown ushers them back to daily life.

> **Cooldown:** The phase of the performance process in which performers move from the world of the performance back to everyday life.

Cooldown is usually not as formal a procedure as warm-up. Part of the reason for this is that once the focused performance is over, people simply let go. But studying this "letting go" reveals a patterned activity. Informal cooldown for the active performers involves gestures that put the role to rest and reawaken the ordinary self. Actors hang up their costumes, take off their makeup, wash, put on street clothes. Athletes visit the training room for rubdowns and attention to injuries. Often a dressing room just after the curtain comes down is relatively quiet. It takes a little bit of time to come back to oneself. When friends invade the dressing room too soon they can feel the actors' tension between wanting to be hospitable and wanting to be alone for a little while.

In ordinary social life, a party can be quite a performance for the hosts. If so, a cooldown usually takes place. After the guests leave, the hosts clean up (or decide to "leave it till morning," a way of saying, almost, that they don't want the party to end). Often, people discuss whether or not the gathering was a "success." After a date, friends ask, "how did it go?" After military action or an intelligence operation comes "debriefing," where descriptions of what happened are carefully recorded for later analysis.

On the spectator side of things, after a performance most often people go out for something to eat and drink – and to talk, not only to evaluate what they've just experienced, but to resume authority over their own time and body. Spectator-behavior often enforces bodily stillness and silence which leave one with a sense of emptiness that demands immediate refilling. For events such as religious services and sports matches that include active audience behavior, even some-times the intake of food and drink, cooldown takes a different path: embraces and greetings after the service, a momentary encounter with the rabbi or minister, a family dinner – which is itself its own performance. At sports, where the generally exuberant behavior includes eating, drinking, and cheering, the cooldown consists mostly of discussing the good and bad qualities of the game just ended.

Sometimes cooldown is more formal. For example, American director **JoAnne Akalaitis** (1937–) gathers the actors for a specific set of cooldown exercises which includes focused breathing and a mental review of the performance just concluded (**see Saivetz box**). In Bali, after trancing, the dancers are "smoked," given incense to inhale, and sometimes a ritual sacrifice is made, all with the goal of bringing the performers back to themselves.

Deborah Saivetz

> ### The Akalaitis CoolDown
>
> In the first of the [cooldown] exercises, the actors lie on their backs with their eyes closed and their arms and legs extended. [. . .] The actors focus on their breath, inhaling through the nose and exhaling through the mouth. They allow their minds to review what they just experienced [. . .]. Akalaitis then talks the actors "through their bodies." Beginning with the soles of the feet, the actors use the breath to become conscious of and release each part of the body.
>
> 1998, "An Event in Space: The Integration of Acting and Design in the Theatre of JoAnne Akalaitis," 149–50

In all these cases, informal and formal, the cooldown is a bridge, an in-between phase, leading from the focused activity of the performance to the more open and diffuse experiences of everyday life.

Aftermath

The continuing life of a performance is its aftermath. The aftermath persists in critical responses, archives, and memories. Most aftermaths are relatively brief or sequestered in personal memories. In modern times, the immediate aftermath consists of the response by the agents of official culture – reviewers and critics. There are then the memories of those participating in the event and those who attended the event. And of course there is the "word-of-mouth" circuit – sometimes people who never went to an event have plenty to say about it. After a time, many of these responses come to reside in the "archive," an umbrella term that means what can be accessed by various performance-forensic means. These include reading old reviews, examining photographs, films, and video, interviewing surviving performers or attendees (if the performance is fairly recent), looking at the scripts or scores, examining performance venues, costumes, and props, and other methods of reconstructing "what happened." This pertains not just to theatrical events, but to performances of all kinds. How many "home performances" have been reawakened by an old photograph, a pair of gloves, or long-forgotten letter discovered in an attic or closet?

Aftermath: The phase of the performance process that may extend for years. The aftermath includes formal and informal responses to the performance ranging from discussions and critical responses in the media to scholarly discussions and archives. Archival materials may include videotapes, films, and sound recordings, printed matter, props or other artifacts, and anything else concerning the completed performance.

the original event might have been. The fascination with the drama of the *Titanic*'s 1912 catastrophic collision with an iceberg in no way has abated (**see Titanic box**). On a less grandiose scale, some artistic events also have a long and influential afterlife. *Ubu Roi* is cited as an initiator and harbinger of the twentieth century avant-garde from surrealism to dada, from symbolism to theatre of the absurd.

There is no fixed limit to an aftermath. In the aesthetic genres, newspaper and media reviews and word-of-mouth are short-term kinds of aftermath. Long-term aftermath includes self-generated documentation (photos, videos, artist's notes, etc.), the impact and influence a work has on other artists, and scholarly articles written about a piece. The aftermath of a work folds back into restagings of classics as well as new work that exits "under the influence of" an older work. Sometimes a particular performance style is very influential and widespread even if, at its point of origin,

The Titanic Sinks on its Maiden Voyage!

Many of those who perished on the ship came from prominent American, British, and European families. [. . .] The glamour associated with the ship, its maiden voyage, and its notable passengers magnified the tragedy of its sinking in the popular mind. Legends arose almost immediately around the night's events, those who had died, and those who had survived. Heroes and heroines [. . .] were identified and celebrated by the press. The disaster and the mythology that has surrounded it have continued to fascinate millions.

2001, *Encyclopedia Britannica Online Exhibit on the Titanic*, http://titanic.eb.com/01_01.html

Performance itself is categorically evanescent. Even the memory of performance fades quickly. Soon enough all but the most famous performances vanish. Events that were shattering and famous in their own time are remembered only when researched. They take on a second or more lives according to who gets hold of, analyzes and reconstructs the archival evidence. Nowadays just about every event is put onto videotape or computer disk. But what is the shelf life of these kinds of storage? Not only the actual operating systems that go out of date rather rapidly, but the attention span of scholars and others. There is much too much out there for most of it to be of use to anyone. Scholars dig through old newspapers or video libraries to pull out long-forgotten reviews or images.

But sometimes the aftermath of a performance is open-ended, generating many new performances that replay with a difference what the authors of the new work presumed

the artist was not well known. From the early 1960s to the late 1980s, performance artist **Jack Smith** (1932–89) staged irregularly scheduled amateurish "theatre evenings" in his living space. Often fewer than 10 persons attended. But a wide range of artists attest to the impact Smith had on their work. Smith pioneered and explored many themes including cross-dressing, queer desire, non-narrative theatre, auto-biographical performance, and radical eclecticism (**see Foreman box**).

Jack Smith (1932–89): Pioneering American performance artist and filmmaker. Smith performed in his loft often to an audience of ten or fewer. He intentionally blurred the boundary between art and life. His films *Flaming Creatures* (1961) and *Normal Love* (1963) featured transvestites, androgynes, and drag queens.

Richard Foreman

A Different Kind of Drama

The situation in *Pearls for Pigs* is that the leading character, the Maestro, after a long career, realizes he hates the theatre. And what he hates it for is the way in which it suppresses the possibility that impulse – human impulse – might be allowed to disrupt the performance. [. . .] There is no story in my plays, because IMPULSE is set free to deflect normal linear development. [. . .] IMPULSE, of course, need not mean hitting someone on the nose – it may also mean reaching for an unsettling idea, or letting words surface from the unconscious. The point is – ART IS THE PLACE TO ALLOW THIS, WHICH CANNOT REALLY HAPPEN IN LIFE, TO HAPPEN IN ITS FULL, RICH, RADIANT, ABUNDANT GLORY. [. . .] But – HERE'S THE IMPORTANT PART – these manifestations of impulse are not just narrated – THE SAME IMPULSE THAT PUSHES THE CHARACTER INTO "ACTING-OUT" ALSO TWISTS AND CONTROLS THE ARTISTIC STRUCTURE, so that the form and sequencing of the play itself reflects that impulsive, usually suppressed, energy of the human mental/emotional apparatus. And it's that isomorphic relationship between form and content that often perplexes people about contemporary art. [. . .] But of course, that happens all the time in drama and film and the novel. But there now exists a large group of so-called "difficult" or transgressive artists who believe that such a strategy no longer suffices to introduce a powerful and effective "impulse" therapy to audiences desperately trying to control their own impulsive tendencies [. . .].

1998, "Program Notes on *Pearls for Pigs*," 157

The aftermath can impact the performance itself, sometimes catastrophically. Bad reviews can close a Broadway or West End show. Or a director may take in the reviews, have an ear tuned to the word-of-mouth, listen to the opinions of friends, and make adjustments in the mise-en-scène. Paradoxically, previews and out-of-town tryouts give useful "aftermath information" before a production actually opens. In all performances – social, political, and professional as well as in the arts – the aftermath records how people react to and feel about an event.

Legal systems function largely in terms of aftermath – cases are decided by "precedent": the case at hand determined on the basis of decisions made earlier in similar cases. Surgery – dramatic and highly ritualized in the operating theatre – is judged "successful" mainly in terms of its aftermath. Was the problem addressed by the operation fixed?

When things go wrong, managing the aftermath – or "spin control" – comes into play. Politicians and CEOs pay public relations people big money to manage aftermath. "Spin" is making a performance mean what the client wants it to mean rather than what an objective observer might find. Tension between handlers and the press is focused on this issue of who controls the spin, the aftermath. A lot is at stake because whoever wins the spin war has a leg up on controlling an event's long-term meaning and significance.

At another level altogether, mythic events exist almost entirely as aftermaths generating myriads of "new" performances. Literally tens of thousands of dramas, movies, paintings and sculptings, novels, and re-enactments have reconfigured events such as the American Civil War, the Passion of Jesus Christ, the Trojan War, or the conflict between the Pandavas and Kauravas as told in the Sanskrit epic, *The Mahabharata*. Once a line of performances is established, the "source" becomes not the event itself – frequently exactly what happened is in dispute or cannot be determined with any historical clarity – but other performances. The archetypal actions of a culture are burned into public memory by means of rituals, re-enactments, and iconic visual arts. "Fact" gets absorbed into collective performed memory. What do you imagine Atlanta in flames in November, 1864 during the American Civil War looked like? The image that comes to mind is most likely drawn from the film, *Gone With the Wind*. Who knows what Jesus' Last Supper "really" looked like? Most people imagining that seder see in their mind's eye **Leonardo da Vinci**'s (1452–1519) famous 1498 painting – or one of its many copies and poster prints (**see figure 7.16**).

Leonardo da Vinci (1452–1519): Italian "Renaissance man" – sculptor, painter, drawer, engineer, and scientist. Among his best-known works, *The Last Supper* (1495–97) and *Mona Lisa* (1503–1506).

fig 7.16. Leonardo da Vinci's 1498 wall painting, *The Last Supper*. Although probably without any historical relationship to the way Jesus and his disciples actually appeared and behaved at that Passover seder, this picture has dominated the popular imagination regarding Jesus and his disciples. As displayed on the internet at http://www.ibiblio.org/ wm/paint/auth/vinci/lastsupp.jpg.

Rules, Proto-Performance, and Public Performance

One cannot stage anything from a play to a religious ritual to a public ceremony to a trial or a party without rules – also called conventions, precedents, liturgies, manners, etc. These rules are not the "performance itself" but guidelines connecting every performance to the past, the tradition, and to the future – performances that will occur after the one at hand is over. Rules instruct all those involved in a performance – the players, the spectators, the production team – about what can and cannot be done. Rules may be invariable or loose, leaving little or much room for spontaneity and improvisation. In sports, for example, the rules always leave plenty of room for individual prowess – although some sports encourage improvisation more than others. Basketball leaves a lot more room for creative movement than the 50-yard sprint. And of course, rules are sometimes broken – both by cheating and as a way of creating a new situation. But this "violation of the rules" does not eliminate either the need for rules or their generally prevailing force. In fact, one might say that true creativity, which is extremely rare, is a play which makes necessary a revision of the rules, not just a shrewder way to play within the rules. In the arts, the avant-garde defines itself as "cutting edge," as breaking rules in order to discover new ways of doing things. But a close examination of the history of the avant-garde reveals mostly replays and variations on known themes and procedures rather than actual newness.

What of free, spontaneous performances such as improvisatory theatre, music, and dance or children's make-believe games? Only a little investigating shows that even these apparently free interactions are guided by conventions and accepted procedures – including the repetition of many packaged bits and routines. In fact, every performance, indeed every social interaction, is guided by a network of expectations and obligations. Each participant expects certain things to happen and wants assurance that other things won't happen. Dark play (see chapter 4) is playing that subverts the rules, but even dark play obeys its own conventions.

The Performance Quadrilogue

The performance process can be studied not only as a multi-phased time-space sequence, but also as the dynamic relationship among four categories of players:

1 sourcers (authors, choreographers, composers, dramaturgs, etc.)
2 producers (directors, designers, technicians, business staff, etc.)
3 performers
4 partakers (spectators, fans, juries, the public, etc.)

Roughly speaking, sourcers write, research, or in other ways find the actions to be performed. These sources are the raw materials for the performance – a play, a personal recollection, a scenario, or anything at all that is used in making a performance. During the workshop and rehearsal process, sources are revised or even discarded; new sources can always be found or brought in by the producers and performers as well as by the sourcers. Producers serve as facilitators guiding the shaping of the sources into a "finished performance." Producers work most closely with the performers, but also with the sourcers and sometimes even with the partakers. Producers are "link" persons, building bridges, making connections. Performers play the actions for the public. Partakers not only receive the actions, but may also participate in the actions. If they do participate, partakers at least temporarily become performers. A person may belong to more than one of these categories. Someone checking himself in a mirror as he dresses for a date plays all four roles. A performance artist like Spalding Gray is sourcer, performer, and producer (though Gray also works with producers other than himself). A group may do some or all of the sourcing, performing, producing, and partaking collectively.

> **Dramaturg:** A person who works with the director in a wide variety of ways. Dramaturgical work includes researching the historical and cultural contexts and past production history of the dramatic text, working closely with the director in interpreting the dramatic text, and writing program notes. During rehearsals, the dramaturg may offer detailed criticism of the ongoing production process.

This "performance quadrilogue" can be represented as a rectangle with every point connected to every other point (**see figure 7.17**). Theoretically, all connections are given equal weight. But in actuality, each performance enacts a specific route around the performance quadrilogue. The route taken around the quadrilogue, and the primacy or dominance of one player category over one or more of the others, reveals a great deal about the performance process of that particular performance or genre of performance.

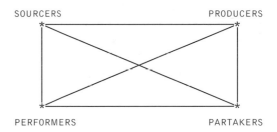

fig 7.17. The performance quadrilogue – with all connections potentially available. Drawing by Richard Schechner.

Take mainstream theatre, for example. This kind of theatre begins with a sourcer, a playwright whose play is selected by the producers (a stage director and/or the person in charge of the money). Next, the producers assemble an artistic production team consisting of actors, designers, and technicians. The job of this team is to transform the play into a public performance. The result of this collaboration is a specific theatre event offered to the partakers – the "Z-path" around the performance quadrilogue depicted in **figure 7.18**. No direct line connects the sourcers to the performers or to the partakers; or the producers to the partakers. In this kind of theatre, although the playwright is the originating source, the most important persons are the producers and the performers.

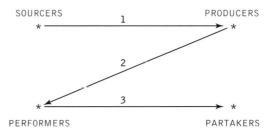

fig 7.18. The Z-path route around the performance quadrilogue signifying the way mainstream theatre works. Drawing by Richard Schechner.

In Z-path performance, the producers may even be more important than the performers. This is because the producers interpret the sources on the one hand and control the actions of the performers on the other. No one exercises control over the producers. They remain relatively free throughout the process. Directors such as Peter Brook and **Peter Stein**

(1937–) work this way. These artists interpret dramas working from the principle that a play cannot speak for itself (**see Carlson box**). Brook was attacked for the way he treated the Indian epic in his production of *The Mahabharata*. The attacks basically claimed that Brook did not respect the "Indianness" of his source material. Although some directors claim that they do what the "author intended," unless the author is alive and actively involved in the rehearsal process, most directors take for themselves the right of interpretation. Of course, the public knows this. People go to the productions of specific directors to find out how a Brook or a Stein "handles" certain texts and source materials.

Peter Stein (1937–): German theatre director whose productions include Ibsen's *Peer Gynt* (1971), Wagner's *Das Rheingold* (1976), Chekhov's *Three Sisters* (1984), and Goethe's *Faust* (2000).

Marvin Carlson

A Play Cannot Speak for Itself

Even today, one encounters those who urge that the theatre produce plays by Shakespeare "straight" or "as the author intended," or to "let the plays speak for themselves," as if unmediated performance were desirable or even possible. Peter Brook has responded to this common advice as succinctly as anyone. "A play cannot speak for itself," he says; one must "conjure its sound from it." Similarly Tyrone Guthrie has warned that the attempt to avoid interpretation usually results in the imitation of previous interpretations which have grown comfortably familiar. It is important to remember that the performed play, unlike the painting, comes to us not as a specific object, but only through a performance tradition.

1990, *Theatre Semiotics*, 116

Visionary Russian director **Vsevelod Meyerhold** (1874–1940), himself a masterful interpreter of dramatic texts, theorized about empowering the actors. He conceptualized a "theatre of the straight line" (**see Meyerhold box**) where the producers absorb the work of the sourcers, passing on their interpretation to the performers. Decisively, late in the rehearsal phase, the producers step aside so that the

performers face the audience directly. Meyerhold rarely followed his own advice.

Vsevolod Meyerhold (1874–1940): Russian actor and director. After the Russian Revolution of 1917, Meyerhold developed "biomechanics," a system of kinetic acting using highly stylized, expressive movements which he felt were just right for the new proletarian age. In 1940, Stalin's police shot him dead. His key writings have been translated into English as *Meyerhold on Theatre* (Braun, 1969).

Vsevelod Meyerhold

Theatre of the Straight Line

A straight, horizontal line with the four theatrical elements (author, director, actor, spectator) marked from left to right represents [. . .] what we shall call the "theatre of the straight line." The actor reveals his soul freely to the spectator, having assimilated the creation of the director, who, in his turn, has assimilated the creation of the author.

[. . .] The actor's art consists in far more than merely acquainting the spectator with the director's conception. The actor will grip the spectator only if he assimilates both the director and the author and then gives of himself from the stage.

1969 (1907), from Edward Braun (trans. and ed.), *Meyerhold on Theatre*, 50–51

Coaches of athletic teams have much less control over what happens on the field. After long periods of training and practicing, the actual playing belongs to the players. Single-person sports — golf, racing, singles tennis — are almost entirely in the hands of the individual athletes. Their situation approaches that of Meyerhold's theatre of the straight line. Even team sports come close to what Meyerhold wanted. Because of the adversarial nature of sports, games often go off in their own direction. Coaches try to maintain tight control — in football this has gone as far as installing small radio receivers in the helmets of quarterbacks so that plays can be sent in from the sidelines. In sports, intricate systems of "signs," codes known only to the team, convey instructions from the coaches to the players. But the unpredictability of sports often takes over. This appeals to fans because spectacular and unexpected plays, errors, willful risk-taking, and surprising moves by the other side provide many thrills.

Some "auteur" producers-sourcers, **Robert Wilson** (1941–) and **Richard Foreman** (1937–), for example, source, design, and direct their own works, thereby controlling every detail of what the partakers experience (**see figures 7.19, 7.20**). Although Wilson has many collaborators – including composer Philip Glass – the works project a very identifiable "Wilson" style. Foreman is even more singular in his control of what the partakers get. He writes, designs, and directs his productions. It is Foreman's voice that is heard on tape. In his earlier work, Foreman himself ran the sound cues and placed himself in the theatre so that the audience could see him as well as the actors on stage. In recent years, Foreman has employed others to operate the technical equipment. All in all, the auteurs' route around the performance quadrilogue is not a "Z" as in mainstream theatre, but a gathering up of all elements to themselves (**see figure 7.21**). To some degree, in this kind of theatre, what the partakers experience is the auteur's vision which the auteur controls as carefully as a painter controls his canvas or some filmmakers their films. Performers in this kind of theatre are not free agents; they may feel more like living puppets – the "über marionettes" that early twentieth-century theorist and director **Edward Gordon Craig** (1872–1966) dreamed of for the theatre.

Robert Wilson (1941–): American opera and theatre director and visual artist, known for his spectacular large scale performance pieces, including *Einstein on the Beach* (1976), *the CIVIL warS* (1984), *The Black Rider* (1990), and *August Strindberg's Dream Play* (1998).

Auteur: A French term meaning "author" originally signifying film directors who exercised complete control over their films comparable to the control literary authors have over their works. Auteur is a term used today to designate theatre, dance, or film artists who exercise such control.

fig 7.19. Robert Wilson's *Einstein on the Beach*, 1976. This production was directed and designed by Wilson, with music by Philip Glass, and choreography by Andrew de Groat. Photo courtesy Richard Schechner.

Richard Foreman (1937–): American playwright, theatre director, and theorist. Foreman has written more than 50 plays — most of which he has directed. His plays include *Sophia=Wisdom* (1972), *Rhoda in Potatoland* (1975), *Penguin Torquet* (1981), *Now That Communism is Dead My Life Feels Empty* (2001), and *Maria del Bosco* (2002). His books include *Plays and Manifestos* (1976), *Unbalancing Acts* (1992), and *Paradise Hotel* (2001).

fig 7.20. Richard Foreman's *Sophia=Wisdom*, 1972. Everything you see in this scene was conceptualized and even actually built by Foreman. The actors function to some degree as extensions of Foreman's consciousness. Photo courtesy of Richard Foreman.

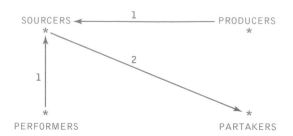

fig 7.21. Auteur-director route around the performance – the way Robert Wilson and even more so, Richard Foreman, work. Drawing by Richard Schechner.

The performance of music spans the possibilities. Rock musicians often compose many of the songs they perform as well as staging their shows, thus combining sourcer, producer, and performer. Classical orchestral concerts, on the other hand, maintain a rather strict separation of tasks. The composer provides the source material; the conductor often radically interprets the score (but does not change the notes); while the orchestra members are given less latitude for individual interpretation than actors. However, soloists are expected to put their own stamp on the music. In dance, there is a similar wide span of practices. Many modern and postmodern dancers choreograph their own dances, while ballet dancers are more likely to perform the compositions of others.

From Performance Montage to Desktop Theatre

Montage, a powerful and widely used technique in visual media and theatre, was developed in the 1920s by filmmaker **Sergei Eisenstein** (1898–1948), at one time a student of Meyerhold's. A montage is a way of "speaking" with images rather than words. In a montage many different shots are spliced together in quick sequence to form a coherent whole that is more than any of its parts. The shots used in a montage may be of different subjects and from different locations. The unity is a result of very careful editing. Thus a montage is a way of constructing new meanings from numerous disparate sources or bits. In the 1960s, Jerzy Grotowski led the Polish Laboratory Theatre in developing performance montages drawing on a wide variety of sources ranging from the personal associations of the actors to materials taken from dramas, literature, music, and the visual arts. The performance montage method is at the heart of Grotowski's best-known works, *Akropolis*, *The Constant Prince*, and *Apocalypsis cum Figuris*. Even when working with a dramatic text, such as **Pedro Calderón de la Barca**'s (1600–81) *The Constant Prince*, Grotowski treated the play as a "scalpel" which the performers used to cut to deep levels of self-awareness (**see Grotowski box 1**). After Grotowski, many others in theatre, dance, and performance art followed suit in using both performance montage and highly personal materials.

Sergei Eisenstein (1898–1948): Russian film director, former student of Meyerhold, inventor of montage editing. His films include *The Battleship Potemkin* (1925) and *Aleksandr Nevskii* (1938).

Pedro Calderón de la Barca (1600–81): Spanish playwright and priest known for his highly romantic treatment of faith and loyalty to the Spanish crown. Author of many plays including *The Constant Prince* (1629) and *Life is a Dream* (1635).

Jerzy Grotowski

A Great Text is a Scalpel

All the great texts represent a sort of deep gulf for us. Take *Hamlet*: books without number have been devoted to this character. Professors will tell us, each for himself, that they have discovered an objective Hamlet. They suggest to us revolutionary Hamlets, rebel and impotent Hamlets, Hamlet the outsider, etc. But there is no objective Hamlet. The work is too great for that. The strength of great works really consists in their catalytic effect: they open doors for us, set in motion the machinery of our self-awareness. My encounter with the text resembles my encounter with the actor and his with me. For both director and actor, the author's text is a sort of scalpel enabling us to open ourselves, to transcend ourselves, to find what is hidden within us and to make the act of encountering the others; in other words, to transcend our solitude. In the theatre, if you like, the text has the same function as the myth had for the poet of ancient times. The author of *Prometheus* found in the Prometheus myth both an act of defiance and a springboard, perhaps even the source of his own creation. But his *Prometheus* was the product of his personal experience. That is all one can say about it; the rest is of no importance.

2002, *Towards a Poor Theatre*, 57

In the final phase of his work during the 1990s, Grotowski adapted the performance montage technique to his collaboration with Thomas Richards on "Downstairs *Action*" (no longer done) and the related performance that followed, "Main *Action*" (still performed). The montages for these performances began with Richards linking personal associations with specific physical actions. These formed a positive feedback loop: the more clear and precise the memory, the more exact the physical action; the more precise the physical action, the more clear the memory becomes. The physical actions were then made into a precise, repeatable score. Richards subsequently taught this technique to other members of the Grotowski Workcenter in Pontedera, Italy. The resulting score is more than personal because while the performers were working on personal associations they were also mastering songs and movements taken from traditional performances both ancient and contemporary – in Richards' case, songs from Haiti (which "vibrated" with Richards' Caribbean heritage). Finally, the scores of different performers are enacted simultaneously. There is give-and-take among the performers; they sing the same songs; they develop their movements in relation to each other. But they are not performing a single-sourced drama that tells a coherent story. They are each performing their own personal scores inflected with the cultural performance materials. This way of performing is personal, intense, and hermetic. Witnesses to work such as this are not usually aware of Richards' personal associations or the associations of the other performers. Those attending "Main *Action*" experience a seamless flowing of movement and song (**see Richards box**). Even Grotowski, the guiding genius behind the performance, is not present in it. The Richards group has achieved the kind of "straight-line theatre" Meyerhold envisioned.

Fewer than a dozen persons are allowed to witness "Main *Action*" at any given time. These spectators sit on folding chairs in a room that could accommodate many more people. The idea is to share on an intimate scale. Although there is no audience participation in the conventional sense, there is a kind of inclusion rarely felt in orthodox Western performing arts. The mood created for experiencing "Main *Action*" is an extension of Grotowski's earlier experiments in environmental theatre (**see Grotowski box 2**). Grotowski tried any number of arrangements of space to foster different relationships between spectators and performers (**see figure 7.22**). But in his "theatre of productions" phase, Grotowski

Thomas Richards

Grotowski's System of Montage

One of the differences between Stanislavsky's and Grotowski's use of physical actions lies in the technique of montage. All of my associations and actions revolved around this personal event, and that was my secret. No one who watched us do the "Main *Action*" would ever know that. They, by means of the complete montage, would receive an entirely different story. While I followed my series of physical actions related to my father, next to me an actress followed another, completely different: *her own personal story*. But, because of the precise coordination in timing and rhythm of some of our actions, and because of the proximity of her and myself, a person looking would perceive our actions as being interrelated. They would see one story which had to do with the two of us together, when in reality we were following two *completely different lines of associations and actions*, which were separate. The actress did not know the memories on which I was working, and I did not know the ones on which she was working.

From the work on this "individual structure," I discovered in practice that I should not tamper with the emotions at all. I should not even worry about them. The key to physical actions lies in the body's process. I should simply do what I was doing, and each time I repeated the "individual structure," remember more and more precisely the way in which I had done what I had done. Let the emotions be. I knelt down like this. My father was lying like this. I reached out to him and my hands were curving like this. I touched him. To massage him I have to press with my hands in a specific way. If I feel nothing, I feel nothing. My emotions are free. I would try to remember anew this *way of doing* each time I executed this "individual structure" in the "Main *Action*."

1995, At Work with Grotowski on Physical Actions, 65

Jerzy Grotowski

Performer–Audience Relationships

[. . .] for each production, a new space is designed for the actors and spectators. Thus infinite variation of performer–audience relationships is possible. The actors can play among the spectators, directly contacting the audience and giving it a passive role in the drama (e.g. our productions of Byron's *Cain* and Kalidasa's *Shakuntala*). Or the actors may build structures among the spectators and thus include them in the architecture of action, subjecting them to a sense of the pressure and congestion and limitation of space (Wyspianski's *Akropolis*). Or the actors may play among the spectators and ignore them, looking through them. The spectators may be separated from the actors – for example, by a high fence, over which only their heads protrude (*The Constant Prince*, from Calderón); from this radically slanted perspective, they look down on the actors as if watching animals in a ring, or like medical students watching an operation (also, this detached, downward viewing gives the action a sense of moral transgression). Or the entire hall is used as a concrete place: Faustus' "last supper" in a monastery refectory, where Faustus entertains the spectators, who are guests at a baroque feast served on huge tables, offering episodes from his life. The elimination of the stage–auditorium dichotomy is not the important thing – that simply creates a bare laboratory situation, an appropriate area for investigation. The essential concern is finding the proper spectator–actor relationship for each type of performance and embodying the decision in physical arrangements.

1968, *Towards a Poor Theatre*, 19–20

fig 7.22. Jerzy Grotowski experimented with different ways of having performers relate to spectators. Although in his theatre of productions phase (1957–69), he never had actual "audience participation," frequently spectators felt as if they were part of the action. Grotowski never used the orthodox proscenium stage.

Akropolis, 1962–65, (above) went through five versions. The production was very loosely based on a play by the man who was one of the founders of modern Polish theatre, Stanislaw Wyspianski (1869–1907). The performance by the Polish Laboratory Theatre under Grotowski's direction took place all around and in the midst of the audience. Photograph courtesy of Eugenio Barba.

Dr. Faustus, 1963, (left) based on Christopher Marlowe's Elizabethan play. The scenic arrangement was two tables around which the spectators sat and on which the performers played. Photograph courtesy of Eugenio Barba.

never used actual audience participation. Interacting directly with the "invited" came during later phases of Grotowski's work. These later phases will be discussed in chapter 8. In any event, audience participation was not, of course, Grotowski's invention. Meyerhold and others experimented with it in post-revolutionary Russia. Participation was a hallmark of many Happenings and theatre events from the 1960s to the present, including some of my own environmental theatre work (**see figure 7.23**). Today's interactive installations and internet performances, where partakers are co-creators, are a continuation of this tradition. One such internet performance is "Desktop Theatre," challenging many assumptions about what theatre is, how it is enacted, and who its performers are. Desktop Theatre is played by persons in far-flung locations using ikons on their computer screens as characters/avatars (**see Jenik box**). Beginning with a version of *Waiting for Godot*, aptly titled *waitingforgodot.com*, Desktop Theatre has since staged its own original plays as well as initiated works involving collective creativity.

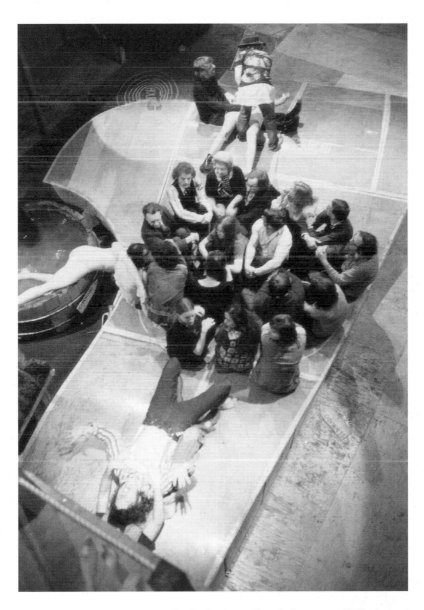

fig 7.23. Audience participation in The Performance Group's *Commune*, 1972, directed by Richard Schechner. Here a small group of spectators is "guarded" by the performers. The spectators represent Vietnamese villagers, the performers, the U.S. military and, in the scene above, the Charles Manson commune and those Manson murdered. Photograph by Richard Schechner.

Adriene **Jenik**

Desktop Theatre

What constitutes theatre? How might drama be expressed when separated from the body, the voice, and shared space? Can poetic speech and changes in expression or gesture attract and sustain group attention in an arena of constant distraction? What new languages exist in this forum? How might theatrical play be used to examine the striking shift in consciousness ushered in by ubiquitous computing? [. . .]

waitingforgodot.com was performed using the Palace visual chat software [. . .] that has since become the venue for most Desktop Theatre productions. The Palace is a software application that provides access to a network of servers that host individual "palaces." These palaces are in turn made up of linked "rooms" designated by 512 × 384 pixel (approximately 6 [x] 4.5 inches) background images that represent a room, a place, a planet, or dimension. Each of the live connected chatters is visible through a small representative image or avatar. [. . .] Avatars can be borrowed or collected from the myriad palaces built for this purpose or can be constructed and designed by the user from scratch. [. . .]

Palace culture is dynamic, ever-changing, and [. . .] largely heterogeneous. There are popular "social" palaces, which consistently host more than 200 chatters at a time, as well as adult palaces and palaces hosted by celebrities, rock groups, TV shows, and films. There are also hundreds of personal and educational palaces. [. . .] After both observing and participating in conversations with palacians in this environment, we were struck by the inherent expressive potential found in the software, but were dismayed by the level of dialogue and activity we found. [. . .] Thinking that introducing an external narrative or drama might provoke more interesting exchange, we began to develop our version of Beckett's *Waiting for Godot*. [. . .]

As we began working with the text, it proved eerily well-suited to chatroom delivery. In producing *waitingforgodot.com*, our first task was to read and discuss the text, and then edit or "compress" it into a format suitable for our venue. In doing so, we tried to remain true to Beckett's overall rhythm and dramatic arc even as we cut and reformed whole sections of the text. We then fashioned simple "everyman" avatars from the basic Palace character known as the "roundhead." [. . .] We concentrated our efforts on the production values of a virtuosic cut-and-paste performance, literally copying the text from a text document, and quickly pasting it into the chat input window. Once input, the text appeared as if "spoken" from a speech bubble attached to the characters onscreen and was simultaneously "spoken" out loud, through the computer's text-to-speech capabilities. Other chatters in the room would alternately comment on our presence, leave in confusion, or join in the piece by trying to help us locate "godot" on the server. [. . .]

In another, more ambitious experiment, *INVISIBLE INTERLUDES I: Santaman's Harvest*, [. . .] we added cast members and improvisational elements. [. . .] In the largest and most tightly scripted of the scenes, there were a total of 11 actors performing at once – in four time zones! [. . .] With our avatars (even the crudely rendered 2D images we encounter on the Palace) we enter a psychic space in which we become our masks. Anyone who spends time in these parallel worlds understands, perhaps implicitly, that one makes accommodations to one's avatar. [. . .] The most recent examples of Desktop Theatre practice are activities that represent alternative models of online play. [. . .] We have begun to perform a series of "dream-plays." The practice, which can be seen as a globally experienced hybrid of sand-play therapy, charades, and surrealist games, takes place in our own "dream-room" [. . .] as well as in the public palaces with dreamers from all over the world. As we solicit dreams from passersby and act them out using available props, improvisational acting, and [computer] painting tools, we meet each other in a true exchange of deeply felt desires and fears, and share the transformative power of collective creativity.

2001, "Desktop Theatre," 96, 98–100, 107, 109

Experimental in One Context, Ordinary in Another

What is experimental in the performing arts is commonplace in sports, pop-music concerts, and religious services. Here the partakers are very powerful event-shapers. Every athlete knows the "home-field advantage," which is not due to any difference in rules or playing surface. The roaring enthusiasm of the fans energizes the players for the home team, lifting the level of their performance. In much the same way, pop-music groups are driven by the crowds cheering, singing along, and pressing onto the stage. More informally, raves and even ordinary parties consist of multiple performances enacted by the partakers. To move from popular culture to religion, even the tamest church service includes abundant responsive reading, rising, sitting, kneeling, and embracing – actions and gestures that draw congregants into the service and closer to each other. Holiness churches go much further, with people suddenly "falling out" into trance, dancing in the aisles, or erupting into "tongues," a direct vocalization of the divine that has no verbatim translation. This kind of sacred performance can be viewed on television any Sunday of the year. In initiation rites and shamanic cures the partakers actively participate by laying on hands, singing, or assisting the shamans. In some cases, the participation is so total that it is difficult to distinguish performers from partakers (**see Read box**).

Kenneth E. **Read**

Collective Creativity in New Guinea

The house was packed to its capacity, but in the blackness I was unable to discover so much as a single feature of the man who sat beside me. Almost immediately, enveloped in disembodied voices, I felt the first stirrings of a curious panic, a fear that if I relaxed my objectivity for so much as a moment I would lose my identity. At the same time the possibility that this could happen seemed immensely attractive. The air was thick with pungent odors, with the smell of unwashed bodies and stranger aromatic overtones that pricked my nostrils and my eyes. But it was the singing, reverberating in the confined space and pounding incessantly against my ears, that rose to cloud my mind with the fumes of a collective emotion almost too powerful for my independent will. Momentarily the night vanished, and my purpose, even the circumstances of my presence in the village, were no longer important. I stood poised at a threshold promising a release from the doubts and anxieties that separate us from one another, offering, if one took the step demanded, a surety, a comforting acceptance such as those who share an ultimate commitment may experience. [. . .]

The songs followed one another without a perceptible break, a single shrill and keening voice lifting now and then to point the way to a new set. As the others joined in strongly, I felt close to the very things that eluded me in my day-to-day investigations, brought into physical confrontation with the intangible realm of hopes and shared ideas for which words and actions, though they are all we have, are quite inadequate expressions. In analytic language, the situation could be accommodated under the rubric of a rite of separation – an event by which a young girl in her father's house, surrounded by her kinsmen, was brought to the morning of the day when she must assume a new status and be transferred to her husband's people, but its quality could not be conveyed in any professional terms. While the voices swelled inside the house, mounting to a climax, the barriers of my alien life dissolved. The sound engulfed me, bearing me with it beyond the house and into the empty spaces of the revolving universe. Thus sustained, I was one of the innumerable companies of men who, back to the shrouded entrance of the human race, have sat at night by fires and filled the forest clearings and the wilderness with recitals of their own uniqueness.

1965, *The High Valley*, 251–52

Trials are much tamer. In fact, because the authority of the state is on display, the decorum of the courtroom is tightly monitored. Spectators are expected to hold back their reactions, which are sometimes extremely emotional. Although jurors have been known to weep and witnesses to break down on the stand, for the most part, trials are subdued (the movie and media versions being very much more melodramatic than the actual thing). However, as noted in chapter 6, an adversary trial is the enactment of two simultaneous dramas. It is the judge's job to keep these dramas moving forward in an orderly fashion. To do so, the judge functions both as referee and as director. The jury consists of partakers of a special kind empowered by the state to pass judgment on the veracity of what they see and hear. A jury's verdict can literally dictate life-or-death. Even in petty cases, however, the story-telling and outcome are of extreme importance to the participants – and, as the daytime mock-courts on television show, of enormous entertainment value. Judge and jury are the "inner partakers" of trials. The public and press are the "outer partakers," participating in the excitement but not the outcome. To make certain that a jury will not be affected by public sentiment, jurors are sometimes sequestered during trials.

The degree to which the operations of the performance quadrilogue are combined in a single person or group and the degree to which they are dispersed vary widely from genre to genre, culture to culture, even occasion to occasion. In everyday life the roles depicted in the quadrilogue are almost always in flux. A short social interaction around the dinner table can include people acting out all four role categories. In fact, "everyday life" might be defined as that social time when people can swiftly move from being a sourcer or producer to being a partaker or performer. The more consciously formal and rule-bound a situation is, the less movement there is among the role categories of the quadrilogue.

Conclusion

Performance processes are dynamic ways of generating, playing, evaluating, repeating, and remembering. Performance processes can be theorized as an orderly sequence of training, workshops, rehearsals, warm-up, performing, performance contexts, cooldown, critical response, archives, and memories. I have developed my basic theory of performance processes from the theatre, the performance genre I am most familiar with. Others may develop and apply a similar processual analysis to all the other genres of performance I am discussing in this book. The three-phase, ten-part sequence is orderly, proceeding from one part to the next. In practice, things aren't so neat. Not all the parts are present in every performance. Noting what is emphasized or omitted can be a powerful analytic tool in understanding specific performances. For example, in modern Western cultures drama is the domain of the playwright. In other cultures, the text of a play, though clearly indicating which words belong to which characters, is actually performed by several persons simultaneously. Thus in Japanese noh drama, the lines uttered by a player may include description as well as dialogue; the dialogue of the main character may be sung by the chorus in the first person (**see Brazell box**). There is no way to know this by reading the dramatic texts. One must know the performance tradition. Another example is the passionate preaching heard in holiness churches. When the reverend gets going, the sermon is more than said, it is sung; and the preaching is met with the cadenced responsive shouts of the congregation, which uplift and drive the preacher. In this kind of church, the warm-up takes place as part of the sermon, the performance swells until it fills the whole space, and the aftermath lives in the spirit the congregants take with them when the service is over. Many other similar examples of how the performance processes are adapted and shaped to suit particular occasions could be offered.

Karen Brazell

The Scripts of Japanese Traditional Theatre

The scripts of Japanese traditional theater are not solely, or even primarily, concerned with reproducing ordinary dialogue. That is, in addition to dialogue, they also include descriptions of and commentary on the setting, the stage actions, and the characters. The lines may be in poetry or metered prose and may be sung, chanted, or spoken, often with patterned intonation. The words uttered by a particular actor are not limited to lines that his character might "logically" or "naturally" speak;

that is, the actor is not restricted to remaining "in character." Moreover, a chanter or chorus may recite large parts of a play, including the first-person utterances of the characters, in which case the reciter(s) may momentarily take on the voice of one or another character. These reciters, however, are never personified storytellers; the noh chorus is not a group of townspeople commenting or elaborating on the action [. . .]. Rather they are stage figures voicing the text, a text that is not limited to creating naturalistic characters or sustaining fixed points of view. [. . .] This fluid narrative stance is exploited in both verbal and visual enactments of theatrical texts. Moments occur [. . .] when the text speaks without apparently being spoken; that is, the words are voiced by the performers, but no character or clearly defined narrator is speaking them. Released from the limitations of direct mime and defined narrative voice, playwrights and/or actors can manipulate the presentation of the text for aesthetic effects and practical purposes.

1998, *Traditional Japanese Theater*, 24–25

If performance processes can be understood as a ten-part sequence, they also can be understood as a complex relationship among four types of "players" – sourcers, producers, performers, and partakers. Sourcers write, research, or in other ways make or find the actions to be performed. Producers guide the shaping of the actions into something suitable for a performance. Performers enact the actions. Partakers receive and/or interact with the actions. A single person may belong to more than one of these categories; a group may do the sourcing, performing, producing, and partaking collectively. The possibilities are without end.

THINGS TO THINK ABOUT

1. Recall a performance in which you were a performer or spectator. Explain what you did or saw in terms of proto-performance, performance, and aftermath. If you have enough information, discuss the performance process in terms of training, workshop, rehearsal, warm-up, public performance, context, cooldown, critical response, archiving, and memories.
2. How might expanding the idea of the performance process to include more than just the "public performance" enhance your understanding of events? Is this understanding limited to aesthetic events? How might knowing the performance process help you understand a performance of everyday life, a courtroom trial, or a medical procedure?

THINGS TO DO

1. Begin working on a scene from a drama or even the restaging of a performance in everyday life (getting ready for a date, a supper party, a legal proceeding). But instead of aiming for a finished performance, invite your audience to a rehearsal. In fact, never finish the scene. Discuss the "rehearsal process" and how it differs from a "finished performance."
2. Using "aftermath information" – newspaper accounts, reviews, opinions of people who have attended the event, scholarly articles, photos, videotapes, etc. – reconstruct a key scene or turning point. Perform that scene or turning point. Do you think such a reconstructed performance is an accurate rendition of the "original"?

SUGGESTED READINGS

De Marinis, Marco. "The Performance Text." *The Semiotics of Performance*. Bloomington: Indiana University Press, 1993. 47–59.

Meyerhold, Vsevolod. "First Attempts at a Stylized Theatre." *Meyerhold on Theatre*. Edward Braun, ed. and tr. New York: Hill & Wang, 1969. 49–58.

Okpewho, Isadore. *African Oral Literature: Backgrounds, Character, and Continuity*. Bloomington: Indiana University Press, 1992. 21–25.

Read, Kenneth E. "Asemo." *The High Valley*. New York: Scribner, 1965. 129–40.

8 GLOBAL AND INTERCULTURAL PERFORMANCE

Globalization's Throughline

Globalization's throughline (to use Stanislavsky's term for the overall intention or objective of an action) is to integrate all systems – information, economic, military, ideological, social, political, and cultural – along the lines of "high performance." If successful, the result will be a worldwide network of maximum productivity. While globalization allows, even encourages, "cultural differences" at the level of daily behaviors, spoken languages, foods, clothes, lifestyles, artistic works, and so on, its underlying system is unified and transcultural. Whether this is good for most of the world's people in terms of eliminating poverty, disease, overcrowding, wars, resource depletion, and the other threats to the planet is, of course, debatable.

Globalization: The increasing interconnection and interdependency of economic, social, cultural, technical, and ideological systems.

Intercultural performance needs to be studied along with globalization because it arises as responses to and in some cases as protests against an increasingly integrated world. Both globalization and intercultural performance have historical antecedents. Globalization in colonialism and imperialism, intercultural performance as an outcome of "contact" among the world's peoples. Clearly, these phenomena are themselves linked.

Intercultural: Between or among two or more cultures. Intercultural performances may emphasize the integrative or the disjunctive.

Types of intercultural performances range from the Olympics and tourism to the intercultural performances of everyday life resulting from the rapid global circulation of styles, musics, media, and more. In terms of aesthetic performances there are four kinds of intercultural performance and performance research:

1 Research into artistic processes which can be either "vertical" or "horizontal." The goal of vertical research is to discover performances or performance fragments that have survived from very early times. This research occupied Jerzy Grotowski during the last 25 years of his life. Horizontal research compares the codified or "extra-daily" practices of contemporary performances in order to identify what is general or universal. This is the aim of Eugenio Barba's International School of Theatre Anthropology (ISTA).

2 Tourist shows that simultaneously preserve, distort, and display traditional performances, daily life, or anything else that may be packaged and sold to an ever-increasing audience of world travelers.

3 Hybrids and fusions that intentionally combine diverse cultural elements. Here the colonial horror of "impurity" or "mixing" is subverted, overturned, and developed. A large and increasing number of artists are doing this kind of postcolonial, postmodern work, which ranges from the respectful to the ironic and parodic.

4 Community-based performances emphasizing local challenges to globalization. This kind of work is what **Suzanne Lacy** (1945–) calls "new genre public art."

Vertical/horizontal intercultural research: Vertical research seeks "original" or "true" universal performances in the convergence of past cultural practices with individual "deep" experiences. Horizontal research locates transcultural or universal "truths" in similarities among contemporary cultures.

Suzanne Lacy (1945–): Conceptual/performance artist who addresses social issues such as racism, homelessness, aging, and violence by engaging local people in site-specific work. Editor of *Mapping the Terrain: New Genre Public Art* (1995).

The intercultural performances of everyday life are a vast number of styles, habits, mixes, hybrids, and fusions that affect the way people dress, talk, eat, interact, worship, celebrate, and are entertained. Some see this hybridity as evidence of Western and especially American cultural imperialism or as a negative result of colonialism (**see Chin box**). Others see it as an opportunity for creativity and dynamic growth. But whether one regards what's happening as positive or negative, there is no place on earth not being influenced and changed by activities going on elsewhere. Some places and people may appear "far away" or "other" from the vantage of the metropolis. But networked communications, the circulation of material goods and techniques, curiosity about everything, fascination with novelty, and of course global popular culture are discernible everywhere.

Daryl Chin

The Duplicity of Interculturalism

The idea of interculturalism is one which is, in a sense, duplicitous. One question which must be addressed is the presence of a dominant power structure, and the presumptions of that power structure. In the context of the United States, the cultural power structure is one which is dominated by the ideology of a specifically white, Eurocentric, specifically capitalist establishment. In addition, all questions regarding interculturalism must be complicated by the pervasiveness of a commercialized popular culture. For those who have grown up with the artifacts of the American cultural establishment, the effects have become endemic, pervasive, and all-encompassing. [. . .]

Interculturalism hinges on the question of autonomy and empowerment. To deploy elements from the symbol system of another culture is a very delicate enterprise. In its crudest terms, the question is: when does that usage act as cultural imperialism? Forcing elements from disparate cultures together does not seem to be a solution that makes much sense, aesthetically, ethically, or philosophically. What does that power prove: that the knowledge of other cultures exists? That information about other cultures now is readily available?

1991, "Interculturalism, Postmodernism, Pluralism," 87, 94

Scenarios of Globalization

If globalization were treated "as" performance, what kind of performance would it be? There are competing scenarios. The boosters of globalization envision a Hollywood production full of high tech special effects starring American superheroes who dissolve national, cultural, and economic boundaries as they spread free market capitalism to every corner of the world (see **Friedman box 1**). Another scenario retells the David versus Goliath story as the struggle of millions of individuals using the internet as a global participatory forum creating new cultural myths battling against corporate conglomerates determined to privatize culture and copyright ideas (**see Jenkins box**).

The detractors of globalization see it as a plot to increase Western, and especially American, hegemony militarily, economically, politically, and culturally (**see Gómez-Peña box 1**). These opponents to globalization regard the fancy talk about "technology transfers," "free trade," and "democracy" as a show staged to distract attention from what's really happening: an ongoing process of accumulating and centralizing wealth and power. For example, aid to developing nations takes the form of loans structured by the World Bank, the International Monetary Fund, etc. so that the poor nations subsidize the rich ones by paying interest on debts they can never retire. Furthermore, many of the projects supported benefit mostly large contractors and the elites of the receiving nations. Resistance to globalization is dealt with harshly by means of economic pressure and/or military action.

The result is that on a global scale, wealth today is more unevenly distributed than it has ever been (**see Friedman box 2**). Globalization feeds on disparities of wealth, power, information, and access. To win the game of globalization, players must make sure there is no actual "level playing field." Manufacturing must occur where labor is cheapest and consumption where wealth is concentrated. In regions where a middle class is developing, billions of people are left out. These live in the poorest parts of the Third World, rural areas or slums within or surrounding burgeoning cities. Even the richest nations – the USA, for example – contain large pockets of poverty. "Guest workers" and "migrant laborers" are often little more than indentured servants. Slavery – for work and for sex – is far from extinct. Many outspoken artists such as Nigerian **Wole Soyinka** (1934–) and Kenyan **Ngugi wa Thiong'o** (1938–) have been forced into exile, the performance spaces of the postcolonial state closed to them. The state wants to confine, the artist desires openness.

Thomas Friedman

Three Cheers for Globalization

The globalization system [. . .] has one overarching feature – integration. The world has become an increasingly interwoven place, and today, whether you are a company or a country, your threats and opportunities increasingly derive from whom you are connected to. This globalization system is also characterized by a single word: the *Web*. [. . .]

The driving idea behind globalization is free-market capitalism – the more you let market forces rule and the more you open your economy to free-trade and competition, the more efficient and flourishing your economy will be. Globalization means the spread of free-market capitalism to virtually every country in the world. [. . .]

Unlike the Cold War system, globalization has its own dominant culture, which is why it tends to be homogenizing to a certain degree. [. . .] Culturally speaking, globalization has tended to involve the spread (for better and for worse) of Americanization – from Big Macs to iMacs to Mickey Mouse.

Globalization has its own defining technologies: computerization, miniaturization, digitization, satellite communications, fiber optics, and the Internet, which reinforce its defining perspective of integration. Once a country makes a leap into the system of globalization, its elites begin to internalize this perspective of integration, and always try to locate themselves in a global context. [. . .]

Today, more than ever, the traditional boundaries between politics, culture, technology, finance, national security, and ecology are disappearing. You often cannot explain one without referring to the others, and you cannot explain the whole without reference to them all. [. . .]

I believe that this new system of globalization – in which walls between countries, markets, and disciplines are increasingly being blown away – constitutes a fundamentally new state of affairs.

2000, *The Lexus and the Olive Tree*, 8–10, 20, 23

Henry Jenkins

Participatory Culture on the Internet

One of the real potentials of cyberspace is that it is altering the balance of power between media producers and media consumers, enabling grassroots cultural production to reach a broader readership and enabling amateurs to construct websites that often look as professional and are often more detailed [. . .] than commercially-produced sites. In such a world, the category of the audience, as a mass of passive consumers for pre-produced materials, may give way to the category of cultural participants, which would include both professionals and amateurs. [. . .] Grassroots groups are seizing the potential of the internet to transmit their materials, to reach a much larger public with their ideas, and they are thus making their own cultural appropriations and productions more visible than ever before. [. . .] Such an argument rejects the idea of a definitive version produced, authorized, and regulated by some media conglomerate. Instead, it pushes towards a world where all of us can participate in the creation and circulation of central cultural myths. [. . .]

The result is a likely legal battle over the question of who owns our culture and who will be allowed to participate within it. We are on a collision course between technologies that encourage collaboration and full participation in cultural production and economic and legal structures which are pushing to further privatize our culture. [. . .] We are going to be watching increasingly bloody fights about intellectual property rights in digital media over the coming decade and those fights are going to determine – in part – the cultural logic that will structure the 21st century.

1998, "The Poachers and the Stormtroopers: Cultural Convergence in the Digital Age," http://commons.somewhere.com/rre/1998/The.Poachers.and.the.Sto.html

Guillermo Goméz-Peña

Globalization's Dark Side

Phase one of the much-touted project of globalization has now been thoroughly completed: macro-economic communities such as the European Union and NAFTA have replaced the "dated" functions of the nation state. Politicians are now "trading partners," and their religious *dictum* is called transnational "free trade" ("free" meaning that it benefits only those who have the power to determine its terms). The "information superhighway," the Internet, e-commerce, cable TV, and "smart" tourism have ideologically narrowed the world and the word. Effectively, "the world" is now "at our fingertips," or at least that's how we're invited to (mis)perceive it so long as we are members of that elite micro-minority which stands on the benign side of globalization. The dark side of this project, however, is implacable. Entire Third World countries have become sweatshops, quaint bordellos, and entertainment parks for the First World and for the inhabitants of the Southern Hemisphere the only options for participating in the "global" economy are as passive consumers of "global" trash, or providers of cheap labor or *materia prima*. Those excluded from these "options" are forced to become part of a transnational economy of crime (sex, drug and organs trafficking, child labor, kidnappings, *fayuca* [smuggled goods], etc. Many will cross the border North in search of the source of the rainbow, only to find racial hatred and inhumane working conditions.

Now that humanistic concerns are perceived as passé, U.S., European, and Asian corporations and governments are no longer accountable to anyone. The "global" goal is to add several zeros to their accounts by simply pressing a button. It is savage capitalism at its most efficient and diabolical: virtual operators discretely trading capital, products, weapons, and hollow dreams; and starving or killing their inconsequential victims in the ether of virtual space, a parallel "world" devoid of ethical or ideological implications, of tears and blood. It's economic-darwinism.com. Only the digitally fit will survive. [. . .] Compassion and philanthropy aren't part of the "global" agenda. In fact, governments and corporations (increasingly more intertwined with and indistinguishable from one another) have effectively designed a high tech prison industrial complex to keep the excluded from bothering us and at the same time to make money off of them. In the U.S., not coincidentally, the prison population is disproportionately black and Latino. This mega-industry has an intricately symbiotic relationship with other equally macabre "industries" such as law enforcement, the border patrol, gun manufacturers, the courts, and of course, the media, where "bad guys," cops, lawyers, and judges all get to have their own TV shows and entertain America.

2001, "The New Global Culture," 9–10

Thomas Friedman

Global Inequities

According to the 1999 United Nations Human Development Report [. . .] OECD [developed nations] countries, with 19% of the world's population, account for 91% of [Internet] users. Bulgaria has more Internet hosts than the whole of sub-Saharan Africa, excluding South Africa. The United States and Sweden have 600 telephone lines per 1,000 people, while Chad has 1 telephone line per 1,000. South Asia, with 23% of the world's people, has less than 1% of the world's Internet users. English is used in almost 89% of Web sites, although fewer than one in ten people worldwide speak the language. Industrialized countries hold 97% of all patents worldwide. [. . .]

[T]he fifth of the world's people living in the highest-income countries had 86% of the world's gross domestic product, 82% of the world export markets, 68% of foreign direct investments, and 74% of world telephone lines. The bottom fifth, in the poorest countries, had about 1% in each of these sectors. Not surprisingly, the wealthiest fifth consume 45% of all meat and fish, while the poorest fifth consume less than 5%. And the gap has been widening. In 1960 the 20% of the world's people who live in the richest countries had 30 times the income of the poorest 20%. By 1995, the richest 20% had 82 times as much income.

2000, *The Lexus and the Olive Tree*, 319–20

Wole Soyinka (1934–): Nigerian writer-in-exile and winner of the 1986 Nobel Prize in Literature. Author of the plays *The Swamp Dwellers* (1959), *Kongi's Harvest* (1965), and *Death and King's Horseman* (1976). Soyinka's books include *Myth, Literature, and the African World* (1976), *The Open Sore of a Continent: A Personal Narrative of the Nigerian Crisis* (1996) and *Arms and the Arts — A Continent's Unequal Dialogue* (1999).

Ngugi wa Thiong'o (1938–): Kenyan writer and political activist. In the 1970s, he was a key member of the Kamiriithu Community Center and theatre, a collective effort to develop an authentic Kenyan peoples theatre in the Gikuyu language. In 1977, Ngugi's *Ngaahika Ndeenda* (I Will Marry When I Want To) was performed in Kamiriithu's open-air theatre. After being imprisoned, Ngugi was driven into exile and the Kamiriithu theatre was literally levelled by the government in 1982. A novelist, essayist, playwright, and filmmaker, Ngugi's works include *Detained: A Writer's Prison Diary* (1981), *Decolonising the Mind* (1986), *Moving the Centre* (1993), and *Penpoints, Gunpoints, and Dreams* (1998).

Cultural Impositions and Appropriations

Which scenario is being enacted? No definitive answer can be given. The disadvantage of most of the scenarios is that they are extremely reductive. However one approaches the question, it's not as simple as one culture imposing itself on the others. One must remember that the USA is itself increasingly multicultural. The so-called white majority will soon be a minority. "So-called" because, as Adrian Piper so dryly proves in *Cornered*, the concept of race is culturally constructed: a social circumstance, not a genetic fact. Therefore, questions of race, ethnicity, and the inflow of new citizens are tightly related to each other. How will American society — and other societies also — accept/reject, integrate/isolate bearers of multiculturalism in terms of languages, religions, histories, races, lifestyles, ethnicities, economic opportunity, political liberty, and social justice?

Furthermore, with regard to the USA, many of its cultural exports are already intercultural. For example, American pop music is thoroughly Africanized, its theatre heavily influenced by Asia. Because so many different kinds of people live in the States, Americans are relatively open to assimilating cultural practices. One might even go so far as to argue that there is no American culture comparable to French or Japanese cultures, for example. This very emptiness accounts for America's cultural accessibility, porosity, and exportability. It is one of the reasons why American culture, which does not exist, is so active globally.

Is Globalization Good or Bad?

Is globalization "good" or "bad"? Good for what, bad for whom? Kenyan playwright and novelist Ngugi wa Thiong'o accuses the West, and especially the USA, of dropping a "cultural bomb" on the struggling peoples of the world, destroying indigenous languages and practices, making it much more difficult, if not impossible, for these peoples to fulfill what **Franz Fanon** (1925–61) called their "passionate search for a national culture" (**see Ngugi and Fanon boxes**). Discovering, making, or reawakening a national culture means resisting alien cultural practices first imposed by colonialism and then seductively proffered by globalization. It also means confronting hard questions. Can there be a "national culture" without a nation? Doesn't globalization eat away at the very basis of nationhood? Resistance is not easy, especially when giving in is a way of earning necessary hard currencies such as American dollars or Japanese yen. Defending against the cultural bomb takes many forms. In Japan, traditional arts such as noh and kabuki are designated "national treasures," their master artists awarded the title of "living national treasures." These arts and artists receive substantial subsidies. In the developing world where money is hard to come by the choices are stark: touristic reformation, commercialization, or extinction.

But it is not only, or even mostly, the arts that are under pressure. In fact, a number of governments and foundations find ways to preserve what are deemed to be very important national, regional, or local traditional performances. The practice of everyday life is something else. For example, the wearing of traditional clothes. It seems the more global the location, the more Western the dress. In Tokyo, Shanghai, or Singapore, few wear kimonos or traditional Chinese or Malay clothes. This garb is reserved for ceremonial or religious occasions. Worldwide, where the weather permits, young children wear short pants or dresses. Older kids and youths put on jeans, T-shirts, and blouses. Even in India, in the cities especially, saris, dhotis, and lunghis are giving way to Western-style clothes. In Africa, there is a wide variety of dress, from dashikis to Levis. Food habits as well are changing in accord with global tastes. Then there is the question of language, with the use of English as the lingua franca. This has led to an explosion of literature in India, Anglophone Africa, and the Caribbean that is English but not British. Although the European languages, Chinese in its several

Ngugi wa Thiong'o

The Cultural Bomb

Imperialism, led by the USA, presents the struggling peoples of the earth and all those calling for peace, democracy, and socialism with the ultimatum: accept theft or death. The oppressed and the exploited of the earth maintain their defiance: liberty from theft.

But the biggest weapon wielded and actually daily unleashed by imperialism against that collective defiance is the cultural bomb. The effect of a cultural bomb is to annihilate a people's belief in their names, in their languages, in their environment, in their heritage of struggle, in their unity, in their capacities and ultimately in themselves. It makes them see their past as one wasteland of non-achievement and it makes them want to distance themselves from that wasteland. It makes them want to identify with that which is furthest removed from themselves; for instance, with other peoples' languages rather than their own. [. . .]

The real aim of colonialism was to control the people's wealth: what they produced, how they produced it, and how it was distributed; to control, in other words, the entire realm of the language of real life. [. . .] Economic and political control can never be complete or effective without mental control. To control a people's culture is to control their tools of self-definition in relationship to others.

For colonialism this involved two aspects of the same process: the destruction or the deliberate undervaluing of a people's culture, their art, dances, religions, history, geography, education, orature and literature, and the conscious elevation of the language of the coloniser.

1986, Decolonising the Mind, 3, 16

Frantz Fanon

On National Culture

[. . .] this passionate search for a national culture which existed before the colonial era finds its legitimate reason in the anxiety shared by native intellectuals to shrink away from that Western culture in which they all risk being swamped. Because they realize they are in danger of losing their lives and thus becoming lost to their people, these men, hotheaded and with anger in their hearts, relentlessly determine to renew contact once more with the oldest and most pre-colonial springs of life of their people.

Let us go further. Perhaps this passionate research and this anger are kept up or at least directed by the secret hope of discovering beyond the misery of today, beyond self contempt, resignation, and abjuration, some very beautiful and splendid era whose existence rehabilitates us both in regard to ourselves and in regard to others. [. . .] It was with the greatest delight that they discovered that there was nothing to be ashamed of in the past, but rather dignity, glory, and solemnity. The claim to a national culture in the past does not only rehabilitate that nation and serve as a justification for the hope of a future national culture. In the sphere of psycho-affective equilibrium it is responsible for an important change in the native. [. . .] Colonialism is not simply content to impose its rule upon the present and the future of a dominated country. Colonialism is not satisfied merely with holding a people in its grip and emptying the native's brain of all form and content. By a kind of perverted logic, it turns to the past of the oppressed people, and distorts, disfigures, and destroys it. [. . .] The effect consciously sought by colonialism was to drive into the natives' heads the idea that if the settlers were to leave, they would at once fall back into barbarism, degradation, and bestiality. [. . .]

We have noticed, on the eve of the decisive conflict for national freedom, the renewing of forms of expression and the rebirth of the imagination. There remains one essential question: what are the relations between the struggle — whether political or military — and culture? Is there a suspension of culture during the conflict? Is the national struggle an expression of a culture? [. . .] In short, is the struggle for liberation a cultural phenomenon or not?

We believe that the conscious and organized undertaking by a colonized people to re-establish the sovereignty of that nation constitutes the most complete and obvious cultural manifestation that exists. It is not alone the success of the struggle which afterward gives validity and vigor to culture; culture is not put into cold storage during the conflict. The struggle itself in its development and in its internal progression sends culture along different paths and traces out entirely new ones for it. [. . .] This struggle which aims at a fundamentally different set of relations between men cannot leave intact either the form or the content of the people's culture. After the conflict there is not only the disappearance of colonialism but also the disappearance of the colonized man.

1963, *The Wretched of the Earth*, 210–11, 245–46

Frantz Fanon (1925–61): Martinique-born anti-colonial theorist who lived mostly in France but concentrated his attention on Africa. His books include *Black Skin, White Masks* (1952, Eng. 1967) and *The Wretched of the Earth* (1961, Eng. 1963).

variants, Indian languages, Arabic, and other tongues are thriving, vast numbers of people find it necessary to acquire English in order to participate in the global multilogue. And a number of languages are in danger of extinction. Many Native American languages are gone or nearly so. The same is true in Africa. Wouldn't the extinction of several hundred or even thousands of languages impoverish the human imagination?

By far the most pervasive cultural aspect of globalization is the media — movies, television, radio, recordings, and the internet. People everywhere attend the same movies, watch the same television programs, listen to the same music over radio, on tape or CD, or via the internet. Local media adopt global styles so that wherever produced the products are similar. The impact of especially American films and television is strong. Whether dubbed, in English, or subtitled the programs retain their Americanness. The situation of recorded musics is more complex. New styles regularly sweep the world, but without the older "classical" musics entirely disappearing. Also there is a robust amount of local and regional music being performed and broadcast. Scanning the air with shortwave, AM, and FM, at any given time one can listen to everything from The Beatles to Puff Daddy, ragas to Beethoven, chutney soca to the chanting of the Quran.

In the future, the internet may prove to be the most powerful medium because it is so difficult to control. But at present, and for a longer time than its promoters allow, the internet will be available outside the West and Japan to only a relatively small minority. However, even though relatively few people can afford to be online, there are, or soon will be,

not many places or villages without at least one computer connected to the worldwide web. Putting all this together, the question remains whether or not cultural globalization — the hybridities and "world styles" — are really global — the result of contributions made by many individuals and many cultures — or are they a sign of the increasing hegemony of the West, more specifically of the USA? And if so, is there anything that can or should be done about it?

Some believe globalization is the inevitable next step in human social evolution on the way toward the emergence of a single world system. What kind of system? Economic, surely. Possibly political too because "free-market capitalism" and "democracy" go hand-in-hand. But will there also be a single value system based on "human rights"? A single religion? A single popular culture? Will this lead to a general liberation or an ever-tightening interlocked surveillance and control operation — a kind of neo-medievalism? Is this global totalitarianism wearing gloves?

Colonial Mimicry

During colonial times, and even after, a complex kind of intercultural performance occurred when "natives" took, or were awarded the privilege of acquiring, the language, dress, habits, religion, and social values of the colonial rulers. These performances were imperfect simulations, non-Europeans almost passing for European. As culture theorist **Homi K. Bhabha** (1949–) put it, the colonial mimic became almost the same but not quite white; Anglicized, not British (**see**

Bhabha box). But in whom was the failure located? Not in the colonial subject, who often acted more British than the British. The failure to pass was created by the colonial rulers, who made the racial difference, not the acquired skills, the basis upon which to make the final judgment. The rulers could not bear to be perfectly replicated because that would deny them the difference upon which their authority was ultimately based. By means of snubs, slights, discrimination, and outright violence, the rulers reminded the subjects that no level of mastering the "parent culture" could wash out the racial stain. Of course, the rulers' own "racial purity" was an illusion, as is the whole notion of race at the genetic level. It is worth noting that colonial mimicry also can go the other way. In these cases ones who passed were sometimes honored by the colonial power, as was **T. E. Lawrence** (of Arabia) (1888–1935), and sometimes disparaged for "going native." In still another kind of instance, many anthropologists use the "participant observation" method of research whereby to a significant degree they take part in the daily life of the people they are studying.

> **Colonial mimicry:** A performance of everyday life in which colonized persons adopt in part or wholesale the culture of their colonizers.

> **Homi K. Bhabha (1949–):** Indian cultural theorist, a leading figure in postcolonial studies. His works include the edited volume, *Nation and Narration* (1990) and *The Location of Culture* (1994).

> **T. E. Lawrence, "Lawrence of Arabia" (1888–1935):** Welsh soldier and author who served as British liaison to the Arabs during their revolt against the Turkish Empire (1916–22). Lawrence gave his account of that revolution in *Seven Pillars of Wisdom* (1935).

There is more. As with gays recuperating the term "queer," more than a few radicals used colonial mimicry to subvert, challenge, and overthrow the authorities. Many anti-colonial leaders were educated in the very countries against whom they battled. To be educated "in" does not determine the uses to which an education is put. Other leaders, after a period of performing the culture of the colonial power, rejected it and flaunted it simultaneously. Two figures of the Indian independence struggle provide illuminating examples. Few English could act more British than India's first prime minister, **Jawaharlal Nehru** (1889–1964). Nehru was tutored in India as a child by a Britisher; he matriculated in England at Harrow and Cambridge. He mastered English thought, language, and social mien. He became close friends with **Earl Louis Mountbatten** (1900–79), the last British Viceroy of India. With his aristocratic bearing and lucid intellect, Nehru could (and did) outdo the British at the banquet table, the debate lectern, and the negotiating

> **Jawaharlal Nehru (1889–1964):** Served as India's first prime minister from Independence in 1947 until his death. Nehru was a key leader not only of India's independence struggle against Great Britain but of the unaligned nations of the Third World. His books include *The Discovery of India* (1946).

Homi K. Bhabha

Colonial Mimicry

Within the conflictual economy of colonial discourse which Edward Said describes as the tension between the synchronic panoptical vision of domination – the demand for identity, stasis – and the counter pressure of the diachronic of history – change, difference – mimicry represents an *ironic* compromise. [. . .] Colonial mimicry is the desire for a reformed, recognizable Other, *as a subject of difference that is almost the same, but not quite*. Which is to say, that the discourse of mimicry is constructed around an *ambivalence*; in order to be effective, mimicry must continually produce its slippage, its excess, its difference. [. . .] The *menace* of mimicry is its *double* vision which in disclosing the ambivalence of colonial discourse also disrupts its authority. [. . .] *Almost the same but not white*: the visibility of mimicry is always produced at the site of interdiction. It is a form of colonial discourse that is uttered *inter dicta*: a discourse at the crossroads of what is known and permissible and that which though known must be kept concealed; a discourse uttered between the lines and as such both against the rules and within them. [. . .T]he difference between being English and being Anglicized.

1994, "Of Mimicry and Man: The Ambivalence of Colonial Discourse," in *The Location of Culture*, 86, 88–90

Earl Louis Mountbatten (1900–79): Last British Viceroy of India, he turned authority over to the leaders of India and Pakistan in August, 1947. During the Second World War, Lord Mountbatten headed the Allied Southeast Asian Command.

chamber. But Nehru's colonial mimicry did not in the least deter him from his life's task. He was a relentless, intrepid battler for Indian independence. As prime minister, Nehru led the non-aligned nations of the world.

No one could be less like Nehru in appearance and style than his closest ally in the struggle, **Mohandas K. Gandhi** (1869–1948). But at the start, Gandhi was an excellent colonial mimic. He took his law degree from the Inns of Court in London, and when he arrived in South Africa in 1893 to practice law, he looked every inch an Englishman (**see figure 8.1**). But when he was humiliated and physically abused for being Indian no matter how properly English he behaved, Gandhi had a profound change of heart. He learned that "playing at being British" was not in the interest of truth,

Indian independence, his own dignity, or that of the Indian people. The deep pattern of his life took the shape of "not British." His campaigns against colonial rule were exercises in "non-cooperation" — boycotting or rejecting British goods, courts, schools, dress, bureaucracy, food, legislatures, and religion. This did not stop him from using the ideas of Leo Tolstoy, **John Ruskin** (1819–1900), and others when they suited him. And Gandhi's values and political strategies profoundly influenced non-Indians, **Martin Luther King** (1929–68) especially. Gandhi practiced Indian values. He was from boyhood a strict vegetarian. He grounded his actions in Indian religious and philosophical texts, the *Bhagavad Gita* in particular, with its teaching of engaging fully but without hatred in the necessary wars of life. He intentionally made a spectacle of himself. He led marches, went on hunger strikes, challenged the British to jail him, and dressed only in homespun khadi and dhoti (**see figure 8.2**). He impressively staged the negative aspects of British colonialism before a world audience. His *satyagraha* (peaceful struggle) was both actual and symbolic, consisting of "demonstrations" — embodied proofs. For example, in the 1930 protest against the British salt tax, Gandhi led a 241-mile march from Ahmedabad to Dandi on the Arabian Sea coast, where he and his followers gathered sea salt (no tax on that). This symbolic act ignited a general protest against British colonial rule resulting in the imprisonment of Gandhi and more than 60,000 others. The jailings, far from being a defeat for Gandhi's movement, was convincing proof of its mass appeal and deeply rooted strength. Gandhi's performances won the respect of some of his British adversaries and the scorn of others. He pretty well drove them all crazy. But to hundreds of millions of ordinary Indians, Hindus and Muslims alike, this trained lawyer, strong negotiator, nonviolent warrior, and great performer was, simply, the *mahatma*, the "great soul."

fig 8.1. Mohandas K. Gandhi the proper British lawyer in South Africa in the 1890s. Photo courtesy of www.mahatma.org.in

Mohandas K. Gandhi (1869–1948): Indian political and spiritual leader advocating non-violent resistance to British colonial authority. In January, 1948, Gandhi was assassinated by a Hindu fundamentalist. His writings include *Autobiography: The Story of My Experiments with Truth* (1954) which Gandhi updated several times.

John Ruskin (1819–1900): English essayist whose *Unto This Last* (1862), a critique of capitalism, influenced Gandhi during his formative years in South Africa.

Martin Luther King, Jr. (1929–68): African-American religious and civil rights leader, winner of the 1964 Nobel Peace Prize for his efforts to end racial discrimination in the USA. King was assassinated by a white racist in April, 1968 in Memphis, Tennessee.

fig 8.2. Mohandas K. Gandhi striding through Bengal wearing a traditional Indian dhoti, 1946. Photo courtesy of www.mahatma.org.in

Tourist Performances: Leisure Globalization

Tourism is no simple matter. To satisfy an enormous and still rapidly growing market of intercultural, international, intracultural, and intranational tourists, performances of all kinds have been found, redesigned, or invented. There are many kinds of tourism – culture, sports, sex, wildlife, historical, etc. – where at the destination the tourist witnesses or, increasingly, takes part in a performance of one kind or another. While on safari, for example, tourists become hunters-with-cameras, living in a refurbished and toileted "wild." Sports tourists at the Olympics or the Superbowl more than watch athletes. They party, sight-see, vicariously take part in the competition while identifying with their heroes and their city or nation. These tourisms, for we must use the plural to describe them, can transport people to distant places or back in time by means of restorations and re-enactments.

It is common wisdom to disparage tourism and tourist performances as shallow and tawdry, a pastime for the rich and an exploitation of "native" or "local" peoples, their beliefs, and skills. Tourists yearn for the "authentic" and the "real," even as most of them know they are being fed the ersatz and the invented. Although all this is too often true, it is not always the case, nor is it the whole story. In Bali the same kind of performance may be part of a temple ceremony in one instance and presented in unconsecrated space for tourists at another time. The quality suffers, but not as much as those who condemn tourism say. *Ketchak* – the "monkey chant-dance" which re-enacts an episode from the *Ramayana* – is performed by the Balinese both in their own ceremonies and as a big tourist attraction. Ironically, ketchak began in the 1920s as a tourist performance.

There are performances not made for tourists which attract them in droves all the same. Many religious observances are open to visitors – sometimes in the hopes of proselytizing, or to earn money, or just to be hospitable. When tourists enter churches, temples, synagogues, shrines, or mosques are they enjoying (and paying for) an entertainment or experiencing the sacred? Need one strictly separate these orders of experience? And insofar as the tourists are present at the "real thing," what adjustments are made in the performances to accommodate the outsiders? The answer cannot be given in a word because the changes may be subtle and slowly transformative.

There is virtual and media tourism – part of the explanation for the great popularity of film and television is that it gives people a chance to experience "the other" without leaving home. Brazilians watching reruns of *Seinfeld* or Americans watching a National Geographic Special (or any number of programs on the Discovery Channel) are virtual tourists. Surfing the web yields similar opportunities to experience the far away. Does virtual tourism create positive feedback whereby the places depicted attempt to live up to their media images?

But for the most part, tourism involves actual travel. This can take many forms. Pilgrimages, popular the world over, and undertaken by many who are far from rich, combine religious devotion and tourism. Hindus are continually in circulation around India, visiting literally thousands of *tirths* (pilgrimage spots) – temples, caves, mountains, rivers – and performances such as the Raslila at Mathura or the Ramlila at Ramnagar, where I met a man who was carrying his mother around India in a basket so that she could visit as many pilgrimage sites as possible. When I met them in 1978, they had been on the road for two years (**see figure 8.3**). Millions of Muslims make the hajj to Mecca at least once in their lives. Places sacred to Christianity abound, attracting tourists to the Holy Land and to miracle shrines in Europe and the Western Hemisphere. People make these journeys to fulfill a religious obligation and to see the world, sharing in the camaraderie that "going away" awakens – a liminal time-space well known in **Geoffrey Chaucer**'s (1342–1400) fourteenth-century England as recounted in his *Canterbury Tales*.

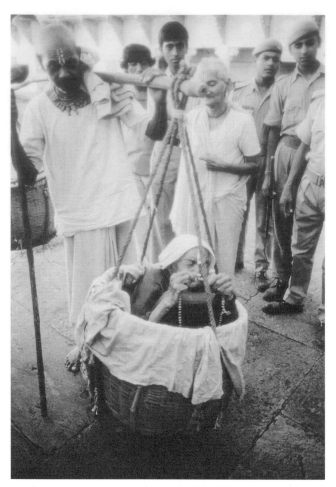

fig 8.3. A devoted son carrying his mother to important pilgrimage centers in India. The journey was to take more than two years. As shown here in 1978 they have arrived at the Ramlila of Ramnagar. Photograph by Richard Schechner.

Geoffrey Chaucer (1342–1400): English poet, best known for *The Canterbury Tales*, written between 1386 and 1400. In this poem, pilgrims on their way to Canterbury, England tell stories to pass the time.

Tourism within nations is at least as big a business as travel among nations. Protecting local peoples, practices, wildlife, or landscapes can turn into selling them, or imitations of them, to tourists. In India, city-dwelling Rajasthanis flock to a specially built "authentic" village to view craftspeople at work and to enjoy music, dance, and supper. The tourists sit on the floor of a large thatch-roofed house eating traditional foods dished onto banana leaves by young women dressed in "traditional" garb. As Jaipur's Rex Tours puts it, "Take a peek into the lives of rural folk, their abodes, social set up, religious beliefs, and innovative cuisine" (**see figure 8.4**). The night I was there most of the tourists were visibly middle class. My

hunch was right that at least some of the visitors were returning to a sanitized version of their own past. "This is very authentic," a man told me. "It is just like the village my parents came from." So why didn't he simply make a trip back to his parents' village? Tourism simplifies, idealizes, and packages. When the show is over, you can wash your hands of the whole thing. The actual village may have been far away or held some disturbing reminders — or even relations to whom he would be obligated. Or maybe his own village had changed so much that the tourist village was a better representation of his past. But most probably, seeing his own experience reified gave him a sense of mastery over his past. He could literally purchase his past. Tourism does that — allows the tourist to purchase the other, the past, the exotic, the sexy, the exciting . . . whatever is up for grabs. And if "purchase" means to buy with money, it also means to get a hold on, to grasp firmly, to be in charge.

fig 8.4. A Rajasthani family as portrayed in a tourist brochure seeking business from Indian as well as foreign tourists. Photo courtesy Richard Schechner.

In Kenya, Mayer's Farm — a homestead owned by white settlers — attracted tourists who wanted to experience "authentic" colonial life including members of the Mayer family and Maasai employees all playing their colonial roles. So for the "eternal past" of the tourist experience, the vanished world was back in place, if only in the realm of the performative make-believe. Mayer's Farm no longer exists — but the Maasai continue to be exploited by hordes of camera-toting tourists who treat them as little more than part of the area's wildlife (**see figure 8.5 and Hamisi box**). What about the economics of this kind of tourism? Much tourism feeds on the needy and, like globalization generally, depends on a sharp imbalance of economic opportunity. The tourist is free-floating, a consumer with a lot of cash (relatively speaking) who could in theory go anywhere. The international tour agency has access to local operators who, in turn, organize the "workers," the Maasai or whoever are the

fig 8.5. Maasai men dancing at Mayer's Farm, a tourist destination in Kenya, in 1983. Although Mayer's Farm has closed, tourist photographers still aim their cameras at the Maasai. Too often, the tourists and tour managers treat "native people" as another form of wild-life – this is an attitude deeply founded in colonialism. Photograph by A. Kent Christensen.

Katuka Ole Maimai Hamisi

Maasai and the Paparazzi

There is a new alternative weapon for lion hunting, the cameras; they are environmentally friendly and require no preparation other than money. The Maasai people are also among the hunted by these "things" as many Western paparazzi found free rides into a land full of exoticism (wildlife and people) where the law to protect indigenous peoples rights and images remains scarce. [. . .] Western paparazzi manipulate and exploit indigenous people such as the Maasai for profit.

It is bothersome when one observes images of the indigenous people and could not see their names. Western paparazzi often fail to distinguish a Maasai from a wild animal. In fact, wild animals are given better recognition than the Maasai. [. . .] For example, chimps have names such as Koko, whales Keiko, even skulls have names, for example, Lucy, etc. Why not the Maasai? The Maasai believe they belong in the human species and deserve full recognition for their existence just as the Westerners do.

Recently, the Maasai came across pictures of their most sacred practices, the circumcision – a rite of passage that is rarely shown to the public, even within its local settings. Generally speaking, this ritual is on view throughout the Western world and the suppliers, i.e. photographers, also known as cultural reapers, continue to celebrate the success of robbing indigenous peoples' cultures. [. . .]

The Maasai question the Western paparazzi's vision of Maasai culture because the paparazzi only see and depict nudity, animalistic and primitive; the paparazzi do not respect the reality of the poor and the cultural differences that exist on this planet. Nudity in Africa and in so many parts of the world is associated with culture and currently with economic disorders that brought about poverty: this disorder is denying the poor people the ability to access better clothing, food, and shelter. It is this poverty that Western paparazzi celebrate and in turn enriches them.

Western paparazzi ignore the fact that much poverty that exists in the world today was fundamentally diffused by their grandfathers, the colonizers. The Maasai people now understand that Western paparazzi are explorers, adventurers, exploiters, manipulators, and in fact a new generation of colonizers. [. . .] The Maasai stress that they do not have a problem with others who wish to learn about their culture, but they have a problem when their culture is inaccurately represented.

2001, "Western Paparazzi in the Maasai Region,"
http://maasai-infoline.org/index.html

destination objects. As in globalized industries, the money is unevenly distributed: the agency and local operators take the lion's share. The Maasai – and their case is not unusual – get less than 10 percent of the tourists' dollars. They are in effect working in a sweatshop.

Visiting the "eternal past" is not just an overseas thing. The Rajasthanis seeking a replica of their own village are matched in the USA by a host of historical re-enactments, theme parks, and restored villages. "Living museums," Plimoth Plantation in Massachusetts and Colonial Williamsburg in Virginia, for example, pride themselves on the historical verisimilitude of their environments. Because no houses survive from the seventeenth-century Pilgrim settlement, Plimoth is not a restoration but a "re-creation." And the location of the present-day Plantation is about a mile from the original site. The "interpreters" – the word "actor" is shunned because it is associated with theatrical inauthenticity – are dressed in period costumes and coached in the language and manners of the New England Pilgrims or the Virginia planters. Interpreters not only improvise dialogue with tourists, but enact specific persons and scenes. At Plimoth, interpreters study "personation biographs" written out in colonial English script describing the settler to be enacted along with a full body portrait (**see figure 8.6**). The interpreter is expected to develop an in-depth characterization and maintain it at all times while on site during the hours that the public is admitted. Needless to say, there are slips and even larger difficulties.

Living museums: Also called "living history" museums, these are historical and/or tourist sites where a specific historical period is recreated in architectural, behavioral, and physical detail. Living museums are often constructed at or near the place where the events re-enacted took place – as at Plimoth Plantation in Massachusetts or Colonial Williamsburg in Virginia.

Plimoth Plantation had a "problem" with how to represent the Wampanoag Native Americans who occupied the land near the Pilgrim settlement. Most tourists come for the Pilgrims, and just as in the colonial past, the natives are pretty well pushed out of the picture. Their "summer settlement" consists of a few tepees. One peculiar detail. A brochure informs visitors that the Wampanoags are "staffed by Native Americans." Why tell us this? Those who interpret the Pilgrims are not advertised as descendants of white Britishers (which most probably most of them aren't). There is both an intercultural apology and a bragging about authenticity

encoded in detail about the "natives." The brochure goes on to invite tourists to "meet the Native American people who have lived for centuries along the New England coast." But are these interpreters from coastal tribes? And what difference would that make when there is no engagement with the circumstances of native "removal" – the wars, the diseases, and the general extermination both cultural and biological that took place? Tourist pleasure trumps historical accuracy even in a museum site that exults in its accuracy. Something similar haunts Colonial Williamsburg.

When Colonial Williamsburg began in 1926, and for many years thereafter, it was a white-only living museum recreating the life of the eighteenth century. African Americans were present, of course, but behind the scenes, mostly as menial laborers. No African Americans were allowed onto the premises as visitors during the period of segregation. But from the 1960s onward, things changed. Yet it was one thing to admit African Americans as tourists, another to integrate their history into a site that depended on slave labor for its very existence. African-American interpretors performed certain aspects of enslavement – working the fields, plantation servants (**see figure 8.7**). Then in the 1990s, it was decided to enact a slave auction. Some of the African-American actors, though recognizing the need for the depiction, felt demeaned and humiliated. But they persevered because they believed that only by performing the auction could people really understand the abomination of African slavery in America.

The Olympics: Globalism's Signature Performance

The modern Olympic Games are the most popular performance event in history, a truly global phenomenon. More than half the world's population witnesses some part of the Olympics via the media. Several million attend the Games in person. The 2000 summer Olympics at Sydney, Australia drew 10,651 athletes competing in 300 events of 28 sports. The athletes came from 199 nations, compared to the United Nations 2001 membership of 189. In addition to athletes, many thousands are involved as press, dignitaries, officials, technicians, snack and souvenir sellers, janitors, housekeepers, performers and other artists, scientists, and commercial exhibitors. Building arenas for the competitions and for housing athletes involves reconstructing large sections of cities, laying down roads and infrastructure, and uprooting neighborhoods. The new construction has reinvigorated fig 8.6. A "personation biograph" of Phineas Pratt used by an "interpreter" at Plimoth Plantation in the 1980s. The actor is called an interpreter in order to distance his "historical re-enactment" from theatre because theatre is tainted "untruth." Photo courtesy Plimoth Plantation.

fig 8.7. The "Slave Quarters" at Colonial Williamsburg as depicted on its official site, history.org, in 2001.

urban areas. But the displacements and profiteering have also evoked strong protests. It all adds up to billions in investments and, during the Games, the spending of even more money by the media, sponsors, and those attending the Games.

The first modern Olympics took place in 1896 in Athens. The brainchild of **Pierre de Coubertin** (1863–1937), the Games featured 245 white male amateur athletes from 14 European nations, the USA, Canada, and Australia. They competed in 45 events of 9 sports ranging from racing and weight-lifting to swimming, tennis, and fencing (where a professional was allowed to compete). In the present-day Olympics, about 40 percent of the athletes are women, people from all over the world compete, and the distinction between professional and amateur has all but vanished because every athlete is either paid or sponsored. When the Games are over, many can look forward to lucrative careers built on their Olympic triumphs. This "impurity" is nothing new. Whatever the rhetoric of the founders, from the start, the modern Olympics combined sport, spectacle, ritual, festivity, performing arts, economics, and politics.

Pierre de Coubertin (1863–1937): Founder of the modern Olympics movement and president of the International Olympic Committee from 1896 to 1925.

And although the International Olympic Committee (IOC) says it wants to keep the Games "above" politics, rifts in the global political landscape are played out at the Olympics. The Games were cancelled three times: in 1916, in 1940, and in 1944 due to the World Wars. Ironically, the 1916 Games were scheduled for Berlin, the 1940 for Tokyo, and the 1944 for London. At Munich in 1972, terrorists murdered 11 Israelis. At the 1976 Montreal Games, 20 teams from Africa (plus Iraq and Guyana) withdrew to protest the New Zealand rugby team's tour of South Africa during the height of apartheid. Taiwan withdrew because it was not allowed to play under the banner of the "Republic of China." The USA and four other nations boycotted the Moscow Games of 1980 to protest the Soviet invasion of Afghanistan. The USSR retaliated by leading 14 nations in a boycott of the 1984 Los Angeles Games.

Despite all this, the Games keep growing in general popularity and national participation. The opportunity to use the Olympics as a showcase is too much to resist. The media event is too popular to forego. Although the original idea was for individuals not nations to compete, the flying of flags, the playing of anthems, the jockeying over where the Games are held, and the keeping of records proclaiming which nation has won the most medals focus attention on national accomplishment.

The modern Olympics were meant to rekindle the spirit of the ancient Olympiads (776 BCE–369 CE), themselves a kind of recreation of the funeral games honoring the slain Patroclus described by **Homer** (8th or 9th century, BCE) in book 23 of the *Iliad*. A key goal of the Olympics, modern and ancient, is to transcend the local and emphasize the "global" (however that is conceived). In ancient times, warfare was suspended for the games. In modern times, the idea is for nations to put aside their differences and sublimate their rivalries in the fields of play. But "the world" of 2002 is not the world of 1896. At the end of the nineteenth century, the world was, or was controlled by, Europe and the European diaspora. But over time, with the end of colonialism and the emergence of multiple players on the world stage, more and more nations joined the Olympic movement.

Homer (eighth or ninth century BCE): Greek poet, composer of the seminal epic poems *The Odyssey* and *The Iliad*. Most scholars believe that Homer, who was blind, performed these works orally.

In terms of the participating athletes, the Olympics are a truly global event. However, at the organizational and structural levels the Eurocentricity of the Games remains intact. First, the IOC continues to be led by Europeans or North Americans. Second, although people everywhere run, jump, swim, play fight, and so on, the Olympic sports based on these activities are European. No effort is made to include non-European sports such as sumo wrestling, Trinidadian stick fighting, or the kind of mixed-terrain long-distance running enjoyed by the Tarahumaras of northwest Mexico. Third, venues remain overwhelmingly Western. Only Seoul in 1988 lay outside the West (if one considers Sydney culturally a Western city). Mexico City, host to the 1968 Games, is both Western and Third World; Moscow, site of the 1980 Games, is a European city even if, at that time, it was capital of the USSR. The 2004 Games will return to Athens.

Thus it was news that in July 2001 the IOC selected Beijing as the site of the 2008 Games. As the decision became known (it was televised on large screens in China), more than 100,000 persons poured onto the streets of Beijing shouting, waving flags, and setting off fireworks (**see figure 8.8**). The joyous celebration was by far the largest free-flowing mass in the streets of the Chinese capital since the Pro-Democracy movement of May–June 1989. That assembly ended bloodily when troops and tanks cleared Tiananmen Square. Clearly the Olympics crowds had the blessing of the authorities. What were they and Chinese officials so happy about? As *The New York Times* put it: "Winning the Olympic bid is much more than a matter of civic or even national pride for people here. [. . .] As host to the Games, China believes it will stand as a respected member of the world community, a position it has long felt the West has denied it." Wanting to be a "respected member of the world community" is to enact a concept made real by globalization.

fig 8.8. Crowds in Beijing celebrating the selection of their city as the site of the 2008 Olympic Games.

Aside from the sports competition, the Olympics have always included sheer spectacle. The first modern Games commenced on Easter Sunday with Athens adorned in colorful bunting, streamers, and green wreaths inscribed with the letters "O.A." (the Greek initials for the games) and the dates "776 B.C." and "A.D. 1896" connecting the ancient to the modern. After the Greek **King George I** (1845–1913) opened the modern Olympic era, cannons were fired, pigeons released, and the Olympic hymn sung. The present era features the arrival of the Olympic torch, elaborate opening-day ceremonies, raising the national flags of winning athletes, playing national anthems, and the constant media drumbeat.

> **King George I of Greece (1845–1913):** Born William, Prince of Denmark, and proclaimed King of Greece in 1863. In 1896, George I inaugurated the first modern Olympics, hoping to restore some glory to Greece.

The Olympics do not stand alone as sports competition. Surrounding the Games are all kinds of celebrations and artistic and commercial events. The 1984 Los Angeles Olympics spawned the "Cultural Olympics," which in turn morphed into the Los Angeles Festivals of 1987 and 1990. The vast conglomeration of performances and exhibitions in 1990 included 550 events in 70 venues with more than 1,400 artists from 21 Pacific Rim countries. Although the 1990 LA Festival may have been the biggest, there are many similar festivals around the world modeled to some degree on the Olympics. This kind of putting together a package of events performed by persons from a variety of nations and cultures is the outcome and continuation of several kinds of events: colonial expositions, worlds fairs, and the Olympics. All of these share a desire to assemble, own, and display the largest quantity and widest diversity of peoples performing either culture-specific (the expositions and fairs) or "universal" activities (the Olympics).

What kind of performance are the Olympics? The Games can't be subsumed under a single category. According to anthropologist **John J. MacAloon** (1947–), the Olympics are a complex interplay of spectacle, festival, ritual, and games (**see figure 8.9 and MacAloon box**). The largest, most inclusive category is spectacle (**see Debord box**). The

> **John J. MacAloon (1947–):** American anthropologist and foremost scholar of the Olympic Games. Author of *This Great Symbol* (1981) and editor of *Rite, Drama, Festival, Spectacle* (1984).

John MacAloon

Genres of Performance in the Olympics

The genres [. . .] spectacle, festival, ritual, game by no means exhaust the roster of performance types found in the Olympic Games. But they are semantically and functionally the most significant. The order in which they are discussed reflects a passage from the most diffuse and ideologically centrifugal genres to the most concentrated and ideologically centripetal. Spectacle and game appeared earliest, festival and ritual consolidated later, in Olympic history. [. . .] These genres are distinctive forms of symbolic action, distinguished from one another by athletes, spectators, and officials alike. While certain features are shared between genres, others are in tension or in opposition, both categorically and in context. [. . .] At the same time, the Olympic Games form a single performance system. The genres are intimately and complexly interconnected on all levels: historically, ideologically, structurally, and performatively. Thus we are forced to recognize that the Olympic Games represent a special kind of cultural performance, a ramified performance type, and we are forced to seek for new models and methods of analysis that will allow us to understand the relationships between the various forms of symbolic action without losing sight of their distinctive properties. [. . .]

By the late 1920s and early 1930s, cultural history had, so to speak, caught up with the Olympic movement. Until that time, the semantic boundary "This is play" had remained more or less intact around the games of the Olympic Games. In turn, this protected the festival frame as well, and it afforded Olympic rituals a certain serenity within which to condense and elaborate. But largely due to the success of the Olympics themselves, a mass efflorescence of organized sport, first in Euro-American cultures, then worldwide, drew down upon the Games of the 20s and 30s ideological, political, and commercial interests of every sort. [. . .]

The professionalization of sports and the transformation of athletes into celebrities, the growing number-fetishism and specialization in athletics, the increased role of technology and hyperextended training periods [. . .], the growth of athletic bureaucracies, the recognition of sport's importance and the incorporation of sports success by the dominant world ideologies, the takeover of the selection, preparation, and financing of the teams by national governments and corporate interests, the counting of medals as propaganda and ersatz warfare, the attempts to co-opt the Games for chauvinistic purposes by host nations, and their use as a stage for "jock-strap diplomacy," saber rattling, regime building, and, finally, terrorism by insiders and outsiders alike: these developments represent in a general way the penetration of the "stuff of ordinary life" into the public liminality of the Games. And as ordinary life has changed, so have the Games been forced to change.

1984, "Olympic Games and the Theory of Spectacle in Modern Societies," 242, 258–59, 262–63

Guy Debord

Spectacle, Society's Real Unreality

The whole life of those societies in which modern conditions of production prevail presents itself as an immense accumulation of *spectacles*. All that was once directly lived has become mere representation. [. . .] The spectacle is not a collection of images; rather, it is a social relationship between people that is mediated by images. [. . .] Understood in its totality, the spectacle is both the outcome and the goal of the dominant mode of production. It is not something *added* to the real world – not a decorative element, so to speak. On the contrary, it is the very heart of society's real unreality. In all its specific manifestations – news or propaganda, advertising or the actual consumption of entertainment – the spectacle epitomizes the prevailing model of social life. [. . .]

The unreal unity the spectacle proclaims masks the class division on which the real unity of the capitalist mode of production is based. What obliges producers to participate in the construction of the world is also what separates them from it. What brings together men liberated from local and national limitations is also what keeps them apart. What pushes for greater rationality is also what nourishes the irrationality of hierarchical exploitation and repression. What creates society's abstract power also creates its concrete unfreedom.

1995 [1967] *The Society of the Spectacle* 12–13, 46

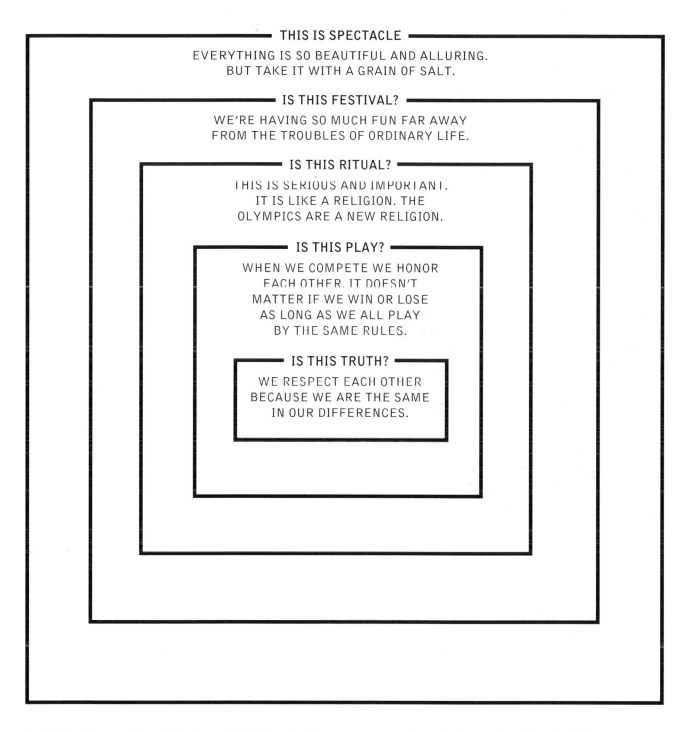

THIS IS SPECTACLE

EVERYTHING IS SO BEAUTIFUL AND ALLURING.
BUT TAKE IT WITH A GRAIN OF SALT.

IS THIS FESTIVAL?

WE'RE HAVING SO MUCH FUN FAR AWAY
FROM THE TROUBLES OF ORDINARY LIFE.

IS THIS RITUAL?

THIS IS SERIOUS AND IMPORTANT.
IT IS LIKE A RELIGION. THE
OLYMPICS ARE A NEW RELIGION.

IS THIS PLAY?

WHEN WE COMPETE WE HONOR
EACH OTHER. IT DOESN'T
MATTER IF WE WIN OR LOSE
AS LONG AS WE ALL PLAY
BY THE SAME RULES.

IS THIS TRUTH?

WE RESPECT EACH OTHER
BECAUSE WE ARE THE SAME
IN OUR DIFFERENCES.

fig 8.9. Each frame contains all the others within it. The entire Olympics are a spectacle inside which is a festival inside which are rituals inside which are the competitive sports inside which is a presumed "core truth." The frames signify mostly a conceptual arrangement, but also to some degree the actual uses of space. That is, the spectacle is everywhere, the festival moves in and out of the various venues and permeates the city beyond. Rituals are enacted side-by-side with spectacles and competitions. The sum total is supposed to be a liminal time of communitas where differences and sameness occupy the space simultaneously.

The question marks represent the change from the founders' desire to enact a truth by means of sports, ritual, and festivity. What has occurred is that only the spectacle – in Debord's sense – continues unquestioned. The other objectives of the Olympics system have been called into question. However, this interrogation has not undermined the Olympics as an event of global magnitude. On the contrary, the questions have only served to enhance the Games because they enact both what they claim they are and what their detractors say they have become. Adapted from John MacAloon's "Olympic Games and the Theory of Spectacle," 1984: 258, 262.

global spectacle of the Olympics is crystallized in the opening-day show, which features thousands of performers, music, dance, and special effects. Spectacle both generates and is part of the overall festivity permeating the Games. Although this festivity is centered in the Olympic city, it extends to many parts of the world, where groups assemble to root for their national heroes. Then come the many rituals of the Olympics. On opening day there are the declaration that the Games are open, the arrival of the Olympic torch from Greece, and the parade of athletes. After each event, the winners are displayed before the crowds as the flags of their nations are raised and their anthems played. The Games close with more rituals and the promise of another Olympiad four years hence. At the center of all this are the games themselves. In appearance these maintain a relative purity determined by the rules. However, because of the intensity of the competition and the huge rewards awaiting both individuals and nations, performance-enhancing drugs and other manipulations are rampant. The ideal of free competition has been corrupted by the demand for victory at any cost. Additionally, all else aside, athletes from poorer nations are at a disadvantage because they cannot afford the kind of training or facilities used by athletes from richer countries.

Grotowski's Vertical Transculturalism

Nothing could be further from the global spectacle of the Olympics than the intercultural explorations of Jerzy Grotowski. Except for one period from the mid-1970s to the early 1980s, he never showed his work to large numbers. But despite this, Grotowski's work is influential globally with adherents in all continents. His methods of textual and scenic montage, actor training, staging, vocal work, and using materials from cultures both ancient and contemporary have influenced a great many in theatre, dance, and performance art – some directly and even more by means of diffusion.

From the very start of his career, Grotowski made connections across cultures and back in time seeking what he believed were deep universal human truths. In 1956, while still a student, Grotowski made his first trip to Asia. Upon his return to Poland, he lectured on yoga and Chinese philosophy. He broadened his interest to include the sacred knowledge of

> **Transculturalism:** Working or theorizing across cultures with the assumption that there are cultural "universals" – behaviors, concepts, or beliefs that are true of everyone, everywhere, at all times.

many cultures, ancient and contemporary. What he learned inflected his theatre work throughout his "poor theatre" phase, 1957-69. Then, at the end of the 1960s, he stopped directing plays. From 1969 to 1983 Grotowski devised paratheatrical experiments, face-to-face encounters between members of the Polish Laboratory Theatre and outsiders some of whom were well-known artists and others students and ordinary persons from many nations. Finally these investigations ran out of energy.

At that point, Grotowski narrowed his focus. He concentrated his work on a few traditional ritual performance specialists from Asia and the Caribbean. This work culminated in Grotowski's 1983–86 "Objective Drama" project housed at the University of California-Irvine. Grotowski wanted to find specific elements of performance that transcended the particular cultures in which they were embedded. In order to do this, he brought traditional performance specialists from Columbia, Korea, Bali, Taiwan, Haiti, and India to work with students. One of these students was Thomas Richards, the young American to whom Grotowski entrusted his most precious performance secrets.

The underlying assumption of Objective Drama and Grotowski's final phase, "Art as Vehicle" (1986–99) is that there is an intersection where the most intimate-personal meets the most objective-archetypal. Locating that intersection demanded what Grotowski called "rendering," used both in its sense of an artist's prepatory sketch (also the Zen "art of the beginner") and in the sense of the distillation of substances into their essences. The substances to be rendered were traditional performances yielding "vibratory songs" and movements and performers yielding their innermost associations. The result was the formation of the Performer performing the *Action* – an attempt to recreate the "origin" of performance (**see Grotowski box**).

One can readily see how Grotowski's ideas are related to globalization. Both are universalistic; both are utopian; both depend on the acceptance of certain transcultural assumptions and methods. Neither could occur except in a period of advanced communications and travel. Globalization at the popular culture level imposes (or seduces people into) a similarity in styles and tastes; at the technical level, requires the use of standardized hardware and software; at the business level, demands adherence to the rules of various world trade protocols. Grotowski's project also leads to standardization embodied by the adherence to a specific kind of training and the nearly absolute dedication to the work. The result is *Action*, an archetypal, ahistorical, finely executed performance.

Jerzy Grotowski

Discovering the Beginning

Performer, with a capital letter, is a man of action. He is not somebody who plays another. He is a doer, a priest, a warrior: he is outside aesthetic genres. Ritual is performance, an accomplished action, an act. Degenerated ritual is a show. I don't want to discover something new but something forgotten. Something so old that all distinctions between aesthetic genres are no longer of use. [. . .].

Essence interests me because nothing in it is sociological. It is what you did not receive from others, what did not come from outside, what is not learned. [. . .]

One access to the creative way consists of discovering in yourself an ancient corporality to which you are bound by a strong ancestral relation. [. . .] Starting from details you can discover in you somebody other — your grandfather, your mother. A photo, a memory of wrinkles, the distant echo of the color of the voice enable you to reconstruct a corporality. First, the corporality of somebody known, and then more and more distant, the corporality of the unknown one, the ancestor. Is it literally the same? Maybe not literally — but yet as it might have been. You can arrive very far back, as if your memory awakes [. . .] as if you recall *Performer* of the primal ritual. [. . .] With the breakthrough — as in the return of an exile — can one touch something which is no longer linked to beginnings but — if I dare say — to *the beginning*? I believe so.

1997 [1988], "Performer," 374–7

But there is a big difference separating Grotowski's from other kinds of globalization. Grotowski's reach is vertical, fetching back in time rather than stretching horizontally across cultures. Grotowski assumes a coincidence of origin and finality. This lack of historicity is the Achilles' heel of Grotowski's final work. Nevertheless, Art as Vehicle is proving influential. Even though *Action* is played for only a handful of people at a time, over the long haul many hundreds have experienced it — especially younger persons not only from theatre but from a diversity of fields. They are impressed by the dedication to the work, the precision of the performance, and the felt presence of the performers, Richards and his

long-time partner at the Grotowski Workcenter, Mario Biagini especially. They are also excited by its utopian spirit. In this regard, Grotowski's late work is analogous to the utopian speculations of Victor Turner at the end of his life. Like Grotowski, Turner sought an "objective" basis for ritual — not in survivals of ancient performances but in brain structure and function. Turner dreamed of a "global population of brains," an organic network that included not only human beings but the whole planet (**see Turner box**). Both Turner and Grotowski saw the best human endeavors as Janus-like, the Roman god who looks back to the "most ancient" and forward to "the newest" at the same time.

Victor Turner

A Global Population of Brains

I am really speaking of a global population of brains inhabiting an entire world of inanimate and animate entities, a population whose members are incessantly communicating with one another through every physical and mental instrumentality. But if one considers the geology, so to speak, of the human brain and nervous system, we see represented in its strata — each layer still vitally alive — not dead like stone, the numerous pasts and presents of our planet. Like Walt Whitman, we "embrace multitudes." [. . .] Each of us is a microcosm, related in the deepest ways to the whole life-history of that lovely deep blue globe swirled over with the white whorls first photographed by Edwin Aldrin and Neil Armstrong from their primitive space chariot, the work nevertheless of many collaborating human brains.

1983, "Body, Brain, and Culture," 243

Barba's Horizontal Interculturalism

Grotowski's project essentializes. *Action* simultaneously enacts the intimate and the "origin" — what in Indian philosophy (certainly an influence on Grotowski's thought) is the union of *atman* (the kernel of absolute in each person) and *brahman* (the universal absolute). Eugenio Barba — who in the 1960s assisted Grotowski and kept in close contact with him since — has from at least 1980 onward developed a particular aspect of the Grotowski work, answering the question:

Where does a performer's "energy" and/or "presence" come from? Barba investigates this not only with his own group, the Odin Theatre, but in the sessions of the International School of Theatre Anthropology (ISTA). ISTA is not a usual school, nor is Barba's "anthropology" the conventional brand.

At ISTA sessions, which last from a few days to a month, Barba brings together a team of performers and performance theorists to advance and demonstrate to a wider public his basic thesis: that there are movements, stances, and rhythms employed by the most accomplished performers in all cultures (**see Barba and Savarese box**). These constitute the "pre-expressive" patterns of "extra-daily" behavior that spectators respond to as the performer's "presence" or "energy."

What are these pre-expressive behaviors? Barba seeks the answer by investigating mostly Asian classical performances. He concentrates not on finished products but on how accomplished performers train and display their bodies. Although he refers to non-Asian genres and performers — ballet, Meyerhold, Stanislavsky, the mime of **Etienne Decroux** (1898–1991), the energetic style of **Dario Fo** (1926–) — these serve mostly as confirmation of principles

Eugenio Barba and Nicola Savarese

Theatre Anthropology

Theatre anthropology is the study of the behavior of the human being when it uses its physical and mental presence in an organized performance situation and according to principles which are different from those used in daily life. This extra-daily use of the body is what is called technique.

A transcultural analysis of performance reveals that the performer's work is the result of the fusion of three aspects which reflect three different levels of organization: 1) The performers' personalities, their sensibilities, their artistic intelligence, their social personae: those characteristics which make them unique and once-only. 2) The particularities of the traditions and socio-historical contexts through which the once-only personality of a performer is manifest. 3) The use of physiology according to extra-daily body techniques. The recurrent and transcultural principles on which these techniques are based are defined by Theatre Anthropology at the field of pre-expressivity.

The first aspect is individual. The second is common to all those who belong to the same performance genre. Only the third concerns all performers from every era and every culture: it can be called the performance's "biological" level. The first two aspects determine the transition from pre-expressivity to expression. The third [. . .] does not vary; it underlies the various individual, artistic, and cultural variants. [. . .]

Applied to certain physiological factors (weight, balance, the position of the spinal column, the direction of the eyes in space), these principles produce pre-expressive organic tensions. These new tensions generate a different energy quality, render the body theatrically "decided," "alive," and manifest the performers "presence," or scenic bios, attracting the spectator's attention before any form of personal expression takes place. [. . .] ISTA's field of work is the study of the principles of this extra-daily use of the body and their application to the actor's and dancer's creative work. [. . .]

Theatre anthropology postulates that there exists a basic level of organization common to all performers and defines this level as *pre-expressive*. [. . .] Theatre anthropology postulates that the *pre-expressive* level is at the root of the various performing techniques and that there exists, independently of traditional culture, a transcultural "physiology." In fact, pre-expressivity utilizes principles for the acquisition of presence and the performer's life. The results of these principles appear more evident in codified genres where the technique which *puts* the body *in form* is codified independently of the result/meaning.

Thus theatre anthropology confronts and compares the techniques of actors and dancers at the transcultural level, and, by means of the study of scenic behaviour, reveals that certain principles governing pre-expressivity are more common and universal than would first have been imagined.

1991, *A Dictionary of Theatre Anthropology: The Secret Art of the Performer*, 7, 187–88

Etienne Decroux (1898–1991): French performer considered "the father of modern mime." Decroux's techniques have been very influential in both dance and theatre.

Dario Fo (1926–): Italian satirical Communist playwright, actor, and director, winner of the 1997 Nobel Prize in Literature. His plays include, in English translation, *The Accidental Death of an Anarchist* (1970), *We Won't Pay, We Won't Pay* (1974), *The Pope and the Witch* (1989), and *The Devil With Boobs* (1997).

Barba derived from working very closely with Asian collaborators such as odissi dancer Sanjukta Panigrahi and buyo dancer Azuma Katsuko (both of whom died relatively young). For example, he claims that the pre-expressive principle of "opposition" is embodied in Indian dance's "tribhangi" position ("three arches"), where the body is bent at three places (neck, torso, hips) to form a figure "S." Barba then illustrates the wide distribution of tribhangi-like poses with photographs of ancient Greek and Renaissance statues, the Aztec goddess Macuilxochitl, ballet dancer **Natalia Makarova** (1940–), actor **Igor Ilinsky** (1901–87), and a 1960s fashion model (**see figure 8.10**). But most of these similarities can be explained by cultural diffusion. There is no need to assert the existence of a universal.

Natalia Makarova (1940–): Russian-born dancer who performed with Russia's Kirov Ballet and later with the American Ballet Theatre.

Igor Ilinsky (1901–87): Russian actor and comedian who worked closely with Meyerhold in developing biomechanics. Ilinsky played Chlestakov in Meyerhold's production of Nikolai Gogol's *The Inspector General* (1926).

More importantly, the dialogue concerning universals would be radically different if Barba paid as much attention to African and African-diaspora performers as he does to Asians. Are the principles of pre-expressivity embodied by Gelede dancers of Nigeria, sambaistas of Brazil, or Trinidad carnival dancers the same as those of odissi in India? If so, in what particular way? Is the tribhangi employed? And why stop there? If one wants universals, examples must be drawn from the widest possible range of cultures. It is not possible to universalize on the basis of a relatively small sampling of examples hand-picked to make a point. This is not to deny that Barba's work is extremely stimulating – and has already proven of great value to theatre artists in various parts of the world. At the same time, the ISTA work is culturally specific. At heart, it exemplifies the Western and now global project of taking from, adapting, generalizing, and exporting the "results" of an analytic process.

Finally, at a theoretical level, the search for universals of performance ancient or contemporary, finished or in formation, transcultural or intercultural, is dubious. Neither Grotowski's performance archaeology in search of practices older and "deeper" (in both senses of that word) than today's practices nor Barba's comparative analysis of Asian and Western genres is likely to come up with anything other than preferences for, and techniques to acquire, specific styles of performing. These may be of artistic merit, but they are not universal in themselves or founded on universal aesthetic principles. Aesthetics, like other aspects of human life, is culture-specific. However, in looking toward Asia for ideas and inspiration, Barba is hardly unique. Many visionary Western theatre artists have, and continue to, look East: Antonin Artaud, Vsevelod Meyerhold, Bertolt Brecht, **Paul Claudel** (1868–1955), Peter Brook, **Lee Breuer** (1937–), **Ariane Mnouchkine**, and **Julie Taymor** (1952–) (a few in a long list).

Lee Breuer (1937–): American director and writer and a co-founder in 1970 of the Mabou Mines experimental theatre company. His productions include the *Animations* series (1970–78), *Gospel at Colonus* (1983), *Epidog* (1996), *Peter and Wendy* (1996), and *Ecco Porco* (2000).

Paul Claudel (1868–1955): French playwright who not only had a deep interest in Japanese noh theatre but wrote noh plays himself.

Julie Taymor (1952–): American theatre and film director and designer. Taymor studied mime in Paris and puppetry in Indonesia, where in the 1970s she started her own group, Teatr Loh. Her more recent work integrates live actors, puppets, and performing objects. Her works include *Juan Darien* (1988), an opera version of *Oedipus* (1992), *The Green Bird* (1996), *The Lion King* (1997), and a film version of Shakespeare's *Titus Andronicus* (1999).

Ariane Mnouchkine (1939–): French theatre and film director who founded the collective ensemble, Theatre du Soleil, in 1964. Productions include *Les Clowns* (1969-70), *1789* and *1793* (1970-73), *Les Shakespeare Cycle* (1981-84), *Sihanouk* (1985), *L'Indiade* (1987-88), *Les Atrides* (1990-93), and *Tartuffe* (1995-96).

fig 8.10. The "tribhangi" position as exemplified in both Asian and Western, high art and popular culture contexts. Shown here are Indian odissi dancer Sanjukta Panigrahi, ballet dancer Natalia Makarova, top row and Russian actor Igor Ilinsky, and an unnamed fashion model, bottom row. Photos courtesy of Eugenio Barba.

Sometimes the encounter though brief and partial is decisive, as was Artaud's experience of Balinese dance-theatre in Paris in 1931. Or it snaps into focus a theory already in formation as it did for Brecht, who in Moscow in 1935 watched Mei Lanfang demonstrate, without costume, lighting, or makeup, a *dan* (female) role from the Chinese theatre, embodying in a definitive way what Brecht called *Verfremdungseffekt* ("alienation effect"). Some artists thoroughly metabolize what they learned in and from Asia, as in the grand spectacles of Mnouchkine's Théâtre du Soleil or the puppet work and visual imagination of Taymor (**see figure 8.11**). Are these activities "Orientalist"? Certainly

most of them would not have occurred except under the aegis of colonialism (even when the artist was actively anti-colonialist). Brook's *The Mahabharata* (1985), an attempt to stage the vast Sanskrit epic, and Mnouchkine's *l'Indiade* (1987), a panoptic performance of a culture and sub-continent, bespeak both the artistic-cultural ambition of these individuals and a more general tendency to control or own the Other that is specific to Orientalism (**see figure 8.12, Carlson box, and Mnouchkine box**). But the process is far from a one-way street (**see Latrell box**). I will discuss these questions further shortly.

fig 8.11. Rafiki watches a herd of gazelles stampede across the African savannah in Julie Taymor's *The Lion King* (1997). Photo by Joan Marcus and Marc Bryan-Brown, courtesy of Julie Taymor.

fig 8.12. Le Théâtre du Soleil's *L'Indiade* (1987) with Andrés Perez-Arya as Mahatma Gandhi. Photo by Michèle Laurent.

Marvin Carlson

Brook's Transnational Theatre

In fact, Brook's *Mahabharata* is absolutely faithful to his entire experimental enterprise, which has been much more directly involved with cultural questions than Mnouchkine's more directly political theatre, but which has from the beginning sought expression which could most properly be characterized not as intercultural but as transcultural. Brook has often spoken of his "international theatre," whose goal is "to articulate a universal art, that transcends narrow nationalism in its attempt to achieve human essence." The fact that nineteen nations are represented by the actors of the *Mahabharata* Brook sees as both a metaphorical and physical indication of the international voice of his theatre. "The truth is global," Brook has observed, "and the stage is the place where the jigsaw should be played." The intention and the strategy is clear, even if the result may be a layering on of cultures rather than a transcendence of them. One Sanskrit scholar, a warm supporter of Brook on the whole, called the idea of an international cast charming, but noted that when one hears a Japanese with a French accent pronouncing an English transliteration of a Sanskrit name, it is hardly surprising that the effect is rather that of a one-man Tower of Babel. [. . .]

The search for the transcultural theatrical experience has occupied Brook's Centre International de Création Théâtrale since its inception [1970]. Indeed it may be said to have been the basic concern of Brook himself for almost two decades, inspiring the research into universal language reflected in *Orghast* and the innumerable performances in remote villages with different cultural backgrounds in many parts of the world. [. . .]

In sum, both the *Mahabharata* and [Mnouchkine's] *L'Indiade* may be seen less as attempts to deal specifically with India or even what the concept of India means to us in terms of difference or otherness than as attempts to utilize images drawn from the Indian experience to construct a theatrical celebration of human brotherhood, either metaphysical or political. Both are appeals to what is imagined to unite all cultures, and this common vision is presented as necessarily positive and grounded on the same bases which ground traditional Western liberal humanism. A potential Otherness of the Indian cultural is absorbed in the universal. For this purpose, the specificity of India itself is not important – China, Southeast Asia, Nigeria, or American Indian myth and history could have served a similar purpose, since the ultimate goal is not to confront the alien element in these cultures but to utilize them as external markers to our own culture upon which to ground a final synthesis. To criticize such productions for failing to speak with the authentic voice of India, as a number of critics have done, is thus to place upon them an expectation quite incompatible with their goals, which are clearly seen by their creators as transcultural rather than intercultural in aim.

1996, "Brook and Mnouchkine: Passages to India?" 88–90

Ariane Mnouchkine

My Source is Asia

Everyone has their sources, that is to say something that sets their imagination to work. In the West we have classical tragedy and the *commedia dell'arte*, which in any case comes from Asia. As far as I am concerned, the origin of theatre and my source is Asia. The West has led us towards realism, and Shakespeare is not realist. For actors who want to be explorers, the Asian tradition can be a base to work from. [. . .]

I do not believe in starting with a clean slate. I don't deny my influences: but you have to know how to choose them if you can.

1996, "The Theatre is Oriental," 96

Craig Latrell

Interculturalism is Not a One-Way Street

We tend to think of "intercultural transfer" or "artistic borrowing" primarily as a one-way phenomenon, something done "by" the West "to" other cultures. Much of the critical rhetoric surrounding this phenomenon has [. . .] an accusatory tone, with Western popular culture pictured as a sort of juggernaut, rolling over helpless local cultures, taking what it wants and in the process ruining fragile indigenous art forms and homogenizing all culture, turning the world into a lowbrow combination of *Baywatch* and Disney. [. . .] Interculturalism is portrayed as something that can only be "explained" by inequities of power between East and West [. . .]. The idea that artists in other societies might be using elements of Western culture for their own reasons is rarely entertained. But why should we deny to other cultures the same sophistication and multiplicity of responses to "foreign" influences that we grant to ourselves in viewing non-Western works? Why should we assume that intercultural transfer is primarily a politically based, one-way phenomenon? [. . .] Why not start with the assumption that other cultures are *not* just passive receivers of Western ideas and images, but active manipulators of such

influences, and that intercultural borrowing is not simply a one-way process, but something far more interestingly dialogic?
[. . .]

   The Minangkabau traditional music ensemble at the tourist center in Bukittinggi, West Sumatra, casually includes in its program a version of a British disco hit (the ever popular *River of Babylon* by Boney M) played on the gongs, considerably altering the disco beat to fit conventional Minangkabau rhythms. In doing so, the musicians are in effect changing the borrowed Western form of disco music as much as they are being changed by it; the resulting hybrid contains elements of both Western disco and Minangkabau traditional music [. . .]. Far from abandoning or tainting formerly pure local forms, the Sumatran musicians are assimilating new influences, and in the process interpreting what they borrow. Such complicated interactions between borrower and borrowed are the rule rather than the exceptions, and narratives of passivity and neocolonialism have little place in this kind of creative activity.

2000, "After Appropriation," 44–47

Integrative Intercultural Performances

Grotowski's and Barba's work are but two examples of the rich variety of intercultural performances (**see Pavis box**). Intercultural performances come in at least two varieties: integrative and disruptive. The integrative is based on the assumption that people from different cultures can not only work together successfully but can harmonize different aesthetic, social, and belief systems, creating fusions or hybrids that are whole and unified. This is not a question of one culture or performance genre absorbing or over-whelming others (as in the "cultural bomb" Ngugi deplores), but of evolving something new from a basis of mutual respect and reciprocity. What Barba attempts at the level of the pre-expressive, the integrators work with at the level of public performance. With regard to rituals and the performances of everyday life, integrative performance hybrids spread on the wings of colonialism, commerce, religion, and the migration of populations.

   Integrative ritual hybrids are so common that they are the dominant mode of actual worship. Even the relatively conservative Roman Catholic Church welcomes elements absorbed over time from a variety of cultural sources. Contemporary Catholic worship in many parts of the world actively includes and integrates local rituals and deities (often transmuted into saints). The Yaqui Waehma is a syncretic ritual drama integrating Native American and Roman Catholic practices. Another example would be the Carnivals of Trinidad or Rio de Janeiro. These integrate African, New World, and European masking, music, dance, and beliefs. Trinidad Carnival also has strong South Asian qualities expressed in music, masking, and dancing. Hinduism has long been receptive to integrating gods and ritual

practices ranging from local spirits and holy places to giving a place to Christian and Old Testament figures. Gandhi was fond of making room for Allah. What is going on in this kind of intercultural performance is a negotiation whereby ideas and practices from both "inside" and "outside" a culture are sorted through, evaluated, interpreted, and reconfigured to suit complex, dynamic situations. The resulting hybrids embody new meanings even as they create new ways of worship and new aesthetics. The process is open ended; change is always occurring.

Hybrid performances: Performances which incorporate elements from two or more different cultures or cultural sources.

   A clear example is the Mami Wata (mother water) worship widespread in sub-Saharan Africa (**see Henry John Drewal box**). This practice mediates between the African and what came to Africa from overseas, transforming aspects of colonial imposition and foreign trade into something positive. When European colonists and Indian merchants moved into Africa, they brought with them new technologies, materials, gods, ritual practices, and beliefs. These fused with indigenous African water spirits. The resulting Mami Wata is a deity who is simultaneously foreign and African, quite literally free-floating, like many of the foreigners in Africa. Mami Wata has no family or social bonds. She rules the waters which surround Africa and articulate the land as rivers and lakes. Mami Wata demands much from her adepts but promises wealth in return. Her worship incorporates African, Indian, and European images and activities – from mermaids

Patrice **Pavis**

What Is Intercultural Theatre?

From our Western perspective, Peter Brook's dramatized adaptation of the epic *Mahabharata* which primarily employed Western performance techniques might be called "intercultural." So might the dramatic and scenic writing of [Hélène] Cixous and [Ariane] Mnouchkine in their staging of Indian history (*L'Indiade*), in which simulated corporeal and vocal techniques were supposed to represent diverse ethnic groups in the Indian subcontinent [see figure 8.12]. Or Barba's rereading of *Faust* for Japanese or Indian dancers. From the perspective of the non-Western *other*, on the contrary, one might examine the ways in which a Japanese director like Suzuki stages Shakespeare or Greek tragedy, using gestural and vocal techniques borrowed from traditional Japanese forms. Or butoh, which acknowledges its debt to German expressionist dance. Although such relationships seem inextricably entangled, there can be no sense in which Asian perspectives are always reversible and symmetrical with those of the West – as a purely functionalist use of the hourglass, turned over and over *ad infinitum*, might lead us naively to believe. Indeed it is perhaps Eurocentrist to imagine that a Japanese perspective, whether that of shingeki ["new" or modern theatre] at the beginning of the [twentieth] century, or that of Suzuki or **Hijikata Tatsumi** (1928–86), [butoh pioneer] in more recent times, also implies the imitation and borrowing of elements from outside its own culture in order to further affirm and stabilize it. [. . .]

"Intercultural" does not mean simply the gathering of artists of different nationalities or national practices in a festival. In this banal sense of *international* (or cosmopolitan), one might say that contemporary theatrical choreographic production has become international, often for simple economic reasons. [. . .]

It is necessary [. . .] to envisage every sort of configuration [. . .] of theatrical interculturalism. Six varieties may be distinguished.

Intercultural theatre. In the strictest sense, this creates hybrid forms drawing upon a more or less conscious and voluntary mixing of performance traditions traceable to distinct cultural areas. The hybridization is very often such that the original forms can no longer be distinguished. [. . .]

Multicultural theatre. The cross-influences between various ethnic or linguistic groups in multicultural societies (e.g. Australia, Canada) have been the source of performances utilizing several languages and performing for a bi- or multicultural public. This sort of exchange is only possible when the political system in place recognizes, if only on paper, the existence of cultural or national communities and encourages their cooperation, without hiding behind the shibboleth of national identity.

Cultural collage. If the intercultural theatre claims to be concerned with the cultural identities of the forms it utilizes [. . .] certain artists, like Robert Wilson [. . .], cite, adapt, reduce, enlarge, combine, and mix various elements without concern for a scale of importance or value. The intercultural becomes the unexpected and quasi-surrealist encounter of cultural debris or – more positively – of cultural material that has been repressed or discredited. [. . .]

Syncretic theatre. [. . .] The creative reinterpretation of heterogeneous cultural material, resulting in the formation of new configurations (for example, the theatre of **Derek Walcott (1930–)** or Wole Soyinka).

Postcolonial theatre. This takes up elements of the home culture (that of ex- or neo-colonization) and employs them from its indigenous perspective, thereby giving rise to a mixture of languages, dramaturgies, and performance processes.

Theatre of the Fourth World. Created by authors or directors belonging to pre-colonization cultures, which have often become minority cultures in relation to that of the colonizers (e.g. the Maoris in New Zealand, Aborigines in Australia, or Indians in Canada and America).

1996, "Introduction: Towards a Theory of Interculturalism in Theatre?" 1–2, 8–10

Hijikata Tatsumi (1928–1986): A founder of butoh, the Japanese dance-theatre that combines traditional Japanese themes and movements with Western experimental performance.

Derek Walcott (1930–): St. Lucian playwright and poet, 1992 winner of the Nobel Prize for Literature. Author of *Dream on Monkey Mountain* (1970) and *The Odyssey: A Stage Version* (1993).

Henry John **Drewal**

Dynamic Hybridity in Africa

In their religious practices involving the water spirit Mami Wata, African peoples from Senegal to Tanzania take exotic images and ideas, interpret them according to indigenous precepts, invest them with new meanings, and then re-create and re-present them in new and dynamic ways to serve their own aesthetic, devotional, and social needs. In so doing, they evaluate and transform external forces, using them to shape their own lives. [. . .] Mami Wata, Pidgin English for "Mother of Water," refers to an African water spirit whom Africans regard as foreign in origin. Africans use the pidgin term to acknowledge the spirit's otherness as well as to indicate its incorporation into the African world. [. . .]

A Yoruba print seller in Togo dramatically illustrates how meanings are constructed and how Mami Wata ritual practices evolve and spread. He uses books on Buddhism, Hinduism, and Occultism as references for his synthesis of foreign and indigenous divinities and the paraphernalia necessary for their worship. [. . .] Since about the First World War, when Indian merchants established firms along the west coast, Africans have been observing their ways, especially Hindu devotions. Many of these rituals are based on the practice of Gujaratis, who predominated among Indian merchants in Africa and were devotees of Lakshmi, the Hindu goddess of wealth [. . .]. Like Mami Wata devotees, Gujaratis place their account books or ledgers on their shrines as objects of veneration. [. . .] These observations and others have resulted in specific ritual practices among Mami Wata worshippers. In Nigeria and Togo, devotees light candles and burn incense during consultation with the spirit called "meditations." One Mina Mami Wata priest displays a photograph of himself taken during his initiation in which he is seated on a Muslim prayer mat in lotus position wearing a turban and signing a *mudra*.

1988, "Performing the Other: Mami Wata Worship in Africa," 160, 174–76

to trance possession to Hindu deities, especially Lakshmi, goddess of wealth. Mami Wata manifests herself in dancing, trance, ventriloquism, and snake charming. Some of her followers dress in combinations of Western, African, and Indian garments, while others present themselves in the lotus position sitting on Muslim prayer rugs signing mudras (**see figure 8.13**).

Such a large number of dance, music, and theatre artists make integrative intercultural performances that it would be impossible to list them all. Three of the better known are Suzuki Tadashi from Japan, **Chandralekha** (birthdate not disclosed) from India, and Philip Glass from the USA. African-American choreographer **Ralph Lemon** (1952–) went on an actual and spiritual journey to Africa and then Asia seeking points of contact out of which to make his trilogy, *Geography* (still in process as of 2001) (**see Lemon box**). In one scene from *Tree*, part two of the trilogy, a Japanese dancer sits listening to a tape of American blues and ballad singer Leadbelly (Huddie Ledbetter) (1885–1949). Immersed in Leadbelly's deep baritone, the Japanese man begins to tap his hand on his thigh, then move his feet. Over the next five minutes, he improvises a dance that is both/neither Japanese nor African American, yet perfectly whole.

The Flying Circus Project of Singapore director **Ong Keng Sen** (1963–) is specifically designed to integrate performance genres/styles from different Asian cultures (**see Ong box and figure 8.14**). Ong's project is fully comprehensible in terms of where and what Singapore is: at the crossroads of trade routes linking Asia, Australia, Africa, and Europe; a city-state consisting of Chinese, Malay, Indian, Indonesian, and European peoples, languages, religions, and aesthetic traditions. Singaporeans are highly conscious of their multiculturality, celebrating rather than denigrating it. They see their ways of handling cultural and technological inputs as a model for future global development elsewhere. Many Singaporeans are also aware of, and not happy with, their

Ralph Lemon (1952–): American choreographer and dancer whose recent work – the *Geography* trilogy (1997–) – emphasizes multicultural and intercultural themes, performers, musics, and dancing. Earlier works include *Joy* (1989) and *Persephone* (1991).

Leadbelly (1885–1949): Born Huddie Ledbetter, this legendary African-American blues and ballad composer and singer was a pardoned murderer and the master of the 12-string guitar.

fig 8.13.

Syncretizing images from a variety of sources, a devotee creates the appearance of Mami Wata by using a black wig, a Western-style dress of imported fabric with a sari-like sash over her left shoulder, an Indian bindu on her forehead and feet, a brace snake in her right hand and holding a trident in her left. The jewelry symbolizes Dan, the celestial serpent. She is seated on a traditional African sacred stool placed on a Muslim prayer rug. Togo, 1975. Photograph by Henry John Drewal.

A formal portrait of a Mami Wata devotee signing an Indian mudra as he sits in a lotus position on a Muslim prayer rug. Togo, 1975. Photo courtesy of Henry John Drewal.

Ong Keng Sen (1953–): artistic director of TheatreWorks Singapore, Ong works interculturally especially with Asian artists. He embraces hybridity. In 1994, he started The Flying Circus Project as a laboratory, to engage the encounter between contemporary urban arts and traditional performance. Ong has also directed and performance curated extensively in Africa, the Americas, and Europe.

Ralph Lemon

How Mysterious We Are to Each Other

Geography, premiered in 1997, featured dancer/musicians from the West Coast of Africa. Fed by West African traditions, religions, and modern sensibilities, the all-male cast performed a passionate theatrical piece, that by conception, explored the nature of race, and unexpectedly evolved into a highly integrated work of spirituality. The performers from Africa fluidly, boldly brought traditions of prayer and "cleansing" to the everyday process of my formal experiments. They did not share my issues with race as an African-American.

After the completion of *Geography Part 1*, I extended my exploration to Asia in search of a perceived belief system. [. . .] I traveled through India, Indonesia, China, and Japan, following the geographical map of Buddhism to Zen, collaborating and sharing questions with performers and musicians contacted throughout the map – a parallel search for diverse but communicable art languages. [. . .] I discovered that the belief systems that I encountered stemmed from the ritual of the art itself, the discipline, the form, thus giving rise to a new exploratory dilemma: How to reconcile ancient traditions with the potential irreverence of [post]modernity dominating a shrinking world? [. . .]

I'm licking my wounds from the amazing onslaught of being in far away places for the past 5 years, experiencing how little of my art past is relevant to the world, and how I can never know another language or culture deeply. But also how essential and common are bodies moving together and laughing.

I found little "spirituality" as theme in *Tree* [part 2 of *Geography*, 1999], which was supposed to be about spirit. [. . .] I find the process is about people, just people. And how mysterious we are to each other.

1999, "Director's Notes," Program for Tree, Yale Repertory Theatre, 9

Ong Keng Sen

Making Intercultural Theatre

My sojourn as a creator, for the past six years [1996–2001], of intercultural projects bringing together traditional Asian arts and contemporary interdisciplinary expression has only just begun. The Flying Circus Project is at the root of my thinking. The Project is an ambitious large-scale laboratory that brings together diverse Asian artists – documentary filmmakers, drag queens, visual artists, rock and computer musicians, disk jockeys, modern dancers, and actors, as well as ritualists, and other traditional performers. For four weeks, different cultures, aesthetics, disciplines, and of course, individual personalities encounter each other in a series of training classes, workshops based on improvisation and reinventing traditional art forms, discussions, and lectures. Thus far, three laboratories have brought together 150 artists from India, Korea, China, Tibet, Taiwan, Vietnam, Cambodia, Laos, Thailand, Myanmar, Japan, Indonesia, the Philippines, Malaysia, and Singapore in a process that I call "cultural negotiation," with no view to end-product or final presentation. The Project has also included a few "guests" from Europe and the USA. The question posed by the Flying Circus Project is, "Can we, as artists from Asia, bring another perspective and forge a different relationship to intercultural performance than what has developed in the United States, for instance?"

In March 2000 I directed *Desdemona* in which 10 artists – actors, musicians, designers, video/installation artists – from India, Korea, Myanmar, Indonesia, and Singapore worked together on stage. *Desdemona* premiered at the Adelaide Festival and then went on to the Munich Dance Festival and the Singapore and Hamburg Festivals. In 2001 it metamorphosed into a visual arts exhibition/performance/outreach program at the Fukuoka Asian Art Museum. [. . .] I wanted to move away from earlier interpretations of *Othello*, especially the obsessive stereotyping of black machismo. What if Othello was played by a woman or by a slight, slender boy? Finally, I cast two Indian performers in this role, a man and a woman: Madhu Margi, a kutiyattam actor, and Maya Rao, a modern theatre actress also trained in kathakali. [. . .]

I wanted to harness a wide range of "contemporary" arts in *Desdemona*. I wanted the contradictions of traditional and contemporary exposed rather than glossed into unity. Maya Rao hinted at Othello, his father, the female within him, and much more. Maya wanted a flow between male and female. Opposed to narrow portrayals of gender that would reinforce stereotypes, she was not costumed/made up to look like a man. Rather than play two characters, she represented the male and female aspects in Othello.

My method of constantly creating different performance drafts, turning written scenes on their heads, developing extensive performance texts, multiple focal points and multiple realities, parallel texts of music and visual arts was difficult for the traditional artists. [. . .] But I was intent on driving a dense, intense, stream of consciousness into the psyche of the two central characters. This required multiple layering, quick shifts into surrealism, abstraction, symbolism, the fracturing of self into different parts and nonlinearity. [. . .] Ultimately, *Desdemona* is a cultural study about a group of Asian artists looking at themselves and rethinking the ways in which Asia has been represented on the stage in the past.

2001, "Encounters," 126–29

fig 8.14. Othello (Madhu Margi) performs the role of the puppeteer manipulating Desdemona (Claire Wong) in Ong Keng Sen's *Desdemona* in the version presented at the Adelaide Festival in 2000. Photograph courtesy of Ong Keng Sen.

authoritarian government. At the same time, they will tell you that this regimented way of life is the price paid for economic success.

Ong's project is an example both of Barba's investigations into Eurasian performance and of Singapore playwright **Kuo Pao Kun's** (1939–) proposal for an "open culture" (**see Kuo box**). The workshops and productions of Flying Circus aim toward but do not achieve seamless integration. As Ong himself notes, "the contradictions of traditional and contemporary are exposed rather than glossed into unity." It takes a longer time and the practice of many artists for whom

the hybrid genre is "natural" for there to be unity. Such is the case of butoh, which combines traditional Japanese approaches to the body, movement, and meditation with impulses drawn from Western modern dance and experimental performance. Similarly, jazz and blues are musical genres with deep roots in Africa and the African diaspora played on Euro-American instruments sung in vocal styles that draw on African and Euro-American traditions. Trinidad's rich musical expression includes "chutney soca," soul-calypso played/sung to a South Asian beat.

Kuo Pao **Kun**

Open Culture – The Global Perspective

Open Culture proposes that the fundamentals of the nurturing process no longer be racially based. Not even bi-culturally and bilingually. A quantum leap must be made onto the global level. Instead of *Multiculturalism* (the twin of *Multiracialism* in Singapore), Singapore's education should begin actively evolving a global awareness. However, while the vision reaches for the global, the footing remains rooted in Indian, Chinese, Malay, European cultures as its primary base or launching point. This will be necessary as a general policy until the people are ready to collectively, and individually, choose otherwise.

Shifting to a global perspective would make it necessary for every student to internalize an overview of the *cultures of the world*. [. . .] This requires an institutional shift in syllabus and allocation of resources to a global perspective. Similarly, the choice of third and fourth languages and cultures must become more open – until it reaches the full spectrum of world cultures. [. . .]

Open Culture is based on several fundamentals: First, every individual should be deeply rooted in at least one culture. Second, every individual should be given the choice to begin one's opening up by first deepening the organic culture one is living by, that is, one's parent culture. Third, the cultural development of the individual should be de-linked from the racial and linguistic origin of the individual. Fourth, every student should be exposed, generally, to an overview of the cultures of the world and, specifically, to at least two cultures in depth. Fifth, the state should recognize culture as a primary, core area of study [. . .]. In short, *Open Culture* contemplates a transcendence of the individual from race and tradition-bound communities to embrace a diverse global community. [. . .]

It is mainly in the realm of culture – especially in intellectual explorations and artistic creations – that the deeper human issues and problems can be identified, analyzed, debated, explored, experimented with, and resolved. For, metaphorically, culture is a huge laboratory and a vast *Play Space* where current ideas and practices are challenged, classical models are re-examined, gut impulses are articulated, fantastic imaginations are exploded, outrageous proposals are tested, and new ways and means are explored. [. . .] *Open Culture* provides resources and provokes dynamic interaction; it is the necessary ambience for enhanced creativity. This very openness, however, also makes it impossible to predict results. *Open Culture* begets Open Futures.

1998, "Contemplating an Open Culture," 57–60

Guillermo Gómez-Peña: Border Wars

Intercultural performances need not aim for integration. Many artists want to expose the difficulties and explore the creative possibilities of playing across national, cultural, artistic, and personal borders. This brand of intercultural performance refuses utopian schemes, uncloaks and parodies power relations, and promotes a critical ideological perspectives. At present, there is no better exemplar both practically and in enunciating its theory than Guillermo Gómez-Peña. Working both solo and in collaboration (especially with Coco Fusco and **Roberto Sifuentes** (1967–)), GGP probes the ambivalences, fears, disruptions, and hilarities occurring when and where cultures collide, overlap, or pull away from each other (**see Gómez-Peña box 2**).

Since the late 1970s, Gómez-Peña has created hybrids made from (in his own words) Mexican *carpa* (urban popular

Border art: Works that seek to blur, challenge, or ironically emphasize distinctions between national and/or cultural identities, calling attention to the arbitrary and socially constructed nature of the nation and national cultures.

Roberto Sifuentes (1967–): Chicano performance artist who has collaborated with Guillermo Gómez-Peña on several works including *The Temple of Confessions* (1994) and *Techno-Dioramas* (1999).

theatre), magical realism, kabuki, and US multimedia with the goal of demolishing monoculture. GGP's early performance world was populated by Mister Misterio, a Mexican detective/poet, Misterio's friend, the burned out ballerina Salome Zentit, a Wrestler Shaman, a multimedia Pachuco, an Aztec princess working as a cabaret chanteuse, and an androgynous Maori warrior opera singer. For some performances, GGP constructed multimedia altars with a video monitor as the main ikon. Before performing, GGP and his co-performers made elaborate rituals to reach a trancelike state but it is not clear if they actually did so or parodied such rituals. But can the distinction between the "real" and the "parody" be definitively made? Later GGP figures include Border Brujo, Warrior Gringostroika, Humble Mariachi Player, and El Mad Mex (**see figure 8.15**). In all these guises and enactments, GGP and his colleagues combine parody, irony, ritual, popular arts, and social commentary.

GGP is a performance artist, critical theorist, poet, and provocateur. He enacts his belief that nomadism and migration are the central experiences of our epoch. In the

Guillermo Gómez-Peña

I Carry the Border With Me

I am a nomadic Mexican artist/writer in the process of Chicanization, which means I am slowly heading North. My journey not only goes from South to North, but from Spanish to Spanglish, and then to English; from ritual art to high technology; from literature to performance art; and from a static sense of identity to a repertoire of multiple identities. Once I get "there," wherever it is, I am forever condemned to return, and then to obsessively reenact my journey. In a sense, I am a border Sisyphus. [. . .]

I make art about the misunderstandings that take place at the border zone. But for me, the border is no longer located at any fixed geopolitical site. I carry the border with me, and I find new borders wherever I go. [. . .]

When I am on the East Coast of the United States, I am also in Europe, Africa, and the Caribbean. There, I like to visit Nuyo Rico, Cuba York, and other micro-republics. When I return to the U.S. Southwest, I am suddenly back in Mexamerica, a vast conceptual nation that also includes the northern states of Mexico, and overlaps with various Indian nations. [. . .]

The work of the artist is to force open the matrix of reality to introduce unsuspected possibilities. Artists and writers are currently involved in the redefinition of our continental topography. We see through the colonial map of North, Central, and South America, to a more complex system of overlapping, interlocking, and overlaid maps. Among others, we can see Amerindia, Afroamerica, Americamestiza-y-mulata, Hybridamerica, and Transamerica – the "other America" that belongs to the homeless, and to nomads, migrants, and exiles.

1996, *The New World Border*, 1, 5–6

mid-1980s, GGP was a founder of the Border Arts Workshop / El Taller de Arte Fronterizo. One of BAW/TAF's actions was placing a table on the beach at Tijuana-San Diego where Mexico and the USA meet. At first the Mexicans sat in Mexico, the North Americans in the USA. Then they "illegally" held hands and passed food across the border; then they rotated the table so that each group sat in the national territory of the other. Whose border is it, anyway?

From 1988 to 1990 GGP was possessed by Border Brujo, a figure of fifteen personae each speaking a different "border language" such as Spanish, English, Spanglish, and tongues. According to GGP Border Brujo was a character, a performance artist, an alternative chronicler of community life, a cultural prisoner, a homeless shaman, and the village fool. He appeared in galleries, community centers, migrant-worker camps, political rallies, museums, and theatres. Border Brujo taught GGP how to cross the borders of cultures, communities, institutions, and territories. Increasingly, he enacted a radical and experimental hybridity (**see Gómez-Peña box 3**).

Guillermo Gómez-Peña

Hybrid Culture is Experimental and Radical

My version of the hybrid is cross-racial, polylinguistic, and multicontextual. From a disadvantaged position, the hybrid expropriates elements from all sides to create more open and fluid systems. Hybrid culture is community-based yet experimental, radical but not static or dogmatic. It fuses "low" and "high" art, primitive and high-tech, the problematic notions of self and other, the liquid entities of North and South, East and West.

An ability to understand the hybrid nature of culture develops from an experience of dealing with a dominant culture from the outside. The artist who understands and practices hybridity in this way can be at the same time an insider and an outsider, an expert in border crossings, a temporary member of multiple communities, a citizen of two or more nations. S/he performs multiple roles in multiple contexts. At times s/he can operate as a cross-cultural diplomat, as an intellectual *coyote* (smuggler of ideas) or a media pirate. At other times, s/he assumes the role of nomadic chronicler, intercultural translator, or political trickster. S/he speaks from more than one perspective, to more than one community, about more than one reality. His/her job is to trespass, bridge, interconnect, re-interpret, remap, and redefine; to find the outer limits of his/her culture and cross them.

1996, *The New World Border*, 12

fig 8.15. Some of Guillermo Gómez-Peña's many guises. All photographs courtesy of Guillermo Gómez-Peña.

El Warrior Gringostroika in his wrestler's mask. Photograph by Eugenio Castro.

Border Brujo and "Aztec" Carmel Kooros draw their weapons.

A Humble Mariachi Player shakes hands with a NAFTA diplomat (Roberto Sifuentes).

El Mad Mex. Photograph by Eugenio Castro.

In 1992–93, in response to the many mainstream celebrations of the 500th anniversary of **Christopher Columbus**' (1451–1506) "discovery" of the "New World," GGP and Coco Fusco devised a performance that parodied how "exotic peoples" were (and sometimes still are) exhibited by and to Europeans and Euro-Americans (**see Fusco box**). Displayed as just discovered "primitive" Amerindians from an island in the Gulf of Mexico, Fusco and GGP lived for three days in a 12-foot square golden cage in Madrid's Columbus Plaza (**see figure 8.16**). After Madrid, the exhibit was seen in London, Sydney, several locations in the USA, and Buenos Aires. The "Guatinauis" carried on their daily lives under the gaze of spectators: sewing voodoo dolls, reciting stories in gibberish, watching TV, lifting weights, and working on a laptop computer. The Guatinauis posed for Polaroid photos. For a small donation, Fusco danced to rap music. At New York's Whitney Museum, a glimpse of "authentic Guatinaui male genitals" cost $5. A handout pinpointed on a map the couple's home island, explaining in ethnographic style who the "specimens" were, their height and weight, what they ate (Diet Coke and burritos), their place in the Guatinaui social hierarchy ("His frequent pacing in the cage leads experts to believe that he was a political leader on his island," "Her facial and body decorations indicate that she has married into the upper caste of her tribe"), and their personalities ("quite affectionate in the cage, seemingly uninhibited in their physical and sexual habits"). Two guards led them on leashes to the toilet and fielded questions from viewers because the "natives" knew no European languages. Many persons knew this was a politically savvy performance, but a surprising number did not – believing that "real natives" were on display. And why not? Exhibiting the "exotic other" is well documented in the colonial archive.

Christopher Columbus (Cristoforo Colombo) (1451–1506): Italian explorer who in 1492, while searching for a westward passage to Asia under commission from Queen Isabella of Spain, "discovered" the Americas by landing on several Caribbean islands. He claimed the "new" lands he touched for the Spanish crown and inaugurated the modern colonial period.

Coco **Fusco**

Two Undiscovered Amerindians Visit . . .

Our plan was to live in a golden cage for three days, presenting ourselves as undiscovered Amerindians from an island in the Gulf of Mexico that had somehow been overlooked by Europeans for five centuries. [. . .] Our project concentrated on the "zero degree" of intercultural relations in an attempt to define a point of origin for the debates that link "discovery" and "Otherness." We worked within disciplines that blur distinctions between the art object and the body (performance), between fantasy and reality (live spectacle), and between history and dramatic reenactment (the diorama). The performance was interactive, focusing less on what we did than on how people interacted with us and interpreted our actions. Entitled *Two Undiscovered Amerindians Visit [.]*, we chose not to announce the event through prior publicity or any other means when it was possible to exert such control; we intended to create a surprise or "uncanny" encounter, one in which audiences had to undergo their own process of reflection as to what they were seeing, aided only by written information and parodically didactic zoo guards. In such encounters with the unexpected, people's defense mechanisms are less likely to operate with their normal efficiency; caught off guard their beliefs are more likely to rise to the surface.

Our performance was based on the once popular European and North American practice of exhibiting indigenous people from Africa, Asia, and the Americas in zoos, parks, taverns, museums, freak shows, and circuses. While this tradition reached the height of its popularity in the 19th century, it was actually begun by Christopher Columbus, who returned from his first voyage in 1492 with several Arawaks, one of whom was left on display at the Spanish court for two years.

1995, "The Other History of Intercultural Performance," 39–40

fig 8.16. Guillermo Gómez-Peña and Coco Fusco as "newly discovered Amerindians" on display in Madrid in 1992. Photograph by Nancy Lytle courtesy of Coco Fusco.

The performance subverted the already blurred boundaries between ethnography, art, and tourism. Reactions were extremely varied. Even those who knew this was an "art performance" readily played the role of colonizer – gazing, probing, objectifying. Some who were taken in tried to free the imprisoned natives; others complained to museum or gallery administrators about the horror of such an exhibition. Many simply enjoyed the exhibit at face value: "interesting, unusual, and rare natives on display." Some wanted to have sex with the Guatinauis. A few thought they were actors working for other artists who conceived the performance but would not participate in it. At the University of California-Irvine, the Environmental Health and Safety Office worried that the excrement of "real aborigines" in the gallery would be a health hazard. The performance exposed uncomfortable parallels between international arts festivals, colonial expositions, museum displays, and tourist expeditions.

If *Two Undiscovered Amerindians Visit* . . . played on the trope of colonial curiosity, objectifying the Other, and the pleasures/horrors of exploitation, the GGP–Sifuentes 1994–96 collaboration, the *Temple of Confessions*, conflated ethnographic and religious dioramas with people's real desire for spiritual experience. GGP and Sifuentes displayed themselves in Plexiglas boxes as scientific specimens of the last two living saints from a "border region." Spectators were invited not only to gaze on these exotic beings but to confess their "intercultural fears and desires" to them.

The performance artists were not prepared for the reception they got when the exhibit premiered at the Scottsdale Center for the Arts near Phoenix, Arizona. Hundreds thronged the exhibit to confess (in GGP's words) "their innermost feelings, fantasies, and memories of Mexico, Mexicans, Chicanos, and other people of color."

As the *Temple* toured Mexico and the USA, the reactions varied from fascination to anger to sharing innermost secrets. The performance itself changed to suit particular circumstances. GGP's trademark cultural pastiche style was in full force: on his ghetto blaster he mixed Gregorian chants with rap, circus music, Mexican waltzes, and Indian blues. He and Sifuentes shared their Plexiglas booths (reminiscent of television quiz shows, Eichmann on trial, church relics, and museum exhibit cases) with roaches, crickets, an iguana, fake "tribal" musical instruments, and various other items eclectically assembled. But, as GGP notes, from a distance the pair looked "authentic." "I could have been an indigenous shaman in a diorama sponsored by the *National Geographic*." Only close up did people see that these performers were Benetton advertisement primitives, more MTV than . . . but who is to say that MTV isn't authentic? Despite this, throughout the two-year life of the performance, GGP wrote, "Visitors attempted to establish a personal 'spiritual' connection with me. Their eyes looked desperately for mine. If I decided to engage in a personalized relation with them (mainly through eye contact, symbolic hand motions or subvocalizing), emotions began to pour from both sides: vulnerability, guilt, anger, tenderness. Some people cried, and in doing so, they made me cry. Some expressed their sexual desire for me, and I discreetly reciprocated. Others spewed their hatred, their contempt and their fear, and I willingly took it. At least a third of the visitors eventually decided to kneel and confess" (*Dangerous Border Crossers*, 38).

Answering Globalization: New Genre Public Art

The real feelings evoked by the ersatz *Temple of Confessions* reveal a need for living contact and interaction, a counterforce to the alienation and homogeny of globalization. Globalization is opposed on many fronts. Political demonstrators disrupt meetings of the WTO and other gatherings of the world's economic masters. Artists expose the contradictions between globalization's hype and the exploitation, displacement, and impoverishment that are what globalization has delivered to most of the world's very poor. But for all the action, there is also a sense of resigned desperation: globalization, like industrialization in the nineteenth century, is not going away. A more positive response has been the growth of community-based, identity-based, and minoritarian performances. These take many forms. In the Third World there is much "theatre for development," some organized by governments, some by NGOs. Theatre for

fig 8.17. Suzanne Lacy's *Whisper, The Waves, The Wind* (1984). Photographs by John Warner. Photos courtesy of Suzanne Lacy.

An overview of the beach and tables where the women sat and talked.

One table with four older women conversing.

Suzanne Lacy

From Private to Public Artist

PRIVATE   PUBLIC

*———————————▶ *———————————▶ *———————————▶*

artist as   artist as   artist as   artist as
experiencer   reporter   analyst   activist

Experiencer. [. . .] In August 1991, I sat for seven days in an abandoned hospital room at Roswell Park Cancer Center in upstate New York, charting the private conversations I had with patients, nurses, doctors, scientists, and administrators. The artwork was located in the interaction between myself as artist and the members of the community, framed by the hospital room and fueled by the human need to reflect on the meaning of one's life and work. [. . .]

Reporter. In the role of the reporter, the artist focuses not simply on the experience but on the recounting of the situation; that is, the artist gathers information to make it available to others. She calls our attention to something. [. . .] Reporting might be compared to aesthetic framing. [. . .] Reporting involves a conscious selection, though not necessarily an analysis, of information. [. . .]

Analyst. From reporting, or presenting information, to analysis is a short step, but the implied shift in the artist's role is enormous. [. . .] As artists begin to analyze social situations through their art, they assume for themselves skills more commonly associated with social scientists, investigative journalists, and philosophers. [. . .] When an artist adopts the position of analyst, the visual appeal of imagery is often superseded by the textual properties of the work, thus challenging conventions of beauty. Their analysis may assume its aesthetic character from the coherence of the ideas or from their *relationship* to visual images rather than through the images themselves.

Activist. The last step along the proposed continuum is from analysis to activism, where art making is contextualized within local, national, and global situations, and the audience becomes an active participant. In seeking to become catalysts for change, artists reposition themselves as citizen-activists. Diametrically opposed to the aesthetic practices of the isolated artist, consensus building inevitably entails developing a set of skills not commonly associated with art making. [. . .] Entirely new strategies must be learned: how to collaborate, how to develop multilayered and specific audiences, how to cross over with other disciplines, how to choose sites that resonate with public meaning, and how to clarify visual and process symbolism for people who are not educated in art.

1995, "Debated Territory: Toward a Critical Language for Public Art," 174–77

Lucy R. Lippard

The Local is the Global

National, global, collective narratives are especially accessible through one's family history – by asking simple questions about why we moved from one block or city or state or country to another, gained or lost jobs, married or didn't marry whom we did, kept track of or lost track of certain relatives. A starting point, for example: simple research about the place where you lived or were raised. Who lived there before? What changes have been made? have you made? [. . .] What Native peoples first inhabited it? [. . .] Do any animals live there? And on a broader scope, are you satisfied with the present? If not, are you nostalgic of the past or longing for the future? And so forth.

Questions like these can set off a chain of personal and cultural reminiscences and ramifications, including lines of thought about interlinking histories, the unacknowledged American class system, racial, gender, and cultural divisions and common grounds, land use/abuse, geography, environment, town planning, and the experience of nature that has made a "return" to it so mythical. When this kind of research into social belonging is incorporated into the interactive or participatory art forms, collective views of place can be arrived at. It provides ways to understand how human occupants are also part of the environment rather than merely invaders (but that too). [. . .] As we look at ourselves critically, in social contexts, as inhabitants, users, onlookers, tourists, we can scrutinize our own participatory roles in the natural processes that are forming our futures.

1995, "Looking Around: Where We Are, Where We Could Be," 115–16

José Muñoz

Mapping Out Alternative Worlds

Minoritarian performance labors to make worlds — worlds of transformative politics and possibilities. Such performance engenders worlds of ideological potentiality that alter the present and map out a future. Performance is thus imbued with a great deal of power. But what is meant [. . .] by "worldmaking"? The concept of worldmaking delineates the ways in which performances — both theatrical and everyday rituals — have the ability to establish alternate views of the world. These alternative vistas are more than simply views or perspectives; they are oppositional ideologies that function as critiques of oppressive regimes of "truth" that subjugate minoritarian people. Oppositional counterpublics are enabled by visions, "worldviews," that reshape as they deconstruct reality. Such counterpublics are the aftermath of minoritarian performance. Such performances *transport* the performer *and* the spectator to a vantage point where transformation and politics are imaginable. Worldmaking performances produce these vantage points by slicing into the facade of the real that is the majoritarian public sphere. Disidentificatory performances opt to do more than simply tear down the majoritarian public sphere. They disassemble that sphere [. . .] and use its parts to build an alternative reality. Disidentification uses the majoritarian culture as raw material to make a new world.

1999, *Disidentifications*, 195–96

development helps people cope with, and where possible take advantage of, the changes being wrought by globalization. Augusto Boal's Theatre of the Oppressed is another response to globalization.

Performance artist Suzanne Lacy has from the early 1970s addressed social issues by devising site-specific performances with local people. In *Whisper, the Waves, the Wind* (1984) 154 older women dressed in white sat at white-cloth-covered tables on the beach at La Jolla, California talking to each other about their lives and especially how it felt to grow old (**see figure 8.17**). Their conversations, microphoned and mingled with the sounds of wind and ocean, were overheard by spectators standing above the beach. Three years later, in *The Crystal Quilt*, Lacy arranged a similar performance after hours in a Minneapolis department store, where 430 older women

dressed in black sat and spoke to each other. The purpose of these performances was to give voice to people and communities often ignored. Over the years, Lacy and other artists have developed ways to involve themselves in different communities. In these involvements, artists can assume several personae: as experiencer, reporter, analyst, and activist (**see Lacy box**).

The movement from the personal to the local to the global embedded in the local is a well-trod path (**see Lippard box**). A large number of community-based performances are based on the premise that what is specific to a place and a community is also generalizable. On one level, it is necessary to preserve the local in the interest of cultural diversity — both actual and virtual diversity. Some minoritarian performances involve "world-making," inventing creative alternatives to mainstream media, values, laws, and styles (**see Muñoz box**). Cultural diversity must be thought of in lifestyle as well as ethnic and religious terms. On another level, giving voice to local issues – such as opposition to a dam that will flood out the farms and homes of thousands, or demanding a boycott of products made by sweatshop or slave labor – transforms the personal into the political as the particular engages global issues. From AIDS activists and Greenpeace staging guerrilla theatre to Palestinians mounting a drama about the destruction of their village by the Israeli army to Northern Irish parading for or against the British presence, performance is a way to embody concerns, express opinions, and forge solidarity. How the environment is managed, wars prevented, occupying armies expelled, or pandemics treated are questions inextricably enmeshed in the globalization process.

Terrorism and Performance

Terrorists use violence as both an instrument of war and as symbolic performance. Although terrorism has been practiced for more than a century, the 11 September 2001 attacks on New York and Washington were different because of their magnitude, the intention to humiliate and destabilize the world's superpower, and the extraordinarily performative quality of the attacks. More than 3,000 persons were killed when commercial airliners were hijacked and then crashed into New York's World Trade Center and Washington's Pentagon building, the headquarters of the U.S. Defense Department (**figure 8.18**). A few weeks after 11 September the spread of anthrax through the mail further increased America's state of anxiety and disorientation (**see McNeil box**). In order both to reassure the American public by "taking action" and to avenge the deaths and damage, beginning in October 2001, the American government orchestrated a war in Afghanistan against the Taliban Islamic fundamentalist government and the Al Qaeda terrorist network of **Osama bin Laden** (1957–). The Taliban was ousted, but bin Laden remained at large. From time to time, bin Laden appeared on videotape praising the attack on America. President **George W. Bush** (1946–)countered with speeches declaring that America will "bring bin Laden to justice, dead or alive."

Both bin Laden and Bush reduced the complexities of the situation to a performative either/or by casting the other side as "evil." Categories such as "good" and "evil" and terms such as "tragedy" and "jihad" (holy war) invoke a highly theatrical protagonist-antagonist conflict. No doubt it is easier to

mobilize popular support – on Main Street America and on the streets of the Third World – by means of theatre than by employing nuanced analyses. In the American media, the destruction of the World Trade Center brought forth repeated allusions to "tragedy." But does this classical category fit what happened (**see Taylor box 1**)?

> **Anthrax:** An acute infectious disease caused by the spore-forming bacterium bacillus anthracis. Anthrax most commonly occurs in cattle, sheep, goats, camels, and other herbivores, but can also infect humans. In 2001, anthrax spores were sent through the mail infecting a number of people in Washington, New York, and elsewhere.

The attacks on New York and Washington were shocking not only because of their audacity and precision but also because the effects were immediate and enormous. America was hit simultaneously in its capitalist and military heart. Air traffic was halted nationally, the vice-president was removed to a "safe location" in case the president were killed, and the president himself was shuttled aloft for a number of hours to avoid being a sitting target. What had been a moderate economic slow down became a full-blown recession. The anthrax bio-warfare further unnerved people. No longer were targets limited to obvious symbols of power. Spreading disease via the postal system – and whatever other means may be employed – makes a most ordinary action, the handling or opening of a letter, potentially deadly. Almost as if to perform the difference between secrecy and display, thousands of American flags were flown all over the country. If capitalism and the "American way of (relatively carefree) life" were their targets, the terrorists scored bull's-eyes.

The media amplified many of these effects. Surely the sudden loss of so many lives is a terrifying event, but within recent times the world has suffered many atrocities of much greater magnitude which the media has paid much less attention to. September 11th was almost immediately translated into a global spectacle of awesomely televisable clips. This specularity was no accident, either on the part of the hijackers or of the media.

The world was given free tickets to a real-life made-for-media movie (**see Gabler box** p. 269). The images from New York uncannily resembled *The Towering Inferno*, the *Godzilla* movies, and other catastrophe films where terrified, panicked crowds flee down the canyons of Manhattan ahead of fire, smoke, and debris. Although the Pentagon was also hit, and a hijacked plane crashed in Pennsylvania, apparently after passengers resisted the hijackers, New York took center stage.

fig 8.18. New York's World Trade Center under attack, 11 September 2001. Photograph by Robert A. Patrick.

Donald G. McNeil, Jr.

Why Does The World Hate America?

T-shirts lionizing Osama bin Laden are hits with those who feel themselves the world's dispossessed and see the terrorists striking a blow against an overweening superpower: in Algerian-populated suburbs of Paris and the Cape Flats of South Africa, in the streets of Cairo and Jakarta. [. . .]

The American notion that anger at America is simply resentment of its culture, that foreigners are unhappy because McBurgers outsells escargots or Stallone outsells Truffaut, is seen overseas as just more American smugness.

When foreign writers complain about America now, their complaints are quite specific, and foreign-policy oriented: America should not silently let the Israelis commit assassinations, bulldoze houses, and colonize Palestinian land; America should pay attention to Muslim fury that American troops occupy the land of the Prophet Muhammad [Saudi Arabia]; America should not bomb dirt-poor Afghan cities with no antiaircraft defenses.

When old sores are scratched, they are usually about American foreign policies: [. . .] the 1973 coup encouraged by Richard Nixon that killed Chile's elected president, Salvador Allende, also began on Sept. 11. Eduardo Galeano, a Mexican journalist, asked why 5,000 New York deaths were televised, but not the deaths of 200,000 Guatemalans "sacrificed not by Muslim fanatics but by terrorist militias supported by successive American governments." A commentary in Britain's left-leaning *Guardian* newspaper said the United States had been "training terrorists" in its Fort Benning, Ga., school for Latin American soldiers and police officers for 55 years and suggested that the British bomb Georgia and also drop packages of nan and curry stamped with the Afghan flag.

2001, "More and More, Other Countries see the War as Solely America's," B1,2.

Osama bin Laden (1957–): A member of one of Saudi Arabia's wealthiest families and founder in 1988 of the Al Qaeda ("the base") terrorist network. Bin Laden is believed to mastermind and finance terrorist actions including the 2001 attacks on New York's World Trade Center and Washington's Pentagon. In 1998, he issued an edict to his fundamentalist Islamic followers: "kill the Americans and their allies, civilians, and military." He is vehemently anti-American, anti-Western, and anti-Israeli. Bin Laden's headquarters were in Afghanistan where he enjoyed the protection of the Taliban regime.

George W. Bush (1946–): 43rd President of the United States and the eldest son of the 41st President, George Herbert Walker Bush. George W. was born in Connecticut but raised in Texas where he worked in the oil business before becoming in 1989 a co-owner of the Texas Rangers baseball team. In 1995, Bush was elected governor of Texas. He won the presidency in 2000 only after the intervention of the United States Supreme Court which stopped the recounting of ballots in Florida (whose governor was Jeb Bush, the President's brother).

The networks contained, packaged, labeled, and capitalized on the attacks and the war that followed. News programs were titled as if they were mini-series: "War on Terror," "America's New War," "Target Terrorism," "America Rising," and the most ironic of all, CNN's and NBC's "America Strikes Back," calling to mind the second of the *StarWars* movies, *The Empire Strikes Back*. What's the sequel, *Return of the Jihad*?

Ironically, even as terrorists oppose globalization, they are creatures of globalization. Without integrated systems of banking, communications, media, and transportation, organizations such as Al Qaeda cannot function. The sternest messages of Islamic fundamentalism are delivered via videotape and disseminated by means of satellite. The fact is that West no longer equals West, South no longer equals South, East no longer equals East. Globalization is not only a system of dominance, it is a system of dissolving boundaries, subverting nations, mixing up populations, and taking advantage of all available technologies. Significant pockets of "West" exist everywhere; and equally significant cultural presences of "non-West" thrive in the West.

Diana Taylor

A Different Kind of Tragedy

When I saw the north tower in flames – about five minutes after the first plane hit – I thought, "God, it's going to take a lot of time and money to fix that." A small community of watchers gathered in the street. [. . .] Others joined us. "Were there people trapped inside?" it finally occurred to us to ask. Traffic stopped. Then the second plane. Another explosion. More people. Even then we didn't start speculating about deliberate terrorists attacks. That happened only after word of the Pentagon filtered onto the street. We stood transfixed, watching, witnesses without a narrative, part of a tragic chorus that stumbled onto the wrong set. The city stopped. The phones went dead, cars vanished, stores closed, the towers folded. [. . .] Some hours later I heard that the attack that we had witnessed was now being called 'war,' albeit a "different kind of war." The world was suddenly being re-shuffled into those who stood by 'us' and those who turned against 'us.'

Tragedy, as an aesthetic category, turns around the challenge of containment. Can Oedipus curb the tide of devastation that has wrecked Thebes? Hamlet's inability to act decisively leads to generalized death and the loss of the kingdom. Yet, tragedy is not just about containment, it functions as a structure of containment. [. . .] The massive potential for destruction depicted in tragedy is contained by the form itself – for tragedy delivers the devastation in a miniaturized and 'complete' package, neatly organized with a beginning, middle and an end. Ultimately, tragedy assures us, the crisis will be resolved and balance will be restored. The fear and pity we, as spectators, feel will be purified by the action.

The events of September 11th, however, make me think that we're not only looking at a different kind of war but also a different kind of tragedy. When people refer to the 'September 11th tragedy,' they usually refer to that awesome spectacle of pity and fear so brilliantly executed by the suicide pilots and so efficiently delivered nationally and globally by the U.S. media. They refer to the hijacked planes and the thousands of victims, whose smiling faces and life-stories appear on Xeroxed sheets taped to phone booths, mailboxes, and hospital walls. President George W. Bush, hastily re-cast as a leader with a definable moral character, sets out to set time right. All of these events are certainly tragic in the popular understanding of the term, and it offers us a language to talk about them. Yet, I think that using tragedy in its aesthetic connotation not only 'structures' the events but also blinds us to other ways of thinking about them.

Take tragedy's organizational timetable: beginning, middle and end. Did the tragic action really start on September 11th? Some might argue that we were hijacked long before September 11th, maybe starting in the fall of 2000 when the elections were pulled off course. Important items on the American national agenda, such as improving education and health-care, for example, went up in smoke. The victims from that catastrophe remain uncounted, although they are certainly identified. New victims are created daily as anti-terrorist legislation, anti-immigrant sentiment, and corporate welfare packages wind their way through the House and Senate. Others might point out that we have been on a seemingly inevitable collision course with Islamic, oil-producing nations for decades. Should the civilian losses they have sustained figure in among the victims? As for the ending, nothing seems certain except that it won't be speedy, make sense, or bring purification and release. [. . .]

September 11th created a revealing paradox. This was an event that, because of the time lag between the first hit and the fall of the last tower, produced a huge number of eyewitnesses. Moreover, they responded as citizens, who wanted to help their fellows by giving blood or volunteering. It soon became clear that their protagonism was not needed. Bush and Giuliani asked people to respond as consumers by visiting malls and attending Broadway plays. When witnesses visited ground zero to commemorate the loss, the Mayor accused them of 'gawking.' We should, it seems, know these events only through the media. In other words, this is an event that has banished and blinded the witnesses, even as it created them. Will purification and release come from participating in polls asking whether we support war efforts?

Talk of 'tragedy', like talk of 'war,' in relation to the September 11th attacks gives the events a sense of clarity, directionality, and moral purpose that they do not have. I only wish they did.

Forthcoming, written for a "Forum on Tragedy" of *Theatre Journal*, in press

Neal Gabler

Terrorism with an Audience in Mind

Over and over Tuesday [11 September 2001], after the planes tore through the World Trade Center towers and then the Pentagon, benumbed spectators said the same words: "It was like a movie."

Which was to say they had seen it before in countless disaster movies. The explosion and fireball, the crumpling buildings, the dazed and panicked victims, even the grim presidential address assuring action would be taken – all were familiar, as if they had been lifted from some Hollywood blockbuster. [. . .]

None of this could have been lost on the perpetrators of this tragedy. American films [. . .] now reach every corner of the world and their images colonize the imaginations of virtually everyone – one reason Muslim fundamentalists so hate America. They certainly understand the power of those visuals. So in attacking the symbols of American finance and American security, it may have been no accident that they chose the language of American movies. [. . .] You have to believe at some level it was their rebuff to Hollywood as well as their triumph over it – they could out-Hollywood Hollywood.

Consider the timing. When the first plane hit the World Trade Center, presumably there would be no camera ready. So the terrorists provided a second attack at a decent interval that they knew would be captured on film or video, and then repeated from many different angles – a montage of death and destruction. It was terrorism with an audience in mind.

2001, "This Time the Scene Was Real," 1.

Conclusion

Given the volatile global situation, what should artists do? Should they cut back on intercultural activities? Or are these precisely the times when such works are most needed? How careful should artists – non-Western as well as Western – be about from whom they borrow, what use they make of the arts and rituals of other cultures, and how individual works might exacerbate or ease the imbalances? Should artists boycott international festivals and tourist performances? Ought the rules governing borrowings differ depending on whether one is a Western or non-Western artist? Most of the heat has been applied to white Western artists such as Peter Brook, Ariane Mnouchkine, Philip Glass, and so on. But what ought one to say to artists of color who are also Western? Can choreographer Ralph Lemon do what Mnouchkine cannot? Is playwright **Suzan-Lori Parks** (1964–) absolved from restrictions binding Brook? What about Gómez-Peña whose work depends upon borrowing, parodic distortion, and making art in the interstices separating/joining Mexican, gringo, and Hispanic cultures? Is there a way of achieving equilibrium in intercultural exchanges (**see Bharucha box**)?

> **Suzan-Lori Parks (1964–):** African-American playwright whose works include *Imperceptible Mutabilities in the Third Kingdom* (1989), *The America Play* (1993), *Venus* (1996), *In the Blood* (2000), and *TopDog/UnderDog* (2001).

Those opposing intercultural works are concerned that Western artists use non-Western materials from which to make their own "original," "innovative," "avantgarde" works, which in turn define the world's arts markets, both economically and conceptually. In other words, the colonial cycle is enacted in the arts market: raw material from the colony at a cheap price, manufactured items back to the colony at a high price. But it is not only Western artists who participate in this cycle. Nor are all the "foreign" materials from outside an artist's own region.

Artists residing in Sao Paolo, Mumbai, Mexico City, Cairo, Johannesburg, Jakarta, and many other places are hooked into global circuits and draw on both foreign and local materials – sometimes freely, sometimes in accord with local restrictions. Even in apparently tightly regulated or oppressive societies, such as Iran or Nigeria, artists have found ways to communicate with like-minded people around the world. The internet provides one avenue, but there are other ways also, some of them secret. In more open societies, the play of differing values and materials is stupendous. Japan is culturally "Japan," but also part of global culture, and I don't mean just economically. Alongside traditional performing arts such as kabuki, noh, and bunraku is a thriving generations-old avantgarde (*engura*, or underground theatre), a more than century old modern theatre (*shingeki*), and the practice of combining the old, new, Western, and Japanese – as in the work of Suzuki Tadashi, **Min Tanaka** (1945–), **Ohno Kazuo** (1906–), and **Kawamura Takeshi** (1959–). Other examples are easy to find in Africa, Latin America, and elsewhere.

Rustom Bharucha

The Possibilities of Equilibrium

What concerns me are not the realities of appropriation but the possibilities of equilibrium, of maintaining and sustaining some kind of balance in what could be called the ecology of cultures. Rivers are said to be in a state of equilibrium when their "load" (of materials) is in direct proportion to their carrying capacity as determined by their speed, volume, and depth. Truly, nature's secrets for sustaining its variable balances are elusive. It is we who destroy these secrets in our zeal to "know," to "develop," to "trade," to "plunder." Indeed, it is with some sadness that I inscribe this process of disruption in my own discourse in order to acknowledge that we are living today with the most acute disequilibrium of cultures. To a large extent, it has materialized thorough the overload of materials from First World economies, which have been indiscriminately imposed on ongoing processes of culture, particularly in those parts of the world and among those indigenous communities who are not in a position to negotiate their increasingly vulnerable positions in the larger context of globalization, the marketing and patenting of biodiversity, and the homogenization of diverse cultural identities.

Can we restore, or more accurately, can we begin to invent a sense of balance in our perception and uses of each other's cultures? If our faith in the dominant mechanisms and institutions of cultural exchange has declined over the years, what are the new agencies of negotiating the transportation and translation of cultures? How do we sensitize ourselves to new principles of vigilance in regulating processes of appropriation and piracy? Can we envision a new ethics of respecting differences in theatre?

1997, "Negotiating the 'River': Intercultural Interactions and Interventions," 32–33

Min Tanaka (1945–): Japanese butoh performer. In 1978, he began the Body Weather Laboratory, a series of physical and spiritual exercises for dancers. In 1996 he started "Dance Resources International."

Kawamura Takahashi (1959–): Japanese experimental playwright and director. Founder in 1980 of Tokyo's Daisan Erotica theatre company whose productions include *Nippon Wars* (1984) and *A Man Called Macbeth* (1990).

Ohno Kazuo (1906–): A founder, performer, and leading theorist of butoh, author of *Ohno Kazuo's Words on Butoh* (in Japanese, 1989). His dances draw on both personal memories and traditional Japanese themes.

In terms of performance studies, the "intercultural question" involves valuing embodied and digital as well as written and archived knowledge. For the most part, at least until the advent of performance studies, Western modes of knowing privileged the written over the enacted, the archive over the repertory (**see Taylor box 2**). But increasingly the embodied – the performed – is being recognized as its own domain of knowledge and experience. It used to be that such a domain existed only during face-to-face contact. But the internet is changing that. Intercultural performance operates both digitally over the internet and in person by means of various exchanges, festivals, and scholarly meetings. Digital knowledge and experience is not a settled category. From one perspective, it appears archival; from another, very "live." Chat rooms, streaming video, instant messaging, live telecasting, and the like occupy a space between actual presence and "finished" works.

Under these circumstances, there is no such thing as cultural purity. All cultural practices – from religion and the arts to cooking, dress, and language – are hybrids. Cultural purity is a dangerous construction because it leads to monoculture, racism, jingoism, and xenophobia. The "natural" proclivity of humankind is promiscuity – which results in an always changing, if sometimes unsettling, diversity. The work of performance studies is to explore, understand, promote, and enjoy this diversity.

Diana Taylor

The Archive and the Repertoire: Performing Cultural Memory in the Americas

The inaugural moment of colonialism in the Americas introduced two discursive moves that worked to devalue native performance: 1. dismissal of indigenous performance traditions as episteme, and 2. dismissal of "content" (religious belief) as bad, as idolatry. These discourses simultaneously contradict and sustain each other. The first posits that performances – as ephemeral, non-written phenomena – cannot create or transmit knowledge. The second admits that performance does indeed transmit knowledge, but insofar as that knowledge is idolatrous and opaque, performance needs to be controlled or eliminated. These discourses, which valorize the written over the performed, set up a false opposition between archival and embodied knowledge, or what I call the "repertoire."

"Archival" memory exists as documents, literary texts, letters, archaeological remains, bones – items supposedly resistant to change. What changes over time is the value, relevance, or meaning of the archive, how the items it contains get interpreted, even embodied. The repertoire, on the other hand, enacts "embodied" memory – performances, gestures, orature, movement, dance, singing – in short, all those acts usually thought of as ephemeral, non-reproducible knowledge. As opposed to the supposedly "stable" objects in the archive, the *actions that are the repertoire* do not remain the same. The repertoire both keeps and transforms choreographies of meaning. Dances change over time, even though generations of dancers (or even individual dancers) swear they're always the same. But even though the embodiment changes, the meaning might very well remain the same.

Certainly it is true that individual instances of performances disappear, and can never be "captured" or transmitted through the archive. A video of a performance is not a performance, though it often comes to replace the performance as a *thing* in itself (the video is part of the archive; what it represents is part of the repertoire). Embodied memory, because it is "live," exceeds the archive's ability to "capture" it. But that does not mean that performance – as ritualized, formalized, or reiterative behavior – disappears. Multiple forms of embodied acts are always present, though in a constant state of again-ness. They reconstitute themselves – transmitting communal memories, histories, and values from one group/generation to the next. Embodied and performed acts, though they belong to the repertoire, in themselves generate, record, and transmit knowledge.

In-between and overlapping systems of knowledge and memory constitute a vast spectrum that might combine the workings of the "permanent" and the "ephemeral" in different ways. In the Western Hemisphere during the past 500 years, both writing and embodied performance have often worked together to layer the historical memories that constitute community. The telling is as important as the writing. Enacted mnemonic rituals and documented records might retain what the other "forgot." These epistemes are mutually constituting. The archive and the repertoire both exceed the limitations of the other, even in the most literate societies. The relationship is certainly not a straightforward binary – with the written and archival constituting hegemonic power and the repertoire providing the anti-hegemonic challenge. Performance belongs to the strong as well as the weak; it underwrites (**Michel**) de Certeau's [1925–86] "strategies" as well as "tactics," (**Mikhail**) Bakhtin's [1895–1975] "banquet" as well as "carnival." Embodied performances, like the archive, have often contributed to the maintenance of a repressive social order.

Even though the relationship between the archive and the repertoire is not necessarily oppositional, written documents have repeatedly announced the disappearance of the performance. Writing has served as a strategy for repudiating and foreclosing the very embodiedness it claims to describe. What is at risk in thinking about embodied knowledge and performance as that which disappears? Whose memories "disappear" if only archival knowledge is valorized? These questions can be addressed by challenging the psychoanalytic claim – from Freud to Derrida – that writing alone preserves memory. Such a challenge is particularly decisive to understanding colonial domination and cultural erasure.

2003, "Acts of Transfer" in, *Hauntology of Performance*

Mikhail Bakhtin (1895–1975): Russian literary and cultural theorist whose work focuses on carnival and other aspects of popular culture. His writings translated into English include *Rabelais and His World* (1968) and *The Dialogic Imagination* (1981).

Michel de Certeau (1925–86): French cultural critic who stressed the importance of the ordinary in understanding postmodern culture. Author of *The Practice of Everyday Life* (1980, Eng. 1984).

THINGS TO THINK ABOUT

1. Has globalization affected you personally? If so, are these effects good or bad?
2. From the point of view of the majority of the world's peoples do you believe globalization is good or bad? Whatever your answer, what can you performatively do either to advance or to stop globalization?
3. Have you ever had an "intercultural moment," when you have miscommunicated or been misunderstood because of a difference in cultures? What did you do in that situation? What should be done in such circumstances?

THINGS TO DO

1. After reading Turner's "Performing Ethnography," use it as a guide to making your own ethnographic performance. How did acting as if you were of another culture help you understand that culture differently than if you just read about it? Did the superficial quality of your enactment actually further distort your understanding of "the other"?
2. Stage a "border scene" in the style of Gómez-Peña. Do it twice, once in class; once in a public space.

SUGGESTED READINGS

Barba, Eugenio. "Theatre Anthropology" Barba and Nicola Savarese, eds. *The Secret Art of the Performer*. London: Routledge, 1991. 8–9.

Bhabha, Homi. "Of Mimicry and Man." *The Location of Culture*. London: Routledge, 1994. 85–92.

Gómez-Peña, Guillermo. "The New Global Culture." *TDR: The Drama Review* 45, 1 (T169) (2001). 7–17, 23–30.

Pavis, Patrice. Introduction. *The Intercultural Performance Reader*. London and New York: Routledge, 1996. 1–21.

Turner, Victor, with Edie Turner. "Performing Ethnography." *The Anthropology of Performance*. New York: PAJ Publications, 1986. 139–55.

APPENDIX

JoAnne Akalaitis (1937–): American theatre director, a founding member in 1970 of the Mabou Mines experimental performance collective. Her productions include Samuel Beckett's *Cascando* (1975) and *Endgame* (1984), Jean Genet's *The Screens* (1989), Georg Buchner's *Woyzek* (1992–93), the *Iphigenia Cycle* (1997), and Philip Glass' opera, *In the Penal Colony* (2000).

Chandralekha is a Cehnnai (Madras), India dancer-choreographer widely known for her experimental and intercultural reinterpretations of traditional forms. Her works include *Angika* (1985), *Bhinna Pravaha* (1993), and *Sharira* (1997).

Edward Gordon Craig (1872–1966): English scene designer, director and actor who staunchly opposed realism. Arguing for the authority of the director, Craig proposed doing away with actors, replacing them with large marionettes. Craig edited the influential journal, *The Mask* from 1908–29. Among his books are *On the Art of the Theatre* (1911, rev. ed. 1957) and *The Theatre Advancing* (1921).

Kalidasa (probably 5th Century CE)· The master poet-dramatist of the Indian Sanskrit tradition. His best-known play, *Shakuntala*, a tale of love lost and then regained, is still often performed.

Kuo Pao Kun (1939–): Chinese born, multilingual Singapore playwright, director and theorist. In 1965 he and his wife Goh Lay Kuan founded the Practice Performing Arts School. He was imprisoned for his views from 1976 to 1980. Kuo's plays include *The Coffin Is Too Big For The Hole* (1984) and the multilingual *Sunset Rise* (1998).

Arthur Schopenhauer (1788–1860): German philosopher whose most important work is *The World as Will and Representation* (1818). A pessimist, Schopenhauer believed that some relief from the pain of living could be found in music, philosophy and art.

Percy Bysshe Shelley (1972–1822): English Romantic poet whose works include the plays *The Cenci* (1819) and *Prometheus Unbound* (1820), and the elegy *Adonais*, written in memory of the fellow poet, John Keats.

Diana Taylor (1950–) is a leading theorist of Latin American and U.S. Latino Performance. Her books include *Theatre of Crisis: Drama and Politics in Latin America* (1991) and *Disappearing Acts: Spectacles of Gender and Nationalism in Argentina's 'Dirty War'* (1994). Chair of NYU's Department of Performance Studies from 1996 to 2002, she is the founding director of the Hemispheric Institute of Performance and Politics.

REFERENCES

Aeschylus. *The Oresteia*. Chicago: University of Chicago Press, 1989.

——. *Aeschylus II: The Suppliant Maidens; The Persians; Seven Against Thebes; Prometheus Bound*. Chicago: University of Chicago Press, 1991.

Alland, Alexander. "The Roots of Art." *Ritual, Play, and Performance*. Richard Schechner and Mady Schuman, eds. New York: Seabury Press, 1976.

Amalarius. *Amalarii Episcopi Opera Liturgica Omnia*. Studi e Testi, 138–140. Città del Vaticano: Biblioteca apostolica vaticana, 1948–50.

Anisimov, A. F. "The Shaman's Tent of the Evenks and the Origin of the Shamanic Rite." *Studies in Siberian Shamanism*. Henry N. Michael, ed.: 84–123. Toronto: University of Toronto Press, 1963.

Anonymous. *Complete Rules of Etiquette and Usages of Society*. New York: Dick and Fitzgerald, 1860.

Anonymous. "Handbook of Appellate Advocacy of the UCLA Law School." nd.

Appia, Adolphe. *Adolphe Appia: Texts on Theatre*. London, New York: Routledge, 1993.

Aristotle. *The Poetics of Aristotle*. Chapel Hill: University of North Carolina Press, 1987.

Artaud, Antonin. *The Theater and Its Double*. New York: Grove Press, 1958.

Associated Press. "NYC Names Decency Panel." 4 April 2001.

Austin, J. L. *How To Do Things With Words*. Cambridge: Harvard University Press, 1962.

——. "Pretending." *Philosophical Papers*. Oxford: Oxford University Press, 1979.

Bakhtin, Mikhail. *Rabelais and His World*. Cambridge: M.I.T. Press, 1968.

——. *The Dialogic Imagination: Four Essays*. Austin: University of Texas Press, 1981.

Banes, Sally. *Terpsichore in Sneakers: Post-Modern Dance*. Boston: Houghton Mifflin, 1980.

Barba, Eugenio. *The Paper Canoe*. London, New York: Routledge, 1995.

Barba, Eugenio and Nicola Savarese. *A Dictionary of Theatre Anthropology: The Secret Art of the Performer*. London: Published for the Centre for Performance Research by Routledge, 1991.

Barba, Eugenio and Ferdinando Taviani. *The Floating Islands*. Gråsten: Drama, 1979.

——. *Beyond the Floating Islands*. New York: PAJ Publications, 1986.

Bateson, Gregory. *Steps to an Ecology of Mind*. New York: Ballantine Books, 1972.

——. *Mind and Nature*. New York: Dutton, 1979.

Baudrillard, Jean. *Simulations. Foreign Agents Series*. New York: Semiotext(e), 1983.

——. *The Illusion of the End*. Stanford: Stanford University Press, 1994.

Beauvoir, Simone de. *The Second Sex*. New York: Knopf, 1953.

——. *The Mandarins*. Cleveland: Meridian Books, 1960.

——. *Force of Circumstance*. New York: Putnam, 1965.

Beckett, Samuel. *Waiting for Godot*. New York: Grove Press, 1954.

——. *Endgame and Act Without Words*. New York: Grove Press, 1958.

——. *Happy Days*. New York: Grove Press, 1961.

Bell, Catherine. *Ritual Theory, Ritual Practice*. New York: Oxford University Press, 1992.

Belo, Jane. *Trance in Bali*. New York: Columbia University Press, 1960.

Benjamin, Walter. *Illuminations*. New York: Schocken Books, 1969.

——. *Understanding Brecht*. London: NLB, 1973.

——. *Reflections: Essays, Aphorisms, Autobiographical Writing*. New York: Schocken Books, 1986.

Bentham, Jeremy. *The Principles of Morals and Legislation*. Buffalo, N.Y.: Prometheus Books, 1988.

Berger, Maurice. "The Critique of Pure Racism: An Interview With Adrian Piper." *Afterimage* 18, no. 3 (1990).

Bhabha, Homi K. *Nation and Narration*. London, New York: Routledge, 1990.

——. *The Location of Culture*. London, New York: Routledge, 1994.

Bharata-Muni. *The Natyasastra*. New Delhi: Munshiram Manoharlal Publishers, 1996.

Bharucha, Rustom. *Theatre and the World: Performance and the Politics of Culture*. London, New York: Routledge, 1993.

——. "Somebody's Other: Disorientations in the Cultural Politics of Our Times." *The Intercultural Performance Reader*.

Patrice Pavis, ed.: 196–212. London, New York: Routledge, 1996.

—. "Negotiating the "River": Intercultural Interactions and Interventions." *TDR: The Drama Review* 41, no. 3 (1997): 31–38.

Birdwhistell, Ray L. *Kinesics and Context: Essays on Body Motion Communication*. Philadelphia: University of Pennsylvania Press, 1970.

Birnbaum, Cara. "How to Wow Anyone You Meet." *Cosmopolitan* (2001).

Boal, Augusto. *Theatre of the Oppressed*. New York: Theatre Communications Group, 1985.

—. *Games for Actors and Non-Actors*. London, New York: Routledge, 1992.

—. *Legislative Theatre: Using Performance to Make Politics*. London, New York: Routledge, 1998.

—. *Hamlet and the Baker's Son: My Life in Theatre and Politics*. London, New York: Routledge, 2001.

Braun, Edward, ed. *Meyerhold on Theatre*. New York: Hill and Wang, 1969.

Brazell, Karen and James T. Araki. *Traditional Japanese Theater: An Anthology of Plays*. New York: Columbia University Press, 1998.

Brecht, Bertolt. *Brecht on Theatre*. New York: Hill and Wang, 1964.

—. *Plays*. London: Methuen, 1987.

—. *The Rise and Fall of the City of Mahagonny; and, The Seven Deadly Sins of the Petty Bourgeoisie*. New York, Boston: Arcade Pub. 1996.

Brentano, Robyn. "Outside the Frame: Performance, Art, and Life." *Outside the Frame: Performance and the Object: A Survey History of Performance Art in the USA Since 1950*. Robyn Brentano ed.: 31–61. Cleveland: Cleveland Center for Contemporary Art, 1994.

Brissett, Dennis and Charles Edgley. "The Dramaturgical Perspective." *Life As Theater, a Dramaturgical Sourcebook*. Dennis Brissett and Charles Edgley, eds. New York: Aldine de Gruyter, 1990.

Brook, Peter. *The Empty Space*. London: MacGibbon & Kee, 1968.

—. *The Shifting Point: 1946–1987*. New York: Harper & Row, 1987.

—. *Threads of Time*. Washington, D.C: Counterpoint, 1998.

Brown, Patricia Leigh. "This Is Extremely Sporting." *The New York Times*, 13 August 2000. Section 4: Week in Review, p. 2.

Buber, Martin. *Eclipse of God: Studies in the Relation Between Religion and Philosophy*. New York: Harper, 1952.

—. *I and Thou*. New York: Scribner, 1958.

—. *The Origin and Meaning of Hasidism*. New York: Horizon Press, 1960.

Burns, Elizabeth. *Theatricality: A Study of Convention in the Theatre and in Social Life*. London: Longman, 1972.

Butler, Judith. "Performative Acts and Gender Constitution." *Theatre Journal* 40, no. 4 (1988): 519–31.

—. *Gender Trouble*. Thinking Gender. New York: Routledge, 1990.

—. "Imitation and Gender Insubordination." *Inside / Out Lesbian Theories, Gay Theories*. Diana Fuss, ed. New York: Routledge, 1991.

—. *Bodies That Matter*. New York: Routledge, 1993.

—. *Excitable Speech*. New York: Routledge, 1997.

Cage, John. *Silence: Lectures and Writings*. Middletown: Wesleyan University Press, 1961.

—. *A Year From Monday; New Lectures and Writings*. Middletown: Wesleyan University Press, 1967.

Caillois, Roger. *Man, Play, and Games*. New York: Schocken Books, 1979.

Calderón de la Barca, Pedro. *Select Plays of Calderón*. London, New York: Macmillan, 1888.

—. *Life's a Dream*. Woodstock: Dramatic Pub, 1990.

—. *Eight Dramas of Calderón*. Urbana: University of Illinois Press, 2000.

Calvin, Jean. *Institutes of the Christian Religion*. Chicago: Encyclopedia Britannica, 1990.

Carlson, Marvin. *Theatre Semiotics: Signs of Life*. Bloomington: Indiana University Press, 1990.

—. "Brook and Mnouchkine. Passages to India?" *The Intercultural Performance Reader*. Patrice Pavis, ed.: 79–92. London, New York: Routledge, 1996.

—. *Performance: A Critical Introduction*. London, New York: Routledge, 1996.

Carroll, Noel. "Performance." *Formations* 3, no. 1 (1986): 63–81.

Carse, James P. *Death and Existence: A Conceptual History of Human Mortality*. New York: Wiley, 1980.

—. *Finite and Infinite Games*. New York: Free Press, 1986.

Certeau, Michel de. *The Practice of Everyday Life*. Berkeley: University of California Press, 1984.

Chaikin, Joseph. *The Presence of the Actor*. New York: Atheneum, 1972.

Chaucer, Geoffrey. *The Canterbury Tales*. New York: Modern Library, 1994.

Chin, Daryl. "Interculturalism, Postmodernism, Pluralism." *Interculturalism and Performance*. Bonnie Marranca, and Gautam Dasgupta, eds: 83–95. New York: PAJ Publications, 1991.

Chute, Marchette Gaylord. *Shakespeare of London*. New York: Dutton, 1949.

Clurman, Harold. *On Directing*. New York: Macmillan, 1972.

Conquergood, Dwight. "Rethinking Ethnography: Towards a Critical Cultural Politics." *Communications Monographs* 58, June (1991): 179–94.

—. "Interdisciplinary Interventions and Radical Research." *TDR: The Drama Review* 46, no. 1 (2002).

Cornford, Francis Macdonald. *The Origin of Attic Comedy*. London: E. Arnold, 1914.

Covarrubias, Miguel. *Island of Bali*. Kuala Lumpur: Oxford University Press, 1972.

Critical Art Ensemble. "Recombinant Theatre and Digital Resistance." *TDR: The Drama Review* 44, no. 4 (2000): 151–66.

Csikszentmihalyi, Mihaly. *Beyond Boredom and Anxiety*. San Francisco: Jossey-Bass, 1975.

—. *Flow: the Psychology of Optimal Experience*. New York: Harper & Row, 1990.

—. *Creativity: Flow and the Psychology of Discovery and Invention*. New York: HarperCollins, 1996.

—. *Finding Flow: the Psychology of Engagement With Everyday Life*. New York: Basic Books, 1997.

D'Aquili, Eugene G., Charles D. Laughlin Jr., and John McManus. *The Spectrum of Ritual*. New York: Columbia University Press, 1979.

Darwin, Charles. *The Origin of Species by Means of Natural Selection*. New York: Modern Library, 1998.

—. *The Expression of the Emotions in Man and Animals*. New York: Oxford University Press, 1998.

Dasgupta, Gautam. "The Mahabharata: Brook's Orientalism." *Interculturalism and Performance*. Bonnie Marranca and Gautam Dasgupta, eds: 75–82. New York: PAJ Publications, 1991.

De Marinis, Marco. *The Semiotics of Performance*. Bloomington: Indiana University Press, 1993.

Debord, Guy. *The Society of the Spectacle*. New York: Zone Books, 1994.

Deleuze, Gilles and Félix Guattari. *Anti-Oedipus: Capitalism and Schizophrenia*. New York: Viking Press, 1977.

—. *A Thousand Plateaus: Capitalism and Schizophrenia*. Minneapolis: University of Minnesota Press, 1987.

Deren, Maya. *Divine Horsemen: the Living Gods of Haiti*. London, New York: Thames and Hudson, 1953.

Derrida, Jacques. *Of Grammatology*. Baltimore: Johns Hopkins University Press, 1976.

—. *Writing and Difference*. Chicago: University of Chicago Press, 1978.

—. *Limited Inc*. Evanston: Northwestern University Press, 1988.

—. *The Derrida Reader: Writing Performances*. Lincoln: University of Nebraska Press, 1998.

Dodds, E. R. *The Greeks and the Irrational*. Berkeley: University of California Press, 1951.

Drewal, Henry John. "Performing the Other: Mami Wata Worship in Africa." *TDR: The Drama Review* 32, no. 2 (1988): 160–85.

Drewal, Margaret. *Yoruba Ritual*. Bloomington: Indiana University Press, 1992.

Durkheim, Emile. *The Elementary Forms of Religious Life*. New York: Free Press, 1965.

Ehrmann, Jacques. "Introduction." *Yale French Studies*, no. 36–37 (1966): 5–9.

Eibl-Eibesfeldt, Irenäus. *Ethology, the Biology of Behavior*. New York: Holt, Rinehart and Winston, 1970.

Einstein, Albert, Max Born, and Hedwig Born. *The Born-Einstein Letters 1916–1955*. London: Macmillan, 1971.

Ekman, Paul. *Emotion in the Human Face*. Cambridge: Cambridge University Press, 1982.

—. "Autonomic Nervous System Activity Distinguishes Among Emotions." *Science* 221 (1983): 1208–10.

—. *Telling Lies: Clues to Deceit in the Marketplace, Politics, and Marriage*. New York: Norton, 1985.

Ekman, Paul, and Wallace V. Friesen. *Unmasking the Face; a Guide to Recognizing Emotions From Facial Clues*. Englewood Cliffs: Prentice-Hall, 1975.

Emigh, John. *Masked Performance: the Play of Self and Other in Ritual and Theatre*. Philadelphia: University of Pennsylvania Press, 1996.

Euripides. *Euripides, Volumes 1, 3, 5*. Chicago: University of Chicago Press, 1955–1959.

Evreinoff, Nicholas. "The Never Ending Show." *Life As Theater*. Dennis Brissett and Charles Edgley eds. New York: Aldine de Gruyter, 1990.

Fanon, Frantz. *The Wretched of the Earth*. New York: Grove Press, 1963.

—. *Black Skin, White Masks*. New York: Grove Press, 1967.

Fischer, Roland. "A Cartography of the Ecstatic and Meditative States." *Science* 174 (1971): 897–904.

Fo, Dario. *We Won't Pay! We Won't Pay!: a Political Farce*. North American version. New York: Samuel French, 1984.

—. *Plays*. London: Methuen, 1997.

—. *The Pope and the Witch*. New York, London: Samuel French, 1997.

Foreman, Richard. "Program Notes on Pearls for Pigs." *TDR: The Drama Review* 42, no. 2 (1998): 157–59.

Foster, Susan Leigh. *Reading Dancing: Bodies and Subjects in Contemporary American Dance*. Berkeley: University of California Press, 1986.

——. *Corporealities: Dancing, Knowledge, Culture, and Power*. London, New York: Routledge, 1996.

Foucault, Michel. *Madness and Civilization; a History of Insanity in the Age of Reason*. New York: Pantheon Books, 1965.

——. *The Order of Things*. London: Tavistock Publications, 1970.

——. *Discipline and Punish: the Birth of the Prison*. London: Allen Lane, 1977.

——. *The History of Sexuality*. New York: Pantheon Books, 1978.

Friedman, Thomas L. *The Lexus and the Olive Tree*. New York: Anchor Books, 2000.

Fusco, Coco. *English Is Broken Here: Notes on Cultural Fusion in the Americas*. New York City: The New Press, 1995.

——. "The Other History of Intercultural Performance." *English Is Broken Here*. Coco Fusco, 37–63. New York: The New Press, 1995.

——. *The Bodies That Were Not Ours*. London, New York: Routledge, 2001.

Gabler, Neal. "This Time, The Scene Was Real." *The New York Times*, 16 September 2001, News of the Week in Review. Op-Ed, electronic archive.

Gandhi, Mohandas. *Autobiography: the Story of My Experiments With Truth*. Washington: Public Affairs Press, 1954.

Geertz, Clifford. *The Interpretation of Cultures*. New York: Basic Books, 1973.

——. *Negara: The Theatre State in Nineteenth-Century Bali*. Princeton: Princeton University Press, 1980.

——. *Local Knowledge*. New York: Basic Books, 1983.

Genet, Jean. *Our Lady of the Flowers*. Paris: Morihien, 1949.

——. *The Maids and Deathwatch*. New York: Grove Press, 1954.

——. *The Balcony*. New York: Grove Press, 1958.

——. *The Thief's Journal*. Paris: Olympia Press, 1959.

——. *The Blacks*. New York: Grove Press, 1960.

Gennep, Arnold van. *The Rites of Passage*. Chicago: University of Chicago Press, 1960.

Goffman, Erving. *The Presentation of Self in Everyday Life*. Garden City, N.Y: Doubleday, 1959.

——. *Interaction Ritual*. Chicago: Aldine Pub. Co., 1967.

——. *Frame Analysis*. Cambridge: Harvard University Press, 1974.

Golding, William. *Lord of the Flies*. London: Faber and Faber, 1954.

Gómez-Peña, Guillermo. *Warrior for Gringostroika*. St. Paul: Graywolf Press, 1993.

——. *The New World Border*. San Francisco: City Lights Books, 1996.

——. *Dangerous Border Crossers: the Artist Talks Back*. London, New York: Routledge, 2000.

——. "The New Global Culture." *TDR: The Drama Review* 45, no. 1 (2001): 7–30.

Gómez-Peña, Guillermo, Enrique Chagoya, and Felicia Rice. *Codex Espangliensis: From Columbus to the Border Patrol*. San Francisco: City Lights Books, 2000.

Goodall, Jane. *In the Shadow of Man*. Boston: Houghton Mifflin, 1971.

——. *The Chimpanzees of Gombe*. Cambridge: Belknap Press of Harvard University Press, 1986.

Gould, Richard A. *Yiwara: Foragers of the Australian Desert*. New York: Scribner, 1969.

Gray, Spalding. *Gray's Anatomy*. New York: Vintage Books, 1994.

——. *Morning, Noon, and Night*. New York: Farrar, Straus, and Giroux, 1999.

Grimes, Ronald L. *Readings in Ritual Studies*. Upper Saddle River: Prentice Hall, 1996.

Grotowski, Jerzy. *Towards a Poor Theatre*. New York: Simon and Schuster, 1968.

——. "Performer." *The Grotowski Sourcebook*. Lisa Wolford and Richard Schechner, eds: London: Routledge, 1997.

Hafner, Kate. "A Beautiful Life, an Early Death, a Fraud Exposed." *The New York Times*, 31 May 2001, sec. Circuits.

——. "Get Hold of Yourself, Lieutenant," www.nytimes.com/2001/06/21/technology/21SIMU.html. 21 June 2001.

Hallett, Garth and Ludwig Wittgenstein. *A Companion to Wittgenstein's "Philosophical Investigations"*. Ithaca: Cornell University Press, 1977.

Halprin, Anna. *Dance As a Healing Art*. Mendocino: Life Rhythm, 2000.

Halprin, Anna and Rachel Kaplan. *Moving Toward Life*. Middletown: Wesleyan University Press, 1995.

Halprin, Lawrence and Jim Burns. *Taking Part: A Workshop Approach to Collective Creativity*. Cambridge: MIT Press, 1974.

Hamisi, Katuka Ole Maimai. "Western Paparazzi in the Maasai Region." http://maasai-infoline.org/index.html, 2001.

Handelman, Don. "Rethinking 'Banana Time'." *Urban Life* 4, no. 4 (1976): 33–48.

——. "Play and Ritual: Complementary Frames of Meta-communication." *It's a Funny Thing, Humour*. Lisa Wolford and Richard Schechner, eds: 185–92. Oxford, New York: Pergamon, 1977.

Handelman, Don and David Shulman. *God Inside Out: Siva's Game of Dice*. New York: Oxford University Press, 1997.

Harbinger, Richard. "Trial by Drama." *Judicature* 55, no. 3 (1971): 122–28.

Harding, Frances. "Presenting and Re-Presenting the Self: From Not-Acting to Acting in African Performance." *TDR: The Drama Review* 43, no. 2 (1999): 118–35.

Hardison, O. B. *Christian Rite and Christian Drama in the Middle Ages*. Baltimore: Johns Hopkins University Press, 1965.

Harrison, Jane Ellen. *Themis; a Study of the Social Origins of Greek Religion*. Cambridge: Cambridge University Press, 1912.

——. *Ancient Art and Ritual*. London: Williams and Norgate, 1913.

Hein, Norvin. *The Miracle Plays of Mathura*. New Haven: Yale University Press, 1972.

Heisenberg, Werner. *Physics and Philosophy: The Revolution in Modern Science*. New York: Harper, 1958.

Heraclitus. *Fragments: the Collected Wisdom of Heraclitus*. New York: Viking, 2001.

Herrick, Robert. *Poetical Works*. Oxford: Clarendon Press, 1956.

Hess, Linda. "Ram Lila: The Audience Experience." *Bhakti in Current Research, 1979–1982*. Monika Thiel-Horstmann, ed. Berlin: D. Reimer Verlag, 1983.

Hobsbawm, E. J. and T. O. Ranger. *The Invention of Tradition*. Cambridge, New York: Cambridge University Press, 1983.

Homer. *The Iliad; and, The Odyssey*. Chicago: Encyclopedia Britannica, 1990.

hooks, bell. *Yearning: Race, Gender, and Cultural Politics*. Boston: South End Press, 1990.

Horace. *The Art of Poetry*. Albany: State University of New York Press, 1974.

Huizinga, Johan. *Homo Ludens*. New York: Harper, 1970.

Huntsman, Jeffrey F. "Native American Theatre." *American Indian Performance: A Reader*. Hanay Geiogamah and Jaye T. Darby, eds: 81–113. Los Angeles: UCLA American Indian Studies Center, 2000.

Hurston, Zora Neal. *Mules and Men*. New York: Harper, 1990.

Hutcheon, Linda. *Narcissistic Narrative: the Metafictional Paradox*. Wilfrid Laurier University Press, 1980.

——. *A Theory of Parody*. New York: Methuen, 1985.

——. *A Poetics of Postmodernism*. New York: Routledge, 1988.

Huxley, Julian. *Evolution, the Modern Synthesis*. London: Allen & Unwin, 1942.

——. *Essays of a Humanist*. New York: Harper & Row, 1964.

Ibsen, Henrik. *The Complete Major Prose Plays*. New York: New American Library, 1978.

Jakobson, Roman. *Fundamentals of Language*. Linguarum, Nr. 1: Gravenhage: Mouton, 1956.

——. *Studies in Verbal Art*. Ann Arbor: Dept. of Slavic Languages and Literature, University of Michigan, 1971.

——. *Main Trends in the Science of Language*. London: Allen and Unwin, 1973.

Jameson, Fredric. *The Political Unconscious: Narrative As a Socially Symbolic Act*. Ithaca, N.Y.: Cornell University Press, 1981.

——. *Postmodernism, Or, The Cultural Logic of Late Capitalism*. Post-Contemporary Interventions. Durham: Duke University Press, 1991.

Jarry, Alfred. *The Ubu Plays*. London: Nick Hern Books, 1997.

Jenik, Adriene. "Desktop Theatre." *TDR: The Drama Review* 45, no. 3 (2001): 95–112.

Jenkins, Henry. "The Poachers and the Stormtroopers." http://commons.somewhere.com/rre/1998/The.Poachers.and.the.Sto.html, 1998.

Jones, Amelia. *Body Art/Performing the Subject*. Minneapolis, London: University of Minnesota Press, 1998.

Josephson, Michael S., Kenneth Klenberg, and Franklin Tom, eds. *Handbook of Appellate Advocacy*. Los Angeles: UCLA Moot Court Honors Program, nd.

Joyce, James. *Finnegan's Wake*. London: Faber & Faber, 1968.

——. *Ulysses*. Reprinted with corr ed. Penguin Modern Classics. Harmondsworth, New York: Penguin Books, 1971.

Kaprow, Allan. *Assemblage, Environments and Happenings*. New York: H. N. Abrams, 1966.

——. "The Real Experiment." *Artforum* XXII, no. 4 (1983): 36–43.

Kaprow, Allan and Jeff Kelley. *Essays on the Blurring of Art and Life*. Berkeley: University of California Press, 1993.

Kendall, Laurel. *Shamans, Housewives, and Other Restless Spirits: Women in Korean Ritual Life*. Honolulu: University of Hawaii Press, 1987.

Kirby, E. T. "The Shamanistic Origins of Popular Entertainments." *TDR: The Drama Review* 18, no. 1 (1974): 5–15.

Kirby, Michael. *Happenings*. New York: Dutton, 1965.

——. *A Formalist Theatre*. Philadelphia: University of Pennsylvania Press, 1987.

Kirshenblatt-Gimblett, Barbara. *Destination Culture*. Berkeley: University of California Press, 1998.

——. "Performance Studies." http://www.nyu.edu/classes/bkg/ps/htm., 1999.

——. "Playing to the Senses: Food As a Performance Medium." *Performance Research* 4, no. 1 (1999): 1–30.

Kolankiewicz, Leszek, ed. *On the Road to Active Culture*. Wroclaw: Instytut Laboratorium, 1978.

Kuczynski, Alex. "On CBS News, Some of What You See Isn't There." *The New York Times*, 12 January 2000, sec. Business, pp. 1–4.

Kuo Pao Kin. "Contemplating an Open Culture: Transcending Multiracialism." *Singapore Re-Engineering Success*. Arun Mahizhnan and Tsao Yuan Lee, eds: 50–61. Singapore: Oxford University Press, 1998.

La Barre, Weston. *The Ghost Dance: Origins of Religion*. New York: Dell, 1972.

Lacan, Jacques. *Écrits: a Selection*. London: Tavistock Publications, 1977.

Lacy, Suzanne. "Debated Territory: Toward a Critical Language for Public Art." *Mapping the Terrain: New Genre Public Art*. Suzanne Lacy, ed.: 171–85. Seattle: Bay Press, 1995.

Langer, Susanne K. *Philosophy in a New Key*. Cambridge: Harvard University Press, 1942.

—. *Feeling and Form: A Theory of Art*. New York: Scribner, 1953.

—. *Problems of Art*. New York: Scribner, 1957.

Latrell, Craig. "After Appropriation." *TDR: The Drama Review* 44, no. 4 (2000): 44–55.

Lawrence, T. E. *Seven Pillars of Wisdom: a Triumph*. Garden City, N.Y: Doubleday, 1935.

Leffingwell, Edward, Carole Kismaric, and Marvin Heiferman, eds. *Flaming Creature Jack Smith, His Amazing Life and Times*. New York: Lookout Book/The Institute for Contemporary Art, 1997.

Lemon, Ralph. "Director's Notes." Program for *Tree*, Yale Repertory Theatre (1999).

Lepecki, Andre. "Skin, Body, and Presence in Contemporary European Choreography." *TDR* 43, no. 4 (1999): 128–40.

Lévi-Strauss, Claude. *Structural Anthropology*. New York: Basic Books, 1963.

—. *The Savage Mind*. Chicago: University of Chicago Press, 1966.

— *The Elementary Structures of Kinship*. Boston: Beacon Press, 1969.

— *The Raw and the Cooked*. New York: Harper & Row, 1969.

Lewis, I. M. *Ecstatic Religion: an Anthropological Study of Spirit Possession and Shamanism*. Harmondsworth, Eng.: Penguin Books, 1971.

Lex, Barbara. "The Neurobiology of Ritual Trance." *The Spectrum of Ritual*. Eugene G. D'Aquili, Charles D. Laughlin, and John McManus eds. New York: Columbia University Press, 1979.

Lippard, Lucy R. "Looking Around: Where We Are, Where We Could Be." *Mapping the Terrain: New Genre Public Art*. Suzanne Lacy, ed.: 114–30. Seattle: Bay Press, 1995.

Liptak, Adam. "When Is a Fake Too Real? It's Virtually Uncertain." *The New York Times*, 28 January 2001, sec. Ideas & Trends, pp. 1–3.

Loizos, Caroline. "Play Behaviour in Higher Primates: A Review." *Primate Ethology*. Desmond Morris, ed.: 226–82. Garden City: Anchor Books, 1969.

Longman, Jere. "Someday Soon, Athletic Edge May be from Altered Genes." *The New York Times*, 11 May 2001, sec. A, D, pp. 1, 5.

Lorca, Federico García. *Collected Plays*. London: Secker and Warburg, 1976.

Lorenz, Konrad. "The Role of Aggression in Group Formation." *Transactions of the Conference on Group Processes of 1957*. B. Schaffner, ed. New York: Josiah Macy, Jr. Foundation, 1959.

—. *On Aggression*. New York: Harcourt, Brace & World, 1966.

—. *The Foundations of Ethology*. New York: Springer-Verlag New York, 1981.

Lyall, Sarah. "A 'Swan Lake' With Male Swans is a Hit in London," 1–3. *New York Times*, 1996.

Lyotard, Jean-François. *The Postmodern Condition: A Report on Knowledge*. Minneapolis: University of Minnesota Press, 1984.

—. *The Differend: Phrases in Dispute*. Minneapolis: University of Minnesota Press, 1988.

—. *Peregrinations: Law, Form, Event*. New York: Columbia University Press, 1988.

MacAloon, John J. *This Great Symbol: Pierre De Coubertin and the Origins of the Modern Olympic Games*. Chicago: University of Chicago Press, 1981.

—. "Olympic Games and the Theory of Spectacle in Modern Societies." *Rite, Drama, Festival, Spectacle*. John J. MacAloon, ed.: 241–80. Philadelphia: Institute for the Study of Human Issues, 1984.

McGrath, John. "Trusting in Rubber: Performing Boundaries During the AIDS Epidemic." *TDR* 39, no. 2 (1995): 21–38.

McKenzie, Jon. *Perform Or Else: From Discipline to Performance*. New York: Routledge, 2001.

McKinley, James C. Jr. "It Isn't Just a Game: Clues to Rooting." *The New York Times*, 11 August 2000, sec. Sports.

McNeil, Donald G. "More and More, Other Countries See the War As Solely America's." *The New York Times*, 4 November 2001, sec. B, pp. 1, 2.

Mamet, David. *American Buffalo*. New York: Grove Press, 1977.

—. *Glengarry Glen Ross: a Play*. New York: Grove Press, 1983.

—. *House of Games: a Screenplay*. New York: Grove Press, 1987.

—. *Oleanna*. New York: Pantheon Books, 1992.

—. *The Old Neighborhood: Three Plays*. New York: Vintage Books, 1998.

——. *The Spanish Prisoner and The Winslow Boy: Two Screenplays*. 1st ed. New York: Vintage Books, 1999.

Mao Tse-tung. *Mao Tse-Tung on Literature and Art*. Peking: Foreign Languages Press, 1967.

Marshall, Eliot. "DNA Studies Challenge the Meaning of Race." *Science* 282, no. 5389 (1998): 654–55.

Maxwell, Ian. "Learning at the Department of Performance Studies." http://www.arts.usyd.edu.au/Arts/departs/perform/Learning%20at%20Perf%20Studies.html, May 2001.

Mei Lanfang. "Reflections On My Stage Life." *Peking Opera and Mei Lanfang*. Huang Zuolin, Mei Shaowu, and Wu Zuguang, eds.: 30–45. Beijing: New World Press, 1981.

Melvin, Sheila and Cai Jindong. "Why This Nostalgia for Fruits of Chaos?" *The New York Times*, 29 October 2000, sec. Arts & Leisure, pp. 1, 31.

Melzer, Annabelle. *Dada and Surrealist Performance*. Baltimore: Johns Hopkins University Press, 1994.

Merback, Mitchell B. *The Thief, the Cross, and the Wheel*. Chicago: University of Chicago Press, 1999.

Miller, Arthur. *Arthur Miller's Collected Plays*. New York: Viking Press, 1957–1981.

——. *Broken Glass*. New York: Penguin Books, 1994.

——. *The Ride Down Mt. Morgan*. New York: Penguin Books, 1999.

Mnouchkine, Ariane. "The Theatre is Oriental." *The Intercultural Performance Reader*. Patrice Pavis, ed.: 93–98. London, New York: Routledge, 1996.

Moore, Sally Falk and Barbara G. Myerhoff. *Secular Ritual*. Assen: Van Gorcum, 1977.

Müller, Heiner. *Hamletmachine and Other Texts for the Stage*. New York: Performing Arts Journal Publications, 1984.

——. *A Heiner Müller Reader: Plays, Poetry, Prose*. Baltimore: Johns Hopkins University Press, 2001.

Muñoz, José Esteban. *Disidentifications*. Minneapolis: University of Minnesota Press, 1999.

Murray, Gilbert. "Excursus on the Ritual Forms Preserved in Greek Tragedy." *Themis: A Study of the Social Origins of Greek Religion*. Jane Ellen Harrison, ed. Cambridge: Cambridge University Press, 1912.

——. *Five Stages of Greek Religion*. New York: Columbia University Press, 1925.

Nehru, Jawaharlal. *The Discovery of India*. New York: The John Day company, 1946.

Nelson, Steve. "Broadway and the Beast: Disney Comes to Times Square." *TDR* 39, no. 2 (1995): 71–85.

Ngugi wa Thiong'o. *Detained: A Writer's Prison Diary*. Nairobi: Heinemann, 1981.

——. *Decolonising the Mind*. London, Portsmouth, Nairobi, Harare: James Curry (London), EAEP (Nairobi), Heinemann (Portsmouth), Zimbabe Publishing House (Harare), 1986.

——. *Moving the Centre*. London, Nairobi, Portsmouth: James Currey (London), EAEP (Nairobi), Heinemann (Portsmouth), 1993.

——. *Penpoints, Gunpoints, and Dreams: Toward a Critical Theory of the Arts and the State in Africa*. Oxford, New York: Oxford University Press, 1998.

Nicoll, Allardyce. *Masks, Mimes, and Miracles*. New York: Cooper Square, 1963.

Nietzsche, Friedrich Wilhelm. *Philosophy in the Tragic Age of the Greeks*. South Bend: Gateway Editions, 1962.

——. "Human, All Too Human." Cambridge: Cambridge University Press, 1986.

——. *Beyond Good and Evil*. New York: Penguin Books, 1990.

——. *Thus Spake Zarathustra*. Mineola: Dover Publications, 1999.

——. *The Birth of Tragedy*. Oxford World's Classics: Oxford World's Classics (Oxford University Press). Oxford, New York: Oxford University Press, 2000.

Northrup, F. S. C. "Introduction." *Physics and Philosophy* by Werner Heisenberg. New York: Harper, 1958.

O'Flaherty, Wendy Doniger. *Dreams, Illusions, and Other Realities*. Chicago: University of Chicago Press, 1984.

Okpewho, Isidore. *African Oral Literature*. Bloomington: Indiana University Press, 1992.

Ong, Keng Sen. "Encounters." *TDR: The Drama Review* 45, no. 3 (2001): 126–33.

Ortolani, Benito. *The Japanese Theatre From Shamanistic Ritual to Contemporary Pluralism*. Princeton: Princeton University Press, 1995.

Osinski, Zbigniew. "Grotowski Blazes the Trails." *The Grotowski Sourcebook*. Lisa Wolford and Richard Schechner, eds: 383–98. London, New York: Routledge, 1997.

Park, Robert Ezra. *Race and Culture*. Glencoe: Free Press, 1950.

Parker, Andrew and Eve Kosofsky Sedgwick. "Introduction: Performativity and Performance." *Performativity and Performance*. Andrew Parker and Eve Kosofsky Sedgwick, eds. New York: Routledge, 1995.

Parks, Suzan-Lori. *The America Play, and Other Works*. New York: Theatre Communications Group, 1995.

——. *Imperceptible Mutabilities in the Third Kingdom*. Los Angeles: Sun & Moon Press, 1995.

——. *Venus*. New York: Theatre Communications Group, 1997.

——. *Topdog/Underdog*. New York: Theatre Communications Group, 2001.

Pavis, Patrice. "Dancing With Faust: A Semiotician's Reflections on Barba's Intercultural Mise-En-Scene." *TDR: The Drama Review* 33, no. 3 (1989): 37–57.

—, ed. *The Intercultural Performance Reader*. London, New York: Routledge, 1996.

—. "Introduction: Towards a Theory of Interculturalism in Theatre." *The Intercultural Performance Reader*. Patrice Pavis, ed.: 1–21. London, New York: Routledge, 1996.

Pelias, Ronald J. and James VanOosting. "A Paradigm for Performance Studies." *Quarterly Journal of Speech* 73 (1987): 219–31.

Pfeiffer, John E. *The Creative Explosion*. New York: Harper & Row, 1982.

Phelan, Peggy. *Unmarked: The Politics of Performance*. New York, London: Routledge, 1993.

—. *Mourning Sex*. London, New York: Routledge, 1997.

Phelan, Peggy and Jill Lane, eds. *The Ends of Performance*. New York: New York University Press, 1998.

Piper, Adrian. "Passing for White, Passing for Black." *Out of Order, Out of Sight Volume 1: Selected Writings in Meta-Art, 1968–1992*: 275–307. Cambridge, London: MIT Press, 1996.

Piper, Adrian, Maurice Berger, and Jean Fisher. *Adrian Piper: a Retrospective*. Baltimore, New York: Fine Arts Gallery, University of Maryland, Art Publishers, 1999.

Plato. *The Republic*. Mineola: Dover Publications, 2000.

Rappaport, Roy A. *Pigs for the Ancestors*. New Haven: Yale University Press, 1968.

—. *Ecology, Meaning, and Religion*. Richmond: North Atlantic Books, 1979.

Read, Kenneth E. *The High Valley*. New York: Scribner, 1965.

—. *Return to the High Valley*. Berkeley: University of California Press, 1986.

Richards, Thomas. *At Work With Grotowski on Physical Actions*. New York: Routledge, 1995.

Roth, Moira, ed. *The Amazing Decade: Women and Performance Art in America, 1970–1980*. Los Angeles: Astro Artz, 1983.

Rothenberg, Jerome, ed. *Technicians of the Sacred: A Range of Poetries From Africa, America, Asia & Oceania*. Garden City, N.Y: Doubleday, 1968.

Rothstein, Edward. "A Jewish Canon, Yes, But Not Set in Stone." *The New York Times*, 24 February 2001, sec. Arts & Ideas, pp. B7, B9.

Ruskin, John. *"Unto This Last": Four Essays on the First Principles of Political Economy*. London: Smith, Elder and Co, 1862.

Sainer, Arthur. *The New Radical Theatre Notebook*. New York: Applause, 1997.

Saivetz, Deborah. "An Event in Space: The Integration of Acting and Design in the Theatre of JoAnne Akalaitis." *TDR: The Drama Review* 42, no. 2 (1998): 132–56.

Saussure, Ferdinand de. *Course in General Linguistics*. New York: Philosophical Library, 1959.

Schaller, George, B. *The Mountain Gorilla*. Chicago: University of Chicago Press, 1963.

—. *The Serengeti Lion; a Study of Predator-Prey Relations*. Chicago: University of Chicago Press, 1972.

Schechner, Richard. *Environmental Theater*. New York: Hawthorn Books, 1973.

—. *The End of Humanism*. New York: Performing Arts Journal Publications, 1982.

—. *Between Theater and Anthropology*. Philadelphia: University of Pennsylvania Press, 1985.

—. *Performance Theory*. London: Routledge, 1988.

—. *The Future of Ritual*. London: Routledge, 1993.

Schechner, Richard and Willa Appel, eds. *By Means of Performance*. Cambridge: Cambridge University Press, 1990.

Schechner, Richard and Mady Schuman, eds. *Ritual, Play, and Performance*. New York: Seabury Press, 1976.

Searle, John R. *Speech Acts: an Essay in the Philosophy of Language*. London: Cambridge University Press, 1969.

—. *Expression and Meaning: Studies in the Theory of Speech Acts*. Cambridge: Cambridge University Press, 1979.

Selbourne, David. *The Making of A Midsummer Night's Dream*. London: Methuen, 1982.

Shakespeare, William. *The Complete Works*. Oxford: Oxford University Press, 1988.

Shephard, William Hunter. *The Dionysus Group*. American University Studies. New York: Peter Lang, 1991.

Shirokogoroff, S. M. *Psychomental Complex of the Tungus*. London: Kegan, Paul, Trench, Trubner, 1935.

Smith, Craig S. "Joyous Vindication and a Sleepless Night in China." *The New York Times*, 14 July 2001, sec. Sports.

Sophocles. *Sophocles II: Ajax, The Women of Trachis, Electra, Philoctetes*. Chicago: University of Chicago Press, 1957.

—. *The Theban Plays: Oedipus the King, Oedipus at Colonus, Antigone*. New York: A.A. Knopf, 1994.

Soyinka, Wole. *Collected Plays*. London: Oxford University Press, 1973.

—. *Death and the King's Horseman*. London: Methuen, 1975.

—. *Myth, Literature, and the African World*. Cambridge: Cambridge University Press, 1976.

—. *The Open Sore of a Continent: a Personal Narrative of the Nigerian Crisis*. New York: Oxford University Press, 1996.

—. *Arms and the Arts – A Continent's Unequal Dialogue*. Cape Town: University of Cape Town, 1999.

Spariosu, Mihai. *Dionysus Reborn: Play and the Aesthetic Dimension in Modern Philosophical and Scientific Discourse.* Ithaca: Cornell University Press, 1989.

——. *The Wreath of Wild Olive: Play, Liminality, and the Study of Literature.* Albany: State University of New York Press, 1997.

Speer, Albert. *Inside the Third Reich: Memoirs.* New York: Simon & Schuster, 1997.

Stanislavsky, Konstantin. *My Life in Art.* Boston: Little, Brown, 1924.

——. *An Actor Prepares.* New York: Theatre Arts, 1936.

——. *Stanislavsky on the Art of the Stage.* New York: Hill and Wang, 1961.

Stebbins, Genevieve. *Delsarte System of Expression.* New York: Dance Horizons, 1977.

Stern, Carol Simpson and Bruce Henderson. *Performance Texts and Contexts.* New York and London: Longman, 1993.

Strasberg, Lee. "Working With Live Material." *TDR: The Drama Review* 9, no. 1 (1964): 117–35.

Sutton-Smith, Brian. *Toys As Culture.* New York: Gardner Press, 1986.

——. *The Ambiguity of Play.* Cambridge: Harvard University Press, 1997.

Sutton-Smith, Brian and Diana Kelly-Byrne. *The Masks of Play.* New York: Leisure Press, 1984.

Suzuki, Tadashi. *The Way of Acting.* New York: Theatre Communications Group, 1986.

Taylor, Diana. *Disappearing Acts: Spectacles of Gender and Nationalism in Argentina's "Dirty War".* Durham: Duke University Press, 1997.

——. "Acts of Transfer." *Hauntology of Performance.* Durham: Duke University Press, in press.

——. "A Different Kind of Tragedy." *Theatre Journal*, in press.

Thompson, Robert Farris. *African Art in Motion.* Los Angeles, Berkeley, London: University of California Press, 1974.

Thoreau, Henry David. *Walden.* Boston: Beacon Press, 1997.

Thornwell, Emily. *The Lady's Guide to Perfect Gentility in Manners, Dress, and Conversation.* New York, Cincinnati: Derby & Jackson, 1856.

Tolstoy, Leo. *War and Peace.* New York: Knopf, 1992.

——. *Anna Karenina.* Oxford: Oxford University Press, 1999.

Toro, Fernando de. *Theatre Semiotics: Text and Staging in Modern Theatre.* Frankfurt am Main, Madrid: Vervuert Verlag, Iberoamericana, 1995.

Turner, Edith L. B. *Experiencing Ritual: A New Interpretation of African Healing.* Philadelphia: University of Pennsylvania Press, 1992.

——. *The Hands Feel It: Healing and Spirit Presence Among a Northern Alaskan People.* DeKalb: Northern Illinois University Press, 1996.

Turner, Victor. *The Forest of Symbols: Aspects of Ndembu Ritual.* Ithaca: Cornell University Press, 1967.

——. *The Ritual Process: Structure and Anti-Structure.* Chicago: Aldine Publishing Company, 1969.

——. *Dramas, Fields, and Metaphors.* Ithaca: Cornell University Press, 1974.

——. *From Ritual to Theatre: The Human Seriousness of Play.* New York: Performing Arts Journal Publications, 1982.

——. "Body, Brain, and Culture." *Zygon* 18, no. 3 (1983): 221–45.

——. *On the Edge of the Bush: Anthropology As Experience.* Tucson: University of Arizona Press, 1985.

——. *The Anthropology of Performance.* New York: PAJ Publications, 1986.

Ueda, Makoto. *Literary and Art Theories in Japan.* Cleveland: Western Reserve University Press, 1967.

Vyasa. *The Bhagavad Gita.* New York: Bantam Books, 1986.

Walcott, Derek. *Dream on Monkey Mountain and Other Plays.* New York: Farrar, Straus and Giroux, 1970.

——. *The Odyssey: A Stage Version.* London, Boston: Faber and Faber, 1993.

Waldrop, M. Mitchell. "Do-It-Yourself-Universes." *Science* (1987): 845–46.

Wilford, John Noble. "In the Dawn of Society, Dance Was Center Stage." *The New York Times*, 27 February 2001, sec. Science, pp. 1–5.

Willett, John. *The Theatre of Bertolt Brecht.* New York: New Directions, 1960.

Williams, Francis Edgar. *Drama of Orokolo: The Social and Ceremonial Life of the Elema.* Oxford: Clarendon Press, 1969.

Wilson, Edward Osborne. *Sociobiology: the New Synthesis.* Cambridge: Harvard University Press, 1975.

——. *On Human Nature.* Cambridge: Harvard University Press, 1978.

——. *Consilience: the Unity of Knowledge.* New York: Knopf, 1998.

Wilson, R. Rawdon. *In Palamedes' Shadow: Explorations in Play, Game & Narrative Theory.* Boston: Northeastern University Press, 1990.

Winnicott, Donald Woods. *The Child and the Family; First Relationships.* London: Tavistock Publications, 1957.

——. *Playing and Reality.* London: Tavistock Publications, 1971.

Wittgenstein, Ludwig. *Philosophical Investigations.* Oxford: Blackwell, 1953.

Wolford, Lisa and Richard Schechner, eds. *The Grotowski Sourcebook.* London, New York: Routledge, 1997.

Wu Tsu-kuang, Mei Shao-wu, Huang Tso-lin, and Mei Lan-fang. *Peking Opera and Mei Lanfang a Guide to China's Traditional Theatre and the Art of Its Great Master*. Beijing: New World Press, 1981.

Zarrilli, Phillip. "For Whom Is the 'Invisible' Not Visible?" *TDR: The Drama Review* 32, no. 1 (1988): 95–106.

—, ed. *Acting (Re)Considered*. London, New York: Routledge, 1995.

—. *When the Body Becomes All Eyes*, New Delhi: Oxford University Press, 1998.

—. *Kathkali Dance Drama*, London, New York, Routledge, 2000.

Zeami. *On the Art of the No Drama*. Princeton: Princeton University Press, 1984.

INDEX

Palecek (Korb stuhl)

100   47,000 - 1
13.5

    47000×135
    47000
    131000
    .23500.0
    6245.00